THE HARPER FACTOR

The
HARPER FACTOR

Assessing a Prime Minister's Policy Legacy

Edited by
Jennifer Ditchburn and Graham Fox

McGill-Queen's University Press
Montreal & Kingston • London • Chicago

ISBN 978-0-7735-4870-1 (cloth)
ISBN 978-0-7735-4871-8 (ePDF)
ISBN 978-0-7735-4872-5 (ePUB)

Legal deposit third quarter 2016
Bibliothèque nationale du Québec

Printed in Canada on acid-free paper that is 100% ancient forest
free (100% post-consumer recycled), processed chlorine free

McGill-Queen's University Press acknowledges the support of the
Canada Council for the Arts for our publishing program. We also
acknowledge the financial support of the Government of Canada
through the Canada Book Fund for our publishing activities.

Library and Archives Canada Cataloguing in Publication

The Harper Factor / edited by Jennifer Ditchburn and Graham Fox.

Issued in print and electronic formats.
ISBN 978-0-7735-4870-1 (hardback). — ISBN 978-0-7735-4871-8 (ePDF). —
ISBN 978-0-7735-4872-5 (ePUB).
1. Harper, Stephen, 1959–. 2. Harper, Stephen, 1959– —Influence.
3. Canada—Politics and government—2006–2015. 4. Canada—History—
21st century. I. Ditchburn, Jennifer, editor II. Fox, Graham (Graham
William), 1974–, editor

FC650.H37 2016   971.07'3   C2016-905039-4
                                          C2016-905040-8

This book was set in Minion Pro Condensed.

Contents

MONEY

PEOPLE

COMMENTARIES

Illustrations

FIGURES

TABLES

Acknowledgments

This book was made possible only by the incredible generosity of its contributors. It is their insights into Prime Minister Harper's legacy in their respective fields that make this volume such a unique contribution to our understanding of the impact of the Conservatives' time in government. Each author has produced a thoughtful—and thought-provoking—analysis that is sure to inform our collective assessment of the Harper decade. For the generosity with which they shared their expertise and insights and the countless hours spent preparing the manuscript, we thank each of them most sincerely.

We also want to thank colleagues and friends who acted as informal advisers on this project, helping us design the frame for the book, approaching prospective contributors, and reviewing any one of several drafts. Your sound advice proved invaluable in getting the book all the way to the printing press. Specifically, we want to thank Manuel Cárdenas for his work in preparing the manuscript for production.

We want to thank our families for their support and understanding during all those hours we spent at a computer instead of at the park or the arena: Greg Loyst, Amaya and Gabriela (Jennifer); and Véronique Mauffette, Sophie, Sarah and Nicolas (Graham). Your love and enthusiasm mean the world to both of us, and we simply could not have done it without you.

Finally, to those who call for a political culture that deals more in complexity and nuances than in binary choices and absolutes, and who demand an approach to public policy that is informed more by evidence than by partisanship, this book is our small contribution to your efforts.

Jennifer and Graham

THE HARPER FACTOR

Introduction

One of the most memorable images from the 2015 Speech from the Throne was that of three right honourable gentlemen laughing and chatting in a moment of uninhibited bonhomie. Former prime ministers Joe Clark, John Turner and Jean Chrétien sat in a corner at the front of the Senate Chamber, watching on as Prime Minister Justin Trudeau took his seat near Governor General David Johnston for the ceremony so steeped in history.

The new Liberal government, for which the cultivation of symbols is a modus operandi, selected the invitees in the Senate Chamber with care. The presence of three former prime ministers with roots in different political parties was surely meant to telegraph a notion of public service that is elevated above partisan considerations, and a spirit of fraternity with those who had previously been called to serve. The gathering before the speech had more the feel of an academic convocation than a political exercise.

It was clear from the opening passages of the Speech from the Throne, however, that the magnanimity on display did not extend to Trudeau's immediate predecessor. Much of the document was a direct repudiation of the government of Prime Minister Harper, defeated a few short weeks before.

"Let us not forget … that Canadians have been clear and unambiguous in their desire for real change. Canadians want their government to do different things, and to do things differently," read the text. "They want to be able to trust their government."[1]

The government immediately set about reversing a number of Stephen Harper's policies. It reinstated the long-form census and committed to establishing an inquiry into murdered and missing Indigenous women. It pledged to limit the use of omnibus bills to pass its legislative agenda through Parliament, and put new constraints on government-funded advertising. Within a month of his swearing-in, Prime Minister Trudeau met with the premiers to discuss how they could work together to reduce greenhouse gas emissions and put a price on carbon. The message was that in tone, and in deed, the Trudeau government aimed to be different.

The 2015 election appears to have been a repudiation of Stephen Harper's government. After almost a decade in power, the former prime minister came to elicit strong feelings in many voters. A few months after the election, Abacus Data surveyed Canadians on their impressions of prime ministers stretching back to Joe Clark. At 55 per cent, Harper received the highest negative response of any of them, and by a significant margin.[2]

What was less clear was whether Canadians were rejecting the man and his way of conducting politics, or his policies as well. Most analyses of Harper's time in office have to date focused on his approach to politics and its supremacy over public policy. But there have been precious few analyses of his actual impact on public policy. What *is* Stephen Harper's record when it comes to public policy?

When he was sworn in as Canada's twenty-second prime minister in February 2006, Harper inherited a country worn down by the scandals and infighting of the previous government. The economy was growing at a healthy clip, but leadership struggles of the Liberal Party superseded most matters of public policy in news coverage of national politics. The sponsorship scandal had gravely eroded public trust in government. Internationally, Canada was at war against the Taliban and al-Qaeda in Afghanistan, and although it was still active in multilateral forums, its influence in the world had begun to wane. At home, the federal government was amassing sizeable budgetary surpluses, and had been for years, but the provinces were struggling to balance theirs. The party system was fragmented along regional lines, and it seemed likely that it would remain that way for some time to come. And although the Liberal government of Paul Martin launched a number of national initiatives, the party's minority status and brief time in office conspired to ensure few of these initiatives would be firmly established by the time the 2005–6 campaign began. Managing Parliament as a minority would certainly pose significant challenges for the Conservatives, as it does for all minority governments, but there was little in the previous government's record to bind Harper's actions once he took office.

The aim of this volume is to assess what Stephen Harper has left to his successors. During his time in office, in what ways did Harper continue along the policy path set by his predecessors, and where did he break from established practice or consensus? And perhaps most significant for supporters and opponents alike, what, if any, long-term impact will he have on public policy in Canada?

These questions first occurred to us over lunch eighteen months before the starting gun went off on the 2015 general election campaign. We shared the reflection that while there was a lot of instant analysis of the Harper government in the form of punditry and editorials, much of it—too much, perhaps—focused on the personality of the man, his temperament and the politics of issues. From there, it was easy for the commentariat to conclude that Stephen Harper was a transformational figure in Canadian politics, whose landscape he had fundamentally reshaped.

Sitting in that restaurant that day, neither of us was entirely convinced of that argument when it came to public policy. We agreed that, in addition to the quality analysis done by others on Harper's politics and the impact of his approach on the party system and the fortunes of its many moving parts, more work needed to be done to better understand the extent to which his decisions as prime minister were actually changing public policy.

We recruited authors from academe, the media, business and the not-for-profit sector and assigned a specific policy area to each one. All contributors agreed to take part in the project long before the outcome of the 2015 election was known and had committed to publishing their analysis regardless of the results. In preparing their chapter, they were asked to reflect on the following questions: What impact had Stephen Harper had on their assigned policy area? In what ways had he changed the approach in relation to previous governments? And what would be the impact of his record on future governments?

As readers will note, the group assembled for this book is politically and philosophically ecumenical. Some contributors have partisan pasts, others well-known views, and others still have seldom if ever expressed their opinions on the Harper government in the public square. That is a deliberate choice on our part. In inviting these individuals to contribute to the book, we were not looking for homogeneity in backgrounds or views on the former prime minister, nor did we feel that absolute neutrality should be the price of admission. What was required was a commitment to consider the evidence before drawing conclusions and to avoid unsubstantiated opinion and partisanship. The result, we think, is a book that will give readers a thoughtful look at what the Harper government set out to do, what it managed to accomplish and what advantages or challenges this will present for the future.

Readers should not assume that we as editors agree with all of the conclusions made by our contributors, nor that the contributors necessarily agree with each other. In assembling the group, we did not aim for consensus. Each author presents an argument that, if spirited at times, is evidence-based. They each provide a unique perspective on their policy area and new insights into what actually happened on Harper's watch.

Stephen Harper's record is decidedly more nuanced than both his admirers and his detractors will concede. As this collection of articles shows, there is good, bad and ugly in almost every policy area Harper had to deal with in his decade in office. This book is therefore not for those who already "know the truth" about Stephen

Harper. It is aimed, rather, at those who are genuinely curious about the impact of Stephen Harper on public policy in Canada. To echo the title of the volume, what has been the Harper Factor?

Jennifer Ditchburn, Editor
Graham Fox, Editor

INSTITUTIONS

1

Unfinished Business: The Legacy of Stephen Harper's "Open Federalism"

Graham Fox

U nfinished business: despite nearly a decade in power, that is the best way to describe the impact Stephen Harper has had as prime minister on the workings of the Canadian federation, its structures and its operations. Ironically, restructuring the power relationships within the Canadian federation—or "rebalancing," as Harper might have put it—was one of the motivating factors behind his entry into politics. It was a defining theme of his political engagement while in opposition, and most importantly, it was a key factor in his first electoral victory in 2006, helping him secure ten crucial seats in the province of Quebec to form a minority government. Yet there is scant evidence that Harper's approach to federalism will have a lasting impact on the conduct of intergovernmental affairs in the years to come, on the forging of common approaches to issues affecting the country as a whole, or on the future of the sovereignty movement in Quebec.

This observation will be jarring to those who have strong views—positive and negative—about the former prime minister. Harper's approach to federalism has been used by both sides as a symbol of the dramatic ways in which he has changed Canada. To his supporters, his abandonment of what they would consider to be "old-style executive federalism," his championing of issues important to Western Canada and his (limited) recognition of the specificity of Quebec were clear signs of the dawning of a new era. To his detractors, his eschewing of First Ministers'

Meetings and his efforts to disentangle federal and provincial jurisdictions weakened our ability to forge a national consensus on important issues and coordinate policy responses from coast to coast to coast.

The evidence suggests that there is some truth to both of those views, but each one fails to paint the complete picture. They also fail to account for the recent history of Canadian federalism and the situation Harper inherited when he became prime minister. The events of the decade before his victory, and his role in them, informed the approach he would take while in government and must be factored into any assessment of whether and how he has reshaped the Canadian federation.

To be sure, while he was prime minister, Stephen Harper took a dramatically different approach to intergovernmental affairs than did his predecessors. Rooted in the views of the Reform Party, he left behind the structures and processes of executive federalism as he understood it and articulated a vision of "open federalism." His refusal to engage premiers as a group also allowed the Council of the Federation to evolve as a stand-alone feature of the Canadian intergovernmental architecture. But his absence from the intergovernmental table also deprived him of any ability to shape the future. While in office, he established few precedents that would bind his successor to his vision of how the Canadian federation is supposed to work. After a period of slow but certain decline, the era of executive federalism dominated by Ottawa came to an end on Stephen Harper's watch, and that is no small thing. But by not institutionalizing any new intergovernmental mechanisms, he has left the design of whatever comes next almost entirely to his successor.

Stephen Harper's Views on Federalism

Most accounts of Stephen Harper's core political beliefs refer in some ways to how the management of the Canadian federation by successive federal governments informed his view of the country and motivated his desire to play an active role in changing it.[1] Ottawa's dominance at the intergovernmental table and the weight of Ontario and Quebec created a deep frustration that Western Canada was being shortchanged and a belief that a significant shift in the balance of power was critical to the country's future.

To be sure, the academic definition of executive federalism is a more neutral concept than how it is usually understood in political circles, and particularly in conservative political circles. The term coined by political scientist Donald Smiley refers simply to the "processes of intergovernmental negotiation that are dominated by the executives of the different governments within the federal system."[2] However, conservatives have for decades lamented that, in Canada, the terms of that interaction between Ottawa and the provinces are too often determined by the federal executive, with the provinces reacting and adjusting to Ottawa's agenda. Thus, their conception of executive federalism includes the notion of Ottawa as the dominant partner. It is that political definition of executive federalism—a system dominated by the federal government—that shaped Stephen Harper's (and many other conservatives') thinking about the Canadian federation, and how it ought to change.

As early as 1987, in a speech to the Reform Party founding convention, the future prime minister was already making the case that the "vested interests of the National Policy, the Welfare State and the Quebec question" would have to "cast aside their narrow definitions of Canada in the interests of the country they claim to love, because that country can no longer be built on the economic exploitation and political disenfranchisement of Western Canada."[3] A few years later, in 1991, the Reform Party's first policy document, on which Harper held the pen, addressed constitutional reform in the opening section: in addition to rejecting the Meech Lake Accord, the platform called for a clear division of powers between federal and provincial governments, and support for the principle of subsidiarity, which holds that the lowest level of government that is capable of discharging a particular duty should be responsible for it.[4]

Those ideals continued to be championed by Harper, first as a Reform MP and then as president of the National Citizens Coalition. Opponents of Stephen Harper's view of the federation often point to the so-called "firewall letter"[5] published in 2001 as an indication of his true intentions regarding federal arrangements, and as a foreshadowing of what would happen if he were ever handed the keys to 24 Sussex Drive. Co-signed with five other adherents to the Calgary School view of Canadian federalism,[6] the open letter to Premier Ralph Klein was a sharp rebuke of the treatment of Alberta by the Chrétien government in the lead-up to and during the 2000 federal election, and an expression of deep frustration that the behaviour had been rewarded with a third majority government.

While the tone of the letter and the insistence with which it urges Premier Klein to isolate Alberta from the rest of the country are perhaps incongruent with aspirations to national leadership, the substance of the letter is far less controversial and absolutely in keeping with Harper's writings up to that point. The letter advocates a more autonomous course for Alberta and taking full advantage of its existing powers as a means to protect itself from federal intrusion into its own affairs. Indeed, most of the policies the authors urged Premier Klein to adopt had, by and large, already been adopted by past Quebec governments. It is therefore difficult to argue that the letter's thesis is inconsistent with established practices of Canadian federalism or that it is a significant departure from the status quo.

As opposition leader, first of the Canadian Alliance and then of the Conservative Party, Harper would build on these foundations and mould them to address the political imperative of creating an electoral coalition that could carry the Conservative Party to power. In addition to Reformers and Progressive Conservatives, that coalition would have to include Quebec nationalists. Over time, Harper's approach would be further developed and refined into the proposal he took to voters in the 2006 election.

The State of the Federation in 2006

Stephen Harper was sworn in as Canada's twenty-second prime minister on February 6, 2006—a decade after the near-death experience of the 1995 referendum on Quebec sovereignty. On October 30, 1995, Quebec voters were asked for the second time in a generation to choose whether to remain a partner in Confederation or secede from Canada. The emergence of then–Bloc Québécois leader Lucien Bouchard as "chief negotiator" of the YES side late in the campaign energized the sovereignist campaign that had until then been disunited and unfocused.[7] What had been expected to be a relatively easy win for the NO side became an intensely competitive campaign in the final lap and, on that fateful night, Canada survived by a mere 54,288 votes.

The reaction from a shell-shocked federal government was swift, if uninspiring. "We will keep open all the other avenues of change, including the administrative and constitutional paths," Chrétien told a rally in Montreal days before the referendum, pointing to a renewal and "modernization" of the federation.[8] On December 13, 1995, his government passed An Act Respecting Constitutional Amendments, which gave Quebec one of five regional vetoes on any future constitutional amendments.

Before long, however, it became clear that the Chrétien government was shifting away from its attempt to renew the federation and accommodate Quebec's traditional demands—widely known in Ottawa circles as Plan A—toward Plan B, a hardline approach that sought head-on confrontations with the Parti Québécois (PQ) government and a more vigorous defence of the status quo. Despite a respectable end result, the 1997 election had been a disappointment for the Bloc, which was still struggling to adapt to Lucien Bouchard's departure for Quebec City in 1996 and to its new leader, Gilles Duceppe.[9] In Quebec City, Bouchard succeeded in securing a second PQ majority government in 1998 but lost the popular vote to Jean Charest, who left his post as leader of the Progressive Conservative Party of Canada earlier that year to lead the Quebec Liberal Party (PLQ). On the face of it, sovereignists were still in charge in Quebec City and a significant force in Parliament, but by 1999, the cracks in the armour were beginning to show.

At the interprovincial level, premiers launched their own attempts at renewing the federation by emphasizing provincial autonomy, interprovincial collaboration and a more coordinated effort to resist Ottawa's attempts to encroach on provincial jurisdiction. The Social Union Framework Agreement (SUFA) was meant to curb Ottawa's intrusion into social policy—largely an area of provincial jurisdiction—by putting limits on Ottawa's ability to use its spending power and providing a framework for Ottawa's participation in social programs. As Alain-G. Gagnon and Hugh Segal point out in their introduction to a collection of essays on SUFA, Ottawa's enviable fiscal position vis-à-vis the provinces increased the threat of encroachment: Ottawa had money to act, and the provinces were struggling with deficits. As a consequence, the appeal of a united interprovincial front increased as well. Earlier iterations of SUFA (the Saskatoon Consensus, August 1998, and the Victoria Proposal, January 1999[10]) reflected a desire by all provinces to combat Ottawa's unilateralism and constrain its spending power; however, the other provinces and territories made concessions to Ottawa during last-minute negotiations that rendered SUFA unacceptable to Quebec.[11] By the time the final text of SUFA was approved on February 4, 1999, Quebec found itself isolated once again: although the rest of Canada had signed on to SUFA, the Quebec government and the PLQ Official Opposition were united in their opposition to it.[12]

A few months later, the federal government went on the offensive again, this time in the form of Bill C-20, known as the Clarity Act. No doubt inspired by Harper's own private member's bill introduced when he was a Reform MP to clarify the rules surrounding secession (Bill C-341, the Quebec Contingency Act, introduced in October 1996), the Clarity Act responded to the Supreme Court of Canada's opinion on a province's right to unilaterally declare its independence. It introduced rules that would govern Ottawa's reaction to the question put in a referendum, the meaning of the results and eventual negotiations.

Unanimously decried by all parties in the National Assembly, the Clarity Act met initial resistance in the Commons that was quickly beaten back, and it eventually passed without controversy. The provocation was deliberate and successful: the Chrétien government had poked the sovereignty movement in the eye, and Quebec voters barely reacted.

The combination of the Clarity Act and the Bloc's showing during that year's election dealt a serious blow to the sovereignty movement, a blow confirmed in October 2000 by Chrétien's third majority victory, which included thirty-six seats in Quebec. Sovereignist leaders had expected a public outcry and did everything in their power to foment one, but it never materialized. Realizing his "winning conditions" were a long way away, Lucien Bouchard resigned his premiership in January 2001. His successor, Bernard Landry, was beaten by Jean Charest and the PLQ in a general election two years later, and the Paul Martin juggernaut was poised to take over the Liberal Party of Canada and sweep the country in the next election.

Soon after becoming Quebec premier, Charest rekindled the premiers' desire to forge closer ties among themselves and facilitate common action on files of mutual interest without requiring a direct intervention by the federal government. Echoing the proposal he had made in 1997 as federal PC leader under the title "The Canadian Covenant,"[13] the new premier led the charge on creating a more formal framework for interprovincial collaboration. Within months of becoming premier, he signed—along with his twelve provincial and territorial counterparts—the founding agreement of the Council of the Federation.[14]

In 2004, the sponsorship scandal severely debilitated the Liberal Party of Canada. The Martin government was reduced to a minority that year and never recovered. The scandal gave the Bloc Québécois a temporary reprieve from its long-term decline, after two elections whose results had not quite lived up to expectations. But it also created an opportunity for Stephen Harper. It was during that minority parliament that he fully developed the approach that would win him ten seats in Quebec and guide his future relations with the provinces and territories.

The decade between the 1995 referendum and Harper's first electoral victory was therefore instrumental in setting the scene for his decade in power. By the time voters headed to the polls in January 2006, the Liberal Party had been crippled by scandal and infighting, the sovereignty movement was adrift and searching for relevance and purpose, and provincial and territorial leaders had formed a new mechanism for collaboration that was deliberately outside Ottawa's sphere of influence. And most importantly, Stephen Harper had a new plan for "open federalism."

The 2006 Federal Election

Expanding on the commitments the Conservative Party had made in its inaugural campaign in 2004,[15] the 2006 campaign platform was considerably more detailed in how a Conservative government would approach the federation. Right from the opening passages, the document committed a new Conservative government to strengthening national unity,[16] but then spelled out explicitly how it would "establish a new relationship of open federalism with the provinces, while clarifying the roles of both levels of government within the division of powers of the Constitution." Specifically, the platform committed the new government to:

> Support the creation of practical intergovernmental mechanisms to facilitate provincial involvement in areas of federal jurisdiction where provincial jurisdiction is affected, and enshrine these practices in a Charter of Open Federalism. We will work with the provinces in areas such as culture, environment, and trade, within the context of the Constitution. Specifically, we will

- invite the government of Quebec to play a role at UNESCO along the lines of its participation in la Francophonie;
- facilitate provincial participation in the development of the Canadian position in the negotiation of bilateral, continental, hemispheric or global trade agreements where provincial jurisdiction is affected;
- work with permanent provincial international trade offices to promote and develop trade opportunities; and
- support the important contribution the Council of the Federation is making to strengthening intergovernmental and interprovincial cooperation, expanding the economic and social union in Canada, and advancing the development of common standards and objectives of mutual recognition by all provinces.[17]

The platform also acknowledged the existence of a fiscal imbalance between the federal and provincial levels of government and committed to reaching a comprehensive, long-term agreement to resolve it. Echoing the demands of the earlier iterations of what eventually became SUFA, it also pledged to curb the federal government's scope of action in areas of provincial jurisdiction by ensuring that new shared-cost programs would require the consent of a majority of provinces and guarantee a right to opt out with full compensation.[18]

On December 19, 2005, Stephen Harper addressed the Quebec City Chamber of Commerce during a campaign stop in "*la Vieille capitale.*" In what became known in political circles as the Quebec City speech, he gave open federalism additional symbolic meaning by linking the foundation of Quebec City to "the birth of the state that became Canada. We must never forget that Canada was founded in Quebec City and founded by Francophones."[19] Emphasizing his desire to work with the Charest government and the Council of the Federation, he committed to recognizing provincial autonomy and respecting their jurisdiction and pledged to give them a greater voice in international affairs when they impact areas of provincial responsibility, including a seat for Quebec at UNESCO. "A Conservative government will offer a complete departure from the approaches of both the federal Liberals and the Bloc Québécois. Instead of the old paternalistic and arrogant attitudes of the federal Liberals and the blind and sterile obstruction of the Bloc Québécois, a Conservative government will practice an open federalism."[20]

A month later, Stephen Harper would be given his first of three opportunities to make good on those commitments as prime minister.

A New Approach for a New Government

Once in government, Harper moved quickly to implement his election platform. While the "five priorities" enumerated during the campaign[21] were given top priority, the new prime minister also moved on the intergovernmental front. A few weeks into his mandate, he seized the opportunity of a Council of the Federation meeting to host an introductory dinner with the premiers. Later that spring, the government of Canada made good on another commitment by signing an accord with the government of Quebec to create the position of a permanent representative of Quebec within Canada's permanent delegation to UNESCO.[22]

The new government was also determined to ensure its victories in Quebec did not turn out to be a temporary improvement in the party's standing in the province. Speaking to the Montreal Chamber of Commerce in April that year, Prime Minister Harper underlined his aim to work toward "[n]ot just rejecting separation […] but by changing the debate, changing the agenda and changing the federation."[23] He went on to call for a new relationship with the provinces—"a relationship that is open, honest, respectful."[24] But more significantly for the actions that followed in the years to come, he underlined that collaboration was at the core of this new relationship. Open federalism, he concluded, was certainly about "being clear about who does what and who is accountable for it," but it was also about "looking forward to what we can accomplish together."[25]

Against this backdrop of openness and collaboration, the new government was also keenly aware of the real possibility that it might not have all that much time before it would have to face voters again. In order to win the next election, tangible progress had to be made on a number of policy priorities: within months, the prime minister would need a record on which he could campaign.[26] Whether one of those early wins could come from the intergovernmental table was very much an open question.

According to a senior federal public servant close to the file who spoke on condition of anonymity,[27] Stephen Harper's approach to the Canadian federation was shaped in no small measure by his personality and by what he had witnessed as leader of the opposition. Describing the prime minister as a "reluctant multilateralist," the official recounted how Harper and his closest advisers came to power intent on not replicating what they considered to be the errors of former prime minister Paul Martin. They viewed the 2004 Health Accord (aimed at improving health systems' performance through predictable, long-term federal funding) and the 2005 Kelowna Accord (whose goal was to improve the living conditions of Aboriginal peoples) that Martin had negotiated as emblematic of the threat First Ministers' Meetings constituted for whoever happened to be sitting in the federal government's chair. With the prime minister outnumbered thirteen to one, the format made it almost impossible for him to not fall prey to the agenda of others. Ottawa's financial contribution at the end of the process would always be larger than originally intended, and ensuring provincial and territorial accountability for federal dollars spent was resisted by premiers at every turn.

This view was reinforced by the experiences of three of Harper's cabinet ministers from Ontario. Jim Flaherty, John Baird and Tony Clement had all been senior ministers in the Mike Harris and Ernie Eves governments in Ontario and brought with them to Ottawa firsthand knowledge of how the federal government can quickly become isolated and be held for ransom at the intergovernmental table. Only when multilateralism was absolutely necessary would Harper engage in this manner.

Moreover, according to this same official, Harper is practical and focused and does not favour "blue sky" thinking or relationship-building for its own sake. As a consequence, he does not view federalism as a policy area unto itself. It is a means to an end, be it related to health care and wait times, internal trade or infrastructure. Thus, one-on-one conversations with a premier who had a focused agenda to deal with a specific matter were frequent occurrences during Harper's tenure—much more so than is commonly acknowledged. In contrast, summitry was to be avoided as much as possible. While all of his recent predecessors had taken a multilateral relationship-building approach to intergovernmental relations, his would be decidedly bilateral and transactional.

The Evolution of Open Federalism over Three Mandates

Rhetorically speaking, Stephen Harper would not deviate from the open federalism proposal outlined in 2006 until the end of his tenure. In 2008, the Conservative platform reiterated the party's commitment to open federalism and declared that "[n]ational unity is stronger than it has been in forty years."[28] It called for the elimination of internal trade barriers. Referencing a 2006 budget paper on the issue, it recalled the government's commitment that it was "prepared to use the federal trade and commerce power to strengthen the Canadian economic union." Noting the progress made since 2007 by provinces and territories, however, it committed to exercising that federal authority only if "barriers to trade, investment and mobility remain by 2010."[29] The same platform also reiterated the party's commitment to a new Charter of Open Federalism, and to limiting federal spending power.[30]

In 2011, the platform added a specific reference to "[w]ork[ing] collaboratively with the provinces and territories to renew the Health Accord and to continue reducing wait times." In the "spirit of open federalism," it noted, the federal government would respect provincial jurisdiction and would negotiate a separate agreement with Quebec.[31] And most succinctly of all, the 2015 election platform made only a passing reference to the workings of the federation and respect for provincial jurisdiction, and committed a new Conservative government only to not entering into a new round of constitutional negotiations.[32]

But if the rhetoric remained constant over nine years, the government's commitment to its implementation clearly eroded as time passed.

The Fiscal Imbalance and Internal Trade

Early in the first mandate, Prime Minister Harper set out to redress two long-standing irritants in federal-provincial relations: the gap in Ottawa's ability to raise revenues in relation to the capacity of the provinces to do the same—known as the vertical fiscal imbalance—and the barriers to internal trade.

The first issue had been a growing concern for provincial premiers since the unilateral cuts to transfer payments imposed by the Chrétien government in 1995. As the federal government's fiscal capacity was restored in the late 1990s and early 2000s, even while provincial governments struggled with their own budget balance, the provinces worried about federal intrusion into areas of provincial jurisdiction now made possible by Ottawa's increased fiscal capacity. The government of Quebec went even further by calling on Ottawa to transfer fiscal room to the provinces to ensure a better alignment of revenue capacity and expenditure requirements for each level of government. As a quid pro quo for resolving the fiscal imbalance, the federal government would expect the provinces to eliminate internal trade barriers.

Writing for *Policy Options*, the magazine of the Institute for Research on Public Policy, in March 2007, I remarked that linking the two issues into one negotiation might not have been popular in provincial capitals, but the fiscal imbalance limited the provinces' capacity to fulfill their obligations to their citizens, and inaction on internal trade impeded the federal government's ability to strengthen Canada's economic union. It was legitimate for Ottawa to want to make progress on both in tandem.[33] The federal government would propose a lasting resolution to the fiscal imbalance, and in return, the provinces would eliminate internal trade barriers.

Moreover, the federal government listed in a 2006 budget paper entitled *Restoring Fiscal Balance in Canada: Focusing on Priorities* the five principles that would guide the formulation of its proposal to the provinces to resolve the imbalance. Notable among them was the insistence on the need for clarity on roles and responsibilities and the "effective collaborative management of the federation."[34] Ottawa would not dictate the solution to the provinces but would ensure mutual accountability through clarity of roles and would adopt a collaborative approach to formulating its proposal. This was the essence of open federalism: a new approach to managing the federation had to acknowledge both the desirability of disentangling roles and responsibilities but also the reality of interdependence.

In the end, real collaboration never materialized and neither issue was resolved satisfactorily. Some action was taken to address the fiscal imbalance, but the gap in fiscal capacity remains to this day, and the corresponding elimination of internal trade barriers has never occurred. This was Prime Minister Harper's first attempt at achieving a "grand bargain" on a complex issue with all of his provincial counterparts. And it would be his last. The outstanding question, of course, is this: Was the fiscal imbalance experience proof that collaboration was destined to be a dead end, or would genuine collaboration have yielded a different outcome for a prime minister still in his early days in office?

Regardless, collaboration would never be attempted in this way again. It should perhaps be of no surprise that, by the 2008 election, only one of the five platform priorities articulated in the 2006 campaign—establishing a medical wait-times guarantee—remained unfulfilled. It was also the only one that required collaboration with the provinces.

Quebec: A Nation within a United Canada

On November 27, 2006, the House of Commons adopted a motion that recognized that "the Quebecois form a nation within a united Canada." The motion had been introduced by the Conservative government on November 22 in reaction to a Bloc Québécois motion tabled a few days prior that had simply called for the recognition that the Québécois formed a nation, with no reference to Canada.

In that short week, the dueling motions caused some difficulty in both the Conservative and Bloc Québécois caucuses. On the Conservative side, the speed with which Harper decided to counter the initial Bloc motion with his own left no time to debate the pros and cons with caucus or even cabinet. While a select few advisers in caucus had been consulted on the motion, Minister of Intergovernmental Affairs Michael Chong learned of its existence during a caucus briefing at the same time as everyone else. Disagreeing with the substance of the motion, and objecting to the lack of consultation on a matter that fell squarely within his portfolio, Chong resigned from Harper's cabinet.

On the Bloc side, as Martine Tremblay revealed in her book *La rébellion tranquille*, there were already significant disagreements in Duceppe's entourage as to whether the original motion should be introduced in the first place. Faced with Harper's countermove, Bloc MPs were divided, upset with their leader and ultimately resigned to the idea that they would have to support the Conservative motion. Regardless of the other details, it was inconceivable that they would vote against any acknowledgment that the Québécois formed a nation.[35]

Notwithstanding the loss of a cabinet minister, Harper won that round against the Bloc Québécois. The tactic was successful, and there is no question that the symbol is a potent one for many Quebec nationalists. The recognition of Canada as a multinational country is also entirely consistent with open federalism, albeit—ironically—much closer to former prime minister Joe Clark's concept of a "community of communities" than the unhyphenated-Canadianism/no-special-status view championed by the Reform Party in its early years.

That said, the haste with which the prime minister decided to ask the House of Commons to pronounce itself on a matter of such deep symbolism, and such difference in opinion, suggests it was a tactical move designed for the needs of the moment, not necessarily with an eye to the future. To wit, other than references over the years to the fact of its adoption, the "nation" motion did not lead to other actions, nor is there evidence that it informed future Harper government decisions. It won the day, but didn't shape the years ahead.

The Global Financial Crisis

Stephen Harper's second term was consumed by the global financial crisis and the precariousness of managing a second minority government. With the threat of an election lurking around every corner, focus was placed once again on files Ottawa could manage so as to show progress when voters were next called to the ballot box.

In November 2008 and January 2009, as the extent of the financial crisis and the impact it would have on the Canadian economy became clear, Prime Minister Harper held his only two official First Ministers' Meetings to coordinate the responses of all governments to stimulate the economy. The concluding press release referred to the need for joint action,[36] but there is little evidence that the federal Economic Action Plan (budget 2009) was designed with meaningful provincial or territorial input, or that its implementation—particularly with regards to infrastructure—was managed successfully with provincial and territorial governments. In fact, the two provincial officials interviewed for this chapter noted significant tensions with their federal counterparts in identifying priority projects and coordinating efforts.

The Council of the Federation

If Ottawa's disengagement from the intergovernmental table frustrated many who would have preferred more proactive federal leadership, it did provide an opening for the Council of the Federation to strengthen ties among premiers and push them toward common action. Ottawa's absence allowed the premiers to make progress on issues that concerned all of them, on their own: from health innovation to internal trade to energy, "pan-Canadian" did not have to mean "federal" in every case. Through the establishment of working groups, premiers were able to share information and coordinate policy responses among themselves. Accountability was assured by individual premiers, assuming the leadership of specific groups and reporting on progress at bi-annual meetings. These working groups also provided an access point for the research community and stakeholder groups to engage in policy development on pan-Canadian issues.

In this respect, Prime Minister Harper's commitment to disentangling areas of federal and provincial jurisdiction and limiting federal action in areas of provincial responsibility was a significant and positive development in Canadian intergovernmental affairs. While we should be careful not to exaggerate the policy successes the Council of the Federation has achieved to date, its intention to disentangle, and the mechanisms it created, may serve the country well in future.

That said, Ottawa's consistent shunning of multilateralism also exposed the limitations of disentanglement, if it is not accompanied by collaboration. Given the complexity of the challenges facing our governments, interdependence is fact of modern federal life. Complete disentanglement may be desirable for those who value black-and-white clarity on who does what, but this "watertight compartments" view of federalism does not reflect the reality of twenty-first-century policy problems.

Confrontation as the Hallmark of Majority Government

Frustrated by two successive minority governments that limited their scope of action, the Conservatives were under great pressure to implement their agenda swiftly following the election of a majority government in May 2011. Patience with any group or body that stood in the way of that agenda had worn thin, and the provinces would not be an exception.

Indeed, two high-level provincial officials from different regions of the country confirm that, following his majority win, Harper became more confrontational with the premiers when policy differences would have impeded his own progress. The commitment to allowing every province to chart its own course remained, but the desire by Ottawa to also go it alone was equally strong.

Signs of this new strain of open federalism were already visible before the 2011 election. Despite provincial protestations to the contrary, the federal government went ahead with the cancellation of the long-form census, knowing full well the impact it would have on a province's ability to design policies and deliver services. In pursuing its law-and-order agenda—long touted as a high priority of the Conservative Party—little regard was given to the impact that changes made to justice policy at the federal level might have on the administration of justice at the provincial level. Provincial officials also remarked that there was little high-level engagement with hesitant provinces on the issue of establishing a single securities regulator. In all these cases, whether Ottawa was correct on the substance of the matter is not at issue; the unilateral approach is. As Roger Gibbins observed in 2008, even Harper's attempt at disentanglement was unilateral.[37] This tendency would only grow after the majority had been secured.

On the health accord, Ottawa ignored its own campaign commitment to work collaboratively with the provinces and territories on health care renewal and instead took a "take it or leave it" approach to the funding formula. To be clear, the formula presented by Finance Minister Flaherty in December 2011 was not a cut in federal transfers for health care[38] and the long-term predictability of it was consistent with the demands of premiers. But the lack of engagement with premiers prior to the presentation of the final offer precluded any discussion, for instance, of how the "one size fits all" approach favoured by Ottawa would impact the level of service to individuals in provinces with an older population. The federal government should not run the health care system, but it also cannot ignore its share of the responsibility to citizens regarding the system's ability to deliver quality care across the country.

If unilateral action in health undermined the principles of open federalism, so too did unilateral inaction on climate change. Climate change is a perfect example of a complex policy issue that thumbs its nose at the division of powers imagined by the Fathers of Confederation almost 150 years ago. Making any progress at all on reducing greenhouse emissions will require policy collaboration at the subnational, national and inter/supranational levels. Not only was there broad consensus within the Council of the Federation that concerted action was required, but they were looking to Ottawa to engage as a full partner. The federal idea (especially in a decentralized federation such as Canada, within which both levels have significant and overlapping responsibilities) should have compelled some measure of engagement by the federal government, but Harper steadfastly refused. Ottawa's aggressive passivity on climate change was a rejection of its own concept of open federalism.

Of course, there were other irritants between Ottawa and the provinces during this period, such as the confrontation with Quebec over long-gun registry data and with Ontario on a provincial pension regime. But while these skirmishes no doubt would have benefited from a closer relationship between governments, they are more akin to disputes between unfriendly neighbours than they are a manifestation of broken federalism. Indeed, in a paper presented to an International Association of Centers for Federal Studies (IACFS) meeting in Montreal in October 2015, Alain-G. Gagnon, political scientist at the Université du Québec à Montréal, noted the frequency with which the federal government became intolerant of dissenting opinion during this period, from Elections Canada to Statistics Canada and from Rights and Democracy to the Veterans Ombudsman.[39] Gagnon's observation raises the interesting question of whether confrontation with the premiers increased because Harper became frustrated specifically with the federal system, or whether the premiers were simply dealt with in the same manner as were other sources of dissenting or opposing opinion.

As Paul Wells noted in *Right Side Up* in 2006, there had never been a grand vision for how the federation would evolve on Harper's watch.[40] Time seems to have borne that out. Absent the discipline that such a vision would impose on individual decisions, circumstances can have an even more significant impact on the course of events. Indeed, as the senior federal public servant interviewed for this chapter put it, there is less theory in Harper's approach to federalism than there is the character of the man and the politics of the issue.

An Assessment of Stephen Harper's Impact on Canadian Federalism

In his compelling biography of the former prime minister, *Globe and Mail* columnist John Ibbitson described the changes Harper introduced to intergovernmental relations (which he suggests might be called "passive federalism") as the "First Big Thing" that he accomplished as prime minister.[41] After decades of tensions, he argued, the relative peace on the intergovernmental front over the Conservatives' nine years in office constituted a significant accomplishment of the Harper government that has led to Canada being more united today "than at any time since the Second World War."[42]

While it is true that no significant crisis erupted around the intergovernmental table after 2006, the absence of crisis is hardly the hallmark of a signature success. Moreover, measured against even that low a bar, the Harper government's public confrontations with the McGuinty/Wynne Liberals in Ontario, the cold relationship with the Charest government in Quebec and the open hostility vis-à-vis the Williams government in Newfoundland and Labrador, or more recently with the Notley government in Alberta, are certainly comparable to the tensions that existed between the Chrétien government and Mike Harris in Ontario or Ralph Klein in Alberta.

So what will be Stephen Harper's impact on the practice of federalism in Canada over the long term?

First, it is important to note that intergovernmental activity is far broader and deeper than First Ministers' Meetings. Contrary to an often-heard complaint that "nothing happened" or that "Ottawa didn't talk to the provinces and territories," there was a lot more going on below the surface than was generally known. In fact, all four officials interviewed for this chapter confirmed that, on an administrative level, there was a great deal of information sharing and policy coordination.

This impression is supported by data compiled by the University of Victoria's Herman Bakvis on the frequency of intergovernmental meetings between 2000 and 2012, which he presented to a round table in Vancouver on October 13, 2015, hosted by the Institute for Research on Public Policy.[43] While first ministers did not meet as frequently as had been the case under Harper's predecessors, ministerial meetings and meetings of officials continued to be held with some regularity. That said, the data only confirms that Prime Minister Harper did not ignore the provinces and territories, as is heard from his detractors. As much as he avoided meeting personally with the premiers as a group, it is demonstrably true that he had closer bilateral relationships with many of them, and his officials maintained some level of multilateral information sharing. But that reveals simply that Harper managed the fact of federalism as all prime ministers must, not that he innovated in the practice of it.

A closer look at the policy achievements reveals a similar picture. Unlike the public breakups over Meech Lake or the tensions over health and social transfers during the 1990s, the intergovernmental front has been relatively calm since 2006. But it is really all one can say, and by the standard he himself set in 2006, Harper had committed to do a great deal more. In the platform that first took him to government, Harper pledged to create mechanisms for the provinces to engage in federal areas of jurisdiction when they would be affected by the outcome of a decision, with a specific reference to international trade agreements. He pledged to support the Council of the Federation, expand the economic and social union and advance the development of common standards and their mutual recognition across the provinces. Despite nine years in government, he accomplished none of these in any meaningful way.

Drawing from his thinking and writing before he became the leader of the Conservative Party, it seems clear Stephen Harper sought to correct three fundamental failings as he saw them of the Canadian federation:

- The power relationship between the federal government and the provinces had to be rebalanced.
- Western Canada needed a stronger voice.
- Accommodation had to be reached with Quebec nationalists.

Rebalancing Intergovernmental Relations

Harper's commitment to limiting federal involvement in areas of provincial jurisdiction as well as federal spending power was a significant departure from the approach taken by Jean Chrétien and Paul Martin. His abandonment of First Ministers' Meetings and his refusal to engage the Council of the Federation also forced the premiers to play a more explicit leadership role within the federation.

Now that they are used to this role, it will be difficult for a future prime minister to put that genie back in the intergovernmental bottle. This consequence of Harper's approach is not likely to be easily reversed by his successor.

A Stronger Voice for Western Canada

The voice of Western Canada was clearly stronger around Stephen Harper's cabinet table than it had been since the days of Brian Mulroney. Highly competent ministers held senior portfolios, and a number of other qualified MPs held senior committee roles in the Commons. Issues important to Western Canadians were treated with the seriousness they deserved, and in a way that was appropriately reflective of the westward shift in economic and demographic power.

At the Council of the Federation table, the voices of Western Canadian premiers were also influential throughout Harper's time as prime minister. Manitoba premier Gary Doer was instrumental in supporting Charest's plan to create the Council in the first place. Saskatchewan premier Brad Wall contributed tremendously to the Council's work on health innovation as a co-chair of the working group, and Alberta premier Alison Redford's personal leadership on the "Canadian Energy Strategy" file ensured the Council would maintain a balanced—and pan-Canadian—perspective on energy and climate change.

These are indeed important successes, but they are not easily attributable to Harper's approach to federalism. At the federal level, these successes are a result of electoral politics and his personal choices on cabinet formation. Stephen Harper should be commended for making sure the West "got in," to borrow a phrase, but it was not a consequence of how he managed the federation. Similarly, his complete disengagement from the Council of the Federation could not have influenced the role Western premiers played within it. In fact, specifically in relation to Alison Redford's proposal to establish a Canadian Energy Strategy, the prime minister was openly hostile.

Accommodating the Aspirations of Quebec Nationalists

As Martine Tremblay has argued, open federalism depolarized federal political debate in Quebec by providing a "third way," between outright independence and centralized federalism.[44] By extension, it also expanded the range of issues on which voters could make their electoral choice. Thus, open federalism loosened the Bloc's firm hold on most seats off the Island of Montreal and the Outaouais. In this way, Stephen Harper broke the post-Meech mould of federal politics in Quebec. But he didn't necessarily break it in his favour.

In the Greater Quebec City Area, where the right-of-centre provincial party Action démocratique du Québec and its successor, the Coalition Avenir Québec, have also been competitive, the fact that the prime minister could move beyond the unity file to appeal to voters on pocketbook issues proved a successful electoral strategy. Over four elections, almost all Quebec Conservatives elected to Parliament came from that region, and owe their seat to that strategy. Elsewhere in the province, however, the re-emergence of the left-right debate benefited other federalist parties. Freed to consider issues beyond the future of the federation, Quebec voters eventually embraced the left-of-centre platforms of Jack Layton in 2011 and Justin Trudeau in 2015 over the Conservative alternative.

Support for Quebec sovereignty also did not increase on Stephen Harper's watch, despite the election of a PQ government in 2012. According to an analysis of public opinion data conducted by Claire Durand of the Université de Montréal, the YES side maintained its support at roughly 40 per cent, with the exception of a short-lived increase immediately after the election of the Marois government. That same analysis shows, however, that the decrease to 40 per cent began before Stephen Harper became prime minister, and there is nothing in the data trend to suggest that his arrival at 24 Sussex changed the trajectory of intentions on the unity question. More likely, support for sovereignty was returning to the norm of 40 per cent, after a post-sponsorship scandal spike.[45]

That said, while Harper may not have had a direct influence on popular support for sovereignty in Quebec, the two officials with ties to Quebec who were interviewed for this chapter both noted that his refusal to pick fights with the Marois government contributed in no small measure to the PQ's inability to increase support for sovereignty. If Ottawa never takes the bait, how will sovereignist leaders convince Quebecers to get mad at Ottawa?

The timing of Stephen Harper's open federalism overture to Quebec was also opportune. By resigning in January 2001 because the winning conditions for independence would not materialize in the foreseeable future, Lucien Bouchard acknowledged publicly what many sovereignists were already thinking: in the short term, neither constitutional settlement nor independence would be possible.[46] In that context, open federalism became a means to change the channel on unity fatigue and the sponsorship scandal. But it was not the instigator of this fatigue or, in the end, its prime beneficiary.

Granting Quebec a seat at UNESCO and recognizing it as a nation in the House of Commons were strong early symbols of Harper's openness to the province's aspirations, but they soon faded in the shadow of cuts to arts and culture, the elimination of the long-gun registry and support for pipelines. In his nine years in power, Harper maintained a foothold in Quebec, but his support never grew much beyond the beachhead in Quebec City.

Conclusion: Where to from Here?

At any given time, Canadian intergovernmental relations are, in a significant way, a reflection of historical context. Canadian prime ministers can only play the hand they are dealt, and change is more often than not incremental. To this rule, Stephen Harper was no exception. His handling of the federation was a product of history—the country's and his own—but in important ways, he failed to answer history's call to have a lasting impact on the management of the federation that he led. Open federalism might have been what Stephen Harper wanted to do, and what he set out to do, but it is not what he is leaving behind.

Had open federalism been practised in the way it was described in successive campaign platforms and speeches, it would have been not just the logical culmination of twenty years of Stephen Harper's thinking, but a doctrine whose time had come. It responded to the sentiment that led to SUFA and would have remedied the failings of the final agreement. It aligned with the desires of nationalists in Quebec who wanted to preserve their autonomy without having to opt for outright independence. And it suited a political coalition that relied on the strength of the regions to achieve power in Ottawa.

To be clear, the intergovernmental record of Harper's nine years at the helm is not without its successes. The growing power of premiers and the corresponding responsibility for outcomes has the potential to ensure future First Ministers' Meetings are different in form and substance from the failed ones of the past. And the end of the Bloc Québécois's monopoly on seats in that province increases Quebec's voice in all federalist caucuses in Parliament and around the cabinet table. But the call for change that could be heard long before votes were cast in October 2015 included a demand for more active federal leadership on issues of importance to all Canadians.

To be implemented successfully, open federalism requires an equal emphasis on disentanglement, decentralization and collaboration. In practice, the overemphasis on disentanglement at the expense of collaboration made policy innovation difficult under Harper's brand of open federalism. As a result, some experts, such as the University of Saskatchewan's Michael Atkinson and Daniel Béland, have argued that we should not mourn its passing.[47] In the view of this author, however, the implementation of open federalism that we have seen over the last decade should definitely be set aside, but the concept itself should be preserved and tried again.

That does not mean going back to the old ways—Ottawa's role in the federation can and should be re-imagined—but deciding on what that new role is and how it is to be exercised requires engagement with the provinces and territories, Indigenous leaders and citizens. The Charter of Open Federalism that Stephen

Harper promised in two election platforms would have been the ideal means to commit to writing the broad parameters of that relationship and the principles that should guide the conduct of intergovernmental relations in Canada.

By not following through on this campaign commitment, Harper denied himself the most promising instrument he had to guide not just his own actions as prime minister, but those of his successors in managing the complex federation that is Canada. Confirming that history enjoys a good dose of irony from time to time, in his nine years in power, Prime Minister Stephen Harper successfully turned the page on Ottawa's approach to executive federalism as practised by the first Prime Minister Trudeau. But by his own decision to not build the institutional support for his preferred approach, he has left the building of the new order entirely to the second.

2

Harper and the House of Commons:
An Evidence-Based Assessment

R. Paul Wilson

Pending democratic collapse at the hands of a despotic prime minister is a perennial theme in Canadian politics. As early as 1905, the *Toronto News* could refer to the prime minister as "almost the absolute ruler of the country" and opine that:

> Canada is governed by two legislatures, one real, the other sham. The sham legislature is composed of the Governor General, the Senate, and the House of Commons. The real legislature consists of a despotic ruler—the Premier; an upper house—the Cabinet; and a lower house—the caucus of the Government members of parliament ... The pretense that the House of Commons exercises real legislative powers is worn very thin.[1]

The editorialist did not believe these democratic defects peculiar to the prime minister of the day, Wilfrid Laurier, but thought them structural since "they will apply to his successor as soon as he is in the saddle." And apply they did. As W.A. Matheson observed, "the Prime Minister has normally been the dominant figure; those prime ministers who failed to be dominant have not been kindly judged by the electorate or by history."[2] What MacGregor Dawson considered the prime minister's traditional "pre-eminence"[3] grew, as Donald Savoie argues, with the higher concentration of power at the centre beginning with Pierre Trudeau.[4] That argument was popularized by Jeffrey Simpson in his 2001 book *The Friendly Dictatorship,* which called Prime Minister Chrétien the "Sun King" of the government and described the "outward appearances" of democracy in Canada.[5]

The long familiar cries of despotism, however, increased in frequency and intensity after 2006 under the government of Prime Minister Stephen Harper. Indeed, they became something of an industry. Back in 2010, Lawrence Martin asserted in *Harperland: The Politics of Control* that Harper "made previous alleged dictators like Jean Chrétien look like welterweights."[6] Martin catalogued what he saw as Harper's "march of audacities" and predicted that his "authoritarian methods" and "authoritarian bent" meant that "the downgrading of democracy would proceed."[7]

But in the year or so leading up to the 2015 general election, bookstore shelves groaned under the weight of volumes decrying Harper as the chief enemy of Canadian democracy. Take, for example, Michael Harris's *Party of One: Stephen Harper and Canada's Radical Makeover,* which presented a long critique of Harper as a "rogue" politician and threat to democracy, capped by an interview with Farley Mowat comparing Harper to Stalin and concluding that he is "probably the most dangerous human being ever elevated to power in Canada."[8] Mark Bourrie's *Kill the Messengers: Stephen Harper's Assault on Your Right to Know* asserted that "the concentration of power at the centre under the control of a single leader smacks of fascism." Bourrie alleged that Harper has "contempt for democratic institutions" and concluded that "rarely has real government of the people been so threatened."[9] In *The Arrogant Autocrat: Stephen Harper's Takeover of Canada,* Mel Hurtig asserted that the Harper government had behaved like an "autocratic, dictatorial regime" and that winning majority power in the 2011 election "allowed him to systematically dismantle our democracy.[10] John Ralston Saul called Harper's style of parliamentary management "a direct negation of our democratic system. Napoleon would have approved. Mussolini would have been jealous. Peron would have been filled with admiration."[11]

This is only a sample. In the fall of 2015 it was not hard to find another half dozen equally condemnatory titles at a friendly neighbourhood bookseller. At least no one can say the Harper government didn't support Canadian publishing.

The indictment against Harper is loud and sustained, but critics, whether in popular books, newspaper columns or academic journals, often repeat the same charges, many of which relate specifically to conduct in the House of Commons. While frequently repeated, however, many accounts seem long on polemics and short on evidence. Therefore, in the spirit of evidence-based analysis, this chapter proposes to test a selection of these claims concerning the Harper government's relationship with members of Parliament: 1) the creation of a "dirty tricks" manual designed to help Tory MPs manipulate and subvert parliamentary standing committee meetings; 2) extreme discipline in whipping the votes of backbench Conservative MPs in the House of Commons; 3) invoking closure and time allocation to cut off debate; and 4) use of omnibus bills to reduce scrutiny of government legislation by opposition MPs. The chapter concludes that, as with other governments, the continued dominance of the executive in the Harper era warrants concern. But while the Harper government undoubtedly used existing parliamentary rules to their advantage, their practices were for the most part consistent with those of other governments. The allegations of despotism are not only unfounded; they are so fantastic as to bolster a diagnosis of "Harper Derangement Syndrome" in many commentators, to the detriment of our democratic dialogue.

The "Dirty Tricks" Manual

In May 2007, *National Post* columnist Don Martin revealed that the Harper Tories had written a "secret guidebook" designed, in his view, to coach Conservative MPs on "how to unleash chaos while chairing parliamentary committees." The 200-page manual, Martin claimed, illustrates "a government preference for manipulative tactics" and "suggests committee leaders have been whipped into partisan instruments of policy control and agents of the Prime Minister's Office."[12] Conservative whip Jay Hill defended the document, saying that "this so-called book of dirty tricks is nothing more than the parliamentary tools that are available to all committee chairs. And 90 per cent, probably, of the information that's contained in that manual is simply the standing orders that all committee chairs should apprise themselves of."[13] Despite these objections, Martin's column became indisputable and enduring evidence of Harper's "undermining of," indeed "disdain for," parliamentary committees.[14] Yet, other than Martin, none of the critics seem ever to have seen the document. The fact that it was not publicly available prompted the Canadian Association of Income Trust Investors to offer a $10,000 cash reward in September 2008 "for the first bona fide copy of this Parliamentary Obstruction Manual."[15]

But Jay Hill was right. A former insider provided a copy of the binder to me, and it shows that while Martin's account was strictly precise, it was also selective. It was, as he claimed, "some 200 pages including background material." But he did not explain that these 200 pages comprised a 37-page large-font PowerPoint deck supported by appendices: a two-page summary of "Bourinot's Rules at a Glance" taken off the Internet, chapters 20 (Committees) and 12 (The Process of Debate) from Robert Marleau and Camille Montpetit's *House of Commons Procedure and Practice* (2000), and excerpts from chapters VIII (Motions) and XIII (Committees) of the *Standing Orders of the House of Commons*. Nor did Martin mention passages which exhorted chairs to

- "listen carefully to what everyone has to say";
- "ensure that everyone has a chance to speak";
- "remain impartial and try not to talk too much"; and
- "work in conjunction with the Clerk to create a balanced witness list."

In an interview, Doug Smith, former policy director to government House leader Peter Van Loan, told me that he wrote the deck himself and compiled the procedural appendices. In his opinion, the manual was "fairly innocuous" and an entirely appropriate training aid to help inexperienced MPs learn their jobs.[16] As Smith explained, in the spring of 2007, just over a year into the new parliament, inexperienced Conservative committee chairs faced the challenge of advancing their party's political agenda in a context where their opponents held the balance of power. The manual was undoubtedly a useful tool for teaching CPC MPs the procedural rules—and how to use them to their advantage. But using the rules to advantage certainly does not constitute "dirty tricks" in an adversarial system.

None of this is to criticize Don Martin. It is hardly unsurprising for a columnist to emphasize parts of a document to get a better story. As Martin himself commented more recently, columnists can write "in a lot more colourful and creative way" than can reporters, and they "do not have to give both sides" of a story.[17] The surprise is how on the basis of his single and uncorroborated account, the "dirty tricks manual" became a central element in the lore of the Harper government.

Party Discipline and Control over Government MPs

It is accepted wisdom that Stephen Harper's "authoritarian tendencies"[18] extended to members of Parliament, and especially to his Conservative caucus. He "put a virtual muzzle on his MPs and a tight leash on his cabinet," argued Chantal Hébert, and "no federal government has ever been run in quite as controlling a manner,"[19] Dan Gardner believed that his "mastery of his party and caucus [was] absolute."[20] Not surprisingly, backbench Conservative MPs were portrayed as intimidated into silence and submission, or, as Lawrence Martin put it more colourfully, as "bobbleheads" and "wind-up dolls pawing at the master's feet."[21]

Certainly CPC MPs sometimes chafed against strict party discipline. In 2006, MP Garth Turner was evicted from the Conservative caucus for breaking confidentiality and later wrote a book condemning the party leadership.[22] In 2013, MP Brent Rathgeber quit the caucus over perceived PMO interference with the standing committee's consideration of his private member's bill C-461, and he also wrote a book complaining about central control over MPs.[23] Frustration surfaced on numerous occasions from social conservative MPs who were discouraged or prevented from bringing forward proposals related to the sensitive abortion issue, which Harper had vowed not to touch.[24] This frustration culminated in what Chantal Hébert called the "first open caucus rebellion" against Prime Minister Harper[25]—if not explicitly against his leadership, then against the party's control over its MPs. The week after Conservative Mark Warawa's private member's motion to condemn "discrimination against females occurring through sex-selective pregnancy termination"[26] was declared non-votable by the House of Commons Procedure and House Affairs Committee, the Conservative whip removed Warawa from the party-approved list of speakers during the time provided for members' statements. Warawa appealed the loss of his speaking slot to the Speaker, claiming that the whip had violated his privileges as a member of Parliament.[27] In doing so, he took attention away from abortion and focused it on party discipline and the fundamental democratic rights of MPs, something with which a much larger group was prepared to express sympathy. In the end, at least eight Conservative MPs expressed public support for Warawa,[28] including Michael Chong, who later that year introduced his Reform Act (first C-559 and later C-586), which proposed measures to curtail the control of leaders and parties over MPs.

Yet evidence for Harper's treatment of MPs does not run only in one direction, and there are also important indicators that the prime minister permitted at least as much latitude to his MPs as other parties—and perhaps more. Analyzing over 162,000 individual votes cast by members of Parliament in the House of Commons between June 2, 2011, and January 28, 2013, *Globe and Mail* reporters Bill Curry and Stuart Thompson found that Conservative MPs were "far more likely than opposition MPs to break ranks with their own party."[28] However, while a single Don Martin column created the lasting mythology of a Conservative "dirty tricks manual," *The Globe and Mail's* detailed statistical report simply vanished into the ether and did nothing to dispel the view that Stephen Harper oppressed his MPs.

Were voting patterns in the first session of the 41st Parliament an anomaly? I have furthered Curry and Thompson's analysis by looking at the second session of the 41st Parliament, which ran from October 16, 2013, until its final sitting on June 19, 2015, prior to dissolution in August for the general election. As table 2.1 shows, altogether there were 467 specific votes in the House of Commons during the session, with MPs casting 123,405 individual votes. Dissent is not common among any party. Out of 37 occasions which saw dissent, only one MP differed from his caucus majority in the context of a government motion.[30] The other 36 times consisted of private members' business (bills and motions), opposition supply day motions and one committee concurrence motion. So party discipline was alive and well.

Table 2.1
Dissenting Votes by Type and Party

Type of Vote		Occasions of Dissent (by Type)	Number of Dissenting Votes Cast by MPs from Party		
			CPC	NDP	LIB
Government Bill or Motion		1	0	0	1
Private Member's Bill	CPC	11	106	17	10
	NDP	10	20	15	0
	LIB	5	12	0	0
Private Member's Motion	CPC	1	1	0	0
	NDP	4	12	0	0
	LIB	0	0	0	0
Opposition Supply Day	NDP	3	4	0	15
	LIB	1	1	0	0
Concurrence in Committee Report		1	27	15	1
Total Occasions of Dissent		37			
Total Dissenting Votes Cast			183	47	27
Number of MPs in Caucus (at Dissolution)			159	95	36
Number of Dissenting Votes per Caucus Member (at Dissolution)			1.15	0.49	0.75

Total number of votes held in House during session = 467
Total number of votes cast by individual MPs = 123,405

Source: Database of House of Commons votes for the 41st Parliament, 2nd session, available on the Parliament of Canada website. Compiled by the author.

But to the extent that dissent occurred in that parliamentary session, it was (consistent with Curry and Thompson's findings) more common among CPC MPs. In total, they dissented from their own caucus majority 183 times. This amounts to a CPC MP dissenting 7.1 per cent of the time (33 separate votes out of the total of 467 votes in the session) or, expressed based on party standings at dissolution, 1.15 dissenting votes per CPC MP. By contrast, NDP MPs dissented 47 times total on 6 of the 467 votes held in the session (1.3 per cent of votes), or 0.49 dissenting votes per NDP MP. For the NDP this amounted to a somewhat different pattern from the first session, where Curry and Thompson found "ironclad discipline" in the party with not a single vote by an NDP MP out of step with the caucus. Liberal MPs dissented from their caucus majority 1.5 per cent of the time (7 out of the total of 467 votes) or 0.75 votes per Liberal MP.

Table 2.2 shows the top ten dissenting MPs in the session as a percentage of votes cast in dissent from their caucus colleagues. The top six are all from the Conservative Party, as well as eight of the top ten, including Gordon O'Connor, who had been the Conservative whip from 2008 to 2013. One MP each from the Liberal Party and NDP made the list. With 10 dissenting votes, CPC MP Michael Chong—who successfully sponsored a private member's bill to limit party control over MPs—had the highest percentage of votes against his party's line.

Table 2.2
Top Ten Dissenting MPs by Percentage of Votes Cast in Dissent from Party Caucus

MP	Party	Votes Cast	Votes against Party	Votes with Party	% Votes against Party
Michael Chong	CPC	465	10	455	2.151
Brad Trost	CPC	441	7	434	1.587
Peter Goldring	CPC	398	6	392	1.508
Mark Warawa	CPC	423	6	417	1.418
Stephen Woodworth	CPC	447	5	442	1.119
Gordon O'Connor	CPC	370	4	366	1.081
Mauril Bélanger	LIB	432	4	428	0.926
Gerald Keddy	CPC	444	4	440	0.901
John Williamson	CPC	448	4	444	0.893
Mark Charlton	NDP	342	3	339	0.877

Source: Database of House of Commons votes for the 41st Parliament, 2nd session, available on the Parliament of Canada website. Compiled by the author.

This is not to argue that discipline is lax among Conservative MPs. In the 41st Parliament they, like all Canadian parliamentarians, toed the party line on the vast majority of votes. Indeed, the fact that dissent was largely restricted to private members' business—when, in theory at least, the whip is not applied—and opposition motions might reveal greater ideological diversity among Conservatives rather than looser discipline. Even if this is true, however, the greater willingness of CPC MPs to dissent from their caucus colleagues certainly mitigates claims of authoritarian control.

Stephen Harper also introduced an important innovation in the relationship between cabinet and caucus: the Minister's Caucus Advisory Committees (MCACs). In August 2010, Harper assigned backbench Conservative MPs and senators to newly created caucus committees that corresponded to House of

Commons standing committees, and he required ministers to consult with these committees prior to taking any proposal to cabinet.[31] While they received very limited media attention,[32] these committees became an important part of the government policy development process since ministers were required to include a report from the committee in their cabinet submission.[33] MPs "got into it with gusto," one former Conservative minister explained, because "they know the PM takes it seriously"[34] and that their views would be considered at the cabinet table. Another MP explained that MCACs "unquestionably" empowered caucus because they allowed MPs to bring their political and regional perspectives to the discussion of policy issues, and gave ministers an incentive to listen and to make changes. "This is a bottom up process, not top down," he explained. "This is a way for the PM to acknowledge that caucus needed more control and input." In his opinion, MCACs were an important legacy for the Harper government: "When writers take on the PM they had better dedicate at least one chapter to this [the MCACs] because it's so significant."[35] Like the CPC voting record, MCACs also present an important counter-balance to the narrative of prime ministerial dictatorship over caucus.

Closure and Time Allocation

As C.E.S. Franks explains in his magisterial work *The Parliament of Canada*, the growth in federal government size and complexity in the 1960s increased the volume of parliamentary business and led to battles between the government and opposition for control of the House of Commons' agenda and timetable.[36] Management of the House is a two-way street. As Franks explains, opposition parties are motivated to delay the progress of legislation in an effort to embarrass or frustrate the government and gain time to rouse public support. For its part, the government responds by either avoiding Parliament or using procedural rules to curtail debate. Such procedural rules are intended, he says, "to ensure fair play, but what to a government looks like a reasonable and fair time to end a prolonged and no longer productive debate can look to the opposition like an unreasonable trampling of their rights of expression and interrogation."[37] Use of such measures, therefore, is bound to be controversial.

A government has two principal options for shortening debate. Closure (under Standing Order 57) ends debate and forces a vote on the motion under consideration that same sitting day. Time allocation allows the government to manage the house schedule through setting limits on debate, and while this can be done by negotiating agreement with all opposition parties (Standing Order 78(1)) or with a majority of them (Standing Order 78(2)), it is most commonly employed by the government unilaterally when agreement cannot be reached. Closure so acts, as O'Brien and Bosc observe, as a "guillotine."[38] Added to the Standing Orders by Prime Minister Pierre Trudeau in 1969,[39] time allocation has become a prominent government tactic in all majority parliaments (and even occasionally in some minority parliaments) since 1974.[40] Its use, however, increased significantly under Stephen Harper's majority government in the 41st Parliament, leading to claims, well summarized by Green Party leader Elizabeth May, that "the House and its members have been deprived of fulfilling constitutional rights, our privilege, and our obligation to hold the government to account, because of the imposition of intemperate and unrestrained guillotine measures."[41]

The increase in instances of time allocation is undeniable. However, François Plante believes, based on his analysis of historical practice, that this is not the whole story. While he found that the Harper government's use of time allocation affected "an abnormally high proportion of bills," he also concluded that there was a "small increase in the time allotted."[42] That is, according to Plante, the Harper government on average allowed more days of debate after imposing time allocation (2.4 days) than any previous government has done back to the 28th Parliament (1968–1972). Used this way, he suggests, time allocation is "more consistent with the concept of a time management tool than an abusive way of gagging the opposition."[43]

Table 2.3
Use of Time Allocation Under Standing Order 78(3)—1993–2015

| Average Number of Debate Days Complete or Underway Average at time of: | | | | | | | |
Parliament	Years	Number of S.O. 78(3) Motions Adopted	Number of Bills Affected	Average Days Debate before Notice	Average Days Debate before Adoption	Avg. Debate Days Allocated	Total Days of Debate
35th	1994-1997	20	14	2.1	2.2	1.5	3.7
36th	1997-2000	30	20	1.4	1.4	1.6	3
37th	2001-2004	12	10	2.5	2.5	1.5	4
38th	2004-2005	0	0	-	-	-	-
39th	2006-2008	1	1	3.0	3.0	1.0	4
40th	2008-2011	3	2	2.0	2.7	1.7	4.4
41st-1st	2011-2013	47	32	1.5	1.5	2.1	3.6
41st-2nd	2013-2015	43	34	1.4	1.4	2.0	3.4

Sources: Data for 35th to 40th Parliaments from François Plante, "The Curtailment of Debate in the House of Commons," *Canadian Parliamentary Review* 36, no. 1 (2013): 34. Data for 41st Parliament compiled by the author from House of Commons Status of House Business report for each session as well as House of Commons Debates. Documents are available at wwww.parl.gc.ca.
Note: Shaded area indicates minority parliament.

Plante's analysis only covered up to June 23, 2012. Does the pattern hold for the entire 41st Parliament? Table 2.3 presents Plante's data for the 35th to 40th Parliaments, along with updated information for the two sessions of the 41st Parliament when the Conservative Party held a majority of seats, from June 2, 2011, until dissolution of Parliament on August 2, 2015, for the general election. As the table shows, the Harper government on average allowed 2.1 days of debate after each vote of time allocation in the first session of the 41st Parliament, and slightly less (2 days) in the second session. Including time spent in debate prior to the 78(3) vote, the Harper government on average allowed 3.6 days of debate in total on time allocated bills in the first session of the 41st Parliament and 3.4 debate days in the second session. By comparison, the Chrétien majority government tended to allow more days of debate prior to introducing time allocation, but fewer days afterwards, and so on average total debate on time allocated bills in the 35th, 36th and 37th Parliaments was, respectively, 3.7 days, 3 days and 4 days. This is consistent with the practice under Harper.

Even though the Harper government allowed similar debate on time allocated bills as the Chrétien government, does the fact that the Conservatives used 78(3) much more frequently mean that overall debate time in the House was curtailed?

As table 2.4 shows, this is not the case. Despite record use of time allocation, the average amount of debate during the Harper majority government from 2011 to 2015 was 3.92 days per bill in both the first and second sessions of the 41st Parliament. As illustrated by figure 2.1, this is higher than all other sessions since 1994 except for the first Harper minority session (39-1) and two sessions under Chrétien (36-2 and 37-1), all three of which had over four days of debate per bill. Debate time under the Harper majority therefore compares very well with practice in recent decades.

Figure 2.1
Average Days of House of Commons Debate per Government Bill

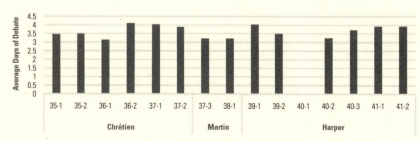

Of course, dynamics in the House of Commons are complex, and more debate is not necessarily a good thing. For example, consensus between parties can mean that bills are adopted with little or no debate—sometimes with unanimous consent in very short order. Conversely, protracted debate can indicate acrimony and a breakdown of negotiations to advance the government's agenda. Undoubtedly, the Conservative government used time allocation to limit debate. But the evidence seems to back up the claim made by House leader Peter Van Loan that the government used it, in part at least, as a "scheduling device" to manage debate[44] and not simply as a way to stifle the opposition. Under Stephen Harper, overall allowance for debate was consistent with that of previous governments and within the normal limits of acceptable parliamentary practice in Canada.

Table 2.4
Average Days of Debate for All Government Bills—1994–2015

Average Days of Debate at Each Stage per Bill						
Prime Minister	Parliament and Session	2nd Reading	Report Stage	3rd Reading	Consideration of Senate Amendments	Total Avg. Debate per Bill
Chrétien	35-1	1.82	0.53	1.11	-	3.46
	35-2	1.32	0.82	1.20	0.17	3.51
	36-1	1.58	0.77	0.78	0.03	3.16
	36-2	1.92	1.10	0.93	0.17	4.12
	37-1	1.71	0.75	1.44	0.15	4.05
	37-2	1.66	0.63	1.29	0.31	3.89
Martin	37-3	1.16	0.44	1.63	-	3.23
	38-1	1.79	0.39	0.96	0.07	3.21
Harper	39-1	1.97	1.12	0.93	0.02	4.04
	39-2	1.62	0.59	1.17	0.13	3.51
	40-1c	-	-	-	-	-
	40-2	1.83	0.29	1.14	-	3.26
	40-3	2.15	0.55	1.00	-	3.70
	41-1	2.29	0.67	0.92	0.04	3.92
	41-2	2.20	0.63	1.09	-	3.92

Source: Compiled by the author from House of Commons Status of House Business report for each parliamentary session (available at www.parl.gc.ca).
Note: Shaded area indicates minority parliament. Analysis considers all government bills initially tabled in the House of Commons in each parliamentary session. Debate on government motions, government Senate bills and all private member's business is not included.
a. Bills which are reinstated after prorogation are not included in calculating the average days of debate per bill for stages at which they are deemed adopted by order of the House.
b. For simplicity, debate on motions to refer bills to committee prior to second reading is included in second reading totals.
c. The government introduced four bills in the first session of the 40th Parliament (November and December 2008) but none was debated prior to prorogation.

Indeed, it is worth noting that under the "sunny ways" of new Liberal prime minister Justin Trudeau, management of the parliamentary calendar continues to look much as it had under the Harper government. For example, the *Status of House Business* report for the first session of the 42nd Parliament shows that, as of June 10, 2016, the Liberal government adopted time allocation motions six times on four separate bills. Excluding three appropriation bills (which are expedited under their own special standing orders), the government used time allocation on three of the four bills which have so far passed in the House of Commons, including C-14, the Medical Assistance in Dying bill. It was Prime Minister Trudeau's personal attempt to speed up the time allocation vote on C-14 which led to his "manhandling" several opposition MPs and subsequent controversy for the government.[45] One can only speculate what critics would have said had Prime Minister Harper physically contacted opposition MPs in order to hasten time allocation.

Omnibus Bills

Critics frequently accused the Harper government of abusing omnibus bills—and in particular omnibus budget bills—in order in order to pass extensive and complex legislative amendments through Parliament without giving the opposition an effective opportunity to respond. C.E.S. Franks has been among the most vocal critics, calling the increase in omnibus budget bills "offensive to the traditions and principles of parliamentary government."[46] The evidence suggests there is room for concern.

Omnibus bills have long been prominent in Canada. The earliest has been identified in 1888,[47] and controversial examples include Pierre Trudeau's criminal law amendments in 1968, his 1982 Energy Security Act, which created the National Energy program and led to the famous "bell-ringing incident," and Brian Mulroney's 1988 act to implement the Canada-US Free Trade Agreement.[48] O'Brien and Bosc say that omnibus bills generally seek to amend multiple acts through "a number of related but separate initiatives," and cite House of Commons speaker John Fraser's 1988 definition requiring "one basic principle or purpose which ties together all the proposed enactments and thereby renders the Bill intelligible for parliamentary purposes." [49] While speakers have repeatedly upheld the legitimacy of omnibus bills, they have also cautioned that there may be a procedural limit to how far the single unifying principle may be stretched: "Where is the point of no return?" asked Speaker Lucien Lamoureux in 1971. "We might reach the point where we would have only one bill, a bill at the start of the session for the improvement of the quality of life in Canada which would include every single proposed piece of legislation for the session."[50] No speaker has yet ruled that the line has been crossed.

Table 2.5
Budget Implementation Acts—1994–2015

Prime Minister	Budget Date	Bill Number	Length at Royal Assent (Pages)	Days of Debate
Chrétien	1994-02-22	C-17	21	7
	1995-02-27	C-76	48	8
	1996-03-06	C-31	53	4
	1997-02-18	C-93	58	3
	1998-02-24	C-36	82	6
	1999-02-16	C-71	27	6
	2000-02-28	C-32	30	6
	2001-12-10	C-49	112	7
	2003-02-18	C-28	133	9
Martin	2004-03-23	C-30	56	5
		C-33	76	4
	2005-02-23	C-43	102	10
Harper	2006-05-02	C-13	186	4
		C-28	134	6
		C-52	134	10
	2007-03-19	C-28	367	8
	2008-02-26	C-50	139	10
	2009-01-27	C-10	528	9
		C-51	52	5
	2010-03-04	C-9	880	12
		C-47	143	6
	2011-06-06	C-3	48	2
		C-13	644	7
	2012-03-29	C-38	425	11
		C-45	414	9
	2013-03-21	C-60	116	8
		C-4	309	8
		C-31	363	9
	2014-02-11	C-43	460	7
	2015-04-21	C-59	158	6

Source: Author's compilation based on Parliament of Canada website (www.parl.gc.ca), principally LEGISinfo and Status of House Business reports for each parliamentary session. Shaded area indicates minority parliament. Page numbers refer to pagination in the print format PDF version.

Since, as O'Brien and Bosc note, "there is no precise definition of an omnibus bill,"[51] this section will study the evolution of budget implementation acts (BIAs) as a proxy in order to assess the comparative use of omnibus bills over time. This is useful since many of the Harper BIAs attracted significant controversy and were seen as stretching the requirement for bills to cohere around "one basic principle." For example, Bill C-9, tabled in March 2010, ran to 880 pages and proposed amendments to a wide range of other statutes whose connection to the budget was not obvious. Among the most controversial were amendments to the Canadian Environmental Protection Act that led environmental groups to claim that the government was "gutting" environmental assessment provisions.[52]

In May 2012 Aaron Wherry of *Maclean's* compared the length of all BIAs back to 1994[53] and demonstrated a trend under Prime Minister Harper toward bigger and more frequent omnibus budget bills. Table 2.5 presents complete data on BIAs up to the 2015 dissolution of Parliament and confirms that the trend Wherry observed in 2012 continued. From 1994 to 2005 each BIA was on average 66.5 pages in length, but from 2006 to 2015 under the Harper government each BIA averaged 305.5 pages. While the Chrétien government only tabled one BIA each year (and none in 2002), the Martin government tabled two in 2004. This became standard under the Conservatives, who tabled two BIAs each year from 2006 on, except in 2008 and 2015, when fall elections disrupted the normal parliamentary calendar. This combination of bigger bills more often meant that the total volume of budget enabling legislation before parliament grew significantly. Figure 2.2 illustrates the increase in pages per year, which reached a high of 1,023 pages in 2010. Altogether, the annual volume of BIA legislation under the Conservative government averaged 550 pages per year.

Fig. 2.2

Total Pages Included in Budget Implementation Acts per Year, 1994–2015

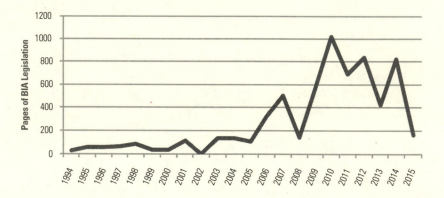

The rules permit such a practice. As explained above, the requirement for "one basic principle" has always been elastic, and while many of the measures are not explicitly spelled out in the budget documents they nevertheless relate to the government's broad fiscal plan since, as James Rajotte, chair of the Finance Standing Committee, argued, "everything the government does is fiscally related because it is dependent on the government allocating resources to it."[54] From the government's point of view, this is an efficient way to proceed. However, it is almost impossible for individual members of Parliament, both government and opposition, to properly understand the myriad provisions in such bills, nor does any single parliamentary standing committee, such as the Finance Committee, which would normally review budget bills, have sufficient expertise to analyze provisions ranging across the spectrum of government policy. Further, as table 5 shows, the time provided for debate does not increase commensurate with the size of the bills.

In 1994, the Chrétien government allowed seven days of debate on C-17, a 21-page BIA. In that context, then–Reform Party MP Stephen Harper objected to the speaker on a point of privilege that "the subject matter of the bill is so diverse that a single vote on the content would put members in a conflict of interest with their own principles," and he asked that government MPs "give serious consideration to this issue of democracy and the functionality of this Parliament now."[55] Harper the Reform MP would not likely have been satisfied with the same seven days of debate for the 644-page C-13 in 2011. Given the challenges for transparency and accountability inherent in such bills, the Conservative government's massive increase in the annual volume of omnibus budget legislation justified significant concern.

Reflection

This chapter has presented a narrow examination of the Harper government's record on a few key points, and on these points the charge of undemocratic behaviour is for the most part unsubstantiated. All prime ministers control their MPs; all use House rules such as time allocation to pass their legislation. The Harper government behaved within the limits of accepted practice in these respects. Of course, saying "everybody else does it" is hardly a strong defence. Neither, however, does it warrant the frenzied vitriol so commonly expressed. In the case of omnibus bills, Harper boldly went where no prime minister had gone before. But even a strong critic such as Franks concedes that an 880-page bill such as C-9 in 2010 "is as much a symptom of underlying problems in our Parliament as it is a problem itself" since our legislative process has "become cumbersome, slow, and unproductive"—the same sort of criticism he made almost thirty years ago.[56]

So why the fury?

First, from the beginning many people in the Harper government viewed them-selves as outsiders and therefore brought a defensive, embattled approach to the job. Their well-documented war with the national press gallery[57] meant that the government frequently refused to explain its choices and seek broader support, or relied on "rote memorization" of carefully scripted talking points rather than argument.[58] As one senior Harper PMO staffer explained, the government was dis-inclined to respond to criticism because "when we're explaining, we're losing."[59] So they stopped talking. This works as a short-term issues-management approach, since if you say nothing, then nothing can be held against you. But this leaves a vacuum that opponents were quite prepared to fill with their narrative. And this narrative was one of democratic abuse.

Second, at times the government abandoned the pretense that Parliament should be taken seriously. While in 1905 the *Toronto News* may have viewed Parliament as a "sham legislature," nevertheless it recognized that there was a "convention of mystification to treat the House of Commons with great respect."[60] Question Period is an apt example. Governments seldom answer questions, but they usually strive to maintain at least the appearance of answering. Paul Wells dubbed Herb Gray, Liberal House leader under Prime Minister Chrétien, "the Gray Fog" for his "fantastic ability to say nothing comprehensible,"[61] yet Gray was widely viewed even by political opponents as respecting Parliament's traditions. This was sometimes not the case under the Conservatives. Instead, the prime minister's parliamentary secretary and chief spokesperson in QP, Paul Calandra, was forced to "unconditionally and unreservedly apologize" for his "behaviour,"[62] which was generally viewed as chronic and disrespectful non sequiturs in response to oppo-sition questions.[63]

This attitude undoubtedly developed following the Harper government's 2006 election when, in a minority position and without natural allies in the House, it used parliamentary tools to advance its agenda rather than pursue consensus entirely on terms dictated by its opponents. In this context omnibus budget bills were an important tactic because the opposition either had to let them pass or precipitate an unwanted election,[64] whereas ordinary bills could be delayed with impunity.

The May 2011 election, however, was a watershed moment. When the Conservatives returned with a majority, they could have chosen a different approach. Instead, they maintained the "command and control" model[65] includ-ing in House management with respect to time allocation and omnibus bills. It is ironic that while an earlier prime minister, Joe Clark, unsuccessfully tried to govern with a minority as if he had a majority, Prime Minister Harper in some respects governed with a majority as if he had a minority, doubling down on the aggressive procedural tactics upon which he had previously relied. But what might be defensible or excused in a minority parliament could be—and was—portrayed as abusive with a majority.

There is another aspect, however. The 2007 committee manual is a small but instructive point. One single newspaper column entrenched the accusation of "dirty tricks" in the popular narrative. This is Stephen Colbert's "truthiness"[66] at work: it fit what critics wanted to believe and became true by repetition, not by substantiation. But a newspaper article conclusively demonstrating that CPC MPs broke ranks more often didn't prove the point and so was ignored. Too often, as Andrew Coyne observed, Harper critics blurred the line "between abuse of power and mere use of power."[67] Numerous commentators including Lorne Gunter have noted the existence of "Harper Derangement Syndrome," a condition in which the "ideological hatred of Prime Minister Stephen Harper" and his policy choices was so acute its sufferers were "prepared to believe the wildest accusations against the man, no matter how thin the evidence."[68] People of good faith may disagree about the policy choices of the Harper government, as with any government, and its style and tone attracted criticism, as the post–2015 election consensus, even among Conservatives, made clear.[69] But examining the evidence shows that its alleged sins against parliamentary democracy were vastly exaggerated. And accusations of fascism? Comparisons to Stalin, Mussolini, Napoleon? Such language has consequences in Parliament and outside and only increases the coarseness and extremism that characterize an alarming amount of our political discourse.

3

Stephen Harper and the Federal Public Service: An Uneasy and Unresolved Relationship

David Zussman

Over the past thirty years, much has been written about the centralization of political power in Canada.[1] In fact, there has been a very active conversation in all Westminster jurisdictions about the growing importance of prime ministers and the consolidation of power through their increased use of political staff and their growing control over the decision-making and appointment processes. The evolution of the prime minister's job to truly being "first among equals" or "primus inter pares" is the result of four important developments in Westminster governments.

The first of these four changes was the development of the Internet as distributor of information and the attendant explosion in the number of experts, commentators and government watchers who had easy access to large and broadly based audiences. Second, was the refashioning of news reporting into 24-7 news cycles that were designed for the increasingly popular all-news TV and radio stations. These news stations created huge content holes, which were filled with easily accessible news items that were inexpensive to produce and interesting to the average consumer. Third was the increase in the number of leadership activities, especially in the international arena, that are now considered major parts of the prime minister's job.[2] Finally, given the increased number of minority governments occurring in parliamentary systems in recent years, many political parties now operate on full election footing even when the real likelihood of an election could be years away.

Each of these developments has its own independent trajectory, but together they have subjected governments and, more specifically, the Office of the Prime Minister to more public scrutiny and accountability than ever before. As a consequence, all prime ministers in Westminster systems seek to mitigate the scrutiny by controlling government messaging and communications to ensure that the public and interest groups see their governments in the most positive way possible.[3]

While these four developments have been hugely consequential to government operations in their own right, they also coincided with the arrival of Stephen Harper in 2004 as the leader of the newly formed Conservative Party of Canada.[4]

The Early Days

When Stephen Harper flew to Ottawa on January 24, 2006, the day after the general election, he had little discernible track record in managing a large, multi-faceted organization. He did not know much about the public service, and what he thought he knew, he did not like. Even in the final days of the 2006 election campaign, he suggested the civil service was partisan. "The reality is that we will have, for some time to come, a Liberal Senate, a Liberal civil service, at least the senior levels where they've been appointed by the Liberals," Harper said.[5]

It has also been reported that his initial views of the impartiality of the public service did not change much during his early meetings with senior deputy ministers, who pointed out to him that his platform agenda was rather thin and would not do much for economic growth (particularly the reduction of the GST). He revealed some of that frustration in a 2007 interview with the CBC's Rex Murphy when he commented that one of the most difficult parts of his job was dealing with the federal bureaucracy. "It's walking that fine line of, of being a positive leader of the federal public service, but at the same time pushing them and not becoming captive to them," Harper explained.[6]

Most people working for the prime minister did not expect his government to survive more than six months before being forced to contest another election and face the prospect of being relegated to the grouping of prime ministers (Clark, Turner, Campbell and Martin) who failed to accomplish much during their terms. However, he survived, learned how to manage diverse political and ideological differences within his caucus, and subsequently led his party to another minority government in 2008, followed by a majority government in 2011. Measured against any traditional indicators, cobbling together all conservative elements in Canada and keeping the coalition together over almost a decade has been a major accomplishment.

The Harper minority government was first sworn into office on February 6, 2006, with a very narrow and limited policy agenda made up of the five priorities on which the Conservative Party had campaigned.[7] In what has become a very characteristic management approach, Harper threw himself into the job of directing the government with his usual forthright style.

In response to the Harper victory, the public service welcomed the new government with greater than usual enthusiasm for a number of reasons. First, the Canadian public service strongly believes in a professional and non-partisan public service, so it was natural that they would want to project a welcoming posture that would include a plan to implement the new government's policy agenda. Second, the federal government policy community was happy to welcome a new set of political actors since they were exhausted and frustrated by the often-chaotic Martin government, where everything was a priority but little was accomplished. The senior public service was still reeling from the 2003 transition to the Martin government, whose political staff appeared intent on undoing the friendly relationship that had been established between the public service and the Chrétien government.[8]

The mood of the Ottawa-based public service was captured in an *Ottawa Citizen* article published in early 2006 where it was noted that "Some quarters of Canada's public service were secretly looking forward to a change in government and getting out from under the mountain of rules and red tape imposed by the Martin Liberals."[9]

While the public service was simultaneously welcoming and somewhat nervous about the arrival of the Harper government, the Harper-led tsunami sweeping in from Calgary was deeply suspicious of the public service—as are most governments when they come to power.[10] This was especially the case for the prime minister, who was never convinced that the welcoming words from the Privy Council Office (PCO) were sincere.[11]

A Snapshot of the Public Service

Given Harper's strong belief in a limited role for government and his trepidation vis-à-vis the public service, how did he reconcile his personal beliefs with the administrative and legal requirements of managing a large public service? This section provides a limited statistical overview of how the public service fared under the nearly ten years of Harper prime ministership using a number of key indicators.[12] The measure is the size of government, defined by the number of federal public servants, the number of executives, the size of the ministry and the number of administrative entities.

Fig. 3.1
Size of the Public Service

Number of Federal Public Servants

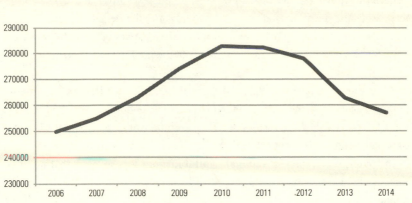

Source: data from Clerk's Annual Reports, available at www.clerk.gc.ca.

Fig. 3.2
Size of the Executive Cadre (EXs)

Federal Government Executives

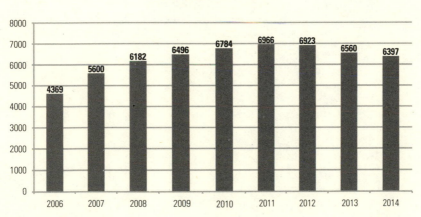

Source: data from Clerk's Annual Reports, available at www.clerk.gc.ca.

The growth of the public service slowed during the Martin years but resumed a steady climb through the minority Harper years, reaching its peak in 2010, as figure 3.1 shows. By 2014, the public service had been significantly reduced, but was still larger than when Harper took office in 2006. A similar but less pronounced pattern of growth and decline can be seen among executives and deputy ministers/associate deputy ministers (figure 3.2). Only after the Deficit Reduction Action Plan (DRAP) exercise in 2011 did the number of executives taper off to its current level. By the end of 2014, the executive ranks of the public service had grown by 37 per cent under Harper.

Over the same period of leadership by Prime Minister Harper, basic demographic trends continued. The proportion of female public servants continued to rise, there was a slow increase in diversity and the workforce got older. Perhaps most surprising is that there continued to be an increase in the concentration of the public service in the National Capital Region. This suggests that no intentional political focus has been brought to bear on the regional footprint of the public service.

Fig. 3.3
Size of the Ministry

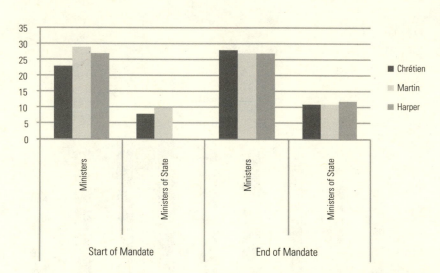

Source: data from Clerk's Annual Reports, available at www.clerk.gc.ca.

The steady increase in the size of the public service after the election of the Harper government in 2006 is also mirrored in the increase in the size of the ministry. As shown in figure 3.3, Harper maintained the same number of ministers as his predecessor Martin, but significantly increased the overall size of his ministry through the appointment of twelve additional ministers of state.

Instead of shedding jobs or limiting the size of the executive cadre, the federal government did move, however, to abolish some federal entities (figure 3.4).[13] Nevertheless, the changes are small in number when compared to the overall number of entities.[14] Overall, government observers assumed that Harper's tenure as leader would coincide with a shrinking of the public service, in keeping with his rhetoric leading up to his election victory. But the evidence indicates that, over Harper's nearly ten years as prime minister, the number of public servants rose steadily until the 2008 global financial crisis forced the federal government to establish the $64 billion Economic Action Plan (EAP) to stimulate employment across the country by financing shovel-ready projects from coast to coast.[15] Only in 2011 did the federal government turn its attention to the size of government, slashing jobs through the DRAP.[16]

Fig. 3.4
Number of Federal Entities

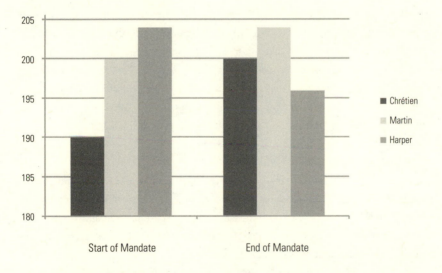

Source: data from Clerk's Annual Reports, available at www.clerk.gc.ca.

Significant Public Service Related Policy Initiatives

Historically, some prime ministers have wished to leave an organizational legacy or a signature project that would underscore their policy priorities. In the case of Stephen Harper, it is hard to discern any particular machinery of government change that would serve to symbolize his policy agenda. In general, he has done some "normal" tinkering to effect policy goals. One example is the merger of the Canadian International Development Agency (CIDA) with the Department of Foreign Affairs and International Trade, and the creation of the Major Projects Management Office. But none of them were anchored by any policy thrust or championed as examples of a new way of governing.

Two important innovative reorganizational changes that the prime minister led were strengthening Departmental Audit Committees (DACs) under the new Federal Accountability Act and amalgamating the many departmental back office administrative and IT systems into a new organization called Shared Services Canada (SSC). However, neither of the two large-scale efforts led to any significant efficiency gains despite their potential as real transformational exercises. At best, the audit committees, which include a large number of expert members from outside government, were a useful sounding board for the deputy minister regarding financial and managerial issues. The SSC lost its way without any meaningful achievements over its four years.

Perhaps more significantly, Justice John Gomery's hearings on the sponsorship program and the commission of inquiry's resulting report gave the Conservative Party plenty of ammunition to attack the Martin government in the 2006 federal election. This in turn led to a series of campaign promises about the need to rid the federal government of "corruption" and mismanagement. It was therefore not surprising that Harper's first piece of legislation was the Federal Accountability Act. At the same time, the government continued to pursue its plans for a more limited role for government by initiating a series of cost containment exercises, which also had a significant impact on the public service.

The Federal Accountability Act

In opposition, Stephen Harper would routinely rail about the corruption in government and how under his leadership, he would make the system more accountable than ever. He made greater accountability and transparency one of his five priorities during the 2006 election campaign and as a result, the Federal Accountability Act (FAA) was his first piece of legislation.

In his March 2006 speech to senior public servants, Harper mixed glowing praise for the work of bureaucrats while underscoring his concern that the public service needed to be more closely monitored. He stated it this way: "we clearly face challenges today in ensuring for the public the highest standards of integrity, effectiveness and accountability."[17]

There were many important elements in the FAA and almost all of them had an impact on public servants in significant ways. For example, the FAA included the creation of five independent oversight organizations (lobbying, conflict of interest and ethics, contracting and procurement, public prosecutions, whistle-blowing and the Parliamentary Budget Office). The legislation increased the scope of access to information, announced the creation of a Public Appointments Commission and reformed political financing. For the public service, the most consequential element in the FAA was the provision that made deputy ministers accounting officers and accountable to Parliament for all activities in their respective departments and agencies.

The accounting officer provision was based on the UK model, which clearly separated the responsibilities of ministers and deputy ministers. This provision made explicit what had been a convention for many years, which was that deputy ministers would be explicitly responsible for administrative matters. While ministers would remain accountable in Parliament for administration and policy decisions, in the end, deputy ministers could expect to be on the pointy end of any questions about the efficiency of their department or agency.

As well, the FAA ended the practice of exempt staff being given preferential consideration for jobs within the public service, and instituted a five-year ban on lobbying for "designated public office holders" after leaving government.

Cost Containment

In addition to attacking the perceived corruption of previous Liberal governments by passing the FAA, the other major policy initiative of the Harper government was a series of cost containment exercises that were all designed to limit the size of the state and constrain spending. Smaller and less intrusive government was a touchstone for the newly created Conservative Party when the merger of the Progressive Conservative Party and the Canadian Alliance created it in 2003. As a consequence, the Conservative government projected an image of being in favour of much smaller government by driving four major cost reduction exercises beginning in 2006. Each exercise had a unique methodology, approach and name: the Administrative Service Review (ASR), the Strategic Review (SR), the Strategic and Operating Review (SOR) and finally, the Deficit Reduction Action Plan (DRAP).[18]

In general terms, the Harper government used these cost containment efforts to achieve a number of different objectives without the guidance of an overarching narrative, except for the occasional reference to "transforming government" and "making government more efficient." Even though cost containment was the primary objective, Department of Finance data suggests that the impact of these exercises in terms of spending cuts is less dramatic that the rhetoric would suggest (figure 3.5).

Fig. 3.5
Government Expenditures

Source: Department of Finance, *Fiscal Reference Tables*, Table 7.

Fig. 3.6
Expenditures as a Percentage of GDP

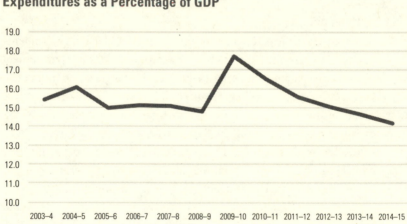

Source: Department of Finance, *Fiscal Reference Tables*, Table 8.

When the Conservatives were first elected in 2006, they inherited an $8 billion surplus from outgoing prime minister Paul Martin. In due course, the surplus soon disappeared as the government implemented a number of targeted tax relief measures that were designed to maintain the support of their voter base. More importantly, the government continued to hire new public servants into positions that supported their high-priority policy areas. In particular, this included new positions in domestic and international security, in law enforcement and in financial oversight.

As a result, government spending continued to rise, from 2006 when Stephen Harper won his first minority government until 2011 when the DRAP, the last of the cost containment exercises, was implemented. DRAP achieved its goals by reducing the size of the federal public service by more than 17,000 jobs and by cutting some programs and agencies (such as the Canadian Food Inspection Agency), thereby altering the shape of the expenditures of the federal government (figure 3.6).

An analysis of the *Public Accounts* figures for Expenditure Object 01 (Personnel), 2006 through 2014, provides evidence of where the government moved to limit human resource costs.[19] For example, the government took action on the ending and cashing out of severance (except for involuntary layoff), increased employee pension contributions toward 50 per cent of current service costs, introduced later eligibility for unreduced pensions for new hires and signalled its intention to reform sick and disability leave to reduce perceived misuse.[20]

However, it is hard to characterize the Harper government as spendthrift, or as having a special agenda against the scale of the federal public service. The Sprott School of Business's Ian Lee observed that although the federal government went through a number of strategic spending reviews and hiring freezes over the past twenty years, there were also periods of growth in the later Chrétien years and under Harper from 2006 to 2011.

Indeed, while the Harper government hired an additional 30,000 employees during its tenure, under its austerity programs it eliminated only 19,000 public servant jobs. Restated, the government was larger under the Harper government that it was under the Chrétien or Martin Liberal governments.[21]

The take-away from the deficit-fighting part of the Harper legacy is that it constrained but did not cut the size of government. Moreover, as the exercise unfolded, the government shifted from characterizing the deficit-fighting as transformational to representing it simply as a cost-cutting effort to balance the budget.[22] In a review of budget reforms of the past thirty years, David Good concluded that "the spending exercise known as Program Review and led by Finance Minister Paul Martin in 1995 was considerably more significant and fundamental than any of the cost containment and expenditure initiatives of the Harper administration."[23]

In summary, after a fairly loose approach to public service staffing in the first few years, the overall pattern was a step-by-step tightening of staffing and compensation arrangements. The change in spending trajectory was driven by a desire to cut the cost of the public service rather than by a genuine desire to refashion it.

The Harper government also reinforced the role of the Treasury Board as government employer and spending guardian by attempting to find ways to cut back on discretionary spending.[24] For example, the annual spending cycle became more systematic than ever with the added rigour of deadlines and spending targets, better systems of approval and accountability for areas expenses such as travel (all must now be approved at the assistant deputy minister level), and the addition of a number of ministerial committees dedicated to improving administration.

Herein lies an interesting feature of the Harper legacy where the rhetoric does not necessarily square with the facts. On the one hand, driven by distrust of the public service and an ideological commitment to small government, Harper saw the size of the public service grow during his almost decade in power. In Lee's view, "the bark of the Harper government—like the Mulroney government—has been much worse than its bite."[25]

As for the public service, it endured more than five years of cutbacks and cost trimming, especially with regards to hospitality and travel. The Deficit Reduction Action Plan of 2011 was an additional burden and was traumatic for the public service because the process and the criteria for cutting were ambiguous and constantly changing. Deloitte, a professional services firm, did a major portion of the complex analysis and strategic thinking for the plan. The implication was that the public service could not be trusted to do the job itself.

While the cost containment exercises were primarily designed to whittle down the size of government, they also had an important impact on the federal public service in three ways. First, over time, public servants saw themselves as victims, with too little time to implement the spending decisions that had been imposed by the prime minister. Second, on the basis of the rushed and uneven decision-making process, public servants eventually concluded that the government was not as interested in the innovation and transformation it had championed in its communications. And, finally, it became very apparent by the end of the process that the Prime Minister's Office (PMO) and ministerial exempt staff had a disproportionate influence on spending decisions at the expense of departmental policy and finance groups.

Moreover, the nature and economic value of the cost containment exercises led to a very public confrontation between the prime minister and the Parliamentary Budget Office (PBO). As the first head of the PBO, Kevin Page took the government to task for its lack of transparency and unwillingness to release important financial data. The often bitter interchange between the principals heightened the fear among public servants of arbitrariness in decisions, and contributed to the widening trust gap between ministers and public servants.[26]

Dynamics between the Prime Minister and the Public Service

While the broad-stroke analysis of the Harper years does not reveal evidence of an explicit effort to reduce the size of the public service, one outcome of the many cost reduction exercises has been to shake the confidence of the public service and create a climate of uncertainty and fear of job loss.

It did not take long after the 2006 federal election before there were signs of discord between the new Harper government and the senior ranks of the public service. In fact, Paul Tellier, former cabinet secretary and co-chair of the Prime Minister's Advisory Committee on Public Service Renewal, was among the first to signal that problems were everywhere. In his initial report to the prime minister, Tellier asserted that relations between politicians and the senior levels of bureaucracy "have never been more strained."[27]

This sentiment was echoed by Arthur Kroeger, the former "dean" of the deputy minister community, who provided some context to the generally poor relations between the Harper government and the public service. In 2006, he observed that "Relations between politicians and bureaucrats, especially at senior levels, have never been worse."[28]

Discussions about the ideal nature of the administrative political interface in Westminster systems have been the subject of many conversations in recent years. Generally, over the past three decades, there has been a steady increase in the role and scale of political staff in all Westminster jurisdictions and most OECD countries.

What is new and significant is that political advisers have become institutionalized across many countries. Their numbers have grown, their influence has amplified and their role within the machinery of government has in some countries been applauded and in others been condemned.[29]

In Canada, it could be argued that the role of political staff grew exponentially under the Harper government. The best strand of evidence might be the 2015 testimony of one-time Harper chief of staff Nigel Wright and other PMO employees at the criminal trial of Senator Mike Duffy. Those staffers detailed the centralizing and controlling behaviour of the Harper PMO. According to Chris Woodcock, the PMO's former director of issues management, the constant intrusion of the office on day-to-day departmental operations was justified in this way:

In the current environment, the Prime Minister is accountable for anything from a decision made by a low level public servant on a particular file to major issues to policy. My job was to make sure that we understand all those different issues and that we deal with them and managed those issues effectively.[30]

While the centralization of power in the PMO did not start with the Harper government, it is now regarded as the most centrally controlling governance system that has ever been devised in Canada. There are a number of reasons for this. First, Harper had a very targeted agenda, which on major policy issues was not informed by public service advice. Instead, the public service was often seen as an impediment to moving his agenda to the implementation stage. Second, Harper was skeptical about the neutrality of the public service and did not feel constrained by longstanding conventions and protocols that had defined the relationship of the government with Parliament and the public service for more than fifty years. Finally, Harper's insistence to be at the centre of the decision-making process without benefiting from the challenge function provided by the public service ensured that senior public servants always found themselves looking in at the action from distant bleacher seats.

One institutional consequence of the strengthening of the PMO has been the systematic bypassing of the formal cabinet decision-making process, eschewing the use of memoranda to cabinet and formal cabinet agendas. Whether Harper was motivated by a desire to avoid potential conflicts within cabinet or to limit input from ministers, the net effect was a weakening of cabinet government and a further distancing of the public service from the government.

Over time, Harper used the PMO to institutionalize the previously informal system of pre-cabinet consultations by taking firm control over policy matters that were important to him. What finally emerged under Chief of Staff Guy Giorno (and fashioned on a system developed by Ontario premier Mike Harris) was a process known as "Four Corners," in which the PMO, the Privy Council Office and the relevant ministers' political offices and departmental officials met to decide on the government's course of action. Over time, as the prime minister became more experienced in managing the government, the pre-cabinet meetings moved from being a consultative, facilitative system to a decision-making one—as Harper's policy preferences were communicated through the attending PMO staff. Not only did the Four Corners practice weaken the pivotal Westminster principle of cabinet collective decision-making, but in term of policy development, it also marginalized the advisory role of the public service in favour of the policy preferences of the prime minister.

At the same time, the demise of the traditional daily "triangulated" meetings with the prime minister, the clerk of the Privy Council and the chief of staff served to further weaken the public service's opportunity to provide policy input on a routine basis. For the four cabinet secretaries who served Harper, the reduction in their opportunities to meet with the prime minister and his political staff meant that they had fewer opportunities to participate in the government's most important decisions. In the end, the Four Corners process and the dispensing of the daily PMO and clerk meetings had the lasting effect of marginalizing the public service with regards to policy development especially after the 2011 majority government election.

Relations: Cabinet Ministers and Public Servants

The centralization of power in the hands of the PMO has had a secondary knock-on effect on the hiring and conduct of exempt staff in ministers' offices. These individuals were working within a minority government scenario beginning in 2006, had limited post-employment prospects due to the provisions of the Federal Accountability Act and in the early Harper years were reported by the senior public service to be younger, less experienced and more partisan than staff from previous governments. With the PMO systematically directing the activities in ministers' offices, ministerial exempt staff kept the bureaucratic system highly responsive to the rhythm and agenda set by the prime minister.

The traditional model that had defined the political–administrative interface for so many years before Harper came undone when the "boys in short pants"[31] no longer played the role of enablers between ministers and the public service.[32] Instead, their task was to implement PMO directives, to identify and deal with critics inside of government,[33] to ensure that the communications plan was meticulously implemented and to suppress potentially negative information within the system. The extreme end of this was seen in 2009, when a political staffer in the office of the minister of public works ordered public servants to "un-release" records being mailed out under the Access to Information Act.

In 2008, the well-respected journalist Susan Delacourt captured this dynamic in the following way:

> There now seems to be little doubt that Prime Minister Stephen Harper's government sees itself in a constant, them-and-us struggle with official-dom in the national capital. ... These have been the high-profile cases, but there are repeated, pervasive stories of the government's attempts to keep its thumb on the bureaucracy—everything from its early refusal to allow a civil servant in the environment department to talk publicly about a novel he'd written, to tales of bureaucrats having to clear the tiniest statements through the Privy Council Office.[34]

To ensure this style of governing was kept within the thin walls of Ottawa officialdom, the government made a concerted effort to centrally control government communications and information. This single-minded approach prompted Robert

Marleau, the former information commissioner, to comment, "There is less information being released by government than ever before."[35]

At the same time, public servants were also publicly blamed for news stories that became an embarrassment to the government. For example, bureaucrats at Citizenship and Immigration who were asked at the eleventh hour to plan a live citizenship ceremony at the Sun TV network were later blamed when it was revealed fellow public servants stepped in to fill vacant spots at the event. Health Minister Rona Ambrose criticized her own bureaucrats in 2013 for approving access to prescription heroin for BC addiction researchers under the department's Special Access Program.

Muzzling of Scientists and the Issue of Evidence

Space does not allow a more complete characterization of the conflict between the scientific community and the Harper government over its nearly ten years in office. The tension arose when the political staff controlled the flow, pace and volume of information from a department to the outside world. It is important to note that there has always been some tension between government scientists and their political masters with regard to their ability to act and speak independently of the government of the day. However, under previous regimes, this tension was left to the senior managers of departments to resolve on their own. The new practice of having ministers' offices approve every press release and all public appearances for diplomats and scientists put a damper on the customary independence of these professionals.

Inexperienced and hyper-partisan ministerial staffers who were placed in ministers' offices by the PMO and were accountable to the PMO for their respective ministers' behaviour heightened the conflict. One can see that the danger of this kind of management style is that staff who are appointed without any job security might feel obliged to "jump as high as necessary" in order to satisfy a demanding and impatient employer (the PMO).[36]

Naturally, all of these tensions and failures to establish a working level of trust and respect between the exempt staff and the senior ranks of the public service had a detrimental impact on the entire public service. A 2015 report by the Association of Professional Executives of the Public Service of Canada (APEX) found that 75 per cent of respondents saw their work as having been deteriorated. "They also reported that real or perceived criticism of public servants from the political level works to reduce their engagement and sense of loyalty."[37]

Yet despite the tensions, Harper maintained the practice of appointing deputy ministers from among the senior ranks of the public service[38] and the legal prohibition on political interference in the appointment or promotion of public servants was respected with few known exceptions.

As a result, the basic structure of government remains the same, but the dynamics that characterize the day-to-day functioning of government have deteriorated. In response to these developments, Ralph Heintzman, a former senior public servant, has argued recently that the traditional model is broken to the extent that we need to produce a new "moral contract" and a Charter of Public Service to remedy the current problems.[39]

Discussion

At the beginning of his time in office, Harper went on a spending spree, consuming the $8 billion surplus that he inherited from the Martin government by introducing tax cuts, including to the GST, and new targeted spending in such areas as defence, correctional services, auditing and tax compliance, and public security. He then began to look for other ways to scale back the ambition of government. As Paul Wells noted about the Harper agenda: "the point was to get money out of Ottawa, to reduce surpluses and restrict the ability of the government—any government—to introduce elaborate new social programs."[40]

While the public service was learning to live with the Harper government, it also came under growing pressure from a number of new forces independent of Stephen Harper that were placing it in a precarious situation. These were the changing work environment that was a result of developments in information technology and the inflow of young technology-savvy workers, new post-Gomery rules that created a complex web of administrative rules and the arrival of new external policy advisers in the form of private consultants and think tanks.[41]

Given the weakened fiscal capacity of the federal government and the multiplicity of issues challenging the health of the public service, there is no evidence that the prime minister responded to the challenge to address the new reality. In fact, the evidence suggests that, despite nearly a decade as prime minister, he still saw himself as an outsider, or least saw the political benefit of portraying himself as one.

During a 2013 speech to the Conservative Party convention, Harper came back to some of the same messages that cast public servants as elites and removed from the interests of Canadians:

In our party, public service must mean private sacrifice. That's why Laureen and I first left our home here in Calgary. We didn't go to Ottawa to join private clubs or become part of some "elite." That's not who you are; it's not who we are. We are in Ottawa only so the Government of Canada can serve you. ... We took money out of the hands of the lobbyists, academics and bureaucrats and we gave it to the real childcare experts—their names are Mom and Dad.[42]

The distrust of the public service appeared to run deep in the psyche of this government when in 2013, Erica Furtado of the PMO's issues management group distributed a memo to exempt staff on what to include in the transition books that are given to new ministers. The *Toronto Star* reported that the "transition binder check list" included the items "What to avoid: pet bureaucratic projects," and "Who to avoid: bureaucrats that can't take no (or yes) for an answer."

Even the day before the 2015 election, Harper again suggested that the public service was an impediment to progress. "We want this government to keep moving forward," Harper told supporters in Newmarket, Ontario. "We do not want to go back to the days where the government ran for a handful of Liberal special interest groups and the bureaucracy."[43]

Conclusion

Stephen Harper campaigned as an outsider, arrived in Ottawa as an outsider and ten years later continued to see himself and his party as outsiders. He was also confident and resolute in his plan to refashion Canada with his own agenda—a small and less activist-minded government being central to this view, with a special emphasis on a punitive criminal justice system, saber-rattling foreign policy and incremental economic policies.

With a strong personal policy agenda, he made little effort to capture or to reform the public service in a way that might reflect his views of government. Instead, he worked alongside it, attacked and demeaned those in government that may have challenged his government's decisions, attempted to make government more efficient through cost containment and dutifully accepted the policy advice offered up by the policy units within the public service without any real engagement with them.

In his attempt to change the Canadian narrative during his tenure, he captured and controlled the government-wide communications function to ensure a consistent and timely message and also challenged the value of the evidence produced by the public service by limiting the roles of those who produce information, analysis and advice.

When he and the PMO were not able to control the messages emanating from the public service (because of their legislative independence or the contrariness of the incumbent), the government applied the full weight of its office to attack the integrity of those with whom they disagreed and, when possible, to fire them or stop their reappointment.

Linda Keen, the former head of the Canadian Nuclear Safety Commission, was characterized as an unqualified Liberal hack and then fired for making a decision that the government ultimately agreed with. Former chief statistician Munir

Sheikh resigned his post after then–industry minister Tony Clement publicly suggested that bureaucrats supported a voluntary household survey as an adequate replacement for the mandatory long-form census. Chief Electoral Officer Mark Mayrand was characterized as power hungry for criticizing the government's Fair Elections Act.

In the end, the public service has been the target of a series of blows, injuring and bruising it, but not destroying the institution. The Harper government had the view that the public service was elitist and Liberal. Rather than try to change it, the Conservatives chose to create a counterweight in ministers' offices and to find policy advice outside of the public service. Only when it turned its attention to deficit reduction in 2010 did job cuts and compensation compression became part of the narrative. At no time did the public service, as an institution, become a direct target.

The Harper legacy reflects an uneasy relationship that has been forged by the many ways he brought the system under his control in order to deliver his policy agenda and maintain strict discipline within his ministry. The burning question is whether the changes that became part of the daily routine of government, such as bypassing policy advice, limiting the role of ministers, controlling all communications, attacking the integrity of those who question government decisions and imposing the will of the prime minister on all aspects of governing, were only a temporary reflection of his prime ministership, or have fundamentally transformed the federal public service.

Appendix: Institutions Affected by the Harper Government

CBC/Radio-Canada
Centre for Rights and Democracy
Court Challenges Program
Canadian Radio-television and Telecommunications Commission (CRTC)
Employment Insurance Board of Referees
Office of the Commissioner of the Environment and Sustainable Development
Health Council of Canada
Immigration and Refugee Board
Library and Archives Canada
National Capital Commission
National Council on Welfare
Nutrition North Canada
Office of the Inspector General
Parole Board
Port Authorities (under Transport Canada)
Security Intelligence Review Committee
Social Security Tribunal
Statistics Canada

4

Government News Management and Canadian Journalism

Jennifer Ditchburn

Radio-Canada reporter Marie-Paul Rouleau committed a terrible faux pas inside Vietnam's presidential palace, one that had an instant blowback on the rest of the Canadian journalists travelling alongside her. She didn't break a Ho Chi Minh sculpture, or slag a national institution, during that Hanoi stop in November 2006. No, Rouleau made the mistake of asking Prime Minister Stephen Harper a question as he strode through the building with counterpart Nguyen Tan Dung.

Within minutes of the incident, the rest of the Canadian press corps was put on notice by Harper's then–press secretary Dimitri Soudas: there would be no more access to the prime minister, apart from a closing news conference at the Asia-Pacific Economic Cooperation summit.

The Canadian journalists (including myself) had to think creatively in order to feed the ever-hungry outlets back home.

And so we waited patiently inside the friendly New Zealand embassy in Hanoi for Harper to arrive for a photo opportunity with his kiwi counterpart. On another leader's turf, he was unable to ignore questions about how millions of British Columbians back home were under a boil water advisory. Later, while the Canadian officials were mum, Chinese and South Korean spokespeople helped fill in the blanks on the summit—including revealing the fact that Canada had recently sent an envoy to North Korea.[1]

Fast-forward nine years to the end of the Harper mandate, and the basic modus operandi of the Prime Minister's Office when it came to media relations and news management had not changed. During the 2015 Summit of the Americas in Panama, Harper's team did not tell Canadian journalists travelling with him about a highly anticipated private meeting with Cuban president Raúl Castro, leaving them to learn about it through a photograph on the Cuban government's state-run media website.[2]

There are different ways to consider news management under Stephen Harper. The easy way is to ascribe all of the changes to the man himself and his personal view of the media as an obstacle to overcome. Former National Citizens Coalition confrere Gerry Nicholls said Harper "didn't trust the media to get our message out. And he believed it was a mistake to get too friendly with the press."[3]

Harper most certainly left his mark on media relations, moving from a system focused on persuasion and "spin" to one that emphasized the throttling of information and access. But that is only part of the picture. This chapter will also take into account the larger historical and political context in which the new strategies were put into place.

An area that has received very little serious attention is how the different approach to news management impacted journalism itself. What has the "Harper Factor" been for the news media? How did journalists change the way they worked? I will address this question partly through a series of interviews I held with fourteen press gallery members between 2013 and 2014, as part of research I conducted for a Master of Journalism thesis at Carleton University.[4] Until March 2016, I had worked as a parliamentary correspondent for nearly eighteen years.

This chapter will also consider the Harper government's policy approach to journalism, and more specifically to the Canadian Broadcasting Corporation, at a time when the news media is struggling financially.

A News Management System Forty Years in the Making

A press gallery dinner pamphlet from 1947 offers some tongue-in-cheek advice for how politicians of the Mackenzie King era should handle the press. "Tell a reporter nothing," read a tip on talking to journalists over the telephone. "Remember that he represents the public and the public must be kept happy. Ignorance is bliss."[5]

Seventy years later, this instruction might inspire a knowing chuckle from reporters. They recognize the politician's reflex to conceal and dissimulate. But in reality, everything has changed about the government's approach to news management. During the long stretch between Confederation and the Louis St. Laurent years, the relationship between government and journalists was underpinned by friendships, business interests and political allegiances. Anthony Westell recounts arriving in the capital in 1956 as a correspondent for a British newspaper and being shocked to discover "there was little machinery for controlling and directing the flow of news."[6]

When Westell referred to the lack of machinery, he wasn't kidding. By the 1960s, only a single person in the entire government was classified as a media relations officer. External Affairs had two press officers, National Defence held regular background briefings[7] and the rest appeared to be handled by a fleet of "special assistants." John Diefenbaker was the first prime minister to hire a formal press secretary, plucked from the ranks of the press gallery.[8]

Meanwhile, the gallery was growing—from 100 members in 1961 to 240 in 1971.[9] Almost half of them worked in radio and television. As well, there were more women. Canadian journalists became less deferential—just consider the rise of programs such as the CBC's provocative *This Hour Has Seven Days*. "After 1960, much of the news media embraced dissent," wrote media historian Paul Rutherford. "Controversy was suddenly a hot item."[10]

Clearly, the scattered, unsophisticated system of communication in Ottawa wasn't going to cut it anymore for governments in the TV era. As Susan Delacourt thoroughly explored in her 2013 book *Shopping for Votes*, parties began to see the value in applying advertising and marketing concepts to their political activities. Enter Liberal prime minister Pierre Trudeau, and some dramatic changes to news management that planted the seeds of Stephen Harper's approach.

In 1969, the Task Force on Government Information released a hugely influential report called *To Know and Be Known*. It scrutinized the way information about the government was disseminated to both the media and Canadian society at large, and baldly concluded that what existed was a "mess" and "supreme disorder."[11] The task force made a number of recommendations, which were rooted in the concept of the public's right to have access to government information as part of a participatory democracy. What would develop over time, however, was less noble.

Trudeau responded by creating Information Canada and later the Canadian Unity Information Office (CUIO), but he did not create a parliamentary body to oversee the changes, as the task force had recommended. Both Information Canada and CUIO later came under criticism in the Commons and in the papers for acting as propaganda arms.[12] The number of information officers in government grew exponentially during the Trudeau years—from 400 identified by the task force to 1,154 by 1976.[13] What also emerged was a centralization of communications and advertising under the Privy Council Office and the Treasury Board Secretariat, a system still in place today.

Conservative prime minister Brian Mulroney (1984–1992) followed Trudeau's path of professionalizing government communications and media relations. An overarching communications policy was established in 1988. Meanwhile, a significant news management infrastructure was being built, imbued with the new corporate spirit that was influencing all government operations. Spending on communications within the federal government grew by 30 per cent between 1987 and 1999. The government's use of advertising and polling was also increasing dramatically.[14]

Meanwhile, the media world saw the rise of the 24-7 news channel—CBC Newsworld hit the airwaves in 1989, and CTV News 1 in 1997. By the time Jean Chrétien's Liberals won power in 1993, the Internet had also arrived on the scene. The pace of news was speeding up.

When I arrived on Parliament Hill in 1997, there was in place a well-organized network of directors of communications and press secretaries in each ministerial office, mostly plucked from party ranks. The prime minister's various directors of communications—Peter Donolo perhaps being the best known—would often call reporters to offer the Liberal government's take on a particular story and argue over different points. Strategic leaks were common, and ministers did frequent interviews.

Most contact with either political or civil-service staff took place over the telephone, although it should be noted that the use of email was just starting to gain momentum in the early part of the Chrétien mandate. It wasn't unusual to speak to a senior public servant or diplomat on the phone or in person for a "background briefing" on a key piece of legislation, or to elicit a same-day response from a departmental spokesperson on a question.

By the time of the 2005–6 election, reporters were dealing with a much more coordinated, multi-layered government communications machine.

And the Canadian government was hardly alone internationally. It was right on trend.

US presidents had long been charting new territory in news management, with Ronald Reagan putting his focus on a more centralized and unified communication system in the 1980s.[15] Democrat Bill Clinton's administration also tried to engage with, and "spin," journalists in order to shape the news—but also sometimes tried to bypass the national media.[16] "You know why I can stiff you on press conferences? Because Larry King has liberated me from you by giving me to the American people directly," Clinton said of the former CNN talk show host.[17]

In the United Kingdom, Tony Blair's New Labour was shaking up the government with a professionalized communications system centred in the Prime Minister's Office.[18] Blair's team—particularly Press Secretary Alastair Campbell—became so synonymous with spin that the era spawned countless books, academic articles, TV shows, movies and parliamentary studies.

In Australia, John Howard adopted much more controlling press techniques, also run out of the PMO. "The key is simply the withdrawal of access," noted Jim Middleton, a television reporter with the Australian Broadcasting Corporation.[19] Howard was also a big fan of "talkback" or talk radio.

Howard's strategies would attract the notice of young Harper marketing whiz Patrick Muttart.[20] And Muttart would be one of the key people responsible for the Conservative Party victory in the general election of 2006, a victory that hinged on message control as part of smart political marketing.

A Shock to the System

Even though the Liberals were shifting how the government interacted with the media, Stephen Harper's victory in 2006 ushered in a new era of news management that caught the press gallery off guard. Where changes before had been gradual, now they had accelerated to warp speed.

To find out what characterized the change in government news management style, I asked fourteen press gallery members a number of open-ended questions, including how they perceived the government's attempt to manage the news product, their opinion on the quality of information they received from both civil servants and political staff, and whether they noted a change in style from the previous government. All the interview subjects, from broadcast and print outlets, had worked on Parliament Hill under at least one other government.

Two main themes emerged from their responses: there had been a curtailment of access to government politicians, and there had been a curtailment of access to the bureaucracy and to government information.

The single anonymous interview subject, who worked for a major national media outlet, summed up the changes as "starving" reporters for information. "They provide as little information as possible about an event or in response to a question or in response to requests for interviews," the reporter said. "My theory is they want to reduce the importance of the fourth estate in Canadians' minds and the only way to do that is to render them useless, so they can speak around them through social media, or talk shows, or advertising."

The Curtailment of Access to Government Politicians

Prime ministers going back to Mackenzie King had spoken to reporters on Parliament Hill before and/or after cabinet meetings, or in the case of the earliest prime ministers, even as they strolled to work.

The preceding thirteen years of Liberal governments had created a routine for journalists, who would arrive on the third floor outside of the prime minister's Centre Block office and the cabinet meeting room to await Jean Chrétien or Paul

Martin. (In the first part of the last century, this happened in the corridors of East Block). A steady stream of ministers had no other way out but to pass the phalanx of reporters gathered at the exit routes.

"Well, that was at least your one shot of the week where you could go stop cabinet ministers and just throw questions at them on the issues you were working on," said CBC Radio reporter Susan Lunn. "There were two microphones and there were probably ten different stories that you were working on, but we had access, fairly regular access to cabinet ministers."

One of the first acts of news management of the new Conservative government in early 2006 was the restriction of reporters' access to those weekly cabinet meetings. In fact, the timing of the cabinet meetings was no longer publicized. Some Conservative ministers were almost never seen by reporters outside of occasional news conferences.

The loss of "cabinet outs" was part of a larger issue identified by the journalists of the general availability of the prime minister and his cabinet. Harper did not hold regular news conferences on Parliament Hill, having used the National Press Theatre only seven times between 2006 and 2009, and not once in the years after. Harper did take questions while travelling abroad or in Canada. But for the many press gallery members whose employers did not have the resources to travel outside of Ottawa, their only opportunity to put a question to Harper was during infrequent bilateral press conferences with visiting foreign leaders. In those cases, media from the respective countries were generally allotted only two questions each and press gallery members collectively agreed on the questions to be asked and the questioners.

This is not to say that Harper was invisible. On the contrary, he held frequent photo opportunities in his office and elsewhere around Parliament Hill, but reporters and camera technicians were instructed not to ask questions. This became an issue in 2013 when CTV cameraman David Ellis asked a question of Harper during a photo opportunity in New York City. The Prime Minister's Office threatened to bar Ellis from a subsequent trip abroad.[21] In my own discussions with Conservative staff members over the years, I have come to understand that Harper disliked unscheduled or unanticipated questions because he viewed them as indecorous.

It's also important to note what took the place of direct contact between government politicians and the press gallery. As mentioned earlier, photo opportunities with no time allotted for questions became de rigueur, but so too did photo opportunities without even the presence of news media cameras.

Initially, the Prime Minister's Office used audio-visual services through the Privy Council Office to record and disseminate video of Harper's appearances abroad and at home, but generally always in the presence of the national media.

In early 2014, the PMO began to post online a video feature called 24/Seven. Some of the footage in the videos came from activities that excluded journalists—such as the cabinet shuffle in March of that year that saw Joe Oliver become finance minister.

More traditional forms of media were also used to bypass national reporters. Stephen Harper favoured talk radio for interviews. He also granted a number of interviews to radio and TV sports programs, but to talk about hockey, football or curling rather than politics. And the Conservative government, as the Blair government in the UK and the Howard government in Australia, turned to small regional or ethnic newspapers for interviews or for exclusive content.

The Curtailment of Access to the Bureaucracy and Public Information

In February 2013, I sent a request to the departmental media relations staff at Natural Resources Canada for information about the parks depicted in a TV ad for the Conservative government's Economic Action Plan. Because the commercial touted a commitment to the national parks system, I wanted to know specifically which national parks were shown in the commercial.

It seemed like a straightforward question.

"Please note that all footage from this campaign was Canadian sourced," was the initial response emailed response back—a response to a question never posed.

The press gallery reporters I interviewed spoke at length about their frustrations in dealing with public servants who worked in government communications, and the inability to easily access government information—even the seemingly anodyne or technical.

The practice of getting background briefings from bureaucrats was not unusual prior to 2006. Lunn of CBC Radio recalled being able to contact the Privy Council Office in the early 2000s to talk to the bureaucrats who were helping to draft new climate change legislation. "If you could at least understand where they were coming from, and understand their difficulties, your story I think was better because it had more context to it. It's very hard now to get through to bureaucrats, to get them to call you back, at least in any kind of official capacity," she said.

The anonymous interview subject said the loss of background briefings was one of the biggest disappointments of the Harper era. "A series of questions and answers volleyed back and forth through email is no substitute for a free-flowing dialogue between a journalist and policy specialist," the reporter said.

The content of those emailed responses was something that stirred passionate responses from the interview subjects. A common complaint was that the answers to seemingly non-political questions put to a department did not match the questions, and smacked of political marketing rather than non-partisan information. David

Akin of Sun Media (now with the *National Post*) mimicked the type of "worse than poor" exchange he would have with media relations staff within the government:

"What's two plus two?"

"Math has been a very important subject to this government for a long time."

"Yes, but what's two plus two?"

"Math has been a very important subject to this government for a long time."

Sometimes, no information is forthcoming at all. Hélène Buzzetti of *Le Devoir* said she once asked the RCMP for basic background information on the sex offender registry on the same day that the minister of public safety was making an announcement, and was told that she needed to speak to the minister's office and its political staff.

One aspect of the new order inside the government's communication system was the introduction of the Message Event Proposal (MEP). All government announcements and public activities needed to be passed first through a template, which set out on paper the parameters for any given event, including the messages to deliver and the type of media coverage desired.[22] The Communications and Consultations Unit within the Privy Council Office oversaw the MEP process, and at least in the early years of the Conservative government the final approval went to the prime minister's chief of staff.[23] This highly centralized exercise didn't only cause information to move much more slowly, but it also may have contributed to a general chill across the public service vis-à-vis media relations.[24]

The "slow-boat approach" to information dissemination, as the anonymous interviewee described it, might seem incongruous with the legions of communications professionals employed by the federal government. As of the end of the 2011–12 fiscal year, 3,865 employees were working in information services roles—a 15.3 per cent increase since 2006.[25]

While there might be substantial numbers of communications personnel to deal with media inquiries, their goal appeared to be to put government activities in the best possible light or not to talk about them at all, rather than to "provide the public with timely, accurate, clear, objective and complete information about its policies, programs, services and initiatives," as the government's communications policy stipulated at the time.

A Rupture

The new way of doing things in Ottawa clearly hit the press gallery hard. Why? Because in the nearly 150 years since Confederation, the government and the media had grown up beside one another in what was essentially a shared culture. Each side built up a set of expectations of the other—expectations that shifted *gradually* with the times.

Communications theorists Jay Blumler and Michael Gurevitch have referred to what happens when expectations are dashed as a "rupture in the role relationship," saying it helps to explain "the note of outrage that is sometimes sounded during adversarial episodes—reflecting the injured party's conviction, not merely that its interests were damaged, but that supposedly moral boundaries were overstepped."[26]

Outrage describes the reaction pretty well. The Canadian Association of Journalists penned an open letter to Canadian journalists in June 2010 about the Harper government, warning of a "genuine and widespread threat to the public's right to know."[27] On two occasions, journalists walked out on Harper events en masse, in protest of the tight controls on their work.

Eleven of the fourteen interview subjects expressed some concern that the key democratic principle of a free press was being undermined, and that ultimately citizens would be the biggest victims. "Because I'm a reporter, I believe that in a democracy information is really the oxygen of a functioning political system, and balanced information and sometimes critical information," said Barry Smith of the *Western Producer*, now retired. "The more information about the people that govern us is restricted or manipulated, I just think the weaker the body politic gets."

So what happened to the press after the Harper government changed the approach to communications? The existing academic literature offers few clues about the effect of government news management on journalistic practice. Blumler and Gurevitch talk about the "journalistic fight back," which mainly consists of writing more process stories, attempting to pull back the curtain on the marketing ploys and strategies of politicians. "Spin" was widely demonized in the British media. American Larry Sabato talks about a "strike back" by disgruntled reporters against the political stage managers.[28] This type of reporting did indeed occur during the Harper mandate—during the 2015 election campaign, several first-person pieces were written about the limits placed on journalists at Conservative events.

But beyond the types of stories that journalists write as they *react* to news management, I would argue that journalists have actually changed the way they work. That has been the main Harper Factor in this area of Canadian life. I describe the altered work process as "journalistic pathfinding."

Journalistic Pathfinding

Elizabeth Thompson of CBC News (with *iPolitics* at the time of our interview) worked for the *Montreal Gazette* during the Oka crisis of the summer of 1990. Reporters who wanted to speak to either the protesting Mohawks or the provincial police officers working in the area during the early days of the crisis found their main access point blocked off. The Sûreté du Québec (SQ), the provincial force, had set up guard gates on the principal road and, according to Thompson, was refusing to talk to journalists or let them through. "What happened was that reporters do as reporters do—they didn't go through the road, so everyone went through the woods, [or] rented boats and got there by water," she explained.

In other words, journalists found new paths to get to the information they needed to tell a story when one or more of the routes was blocked or restricted.

The Collins Dictionary defines pathfinding as "the process of finding a way in new circumstances; trailblazing," and of a pathfinder as "a person who makes or finds a way, especially through unexplored areas or fields of knowledge."

Pathfinding matches the experience of the reporters I interviewed, as well as my own, when examining the different adaptation techniques of journalists. Thompson's anecdote had reporters literally finding physical paths and routes, whereas most of the time reporters rely on more virtual paths to the information they seek. The point is that journalists are active participants in the media-government relationship rather than just passive recipients of information.

And there's an explanation for why journalists keep on looking for the feast, rather than settling for information crumbs. Reporters are inculcated with certain long-held journalistic values at universities and colleges, and within their newsrooms, particularly those values of impartiality, objectivity, accuracy and fairness. We can have a debate over how well those values are reflected in the media, but the point is that if news management appears to obstruct these overarching values, journalists may not be prepared to accept the packaged information provided or the roadblocks set up in front of them.

Dutch scholar Henk Pander Maat, for example, found that reporters will take a product press release and add information to it, often reframing it to turn a promotional release into a negative report.[29] American Scott Althaus observed that US journalists covering the first Gulf War adapted to the tight government control of information by actively seeking out voices of opposition for their stories—or acting as the voice of opposition themselves.[30]

News has to be composed of "new" elements. Politicians who repeat funding or policy announcements are often ignored because the content is not newsworthy. That goes for the boilerplate quotes and information emailed to reporters by political aides or public servants.

Linked to newsworthiness is the constant pursuit of exclusivity and distinctiveness in the news. The fragmentation of the media landscape and the old journalistic "pack" has meant all the players are looking to stand out with original material.

"If someone gets a scoop, the tendency now rather than to say, 'Oh wow, we've got to match that scoop,' is to say, 'OK, it's out there, they're the first to get it, let's go out and get something else,'" said Thompson.

That motivation became clear during the 2015 general election, when most outlets opted not to pay for seats on the leaders' planes for most of the campaign. Instead, they channelled their resources into more original content.

The press gallery interviewees who were confronted with blocked channels of information described two main ways they dealt with the obstacle: through the use of alternative sources, and through the use of documents and data.

Alternative Sources

In 2012, federal-provincial-territorial negotiations were underway for a new five-year agricultural policy called Growing Forward 2. Barry Wilson of the *Western Producer* had a suspicion there would be major cuts in federal spending, but could get neither the minister's office nor the assistant deputy minister to speak to him. Wilson said he intensified his focus instead on the other figures around the table—namely provincial officials and farm lobby groups—to "get around" the federal government's silence.

"What I try to do is cultivate provincial sources, because they're involved in all the negotiations with the feds over policy, certainly work the lobby groups to find out what they're hearing about what's coming up inside government," said Wilson. Ultimately, Wilson was able to get the goods from a source inside the Ontario government.

The theme of seeking out more talkative and informative sources outside of the federal government came up repeatedly. "You also do end runs and try to find people that have some access and some portal into the political machine, and ask them for information when you can't get it other ways," said Jacques Bourbeau, then the bureau chief of Global News. "You have to be nimble. Before, the lines of information were more direct. Now they're more indirect at times."

The reporters referred to NGOs, lobbyists, academics, foreign governments and provincial governments as alternative sources that they began to seek out more routinely. "For the most part, on Aboriginal issues, I just don't bother with them," the *Globe and Mail*'s Gloria Galloway said of the federal government. "I go to the First Nations or the Inuit or Métis."

Said David Akin of international trips with the prime minister: "What is our Canadian government doing? Ask the Chinese, ask the Australians, ask the Brits."

Documents and Data

Human sources of information were not the only path that journalists found to the information they needed. Several of the national journalists I spoke to described an increasing reliance on different types of records to replace the information that they were having a difficult time obtaining through government departments.

The Access to Information Act became a tool for some to get around obstacles. Michael De Souza, who was with Postmedia News at the time of the interview, said he filed dozens of requests every month.

In the case of *La Presse's* Ottawa bureau, an extra staff member was hired to focus exclusively on that method of uncovering government information. Bureau chief Joël-Denis Bellavance said they hired the researcher in 2007 as a direct reaction to the Conservative government's approach to news management.

David Akin said he created an online database of background information by requesting the Question Period notes created for ministers on key policy issues. Rather than wait for bureaucrats to get back to him for rudimentary data, he would have some of it at his fingertips.

The government's statistics on Access to Information requests, published by the Treasury Board Secretariat's Info Source service, shows that inquiries from the media went from 2,835 in 2003–4 to 8,321 in 2012–13, a 210 per cent increase versus a 119 per cent increase overall for requests.

Information Commissioner Suzanne Legault drew a link between the Conservative government's news management approach and the use of the Access to Information pathway in a 2013 interview with CBC Radio. "What I can say is one of the reasons why people make access to information requests is to basically sift through … something that is being massaged as a message as opposed to what are the facts," Legault said.[31]

Of course, the Access to Information Act is no replacement for an open government communications system. Legault has chronicled the frustrations she's had with various departments in her annual reports. Over the Harper years, delays got longer—1,100 days in one case involving National Defence—and the exemption for cabinet confidences was used with more regularity.[32] Some of the reporters interviewed said they didn't bother with requests because the return on their time investment didn't make them worthwhile.

But there's more than one way to ferret news out of documents. Elizabeth Thompson talked about the "hiding-in-plain-sight" school of journalism, which basically consists of poring over public sources of information that might escape the notice of other busy journalists. For example, she will pick through the *Canada Gazette*, supplementary budget estimates and public accounts for new leads. She will also read through the responses given to order paper questions, the inquiries posed by opposition MPs that must be answered by the government within forty-five days.

Other journalists, such as CTV's Glen McGregor, the CBC's David McKie and Canadian Press journalists Jim Bronskill and Jordan Press, regularly use computer-assisted reporting techniques to cover the federal government.

An unintended consequence of the heightened controls over news management during the Harper years might have been to inspire more resourcefulness and creativity amongst national journalists. It has arguably also broadened the spectrum of sources used in reporting.

"I think journalists are a breed that the more barriers you put in front of us, the more dogged we become," said Bourbeau of Global TV.

One Step Forward, Two Steps Back

Journalists might have adapted to their new reality, but there's little cause to celebrate what's unfolded in the overall industry.

Governments are now equipped with armies of communications personnel that vastly outnumber the reporters that cover government. Each month seems to bring more grim news for the major national media outlets, the ones that have traditionally spent serious dollars on serious journalism.

Since I began my research in this area, Postmedia closed their parliamentary bureau. Sun TV no longer exists, and the Sun newspaper chain has been sold to Postmedia, which in turn is drowning in hundreds of millions of dollars in debt. The Canadian Media Guild estimates that the sector shed 10,000 jobs from 2008 to 2013.[33] That there are fewer regional reporters in the press gallery is an old story now—long gone are the correspondents for the *Montreal Gazette,* the *Edmonton Journal*, the *Calgary Herald* and others.

Meanwhile, newsrooms are smaller and reporters have more to do. At the Canadian Press, we were expected to write print stories, record and file audio clips, record and file video clips, and also maintain a social media presence. Reporters at the CBC are now tri-medial, contributing to radio, TV and the website, with some also able to shoot and edit their own TV items. Perhaps it needs to be emphasized that every minute spent doing these new tasks means less time spent tracking down facts and sources.

David Battistelli, the long-time bureau chief of OMNI News in Ottawa, was laid off eighteen months after I interviewed him for my research. He was most pessimistic at the time about the impact that government news management could have on his work product.

"I want people to know that we're in jeopardy of not being able to truly have a responsive journalistic product," said Battistelli. "In the end if we don't have journalists being able to do their jobs without hindrance, interference, control, what have you, then it's going to have an impact on everyone. I want people to know this is not the democratic way."

The Pew Research Center's research on the 2012 American presidential campaign is a cautionary tale. It found that the 48 per cent of the "master narratives" that emerged about Barack Obama and Mitt Romney came from partisan sources, while only 27 per cent came from the news media, a group that included talk-show hosts. Compare that with the 2000 campaign, where the numbers were 37 per cent and 50 per cent, respectively.

"The shrinking role of journalists in shaping the master character narratives of the candidates more likely reflects diminishing reportorial resources in news-rooms and more reliance, on television in particular, of live interview formats in which partisans are invited to deliver campaign messages," read the report from Pew's journalism and media research team.

Public Policy Approaches

Under the Harper administration, there was little to no reflection on supporting journalism or the media sector, as a matter of public policy. There was barely a blink, for example, when the *Lindsay Post* and the *Midland Free Press* shuttered their doors in 2013. Both Ontario newspapers were more than one hundred years old.

The last major parliamentary study on the news media was struck more than a decade ago. The Senate transport and communications committee's 2006 report focused on media concentration and the potentially negative consequence of overly centralized coverage of national and provincial news. One of its principal recommendations was to add a new section to the Competition Act to review media mergers.

The Senate committee's recommendation did not get picked up by the new Conservative government, just as previous governments stretching back to the 1970s had also ignored pressure to do something about concentration.

And so it continues. In 2007, Quebecor purchased the 54 newspapers in the Osprey Media chain. Shaw purchased Global TV from the collapsing Canwest Global Communications empire in 2010, and the Postmedia Network purchased Canwest's chain of newspapers. In 2014, Postmedia bought 175 English-language newspapers and associated websites from Quebecor—the old Sun/Osprey publications.

Television broadcasters have also struggled with a viewership that is increasingly fragmented—audiences can watch shows on their phones, tablets and laptops, and from a variety of new sources including Netflix and Amazon. Funding local news with dwindling ad dollars is much more challenging. Interestingly, that fragmentation was embraced by the Conservative Party during the 2015 election as the rationale for rejecting a consortium of the Canadian TV networks (CBC/Radio-Canada, CTV and Global) as a debate sponsor. The party argued that the public was using different platforms for getting their news, and so the traditional debate hosts should also change.

The starkest example of the financial woes faced by the Canadian news media came during the 2015 campaign. During most weeks, a core of only three national reporters plus a small TV camera pool would travel with the party leaders. The hefty campaign price tags had become impossible to rationalize at $50,000 to $70,000 per person, per leader's campaign.

A bleak discussion paper in 2015 by industry analysts Communications Management Inc. predicted that there would be no more printed daily newspapers or local broadcast TV stations in Canada by 2025, based on current revenue trajectories and the pervasiveness of Internet-based services.

"The current changes in the media ecosystem carry the possibility of profound changes for the way we, as citizens, will pay for and receive journalism," reads the paper. "It is also, therefore, a question about how, and how well, Canadians will be informed in the future."[34]

One of the potential ways to address the impact of media concentration and contraction in the industry is to use public broadcasting as a sort of journalistic bulwark. The suggestion of enhancing public broadcasting and even subsidizing newspapers has come up in discussions about what to do about journalism in the United States.[35][36][37]

But money for the public broadcaster has declined in Canada.

A ten-year summary of government funding, compiled by the CBC in 2013, shows that its parliamentary appropriations were $1.063 billion in 2003-4, and $1.065 billion in 2013-14. Using the Bank of Canada's inflation calculator, the numbers represent a decline of federal support of $220 million.

The appropriation numbers don't tell the whole financial story. Over the past fifteen years, the CBC has had to foot the costs of switching its operations from analog to digital. Like other media organizations, it's also had to deal with a sharp decline in ad revenues since the recession of 2008. Perhaps most devastating was the loss of the contract to broadcast *Hockey Night in Canada*, which represented 40 to 50 per cent of the CBC's annual advertising haul.[38]

A staggering 2,807 job cuts have been announced at the CBC since 2012, to stretch into the year 2020.

A Senate committee specifically studying the CBC issued a report in July 2015 that did not recommend any additional federal funding for the public broadcaster but instead advised that it consult with the government on how to find new sources of funding outside the annual budgetary allocation. It also urged the CBC to focus on "high quality" programming that was not being undertaken by private networks, such as amateur sports and Canadian ballet and orchestra performances, shows that don't necessarily attract big audiences or ad dollars.[39]

"We have been losing a global fight for the continued value of the institution of public broadcasting," CBC president Hubert Lacroix lamented in a September 2015 speech to the Public Broadcasters International Conference in Munich.

"It's a vicious circle. First, we struggle with cuts to our funding. Then as the cuts make us weaker and affect morale, critics, key stakeholders and even some of the citizens we serve question our relevance in a digital world."[40]

The Conservative government appeared more alarmed when Rogers announced in the spring of 2015 that it was closing down the multilingual evening newscasts broadcast by OMNI. Executives were quickly summoned before a House of Commons committee. The Rogers brass reminded the MPs of the dire straits that news programming is in—OMNI's advertising revenue had dropped from $80 million to $22 million between 2011 and 2015.

"What surprises me today is that all of you seem surprised. That's the biggest one for me, because I've been talking about this for the last three years," said Rogers Media president Keith Pelley, as he faced pointed questions from MPs of all parties in June 2015.

"This isn't going to be the only thing that you're going to face going forward in the broadcast industry. OMNI is just the tip of it."

Conclusion

It might seem odd to devote an entire chapter in a book about a prime minister's public policy legacy to news management and the news media. But communications has become so central to governing in this era that it is near impossible to properly analyze a leader and his or her government without taking a look at how they managed the media.

Stephen Harper's approach could be summed up by an image snapped of his PMO team during a trip to the Arctic in the summer of 2014. A pair of his staffers put up bank-style stanchions on the tundra of remote York Sound—an absurd sight, but one that symbolized an attitude that said, "contain the reporters, keep them away, but let them watch a staged event."

People talk about pendulum swings a lot when it comes to news management. They point to Pierre Trudeau, and his general disdain for journalists, as evidence that things can loosen up under a different leader. "Hey! Hey! We have respect for journalists in this country," Justin Trudeau berated a supporter during the 2015 campaign. "They ask tough questions and they're supposed to. OK?" He also pointedly held a news conference in the National Press Theatre two days after the election.

But even if relations with the media become more cordial under a different prime minister, it's difficult to see the modern philosophy behind the approach changing very much at all.

Detailed research by the *Columbia Journalism Review* found that US president Barack Obama had created the most distant relationship with the press in a half century.[41] "In the Obama administration's Washington, government officials are increasingly afraid to talk to the press," Leonard Downie Jr. wrote in a report for the Committee to Protect Journalists. "Those suspected of discussing with reporters anything that the government has classified as secret are subject to investigation, including lie-detector tests and scrutiny of their telephone and e-mail records."[42] Democratic candidate Hillary Clinton was criticized in the summer of 2015 for having her underlings wield a long rope during a parade to keep reporters at a distance.

In Canada, the opposition parties are no strangers to news management. When the NDP were the Official Opposition, for example, they would aggressively challenge media outlets that did not give prominent placement to their leader or their MPs in a story. The Liberals are prolific users of social media to transmit and broadcast messages from their leader directly to the public.

The challenge for future governments is to recognize that stemming the flow of information, and blocking access to decision-makers, has an impact on journalistic practice. The unintended consequence is a press gallery that is perhaps more nimble and creative, while less trusting of government messages. Early indications are that the new Liberal government seems to recognize this, immediately opening up access to ministers, diplomats and bureaucrats as it came into office.

Still, it is difficult to overstate the crisis that federal government communications found itself in when Harper left office. Something is seriously broken when even basic statistics and technical information about programs and policy decisions are withheld, or else packaged in a way that is designed to promote rather than inform. The politicization of the public service's communications role needs to be addressed if we are to live up to the government's stated policy view that "Communications are central to the Government of Canada's work and contribute directly to the Canadian public's trust in their government."[43]

Finally, journalism is a democratic institution that is often overlooked as a public policy concern in this country. Federal politicians have often seemed indifferent to the wider implications of media fragmentation, newspaper closures and the decline of quality reporting, and media organizations are slow to sound the alarm. The demise of the *Guelph Mercury* and the *Nanaimo Daily News* in early 2016 seemed to stir parliamentarians into action. An extensive study into news and local communities was launched by the Commons Standing Committee on Canadian Heritage.

While the appetite for helping private media companies might be non-existent, at a minimum the public broadcaster should be properly supported to ensure the country always has a benchmark of quality national journalism.

Prime Minister Justin Trudeau and those who come after him will face important questions. Who will continue to hold elected officials accountable? What will a weaker, constrained news media mean for citizen engagement? What will the absence of strong, national journalistic voices mean for our sense of national identity and unity?

5

Permanent Marketing and the Conduct of Politics

Susan Delacourt

In the early days of 2007, just as Prime Minister Stephen Harper's government was nearing the anniversary of its first year in power, a noteworthy meeting took place at the Delta hotel in downtown Ottawa.

Two of the sharpest minds in federal politics at the time were having an impromptu get-together. On this chilly January day in 2007, the Conservatives held power in a minority government, which would last until the end of summer in 2008. The New Democrats had third-party status in the Commons. The Liberals, in official opposition for the first time in more than a decade, had just elected a new leader, Stéphane Dion. It was this latter development that prompted the prime minister's deputy chief of staff, Patrick Muttart, to meet with Brad Lavigne, then the director of strategic communications for NDP leader Jack Layton. The two men, though officially rivals, enjoyed a collegial relationship and a mutual interest in keeping Liberals out of power. At the Delta hotel restaurant, Muttart handed Lavigne a copy of an ad that the Conservative party intended to put on the air in the coming days. Lavigne went home that night, fired up the DVD and realized he was seeing something new and startling in Canadian political culture. Conservatives were launching an all-out advertising attack on the Liberals' new leader, to be aired in a non-election period.[1]

The ad used footage from the Liberal leadership debates of the previous fall, featuring runner-up Michael Ignatieff saying, on the environment, "We didn't get it done." Dion himself plaintively replies, "Do you think it's easy to make priorities?" Conservatives would show these ads during the big Super Bowl broadcasts in February and keep bombarding the airwaves with them over the next months to drive home to Canadians that Dion was, in the ad's words, "not a leader."

Harper's Conservatives were not the first governing party to air political advertising on TV between elections. In 2004, in the lead-up to an election they would call in the spring, the Liberals under Prime Minister Paul Martin launched a volley of anti-Harper ads on TV, as well as a website: www.stephenharpersaid.ca. But the ads ended after Martin's government was returned with a minority win in June 2004. Harper's government would be the first in Canada to make between-election advertising a standard occurrence.

Every Liberal leader after Dion was subjected to the same style of advertising barrage. After Dion was gone in 2009, his successor Ignatieff was the target, and within twenty-four hours of his Liberal leadership victory in April 2013, Justin Trudeau was the focus of a new wave of mocking ads by the Conservatives. Ignatieff, in the book he wrote on his bruising experience in politics, described the advertising innovation this way: "Between May 2009 and the election two years later, they ran those ads everywhere, buying airtime on the shows with the highest viewing figures. I couldn't turn on the Oscars without seeing my face in the commercial breaks. I couldn't watch the Super Bowl without being told that I was 'just visiting.' … Normally, governments in Canada get on with governing between elections. They don't run campaigns against opposition leaders. But in the new politics of the permanent campaign, governing is campaigning."[2]

The January 2007 meeting between Muttart and Lavigne captured in a snapshot how the conduct of politics would change while Stephen Harper was in power. These were years when politics was pervasive, personal and polarizing—all part of the "permanent campaign" in which parties never stopped fighting the last, or next, election. They were also years when marketing and advertising assumed a far more prominent place in Canadian politics, with branding, imagery and attack ads used across multiplying channels of communication in the digital universe. So successful was the attack-ad strategy that Harper's rivals ultimately had no choice but to respond with their own ads in between elections too.

Together, political marketing and permanent campaigns would guide the culture of politics in the Harper years, and in all likelihood, they will in the years ahead too. Both trends had parallel developments in other countries. Presidential and congressional races have expanded to near-permanent conditions in the United States, and political-marketing practices have spread to Canada from the US, Britain and Australia, among other countries, over a couple of decades. But the combination of the two trends—a permanent campaign characterized by hardball marketing tactics—put a hyper-partisan stamp on Canadian politics from 2006 onward. And Harper, through the force of his own personality, hard-won experience and approach to political organization, would galvanize those changes on Canada's political landscape.

Branded

When Pierre Trudeau and Brian Mulroney were in power through the 1970s and 1980s, it helped to come to work in Ottawa with a firm understanding of the Constitution. Politics was conducted against the constant drumbeat of the national unity drama with Quebec and the intricacies of any number of demands on Canada's Constitution and its institutions. But Harper arrived in power in 2006 with much of the constitutional dramas behind Canada—indeed, at a time when politicians were rewarded by the public for promising to never open or even speak about the Constitution again.

In its place, a new branch of political science assumed an emerging significance; some might argue that it found a pre-eminent place in our understanding of Ottawa. This was the study of political marketing, much researched and analyzed in the United States and Britain since the time of Ronald Reagan and Margaret Thatcher leading those countries, respectively, in the 1980s. The discipline was virtually unknown in Canada until Harper came to power.

To understand the culture of politics in the Harper years, one needed to have a grasp of the basics of political marketing: branding, advertising and talking to citizens as consumers, with all the modern tools of salesmanship and customer research. One of the leading academic researchers in this emerging field in Canada was Memorial University's Alex Marland, who assiduously tracked how marketing tools had been put to political use in Harper's Ottawa. Marland would eventually conclude that "branding" was the larger term required to describe the transformation of Canadian politics in the Harper years—years that he described as "formative."[3] Marland pulled many of his findings into a 2015 book called *Brand Command,* destined to be a reference manual for how branding and marketing put Canadian politics, as well as government, on a new axis in the country, probably for the long term. "Branding is an unstoppable force in politics and government," he wrote.[4]

Muttart, who had a background in marketing and ad design, is widely given much of the credit for the consumer-friendly overhaul of Harper's Conservative party in the years between the party's unsuccessful 2004 federal campaign and its victory in 2006. Once in power and installed as a strategic adviser in the PMO, Muttart was seen essentially as the "vice-president of marketing" in the government, overseeing the rigorous attention to branding, backdrops and imagery.[5] The idea of a marketing chief in government was new to Canada, as were public-service job titles with "marketing" in them. By 2015, the Canadian government's electronic staff directory listed more than 200 people responsible for some aspect of marketing within government departments; it was an indication, perhaps, of how much the political attention to marketing wisdom had crept into the public service.

Muttart left government in 2009, but attention to marketing and branding remained rigorous, largely because Harper himself shared the view of its importance to his government. "Never once was there a debate about the importance of marketing or the need to use marketing strategies to deliver political messages to Canadians," Muttart said.[6] Muttart believed that Harper's appreciation for marketing techniques came from his immersion in the consumer and television culture of the Baby Boomer generation, as well as from Harper's stint in the 1990s at the National Citizens Coalition, an advocacy organization fond of hard-sell tactics. Muttart had also spent some time learning from political-marketing practices abroad, notably from John Howard's Liberal-National coalition in Australia.

Wherever the marketing techniques originated, they were immediately evident within weeks of Harper's victory in 2006. "We're a different kind of government and we place a heavy value on communications and we like the visuals," Sandra Buckler, then–director of communications for the PMO, said in a meeting with the parliamentary press gallery in early 2006.[7]

Careful attention was paid to the placement of flags and backdrops when the prime minister or his ministers spoke, more than had been witnessed in previous governments. Press releases were issued from "Canada's New Government," and the releases themselves were described as "communications products." A Conservative-blue hue crept into the traditional (and official) red-and-white colour scheme of Canadian government signage and its websites, which were directed to have a "common look and feel." Legislation was given snappy, attention-grabbing names: the "Cracking Down on Crooked Consultants Act" and the "Zero Tolerance for Barbaric Cultural Practices Act," to name just two. Several ministers courted controversy when appearing at events with oversized cheques bearing the Conservative party logo—even when the money was coming from the federal treasury.[8]

It requires a good deal of planning and choreography to put such a strong marketing stamp on so many aspects of government. To that end, the Harper government will be remembered for ushering in what was known as the "Message Event Proposal"—an incredibly detailed form that had to be filled out and cleared by the Prime Minister's Office before any public event held in the government's name, no matter how big or small. The form asked planners to provide details such as backdrops, media lines and strategic objectives, as well as listing which headlines and photographs were desired results in the media. As Marland reports in *Brand Command*, this marvel of micro-management was inspired by the example of Ontario's Progressive Conservative government and overseen in the early days of Harper's government by Muttart. "The introduction of the Message Event Proposal fulfilled its objective of infusing a change to organizational culture in the Government of Canada. The permanent government became more cognisant of the importance that the political government attaches to communications planning and visuals." [9]

Branding can only really be done well in a highly centralized government. As Carleton University's Richard Nimijean puts it, "the brand state requires the centralization of power within the government in order to effectively direct the cohesive implementation of the brand in all government products." [10] So it was good news for Harper that he arrived in power in a government that had already been heading in the direction of centralized command, dating back to the Pierre Trudeau years. The centralizing tendencies of prime minister Jean Chrétien, for instance, were highlighted in Donald Savoie's signature book, *Governing from the Centre*.[11] And Marland, for his part, predicted that the branding and centralization seen in the Harper years would continue.

Top-down Management

Minority government, it goes without saying, keeps all political parties on a campaign footing. When no party knows exactly when Parliament will lose confidence in a government, triggering the launch of an election, it is prudent to remain in constant readiness for a campaign, with party coffers filled and supporters energized.

So it is understandable that the years between 2006 and 2011, featuring two minority governments under Harper, saw the parties scrambling to remain election-ready, taking advantage of all the means available, especially new tools on the digital frontier. Other chapters in this book will explore in more detail how the permanent campaign and its tools crept into the public service and into the government's relations with the media. But for all these developments to have taken place, a strong, central political culture was required. It started with Harper's centralization of his own party's architecture.

Tom Flanagan, the University of Calgary political scientist who also served as a mentor and campaign chief for Harper, has written prolifically on the root-and-branch transformation of the Conservative Party into a perpetual election-fighting machine. In a paper presented to the Canadian Political Science Association conference in Montreal in 2010, Flanagan described the Conservatives' approach with a military metaphor. "Just as chronic warfare produces a garrison state, permanent campaigning has caused the Conservative Party to merge with the campaign team, producing a garrison party. The party is today, for all intents and purposes, a campaign organization focused on being ready for and winning the next election, whenever it may come."[12]

The paper provided a revealing look into the mechanics and motives of a permanent-campaign apparatus and, perhaps most intriguingly, into how Harper's experience in the opposition wilderness had informed the design of the modern Conservative Party.

Harper, wrote Flanagan, deliberately constructed a highly centralized organization when the old Canadian Alliance and Progressive Conservative parties were merged in 2003–4 because of bitter past experience with power struggles in party backrooms. Harper was careful to design a new Conservative Party constitution in which all power was designed to flow directly from (and to) the top. "This desire to exercise unhampered control over the party was also congenial to Harper's basic personality, which is dominant and controlling in all matters in which he is personally involved," Flanagan wrote.[13] The combination of Harper's personality and the reality of the permanent campaign also meant strict message discipline within Conservative ranks and a sharp decline in policy-making at the grassroots—which would continue and amplify when the party came to power. A party constantly on alert for an election cannot afford loose lips or to grow overly committed to potentially unpopular grassroots policies, Flanagan explained.

At first glance, one would not necessarily think that the simple structure of one political party would have a noticeable impact on the overall culture or conduct of politics. But Harper's approach to political organization would be the hallmark of his governance style, and it also came to be seen as a how-to manual for success by his rivals. As such, the changes to the shape of the Conservative Party had a domino effect on the structure of the other parties too.

For instance, when Liberal Party president Alf Apps was stepping down in late 2011 after the party's devastating election defeat that year, he wrote an extensive paper analyzing the Liberals' strengths and weaknesses. "There is much to be gleaned from the CPC (Conservative) example about modern political organizing and campaigning that LPC can and should emulate," Apps candidly wrote.[14] And so the Liberals would emulate the Conservative example. Seeing the leaner and more nimble Conservative organization, the Liberal Party post-2006 would make moves to turn party membership and fundraising into a centralized, Ottawa-based operation. By 2016, after they had reclaimed power in Canada, the Liberals would overhaul their party constitution to do away with provincial and territorial associations altogether.

Harper's changes to the Conservative party were much studied by Layton and his advisers too. When the NDP decided to pull itself into permanent-campaign mode, it also centralized more power with the leader and Ottawa. Lavigne, in his

2013 book *Building the Orange Wave*, described how authority over everything from fundraising to candidate selection was wrested away from provincial NDP organizations and streamlined under central command in Ottawa. Lavigne wrote of the old confederated NDP organization as "an unworkable structure for running a permanent campaign."[15]

Over the years between the 2009 and 2011 elections, the New Democrats paid the Conservatives the immense compliment of imitation—not just in terms of party organization, but with respect to marketing approaches too. Just as Muttart had applied his marketing talents to make Conservative politics consumer friendly and attentive to "branding," so would the NDP. Layton built a platform in 2011 loaded with items targeted at consumers: lowering home heating costs, bank fees and wireless bills.

Liberals too would offer policies that echoed Harper's "boutique" approach to courting selected consumer-voter constituencies. The Liberals' 2011 platform was called a "Family Pack" and included a monthly cheque for caregivers, similar to the Conservatives' $100-a-month payouts for parents. In the 2015 election, Trudeau's Liberals offered tax breaks for teachers who had to buy school supplies out of their own pockets.

Shaking up the Institutions

Throughout Harper's years in power, much of Parliament Hill was under construction as part of a massive Public Works renovation. The scene was a fitting visual metaphor for frequently told stories of siege and struggle between the Harper government and its institutions. Failing to reform the Senate, Harper filled it with political appointees, notably former CTV journalist Mike Duffy—a decision that would ultimately plunge his government into a legal and moral crisis, played out in an Ottawa courtroom even as the Conservatives sought re-election in the summer of 2015.

The Senate was only one of many institutions shaken while Harper was in power, though. Over the course of nearly a decade, Harper would place himself at political odds with the Supreme Court of Canada, the public service, the press gallery, independent watchdogs such as the Parliamentary Budget Officer and, repeatedly, Elections Canada. Two Conservatives—MP Dean Del Mastro and party staffer Michael Sona—were jailed for election-related offences. A cabinet minister, Labrador's Peter Penashue, was forced to resign his seat for irregularities in his 2011 campaign expenses. In 2011, the Conservative Party and its fundraising arm, the Conservative Fund of Canada, were fined for violating election-expense rules in a complex, so-called "in-and-out" scheme in which funds were transferred between local and national organizations.[16]

At the epicentre of the institutional battles was Parliament itself. The theatrics of the daily Question Period in the Commons have always presented opportunities for all parties to perform full-on politics. A frequent question throughout the Harper years, however, was whether the displays were worse or more toxic in the era of the permanent campaign.

In government, it was clear that the Conservatives took a somewhat innovative approach to answering questions, most likely based on their experience in opposition. Queries about government business from the other side were often met with opposition-style research or attacks on the inquiring party. When Liberals and New Democrats were protesting about Canada's temporary-worker policies, for instance, Conservative ministers would rise and reply with evidence of opposition requests for temporary-worker permits for businesses in their ridings. When Liberal MP Bob Rae stood up to ask about the long-gun registry in September 2010, Harper answered him with a volley of questions: "What does the Liberal Party have against law-abiding citizens? What does it have against farmers? What does it have against duck hunters? What does it have against aboriginal Canadians? Why does it not stand up for people in the regions of this country?" Perhaps the most incendiary example of the government's tendency to attack rather than answer came in 2012, when Public Safety Minister Vic Toews said that critics of increased police surveillance "can either stand with us or the child pornographers."

Even away from the Question Period theatrics, opportunities for cross-partisan collegiality among MPs seemed scarcer in Parliament. Ottawa journalist Don Martin uncovered a Conservative manual in May 2007 instructing Commons committee chairs on how to operate hearings to maximum political effect, including selecting witnesses approved by the Conservative Party and from witness lists weighted heavily by Conservative-held ridings. [17] Opposition MPs were sometimes left out of international delegations, notably from a large government-sponsored trip to Israel in January 2014 and a trip to Ukraine a month later, led by foreign affairs minister John Baird. The Prime Minister's Volunteer Awards left opposition MPs off the ceremony guest list in 2012, even when their respective constituents were set to receive the honour on Parliament Hill.

Ministerial announcements, once studiously non-partisan when issued from a government office, often contained a swipe against the opposition Liberals or New Democrats. And where once governments would include opposition MPs in funding announcements in their ridings, the practice effectively ceased after 2006. This development prodded NDP MP Pat Martin into a 2012 Twitter tirade when Vic Toews, then the public safety minister, neglected to include Martin in a government event in his Manitoba riding. "I'm not 'worked up' so much as 'fed up' with the rat faced whores in the [Conservative Party] who neglect to invite me to announcements in my riding," Martin wrote to a journalist on Twitter. (Martin subsequently withdrew from Twitter and apologized for his language.)[18]

The fast-moving, 140-character universe of Twitter often helped to amplify the hyper-partisan climate, as the Pat Martin example illustrates. In instances too numerous to list here, ministers, as well as MPs and staff in all parties, would fire off barbs against each other or get into long spats in full view of all those following on Twitter. Apologies for hasty or ill-considered Twitter posts became common, though they did little to dilute the hyper-partisan stream of commentary on the social medium. On the upside, Twitter was a new window for voters into day-to-day political business in Ottawa. Harper himself paid tribute to Twitter's emergent role in political communication in later years in power, choosing to announce his cabinet-shuffle appointments on Twitter first.

Quantifying the volume of political or partisan discourse is not easy, especially amid the raucous atmosphere of Question Period. One measurable indicator of the partisan preoccupations of the prime minister, though, could be found on the openparliament.ca website, which used an algorithm to track the "favourite words" of individual members of Parliament. This algorithm discounted ordinary or frequently used words, such as "the" or "and" or "Mr. Speaker," to come up with the words most uttered in the official Hansard record of proceedings. In session after session of Parliament after he took power, Harper's favourite word was "Liberal." This continued for some time after the Liberals were knocked to third-party status in the election of 2011, but "Liberal" was eventually replaced by "NDP" as the 2015 election loomed.[19]

Actually, though, it was the fifteen minutes before Question Period that provided another telling measure of the increase in partisan politicking in the House—the time reserved for "members' statements" or SO 31s, short for the Standing Orders of the Commons under which these statements take place every day. Traditionally, members' statements have been used by individual MPs to make laudatory remarks about events or milestones in their own ridings, such as victories of local sports teams or notes of condolence for a loss of a community member.

But after the Conservatives took power in 2006, these members' statements often acquired a harder political edge, with backbenchers reading from scripts that attacked the opposition. The evidence of the script could be found later in Question Period, when similar lines and wording would be echoed by government ministers. The phrase "job-killing carbon tax" was uttered so often in statements or in replies to opposition questions that it became a target of parody.

Evan Sotiropoulos, a master's graduate from the University of Toronto's political science department, carried out a systematic study of members' statements in the 38th and 39th parliaments, from 2004 to 2008, and delivered his findings in a paper presented to the 2009 Midwest Political Science Association in Chicago. Sotiropoulos chose these two parliaments for study because they were both minority governments, operating with the same speaker (Peter Milliken), but one was Liberal (the 38th) and one was Conservative (the 39th). "My extensive review of parliamentary transcripts showed that unparliamentary or partisan discourse is on the rise during Members' Statements in the House of Commons," Sotiropoulos wrote.[20] After analyzing more than 4,000 members' statements from 2004 to 2008, he found that even though the Liberals doubled the number of partisan statements they made when they became the Official Opposition, Conservative MPs were still twice as likely to deliver a political punch."[21] So even when Conservatives crossed the floor from opposition to government, they continued to use these statements for partisan purposes.

Though Speaker Milliken issued a warning against partisan snipes in members' statements in 2009, they persisted. Keith Beardsley, a former aide to Harper in opposition and in the Prime Minister's Office, wrote an enlightening blog post in 2012 on the origins of the sharp politicization of this portion of Commons business. Beardsley said that when the Conservatives were in opposition from 2003 to 2006, they began to realize that they were getting more attention than anticipated for members' statements that came last in the fifteen-minute lineup. This was because journalists and cabinet ministers were filing into the chamber for Question Period as the statements were winding down. As a bonus, MPs could use one minute of time for members' statements, but they had only thirty-four seconds for a question in Question Period. Beardsley, out of government by 2012, wrote how he now looked at this politicization of members' statements as a regrettable development. "The downside to this is that the more you lead off the day with a series of attacks, many of them personal, the other parties tend to respond in kind. In my opinion this has been one of the contributing factors to the caustic atmosphere you now see on a daily basis in the House of Commons."[22]

Harper was an MP on the Reform Party benches from 1993–97 and had seen then–leader Preston Manning attempt to introduce more populist measures into the daily Question Period session. One such idea was for Reform MPs to read aloud questions from citizens. This tactic, like many others, was quickly jettisoned as Reform MPs became accustomed to their jobs in Parliament, and as the Reform Party rebranded itself as the Canadian Alliance. Throughout these years, Harper and Manning had fundamental disagreements about the role of populism in politics; it was just one of many reasons they eventually parted ways, as Flanagan, also a Reform Party founder, has written. In fact, as Flanagan noted in his 2010 paper, "After he [Harper] saw the Canadian Alliance experience of how populism could get out of control, he ultimately ended up with a view of leadership far more aggressive than Manning's."[23]

Dollars and Numbers

Ironically enough, in a digital world that gives citizens and politicians many tools to communicate and even collaborate, Harper's Conservative government was known more for a governing style shrouded in secrecy. Nonetheless, the populist roots of the Reform Party would give Harper the tools for one of the most important innovations of politics in the early twenty-first century—the political database. Because Reform had been built on a wide-ranging network of small donations, it had a ready-made array of names and addresses to plug into the newly emerging technology to track voters and supporters. Flanagan, in his role as Harper's chief of staff in opposition, gave the go-ahead to much of the early work in creating what would be known as the Constituent Information Management System (CIMS), based on an earlier model developed for the Ontario Progressive Conservative party in the 1990s.

The contents of the CIMS database were a closely guarded secret, but some details came to be known through media reports. CIMS initially tracked mainly supporters and donors to the party, then added information based on petitions signed, letters written or party events attended by citizens. Conservative volunteers were encouraged to enter relevant data into the system while out canvassing so that the party could identify which voters should receive specialized, targeted pitches. A voter listed in the CIMS database as a parent of children, for instance, would get messages designed for families. It was called "micro-targeting"—identifying pockets of support and creating policies and pitches just for those voters. In ridings where election races were tight, and with a winner-take-all system, the ability to attract votes from these small constituencies could add crucial seats to a party's results. The irony of the CIMS database, not to mention the strategies around it, was in the way it was turning the art of politics into a highly specialized science. So the same government that had ended the mandatory long-form census and the gun registry—arguing them to be too intrusive—was heavily invested in keeping lists and data on the population when it came to political operations.

The New Democrats and Liberals would create their own databases too, on the heels of the Conservatives' success with CIMS. After the 2011 election, in fact, one of the larger tasks inside all party organizations was loading the databases. Efficiency was also the driving force—Conservatives, with CIMS, could identify their voter base in non-election periods, and then use campaigns to find new support. Thanks to databases, no party had to waste precious time during an election period looking for support they already had. As databases and data analysis grew more sophisticated, all parties could also sort voters by their potential leanings— even ranking them according to how likely they were to lean in any political direction. The proliferation of the databases prompted Canada's Privacy Commissioner to launch a study, led by University of Victoria political scientist Colin Bennett, which called for privacy regulation and oversight of these databases.[24]

Probably the biggest motivation for creating the databases rested in the huge changes to Canada's political-fundraising rules in the early 2000s. The Conservatives came to power on the heels of important new bans and limits on political fundraising in Canada, initiated by Liberal prime minister Jean Chrétien, but enhanced and made more strict when Harper took office. Chrétien had set the individual annual donation limit at $5,000 and the corporate and union limit at $1,000 in changes to the Elections Act in 2003. Chrétien also established a public subsidy to be paid to political parties, amounting to $1.75 a year for every vote they received in the previous election. Harper in turn banned corporate and union donations entirely and cut the individual donation limit to $1,000 (later indexed to $1,100). And then, between 2011 and 2015, the Harper government phased out the public subsidy to the political parties, leaving all of them solely reliant on small donors. The leaner, more centralized party operations they had built in the Harper years would now be an economic necessity as well.

The new fundraising regime played to Conservative strengths, as the party's financial coffers were built mostly out of small donations from the grassroots. It also fundamentally changed the dynamics between the corporate sector and politics. In the past corporate Canada could gain access and influence through big donations to parties. Their influence was now financially negligible.

Ken Whyte, a former journalist and later an executive vice-president at Rogers Communications, wrote in *Maclean's* magazine in 2013 about the shift in political influence in Canada that was thanks to the new fundraising rules. Rogers, as one of the big telecommunications companies, had been one of a number of such companies attacked in government advertising for its wireless fees. The Canadian Council of Chief Executives, alarmed at the attack by the state on the private sector, had written a letter to the government to protest the policy and the tactic.[25]

But as Whyte stood in the back of the room at the Conservative convention in Calgary in 2013, listening to chief fundraiser Senator Irving Gerstein, he realized that the people in Canada with real political clout were the small donors—the hyper-partisans who kept the money flowing to party coffers. "One hundred and fifty CEOs may rule Canadian business, but at $1,200 a head they are worth at most $180,000 to Harper," Whyte wrote in Maclean's. "So 150 of the biggest, fattest CEOs in Canada wield less clout in Ottawa than any 150 Conservative hotheads in my home riding of Edmonton Centre." Whyte, incidentally, did not portray this as a positive development. "We all need to get used to national parties more interested in capitalizing on problems than in fixing them. Get used to reams of government policy inexplicable but for its ability to grease the bagman's gears."[26]

The databases; the new fundraising rules; the hyper-partisan, branded marketing culture—all conspired to sharply divide Canada's political culture into friends and enemies. The old mass-marketing model of politics, in which politicians struggled to find the largest possible consensus for support, was being replaced in the Harper years by the quest to find micro-targeted areas of support, or what Flanagan would call the search for a "minimum winning coalition" in selected constituencies.[27] Where political parties once divided the country into winnable regions, by geography, they now had the technology to go after winnable individuals.

Friends and Enemies

Even some seasoned observers of Canadian politics were struck by the ways in which Canadian politics had been moving away from the constant search for friends and allies. One such observer was renowned pollster and commentator Allan Gregg, who had worked with Mulroney and the Conservatives in the 1980s. "Every party that I've worked for wanted to be more popular. They always wanted more votes," Gregg said. "And these guys [Harper Conservatives] are saying we don't need more votes."[28]

Throughout the years Harper was in power, this would be a familiar criticism—that Canada was being led by a prime minister more interested in cultivating the base than in expanding Conservatives' support across the country. "There has never been a prime minister as utterly contemptuous of people outside his voting coalition," wrote the *Globe and Mail*'s John Ibbitson in his 2015 biography of Harper.[29] The corollary to this assumption was the also-frequent allegation that Conservatives were deliberately trying to suppress the votes of their challengers while trying to maximize their own supporters' participation in politics.

Voter suppression was the central allegation in the so-called "robocalls" controversy after the 2011 election—one in a series of Conservative battles with election authorities. In 2012, Postmedia's investigative journalists Glen McGregor (now with CTV) and Stephen Maher uncovered evidence of mass automated phone calls made to voters across Canada, misdirecting them away from polling stations in the 2011 election. The calls were primarily made to Liberal and NDP supporters, in what Federal Court judge Richard Mosley would call a "widespread" scheme in a 2013 ruling.[30] Michael Sona, a former Conservative Party staffer, was sentenced to nine months in prison in 2014 for his role in making fraudulent calls to voters. The Conservative Party itself, it should be noted, did not face prosecution for any robocalls-related offences and stated repeatedly through its lawyer that any fraudulent calls were not approved or directed by anyone in the party.

The introduction of the Fair Elections Act, intended to set the stage for the 2015 election, revived fears that Harper's government was in the voter-suppression business. Among its many measures, it introduced strict new rules for voter identification at the ballot box and put limits on Elections Canada's powers to promote voter participation. The legislation prompted more than 450 political scientists and other academics to write a letter of protest, and the bill was also widely condemned in newspaper editorials.[31] Once again, Canada's chief electoral officer, Marc Mayrand, found himself in a showdown with the Harper government. In testimony to parliamentary committees and media interviews, Mayrand would point out that this was the first electoral reform in Canada's history that was aimed at limiting, rather than expanding, the voters' franchise. "My biggest concern is that, at the end of the day, Canadians will be denied the right to vote. Even though they are citizens, qualified and perfectly legitimate," Mayrand told reporters after speaking to a House of Commons committee in March 2014.[32] The government's democratic reform minister, Pierre Poilievre, responded to Mayrand's criticism with an attack on the chief electoral officer himself, accusing him of wearing a "team jersey."[33]

The Fair Elections Act ultimately became law with some amendments, but the controversy it provoked served as a useful bookend on the Harper decade in power—a time of tumultuous, often intensely personal, polarized politics, frequently pitting Conservatives against institutions and shaking up the very process used to elect people to Parliament.

How much of this could be attributed to the "Harper Factor"? It is undoubtedly true, as even Harper's old advisers and his biographer, John Ibbitson, seem to agree, that the prime minister himself set the tone for the hardened state of inter-party relations in politics. His own experience in party backrooms and his own approach to leadership further centralized a form of political organization in Canada that would be imitated by his rivals. And while branding, marketing and political polarization were trends that were sweeping democracies in the early 2000s, it was more than an accident that Canada would follow these trends with an enthusiastic proponent of them in the top political job of the country.

In the summer of 2015, nearly nine years after Muttart and Lavigne had met at the Delta hotel for the handover of the anti-Liberal ad, Harper called an election. That long-ago meeting had foreshadowed much of the political setting in which the 2015 campaign would be launched—with Liberals enfeebled by an advertising barrage, and the Conservatives and New Democrats vying to make it a polarized two-party race between the traditional right and left. Politicos of all stripes were braced for a longer-than-usual, harsh campaign, heavy on ads and marketing, and fought in the trenches with data, numbers and micro-targets. In tone and in substance, the 2015 campaign, in other words, would be an accurate reflection of the decade of politics that preceded it.

Perhaps the most revealing review of political conduct in the Harper years, though, was the election result itself, and the large, 184-seat majority win for Trudeau and his Liberal party. In the immediate aftermath, the victory was widely interpreted as the voters' rebuke for Harper's style of governance—a rejection of negative advertising, divisive politics and marketing gimmicks that had characterized the Conservative campaign. In the final weeks of the election, Trudeau had tried to pitch himself as the anti-Harper, in policy and particularly with regard to political opponents. "Conservatives are our neighbours, our cousins, our parents," the Liberal leader said at an end-of-campaign rally in Brampton.

Trudeau, in victory, promised that "sunny ways" would prevail in the new Liberal regime, and even Conservatives, such as Jason Kenney and Diane Finley, talked of the need for their party to embrace "sunnier" or "softer" politics.

Still, the Liberals in power would also prove that some of Harper's innovations in politics were enduring: a strong attachment to images and visuals in the new Trudeau regime, a centralization of the leader's power within the party machine and a fierce embrace of big-data politics as a winning strategy for election campaigns.

"I see images as a way to communicate," Trudeau said in an interview a couple of months after winning the 2015 election. "Understanding how to use everything you can to connect with people, whether it's my speeches … or whether it's images or advertising, that's a way of connecting directly with the people."[34]

Trudeau's principal secretary, Gerald Butts, even more frankly acknowledged how Harper's conduct of politics had a lasting impact on his successors in power. "The Tories methodology wasn't the problem," Butts said. "It was what they were putting it in service of. They used it to pull people apart, but it could be used to bring people together."[35]

THE WORLD

6

Rising Power: Stephen Harper's Makeover of Canadian International Policy and Its Institutions

Colin Robertson

From his first days as prime minister, Stephen Harper's guiding principle in conducting international relations was to support Canada's economic growth. To achieve this goal, he drew on Canada's advantages: our resource wealth, our geographic propinquity to the world's biggest markets, and our pluralism and openness to continuing immigration.

The foreign policy of nations reflects a balance between interests and values. Stephen Harper's redefinition of those interests and values tilted heavily toward *realpolitik* and realizable economic gains. There was little interest in multilateralism, usually portrayed as "going along to get along," with one notable exception: the management of the global financial and economic system. Canadian diplomacy also changed. There was no appetite for the niceties of traditional diplomacy and scant appreciation of Canada's diplomatic service.

Over his three terms as prime minister, Stephen Harper changed the focus and thrust of Canadian foreign policy. He restructured the role of many elements of the machinery of government in the design and deployment of that policy. But ultimately, many of those changes came to undermine his efforts at reaching his foreign policy goals. By the end of his term, his success at meeting the objectives he had set out for his government was decidedly mixed.

The "Harper Doctrine"

Harper's overarching objective was to position Canada as a "rising power," a phrase used in conversation with the author by senior prime ministerial assistants during the Harper years. They drew on Harper's repeated contention that Canada had become one of the "top global performers."

"We know where our interests lie, and who our friends are. And we take strong, principled positions in our dealings with other nations whether popular or not ... and that is what the world can count on from Canada!" Harper said in a speech to the Conservative Party in June 2011.

"These views matter, not just because we now have the tools to act, but also the capacity. ... Because we are no longer in the middle of the pack, but among the world's top performing nations."[1]

That vision of Canada as an international leader through its military presence, through an aggressive trade and economic agenda, and through moral clarity, underpinned the government's approach to international policy. Some have called it the "Harper doctrine," especially when addressing his unequivocal stance on issues such as Israel and Ukraine.[2]

In his first major international policy speech in the fall of 2006, Harper committed to reviving Canada's "entrepreneurial spirit" and to building "the relationships and the capabilities which will allow us to preserve our sovereignty, to protect our interests, and to project our values" in a "shrinking, changing, dangerous world."

He declared that Canadians "don't want a Canada that just goes along; they want a Canada that leads. They want a Canada that reflects their values and interests, and that punches above its weight."

The embodiment of his international policy were three specific benchmarks or objectives enunciated in London in July 2006: asserting Canadian sovereignty in the Arctic, rebuilding the armed forces and establishing Canada's place in the world economically and geopolitically.[3] As we shall see in this chapter, meeting these objectives involved a series of practical changes.

Harper changed the internal institutions that help carry out international policy, such as the Prime Minister's Office and the foreign service. Through the Canada First Defence Strategy unveiled in 2007, Harper promised to re-equip, enlarge and restore the morale of our armed forces after what his supporters characterized as a Liberal-imposed "decade of darkness." (See Chapter 7 for Murray Brewster's full assessment of this area.)

Harper prioritized trade by advancing new deals and by supporting more focused marketing by the Trade Commissioner Service. Economic diplomacy became the driver of foreign policy. In the meantime, relations with two of the world's most important markets, the United States and China, stumbled.

Development assistance was redesigned to advance trade and commerce and complement the activities of Canadian enterprise, especially our mining industry. A specific northern strategy was put in place. Finally, Harper also pursued his own personal global project, the Maternal and Child Health Initiative, which fit perfectly into this overall approach to international policy. And all this was done with a sharply different style from previous governments.

The Harper doctrine had little respect for traditional diplomatic politesse, multilateralism or the United Nations, nor for Canada's foreign service. Speaking to a Jewish audience in Montreal in May 2015, Harper proudly told them, "Gone are the days when Canadian foreign policy was about nothing more than trying to be liked by every dictator with a vote at the UN."[4]

Harper's personal diplomatic style was brash and unapologetic, black and white, ready to stand apart from both international organizations and the Canadian foreign service.

But the Conservative prime minister's style also appeared to alienate some important players on the international stage—namely, our number-one trading partner, the United States, and the partner we need, China.

Managing the Institutions of International Policy

As noted earlier, Harper's particular vision of international policy resulted in significant changes to the institutions that help to carry that vision out. While the scope of the Foreign Affairs Department was broadened to include trade and development, its role was essentially operational. It became a deliverer of services—trade, development, consular—while the policy-making was taken care of primarily by the Prime Minister's Office—although then–foreign affairs minister John Baird was afforded considerable leeway in personally taking initiatives, notably the "dignity" agenda that advanced LGBTQ rights and "girls not brides" agenda internationally, during his tenure as foreign minister.[5]

From Mackenzie King through to Paul Martin, foreign service officers were closely aligned with the prime minister, either on secondment to the office or through the Privy Council Office. While foreign service officers continued to work in the Privy Council Office during Harper's tenure, they did not enjoy the same kind of relationship to the prime minister as in the past.

The Prime Minister's Office

Harper extended the guard rails buffering the civil service and the Prime Minister's Office. Relationships between the political staff and senior civil service that were once porous, informal and frequent became privileged, formal and infrequent. Harper enthusiastically embraced the increased centralization of decision-making and communications within the Prime Minister's Office when it came to international policy.

Meanwhile, the Harper government followed the example of the United Kingdom, Australia and New Zealand in expanding the role of the national security adviser. By 2015, the adviser, who reported to the prime minister and the clerk, oversaw the Privy Council Office secretariats dedicated respectively to defence, foreign policy, security and intelligence so as to bring greater coherence to policy advice within this central agency. In an age of terrorism and protracted conflicts, the national security adviser inevitably ensured that a greater voice for security was heard in all foreign policy-making.

Harper's political staff were partisan, loyal and discreet. On at least two occasions, the chiefs of staff intervened directly to help achieve foreign policy goals. Ian Brodie led a small group to meet with George W. Bush's chief of staff, Andy Card, shortly after the January 2006 election. Nigel Wright intervened with his counterpart, Bill Daley, to ensure Canada was admitted to the Trans-Pacific Partnership prior to the 2011 APEC summit meeting between Prime Minister Harper and President Obama.

The centralization of foreign policy-making in the PMO sometimes slowed down the achievement of their objectives. Departments were obliged to fill in "Message Event Proposals" for all media encounters and public events. The proposals went to the Privy Council Office and then to the Prime Minister's Office for approval by the director of communications. The delays in this process meant opportunities were lost, especially overseas. For example, Michael Wilson was invited to appear on the Diane Rehm National Public Radio morning interview show, shortly after he became the Canadian ambassador to the United States. An inability to move the request quickly through the approval process killed this opportunity.

The requirement for permission to give speeches and then ensure they were centrally vetted had a stifling effect on outreach and public diplomacy. Controlling the message and the media may be possible within the confines of Ottawa, but in the international marketplace it's a buyers' world and there is limited interest in Canada.

Parliament

In opposition, the Conservatives had argued for greater parliamentary accountability promising a greater role for committees, and debate on significant foreign policy issues. They largely delivered on their promise through parliamentary debate and votes, especially during the deployment of Canadian Forces in Afghanistan, Libya and the Middle East.[6]

The Senate and House committees responsible for international affairs did useful work in holding hearings and issuing reports on current issues like ballistic missile defence and relations with, for example, Turkey, as well as providing recommendations to strengthen Canada's relations with Asia-Pacific, Europe and the rest of North America. At their best, the committees heard a range of views from witnesses and worked collegially with members to offer policy prescriptions in their reports.

But there was also increasingly close political oversight from the PMO on the scope of these committees, both in the House and in the Senate. Then–senator Hugh Segal, for example, "reluctantly" resigned as chair of the Foreign Affairs Committee, and colleague Michael Meighan was removed as vice chair of the National Defence and Security Committee.[7] There were complaints from the opposition parties that the government was neglecting the traditional inclusion of opposition members on missions abroad.

The Liberals had held "take note" debates on the Afghan mission in 2001, 2003 and 2005, and in opposition, Stephen Harper promised a formal debate on military interventions overseas. He followed through. After a six-hour debate in May 2006, the House agreed to extend the mission until 2009,[8] and then after another vote in March 2009, to extend it until 2011.[9] A formal vote was also held in March 2015 to extend the Iraqi mission and widen it to include the bombing of ISIS bases in Syria.[10]

The decision to advise Parliament and permit a government-sponsored vote on what had previously been the prerogative of the prime minister and cabinet reflected a growing sense, not just in Canada but in Westminster-style governments globally, of the need to secure popular support, especially in the case of armed interventions. The appropriate way to achieve this was through parliamentary debate and division.

This "democratization" of foreign policy was inevitable, given the blurring of what was once considered international into the domestic arena and the domestic into the international domain. Domestic departments all have sections devoted to international work and their expertise is both acknowledged and required. Social media reinforces the trend toward "intermestication"—what is international becomes domestic and what is domestic involves the international—especially in their attention to humanitarian crises and terrorist incidents.

The New Department of Foreign Affairs, Trade and Development

A major structural change designed to bring greater policy and program delivery coherence was the reintegration of international trade in 2006 and international development in 2013 into what became the Department of Foreign Affairs, Trade and Development. The new department's resources quadrupled with the inclusion of the Canadian International Development Agency (CIDA). Spending for 2015–16 was planned at just over $5 billion. By comparison, Industry Canada had a budget of just over a $1 billion and National Defence's budget was set at $13.5 billion.

The short-term impact of integration, as is usually the case, was to confuse the affected civil servants and clog the system as new hierarchies were put into place. What was already seen as a constipated process for policy development now had new actors with new ideas. Program delivery now required different, and initially more, approval levels, along with the additional reconsideration of assuring "program coherence." In the future, this integration is likely to create better synergies between the main strands of policy development, especially between trade and development, and better coherence in policy delivery for Canadian missions overseas.

The Foreign Service

Within the civil service, the foreign service has traditionally been the closest to the prime minister. The foreign service was effectively an adjunct of the Prime Minister's Office from its inception in 1909 until 1945, during which time successive prime ministers from Robert Borden to William Lyon Mackenzie King also held the portfolio of Secretary of State for External Affairs.

The foreign service was housed with the prime minister in the East Block of the Parliament Buildings until it moved into the Pearson Building in 1973. Foreign service officers were customarily seconded to the staff of the prime minister, a practice begun under Mackenzie King with the secondment of J.W. "Jack" Pickersgill. A senior foreign service officer always headed the foreign policy and defence secretariat within the Privy Council Office and would accompany the prime minister on travels abroad.

This comfortable relationship endured. Even though Pierre Trudeau once lamented that he could read all he needed to know in the *New York Times*,[11] he relied on the foreign service, especially in the promotion of his valedictory Peace Initiative, in which he personally visited leaders in the Eastern and Western blocs in an effort to lower Cold War tensions and promote nuclear disarmament.

Brian Mulroney had promised "pink slips and running shoes" in his first months of governing, but later his chief of staff, Derek Burney, his lead speechwriter, Paul Heinbecker, and his communications director, Marc Lortie, were all drawn from the foreign service.

Jean Chrétien underlined to his cabinet at their first meeting his expectation of close collaboration with the civil service, and throughout his tenure he personally relied on the foreign service and would regularly call Ambassador Raymond Chrétien to check the pulse in Washington. While Raymond Chrétien was his nephew, he had already achieved a distinguished foreign service career and his appointment to Washington made sense. The family connection was not lost on either Capitol Hill or the White House.

There was nothing comfortable about Stephen Harper's dealings with the foreign service. The relationship is best characterized as one of mutual contempt. Diplomats were perceived as neither effective nor efficient nor loyal.[12]

A strike in 2013 by foreign service officers, unprecedented in length and scope, resulted in picketing at headquarters and abroad. The decision to sell off Canada's historic ambassadorial residences and their artworks, as a demonstration of rectitude and economizing, was also seen as a slap at the diplomats.

There are many reasons behind the broken relationship. There were misunderstandings and delays, often caused by the new chain of communications and the requirement for the Prime Minister's Office to approve what old hands saw as the most pedestrian public affairs activities and initiatives.

No longer did heads of mission feel they had the authority to speak publicly on issues, unless they had secured prior approval. This meant opportunities to provide the Canadian perspective in a timely fashion and in local media were lost.

With the introduction in 2013 of the government's "economic diplomacy" agenda,[13] the ministerial message to diplomats was "take off your tweed jacket, buy a business suit and land us a deal."[14] It was gratuitous (advancing business has always been a top priority for the foreign service) and untrue (those who wear jackets choose blue blazers, not tweeds).

Within the PMO there was dissatisfaction with departmental advice that they often saw as late, inadequate and uninformed—especially in the early days of the Afghan campaign, which was one reason for Harper's commissioning the Afghan Task Force led by John Manley.

A sense developed within the PMO that of all the civil servants, the foreign service was the most antagonistic to the agenda of the new government. At a meeting shortly after the 2008 election, a senior PMO officer swept aside a pile of briefing books provided by Foreign Affairs with the comment, "We thought they were hiding stuff from us because they didn't like us, but looking at this stuff either they are still hiding stuff from us or they simply don't have anything new or innovative."[15]

The selling off of official residences was a major misstep that alienated the foreign service. Presented as an austerity measure, it also reflected the perception that diplomatic life was out of step with the "Tim Hortons crowd."

But the residences are and should be platforms for marketing Canada. As Jean Chrétien observed, "You don't do diplomacy from your basement." The residence in Los Angeles, for example, is a splendid home from which to promote Canada's entertainment industries—film, television, music. While posted there, we would host provincial governments—consecutively, Premier Ralph Klein of

Alberta, Premier Gordon Campbell of British Columbia, Premier Gary Doer of Manitoba and Premier John Hamm of Nova Scotia led delegations with whom we promoted location shooting for film and television. We also served and promoted their respective provinces' products—wine, beer, Crown Royal—and food—beef, pork, seafood. We would host the music supervisors from the major studios, and they'd sit in the living room watching the Junos on the big screen to spot talent. It worked well to promote Canada, and the residence hosted over 300 events during four years. To John Baird's credit, when the business case for retaining the Los Angeles residence as the platform for marketing Canada's entertainment industry was pointed out to him, he took down its "For Sale" sign.

Given the importance to Canada of a reliable foreign service, it is surprising that Stephen Harper did not make better use of the foreign service, which traditionally takes pride in its "special relationship," deservedly or not, with the prime minister.

While most of the responsibility for the failed relationship lies with Harper, the foreign service needs to look at its recruitment, training, management and prioritization of programs and policies. Foreign services everywhere are having to cope with the fact that technology, social media and the expansion of civil society actors have removed their monopoly on insight, advice and knowledge.

Successive waves of cuts, euphemistically called "program review," hollowed out the policy development capacity of the foreign service. Meanwhile, the demands of information technology and human resources, grew in response to greater obligations, such as secure and rapid communications and a surge in accountability requirements. The Harper government's emphasis, at least as it was interpreted by senior departmental management, would be on program delivery and accountability, rather than policy.

Increasingly, policy expertise on international issues lies within domestic departments. For example, when it came time to select a chief negotiator for the Canada-Europe free trade negotiations, the nod went to Steve Verheul, an experienced senior official from Agriculture Canada.

It has been over thirty years since the last serious examination of the conditions of the foreign service, and it's time for a review.

Defence and National Security

Throughout the Harper years, Canada was a reliable ally in defence of collective security. "A handful of soldiers is better than a mouthful of arguments," Harper said in Trapani, Italy, at the base for RCAF CF-18s flying over Libya, "for the Gadhafis of this world pay no attention to the force of argument. The only thing they get is the argument of force."[16]

Canada stood up during the long Afghan campaign and 158 members of the Armed Forces were killed during the combat mission (2002–10).[17] During the Libyan campaign, Lieutenant General Charles Bouchard directed NATO's air campaign. As the Ukrainian crisis unfolded, the government dispatched fighter jets and naval frigates to the theatre. Canadian trainers helped Ukraine, and members of the Canadian Forces were based in Eastern Europe through NATO. Canadian fighter jets and special forces were deployed to combat ISIS in Iraq and Syria.

If mutual contempt characterized the Harper government relationship with its foreign service, the government's relationship with the senior command of the Armed Forces was one of disappointment and a sense of having been let down. The escalating cost and delays to promised multi-billion-dollar procurement projects poisoned the relationship. As *Globe and Mail* national affairs correspondent Jeffrey Simpson observed, "Canada's Conservative government loves the idea of the military; it just doesn't always like the military."[18]

After developing a coherent and credible Canada First Defence Strategy (there was no such effort on foreign policy), as well as a budget that pledged to support the requirements for new military kit, the funding evaporated in subsequent budget restraint exercises and the promised update never materialized. Capital spending dropped on defence to the lowest level since 1977–78[19] and the Parliamentary Budget Office warned that if program costs and budget allocations were not brought into alignment (i.e., more defence spending), there would be a reduction in the capabilities of the current forces.[20]

The government's efforts to rationalize and improve defence procurement included rationalizing shipyards, creating closer ministerial oversight and establishing a Defence Analytics Institute. But the rhetoric never matched performance.

While the Defence Procurement Strategy has had some successes—for example, in the purchase of our airborne lift capacity—David Perry, now a senior analyst at the Canadian Global Affairs Institute, concluded in a 2015 study that "at the political level, trust in the acquisition system has been significantly degraded as a result of multiple failed procurements and negative Auditor-General reports."[21] There were continuing delays around major projects—new fighter jets and warships, supply ships and Arctic patrol ships promised through the National Shipbuilding Procurement Strategy. The delays embarrassed the service commanders, frustrated the senior bureaucracy in the responsible departments, irritated industry and infuriated the government.

International Trade

The Harper government increased our trade commissioners' presence in Asian markets and improved the services provided by the Trade Commissioner Service within Canada. It re-established offices across Canada and created a results-based plan that included, for example, sponsoring Canadian entrepreneurs' involvement with business incubators in Silicon Valley.

Several trade agreements were brought into force (see Laura Dawson's Chapter 9 for a full analysis of the trade record). The Comprehensive Economic Trade Agreement (CETA) with the European Union was negotiated in 2014 but awaits ratification and implementation. The Trans-Pacific Partnership agreement—with eleven Pacific nations including, importantly, the United States, Mexico (thereby effectively updating the NAFTA) and Japan (with whom parallel negotiations on a free trade agreement were also underway)—was concluded during the 2015 election and also requires ratification and implementation.

The government restructured trade development, putting greater focus on priority markets and sectors. The objective was to double small and medium-size businesses' involvement by 2018.[22] The government also restructured its approach to the recruitment of foreign students with an objective of doubling their numbers by 2022.[23]

But there were major setbacks too. Harper wanted to be not only a global power, but also an energy superpower. His government enthusiastically supported Enbridge's Keystone XL oil pipeline but, as we shall see later, did little to allay concerns in the United States about the environmental impact of the pipeline and Canada's own commitment to combat climate change.

International Development Assistance

Re-integration of CIDA within Foreign Affairs, as part of the May 2013 budget, was controversial but sensible. Too often in the field, there was a disconnect over foreign policy objectives and how they meshed with the delivery of development assistance. There was a cultural chasm between the two departments and how they viewed their respective missions.

CIDA was created during the Pierre Trudeau years, emerging from what had been the Aid Office of the Department of External Affairs (it became Foreign Affairs under Jean Chrétien). CIDA was intended to operate in the field as a development delivery agency. Instead, operating from Hull (now amalgamated into the City of Gatineau), across the Ottawa River in Quebec, under the direction of Paul Gérin-Lajoie, a former Quebec education minister, it developed an independent streak and its own distinct culture. Long-term development goals, argued those within CIDA, should not be subject to short-term diplomatic imperatives.

CIDA officers at missions overseas took their cue accordingly, armed with separate and substantial budgets that usually eclipsed those of their diplomatic colleagues. They often operated independently of their ambassador or high commissioner, even though the latter was intended to have overall responsibility. There were awkward conversations with foreign governments about CIDA-funded projects that were perceived as interfering in the host country's domestic affairs.

The re-integration of CIDA and the shift in development philosophy brought criticism from development interests and NGOs. Then–minister Julian Fantino responded that "this is Canadian money" and that those who believe "CIDA only exists to keep NGOs afloat" were wrong. NGOs would not be funded for life, and Fantino said he found it "very strange that people would not expect Canadian investments to also promote Canadian values, Canadian business, the Canadian economy."[24]

This shift in development approach and philosophy is not unique to Canada. The British, Australians and New Zealanders have also incorporated development assistance funding under the direction of their foreign affairs ministries with the goal of instilling a "business" perspective into development.

The CIDA-DFATD merger has still to gel. The policy changes will oblige a change in attitudes as CIDA partnerships are broadened to include business as well as NGOs and multinational organizations.

The OECD reviewed Canadian development policy in 2012 and commended the Harper government's strong stand on human rights, its cooperation with developing countries and its "effective efforts" in Afghanistan and Haiti.[25] It also praised Canada for untying its aid and opening its markets to forty-six developing countries in every sector except supply-managed dairy and poultry.[26] But it warned that aid as a percentage of GDP was still declining and that the system was "cumbersome."[27]

An assessment of Canada's global engagement by Robert Greenhill and Megan McQuillan (calculated as combined spending on official development assistance and defence), determined that as a share of GDP it fell by half, from 2.4 per cent of GDP in 1990 to 1.2 per cent in 2014. Defence spending dropped to 1 per cent of GDP. NATO nations commit to spend 2 per cent of GDP on defence. Development assistance had fallen to .23 per cent of GDP compared to the G7 average of .32 per cent. Canada's global engagement, they observed, is a full 40 per cent lower than the G7 average. Canada, they concluded, had become a "free rider."[28]

The North

Like Diefenbaker, Harper made development of the North a key policy initiative, observing after the 2010 military exercises in the Arctic that "we're doing it because this is about nation building. This is the frontier. This is the place that defines our country."[29]

Harper established an Arctic foreign policy in 2010, setting as his objective a "stable, rules-based region with clearly defined boundaries" and an important environment in which "dynamic economic growth and trade" can take place.[30] Canadian sovereignty claims were extended to include the North Pole.[31] During its chairmanship of the Arctic Council (2013–15), the Harper government established the Arctic Economic Council.

But the promised developments within Canada either were shelved or fell behind schedule. The Arctic base for docking and refuelling in Nanisivik at the eastern entrance to the Northwest Passage didn't materialize.[32] While construction at the Irving shipyard in Halifax of the Arctic offshore patrol ships has begun, they are behind schedule. The *John G. Diefenbaker* icebreaker to be constructed by Seaspan in Vancouver was promised by Prime Minister Harper in 2008 for 2017 but anticipated delivery is now in the 2020s.[33]

Harper's Project: Maternal and Child Health

For Harper, effective results and accountability came through collaboration with private groups like the Gates Foundation, rather than other governments. In Harper's view, governments can provide financial and technical support for development goals, but delivery and field operations are best left to NGOs and the private sector.

It was with this in mind that he pursued the Maternal and Child Health Initiative, a personal policy project that he championed at the G8 summit in Muskoka in 2010. Harper followed through on the project by working at several levels. He co-chaired (with Tanzanian president Jakaya Kikwete) the UN Commission on Information and Accountability for Women's and Children's Health. He hosted the 2014 Saving Every Woman, Every Child global health summit in Toronto.

At multilateral meetings Harper consistently argued for stronger public accountability[34] and greater transparency. Both are key features in the maternal, newborn and child health initiatives.[35] These initiatives also featured another Harper approach—the involvement of the voluntary sector, in this case the Gates and Clinton foundations.

This Harper legacy, while useful and important, does not match that of Progressive Conservative prime minister Brian Mulroney and Liberal Jean Chrétien, who also drew on their place and standing to leave a personal imprint in international policy. Brian Mulroney defied his natural allies, Ronald Reagan and Margaret Thatcher, to reach out to South Africa bilaterally and through the Commonwealth. He also made his contribution to narrowing the East-West divide through adroit diplomacy during the Ottawa Open Skies conference, which proved to be the first step in the reunification of East and West Germany. He earned the accolade of Canada's "greenest prime minister" for his efforts leading to the Montreal Protocol on Substances that Deplete the Ozone Layer (1989) and the Acid Rain Accord (1991).[36]

Jean Chrétien oversaw the human security agenda that led to the landmark 1999 Mine Ban Treaty, the creation of the International Criminal Court in 2002 and the groundwork that led to the G20. Chretien personally led the initiative for investment in Africa at the 2002 G8 Kananaskis summit.

Stephen Harper's Brand of Internationalism

Assessing the Harper record over his decade as prime minister is a study in applied unilateralism whenever possible, and multilateralism when necessary.

Critics have made much of the lost bid for a seat on the UN Security Council in 2010.[37] Canada lost for a variety of reasons: a late campaign waged without the strategic resolution that characterized previous efforts and inept handling of the Arab states. Our inclusion in the Western European and Others Group (WEOG) also puts us permanently at a disadvantage, because the EU increasingly votes as a bloc. If we want a seat on the Security Council more frequently, we should recognize geography and obtain UN permission for us to shift to the Americas group of nations within the UN. It would also oblige us to take a more active role in our hemisphere.

But Harper's attendance at the traditional multilateral talk fests was perfunctory. He missed several of the annual UN General Assembly sessions for leaders, and did not demonstrate any enthusiasm for either the Francophonie or the Commonwealth—because of his belief that they failed to set goals or establish accountability.

In discounting multilateralism, Harper missed opportunities to establish the personal relationships with his foreign counterparts that well served his predecessors. Even with fellow conservatives, Stephen Harper kept his distance, turning down the invitation from George W. Bush and John Howard to take on chairmanship of the conservative International Democrat Union after Howard was defeated as Australian prime minister in 2007.

Nor did the Harper government try to place Canadians in international institutions. Michaëlle Jean, secretary general of the Francophonie, is the only Canadian whom the Harper government has visibly supported for an international leadership position. Too bad, as Canadians derive a sense of our identity how we are seen abroad. It is also through that presence that we contribute to international order.

The Impact of the "Harper Doctrine" on Bilateral and Hemispheric Relations

The United States

Harper was determined to restore the Canada-US relationship, but a decade later it was even cooler than when he had first taken office.

He initially took to heart the Brian Mulroney axiom that the initiative for action with the USA, no matter how frustrating, always lies with the Canadian side. Opening the border for swifter passage of goods and people is a constant Canadian priority, and Harper carried on Canadian support for the North American Security and Prosperity Partnership initiative begun under his predecessor Paul Martin with presidents George W. Bush (USA) and Vicente Fox (Mexico).

With the change of US administration, Stephen Harper put border access at the top of his list during President Barack Obama's February 2009 visit to Ottawa and then pushed it again with Obama at the Toronto G20 summit in 2010. Launched in December 2011, the "Beyond the Border" and regulatory coordination initiatives have made progress.[38] People and goods are moving across the border more quickly, but progress has been slow. A Statistics Canada study showed that it cost 25 per cent more to move goods across the border between 2001 and 2009 than to move them the same distance within Canada.[39]

Harper also acknowledged Brian Mulroney's advice[40] that the most important relationship for every prime minister is that with the US president, but he ultimately failed to follow through. Almost immediately after his January 2006 victory, he rebuked American ambassador David Wilkins over US policy in the Arctic.[41] He later declined George W. Bush's invitation to his ranch in Texas.

Both Barack Obama and Stephen Harper achieved power as underdogs and retained office in subsequent elections. Deliberative, disciplined and determined, each likely thought himself the smartest person in the room. Despite their differences in political philosophy, Obama and Harper worked together on the big issues of global financial crisis, peace and security (although they differed in their tone on Israel) and kept the border and regulatory initiatives moving forward.

Their mutual failing was on the Keystone XL pipeline project.

Keystone XL is a lesson in how not to conduct bilateral relations. Harper antagonized President Obama by calling the pipeline's approval a "no-brainer" and saying he wouldn't "take no for an answer."[42] Obama annoyed Harper with his remark, "Understand what this project is: It is providing the ability of Canada to pump their oil, send it through our land, down to the Gulf [Coast], where it will be sold everywhere else. It doesn't have an impact on US gas prices."[43] Of American presidents since Franklin Roosevelt, Barack Obama appeared to exhibit the least appreciation of the strategic importance of Canada to the US.

For too long, Keystone dominated the bilateral relationship. The time devoted to secure the Keystone permit would have been better spent on other issues, including country-of-origin-labelling, or border infrastructure and the financing of the new Gordie Howe International Bridge between Windsor and Detroit. The government passed up an opportunity to collaborate through co-presidencies on the Arctic Council, as the Nordic nations had done in the previous years, in part because of the rancour over Keystone.

China

With China, Conservative anti-communist ideology met Conservative economic aspirations. There were heated debates within caucus and cabinet around Tibet and Taiwan, and the Chinese treatment of dissidents, especially the Falun Gong spiritual movement. Pragmatism eventually prevailed,[44] although it took nearly five years, earning Harper a public rebuke during his first visit to Beijing in December 2009 from Chinese premier Wen Jiabo for taking "too long" to visit.[45]

Speaking in Guangzhou in February 2012, Harper described the entrepreneurial spirit of the southern Chinese province and the contribution that its people have made to Canada. He acknowledged the "enormous differences" between the two countries but noted the similarities: "both ambitious, outwardly focused, trade-oriented, eager to strengthen our partnership." He pitched for more trade, investment and tourism and for Canada as a place for Chinese students to further their education. Harper spoke of Canada's assets: natural resources "that made the nation an emerging energy superpower," a skilled pluralistic work force and low tax rates.

Notwithstanding the arrival of the pandas at the Toronto Zoo,[46] the China relationship remains incomplete, and unlike Australia and New Zealand, Harper did not achieve a free trade agreement, held back by ideological distrust of "communist" China and complicated by Chinese expansionism in the North and East Pacific.

The other major Asian relationships are back on track after a series of minority governments curtailed the ministerial visits essential to sustaining and development business in Asia. Relations with India under Prime Minister Narendra Modi have significantly improved, including the negotiation of a uranium supply deal.[47]

Russia

In 2006, Stephen Harper accused Vladimir Putin's government of "self-serving monopolistic political strategies" after it shut off gas supplies to Ukraine.[48] During the 2014 invasion and later annexation of Crimea and incursions into Eastern Ukraine, the Harper government was at the forefront of those encouraging and then imposing sanctions on Russia.

While he consented to shake hands with President Putin at the 2014 G20 summit in Brisbane, he told the Russian president, "You need to get out of Ukraine."[49] The Harper government's reaction reflected a combination of factors: anti-communism, the 1.3 million Canadians claiming Ukrainian descent, many of whom had settled in Western Canada, and Stephen Harper's own personal dislike of Vladimir Putin that dated to their initial encounters at international summits.

Iran

The Harper Government abruptly terminated diplomatic relations with Iran in September 2012, citing Iran's nuclear program, its support for terrorism, its anti-Israel activities and its abuse of human rights. It followed on a series of increasingly strict sanctions in alignment with UN resolutions over Iranian nuclear development and human rights abuses.

After the negotiation of the Iranian nuclear framework deal in November 2013, Canadian sanctions remained in place, with the Harper government saying they were "deeply skeptical" and that "actions would speak louder than words." The approach reflected the continuing sense of the Harper government that "Canada views the government of Iran as the most significant threat to global peace and security in the world today."[50]

Israel

On Israel, Stephen Harper was unequivocal: within whatever borders, in whatever form, it must be supported. As Harper told Israel's Knesset in January 2014, the Jewish state's critics, especially those in the West, are guilty of moral relativism: "People who would never say they hate and blame the Jews for their own failings or the problems of the world instead declare their hatred of Israel and blame the only Jewish state for the problems of the Middle East. ... Such 'going along to get along' is not a 'balanced' approach, nor a 'sophisticated' one; it is, quite simply, weak and wrong."[51]

The Knesset speech captures Harper's personal diplomatic style: brash and unapologetic, ready to stand alone, and the pursuit of this policy and its objectives would be accomplished regardless of the advice of Canada's diplomats. The problem with the Harper government's support without qualification for Prime Minister Benjamin Netanyahu is that it effectively alienated Canada from any other involvement on Middle East issues. We gave up our reputation as bridge builder and helpful fixer for that of booster and scold. Whether this ultimately served Israeli interests (as opposed to those of Netanyahu and the Likud Party) or Canadian interests is doubtful.

Latin America

In 2007, Stephen Harper set out to make Canada's relationship with Latin America a priority, mentioning it specifically in the Speech from the Throne. He announced an Americas strategy and worked to forge ties with Mexican presidents Vicente Fox and Felipe Calderón, while supporting peace, development and trade in Colombia. A secretary of state for the region was appointed, and in 2015 Canada obtained observer status within the Pacific Alliance—a freer trade bloc consisting of Mexico, Peru, Colombia and Chile

But within a few years, even the department itself was calling the strategy a hollow promise. Funding evaporated for FOCAL, an Ottawa-based think tank supported through the Mulroney, Chrétien and Martin governments, and it closed down. The department's 2011 audit of the Americas strategy said there was poor understanding of the objectives and little coordination. The analysis also said that Canadian missions weren't given enough resources. It warned that Canada's influence in the region could be waning.[52]

The awkward imposition of a visa requirement on Mexican visitors in July 2009 chilled relations with a critical political and trading partner, and while the lifting of the requirement (slated for December 2016) was a welcome move, the Mexican relationship needs a comprehensive strategy.

Africa

Africa ranked low in terms of attention. Outside of international summits, Stephen Harper spent little time visiting Africa in comparison to previous prime ministers.[53]

Meanwhile, Canadian investments, especially in the mining sector continued to expand. Canada, for example, has become the largest foreign investor in Madagascar and Burkina Faso.[54]

South Africa was accorded priority status during Ed Fast's trade mission in June 2014 in reflection of its "broad Canadian interests" and an Export Development Corporation office was promised for Johannesburg.[55]

Conclusion

In a world that is a dangerous and volatile place, Stephen Harper can argue that his policies have kept Canada safe and generated an economic return through the revitalization of the Trade Commissioner Service and the expansion of trade agreements, notably with the European Union (CETA) and the Pacific (TPP) and through the Beyond the Border initiative with the US. Immigration increased with an emphasis on those with desirable skills.

Structural reforms were designed to bring greater cohesion between trade, development and foreign policy. Defence policy was clear and Canadian Forces pulled their weight in Afghanistan, Libya and the fight against ISIS. All of this was designed, according to Harper, to make Canada "the best country in the world … a confident partner, a courageous warrior, a compassionate neighbour."[56]

But of Canada's modern prime ministers, Harper's internationalism more closely resembles that of John Diefenbaker, not generally judged to have conducted a successful foreign policy. As with Diefenbaker, Stephen Harper's often black-and-white approach to international relations made achievement on the international stage difficult.

Boycotting the Commonwealth Heads of Government summit,[57] for example, has not improved human rights in Sri Lanka. Better to go and express our strong views, as did then–British prime minister David Cameron, than to absent the field.

Similarly, breaking relations with Iran eliminated our capacity to influence policy through an onsite diplomatic presence. While the government deserves credit for its subsequent efforts to utilize digital media in support of Iranian dissidents,[58] the Harper government severely curtailed public diplomacy.

Foreign diplomats regretted the lack of Canadian commitment to multilateralism and the vacating of our traditional role as bridge and helpful fixer. "What happened to Canada?" was a common question from representatives stationed in Canada. To the foreign diplomatic community, Canadian foreign policy had become narrow, self-centred and self-congratulatory.

The Harper government was occasionally also mean-spirited—it successfully lobbied for the early departure of a British high commissioner who was deemed too outspoken in his advocacy on climate change. The Conservatives shunned at various times both the US and Mexican ambassadors—hardly a way to generate neighbourliness.

Pierre Trudeau, Brian Mulroney and Jean Chrétien developed and successfully used a Rolodex of personal contacts with current and previous world leaders that crossed the boundaries of east and west, north and south, developed and developing nations. One might wonder, who would Harper have called, or would he have even placed the call?

Even on those issues he personally championed, maternal and child health, Ukraine and Israel, Stephen Harper seemed unwilling to either act as spokesman for the West or to summon other leaders to collective action. Nor, like Diefenbaker, did his personal commitment to the North amount to much more than annual summer jaunts to participate in military exercises.

In international institutions, our diplomacy punches below its weight. The Canadian foreign service is under-resourced and under-utilized. The capacities and capabilities of Canada's Armed Forces are stretched and wearing out, especially those of the Royal Canadian Navy.

"Not going along to get along" was sophomoric and inadequate as a principle for Canadian international policy. It failed to win friends or influence others, and it reduced Canada's leverage in bilateral and multilateral relations. It did not establish the conditions to achieve Stephen Harper's goal of positioning Canada as a rising power.

It was not the "low, dishonest decade"[59]—Jim Eayrs' description (drawing from the poet W.H. Auden) of Canadian foreign policy in the 1930s—but the Harper years in foreign affairs were narrow, binary and pugnacious.

The task ahead for Justin Trudeau, and for future governments, is threefold.

First, there is the unfinished business of securing better access for Canadian products and services into foreign markets. The Beyond the Border and regulatory initiatives with our most important partner and ally, the United States, need revitalization. We need to develop and follow through on an Americas strategy, starting with Mexico.

Given that sixty cents on every dollar that Canada generates depends on foreign trade, the trade agreements with the European Union and Pacific nations need to be implemented. This will oblige explaining why trade matters at home and then actively marketing Canadian goods and services abroad. We need to make Canada a magnet for tourists, students, investors and talented immigrants.

Second, Trudeau needs to re-establish Canada's credentials as a valued and helpful internationalist nation. It begins with personal commitment through active participation in summits and the cultivation of foreign leaders. It means active, constructive involvement in multilateral theatres, especially the United Nations. Trust and confidence in the foreign service, as the delivery mechanism, will need to be restored. A good start was made through Trudeau's letter to Canada's envoys, telling them that "you will have a government that believes in you and will support you in your work around the world."[60] But the foreign service also needs serious review and reform to ensure it can both devise and deliver on government policies.

Finally, to make "Canada is back"[61] more than a clever social media slogan will require hard-headed choices—a prioritization of Canadian interests and determination of the Canadian niches. It will oblige ongoing attention by the prime minister, a "Team Canada" approach that includes premiers, business and civil society and, inevitably, more money for defence, development and diplomacy.

7

The Strange Voyage:
Stephen Harper on Defence

Murray Brewster

Never, never, never believe any war will be smooth and easy, or that anyone who embarks on the strange voyage can measure the tides and hurricanes he will encounter. The statesman who yields to war fever must realize that once the signal is given, he is no longer the master of policy but the slave of unforeseeable and uncontrollable events.

— *Winston Churchill*

For Stephen Harper, the strange voyage was the five-year Canadian Forces combat mission in Afghanistan. It had a seminal influence on his government and its legacy. The war in Kandahar, and its aftermath, shaped not only the political agenda and defence policy, but aspects of social, fiscal and procurement administration in obvious and not so obvious ways.

Harper embraced both the Canadian military and the war he'd inherited from the Liberals in 2006. Harper and the Conservatives knew that associating themselves with strong institutions was red meat for the party's base of support. It was a lesson ripped straight from the Republican Party playbook in Washington.[1] The bread and butter of retail conservative politics in America was support for the troops, for law enforcement, and for anyone in uniform and the institution they served. Canadian conservatives had long been pro-military, but that message under Progressive Conservative governments had never been delivered so clearly or as bluntly as it was under Harper's united right. Brian Mulroney was the prime minister of free trade, the GST, and the first Gulf War, but when it came to the liberation of Kuwait, he purposely left the messy, dirty ground combat to the Americans, the British and other allies.

Kandahar, more than anything else, was Stephen Harper's war. It was made so in the first weeks of his mandate when he delivered a firebrand speech at Kandahar Airfield.

"There may be some who want to cut and run. But cutting and running is not your way. It's not my way," he said on March 13, 2006.[2]

"Cut and run" would surface over and over again as a prime example of Harper the war monger. But to accept such a paper-thin interpretation is to miss the point entirely. It was not meant to be some kind of weighty, Ronald Reagan–style "tear down this wall" moment. Harper wasn't speaking to history. He was speaking to voters at home, who had just elected him to a tenuous minority government. That speech, delivered half a world away in front of the troops, was intended not as a warning to the Taliban, but as an article of faith for the political base at home.

At that point in time, the NDP had not yet laid claim to the "bring the troops home" mantle, but they were headed there. By defining himself politically at the outset, Harper effectively sowed the seeds of division; it was the initial taste of not only how he would handle the war, but also how he would approach matters of national defence and security.

The problem Harper likely didn't realize then, but no doubt came to appreciate later, was that war was not like trade, economic or even tax policy, with predictable, scientifically measurable outcomes.

Kandahar, within weeks of Harper's speech, became that series of unforeseen and uncontrollable events Churchill once described, events that would preoccupy Harper throughout his minority government. Fallout from the war in terms of dealing with veterans would prove to be a further distraction and politically damaging during majority government years. Coming into office, Stephen Harper had big plans for the Canadian military, not only as a political vehicle to promote his brand, but also a place for institutional reform. National defence, the single biggest non-discretionary line item in the federal budget, had too many bureaucrats and not enough boots. The enormous political focus on Kandahar would postpone, and in some cases derail, his ambitions.

Kandahar the Conundrum

The first Canadian boots on the ground in Afghanistan landed in the fall of 2001 following the 9/11 terrorist attacks and came in the form of Special Forces: the country's elite counter-terrorism unit, Joint Task Force 2 (JTF 2).[3] A deployment of regular army troops followed in the spring of 2002 for a six-month mission in Kandahar to help the US mop up the remnants of the Taliban and al-Qaeda. Another contingent later deployed to Kabul as the international community tried to stabilize the ethnically and politically fractured nation. By the time Paul Martin's minority government decided to return to Kandahar in 2005, the Taliban was already showing signs of renewed life, particularly in the Pashtun-dominated south. Canadian military commanders put in charge of the volatile province were warned prior to the deployment of their 2,500 troops that a surge was imminent and that the hardline Islamic group would fight hard for the country's second-largest city because it considered it to be the Taliban's spiritual home.[4] It is unclear whether these blunt, specific warnings were ever communicated to Harper's incoming administration.

Within weeks of the February 2006 deployment of Canadian troops, the Taliban unleashed a springtime campaign of car bombings and suicide attacks that morphed into an annual orgy of violence known as fighting season. The Conservative strategy at the time was to push through an extension to the mission—something that turned the political divide into a canyon. By the fall, the NDP's Jack Layton demanded the troops be brought home immediately. The deadly conflict was treated as a political wedge issue at home by both sides. There was no attempt at consensus-building, something Layton laid at the foot of the prime minister, who he believed should have—at least on this one issue—sought to include opposition parties in some form of war council. In a 2011 interview, he claimed never to have had a private conversation with Harper about the conflict and to have been brushed aside when the subject was brought up. "We're going to have to just agree to disagree on that, Jack," he quoted Harper as saying.[5]

It often seemed that the political debate in Ottawa—first the question of whether Canada should leave or stay, and later the toxic crisis over Afghan detainees—overshadowed events taking place in Kandahar. Duels on the floor of the House of Commons often supplanted news from the front, and the longer the war dragged on, and the higher the casualty count rose, the more Canadians became uneasy.

A series of public opinion surveys conducted by National Defence tracked Canadians' anxiety and showed a pining for the days of peacekeeping. The notion—some would call it the myth—of Canada as a peacekeeper was deeply engrained in the national psyche and very hard to dislodge. Focus group participants were asked in a March 2008 Ipsos Reid survey what image came to mind from the word "soldier," and one respondent said: "I do not picture a Canadian soldier carrying guns."[6] The consistency of responses over the years led the same pollsters to observe in 2009, "Recent attempts at repositioning this traditional role toward one that emphasizes a more activist approach which includes the use of force have met with relatively little interest and still less acceptance."[7]

The cherished public notion of Canada as a peacekeeping nation is occasionally greeted with derision by some academics and by some inside the military, which was of the view publicly and privately that the era of traditional UN, Pearson-style peacekeeping faded with the ending of the Cold War.

"There is unfortunately a pacifist mentality in Canada that believes that only the most benign form of peacekeeping is fit duty for Canada's soldiers. This attitude meshes seamlessly with the anti-Americanism that asserts regularly that Canadian cooperation with Washington in any military activity (let alone anything else) is inevitably wrong and designed to serve the evil ends of US imperialism," historian Jack Granatstein wrote in the *Globe and Mail* in September 2007.[8]

If Conservatives need a policy lesson in the vagaries of war, the only thing they need to do is speak the name Richard Colvin, the foreign service officer responsible for much of their deepest grief on the Afghan file. His allegations of political indifference and institutional negligence on the question of alleged torture of Afghan prisoners rocked the government to its very foundations. The fallout from his testimony was one of the driving forces that led to the prorogation of Parliament in December 2009. A government's refusal to turn over documents related to the detainee file was the fuse that lit the prorogation bomb. Colvin's appearance before a House of Commons committee poured gasoline on an issue that had smoldered and flash-flared in public for two years. Colvin said Canadian "complicity in torture" ultimately undermined the country's nation-building efforts in Kandahar and had turned the local Afghan population against the NATO mission. He claimed he'd red-flagged the treatment of detainees as far back as 2006, but his warnings had been ignored by the military and the Conservative government. Colvin also declared that innocent people had been swept up in the dragnet of counter-insurgency operations.[9]

Colvin's testimony represented the climax of a mangled policy on the treatment of prisoners, the murky roots of which went back to the waning days of Paul Martin's administration. At that time, on the eve of the deployment to Kandahar, the government signed an agreement with the Afghans that required Canadian troops to transfer prisoners to local authorities. Unlike the British and the Dutch, who were also in the process of pitching tents in southern Afghanistan, the Canadian deal did not grant Canadian diplomats or soldiers the automatic right to check on the well-being of those detainees. It was a critical oversight.[10] Human rights groups feared that, given a host of international reports and red flags, prisoners handed over by Canada faced the very real likelihood of being tortured at the hands of their Afghan jailers and fellow countrymen. That would be a violation of international law.

The fears of human rights groups manifested themselves in headlines during the spring of 2007 with a *Globe and Mail* report that interviewed dozens of former Canadian-captured prisoners who claimed abuse.[11] The screaming headlines led to screaming in the Commons, which after weeks of negative publicity led to a revised transfer agreement with Hamid Karzai's government in Kabul that granted the right of inspection.

The Conservatives used the detainee issue to further drive in the political wedge over Afghanistan and were loath to admit that the policy was flawed.

"I can understand that the leader of the Opposition and members of his party feel for Taliban prisoners. I just wish occasionally they'd show the same passion for Canadian soldiers," Harper said on March 22, 2007, in response to a question from Liberal leader Stéphane Dion.[12]

It was a heaping handful of political poison to spread on the notion of bipartisanship and a particularly curious tactic, given that Harper's political survival depended on the Liberals voting with him on matters of confidence.

By the summer of 2007, the war in Kandahar had become so toxic Harper reached out to John Manley, Jean Chrétien's former deputy prime minister, to form a blue-ribbon panel to recommend a future course free of partisan taint. Manley delivered his report in January 2008. It recommended that Canada establish a more robust diplomatic and civilian presence and remain in a combat role in Kandahar as long as NATO coughed up reinforcements. Manley also concluded that the stalled procurement of CH-47 Chinook battlefield helicopters and remotely piloted drones could not wait for the Ottawa bureaucracy to sort itself out. The military needed to acquire the helicopters and drones urgently or abandon the mission. The Harper government acquired the equipment in separate deals with the US and Israel. With recommendations and promises that the mission would focus on training Afghan forces, the prime minister asked for an extension to the deployment until the middle of 2011.[13] He got it with the support of the thoroughly cowed Liberals, who vacillated between endorsement and opposition.

The populist policy of consulting with Parliament on military deployment, something that is strictly the prerogative of cabinet, was a hallmark of Harper's tenure. It was never a specific electoral promise, and Harper certainly didn't have to do it, but it fit within the Reform/Canadian Alliance notion of grassroots democracy. Consultation, however, gave opponents of the war a platform, a spotlight and airtime they might otherwise not have had. It further contributed to political polarization and helped solidify skepticism almost as much as the steady stream of television images showing the return of fallen soldiers, a phenomenon dubbed by defence academics as "the Trenton Effect."[14] The repatriation ceremonies, which took place at the country's largest military air base in Trenton, Ontario, were the subject of intense media coverage. Recognizing the damage this coverage could do to public morale, the Harper government attempted to bar reporters from covering the events in early 2006, only to face a public backlash. The decision to allow—or disallow—media was ultimately left up to the families of the dead, and many permitted the coverage. The public revulsion at the sight of so many coffins was another one of those unforeseen circumstances. And it was a matter of great frustration in both political and military circles, where senior leaders said they believed media coverage of the war to be unbalanced. Whether those leaders ever stopped to consider their own restrictive institutional communications policies, particularly at the Department of Foreign Affairs, or the Harper government's genuine unwillingness to engage in debate outside of its own carefully scripted talking points is something that's unclear. Nonetheless, they complained the public narrative as shaped by the media was weighted too much on the casualties and not enough on the good deeds that took place.

To remedy that, as part of the policy-retooling that went on post-Manley, there was a "civilian surge" at the provincial reconstruction base in Kandahar, where embedded media were fed a steady stream of development and diplomatic stories, all of which were carefully shaped and shepherded by a task force set up within the Privy Council Office under the auspices of veteran civil servant David Mulroney.[15] The Department of Foreign Affairs held regular briefings to answer the specific Manley commission criticism that the government was not communicating enough. But the briefings lasted only a few months before the task force began to rely on regular reports for public consumption. The slick, glossy publications tracked specific policy benchmarks that had been established, including "signature" development projects such as the $50-million refurbishment of the Dahla Dam irrigation project in northern Kandahar (an initiative criticized as ill conceived and unsustainable in the long term).

The corruption-laced 2009 Afghan presidential election, which returned Hamid Karzai to power, appeared to have an enormous impact on the Harper government's attitude towards the whole endeavour, and Canadian political messaging took on a more sober, even hostile tone. Lauded as the saviour of Afghanistan and a modern-day freedom fighter before his 2006 speech to Parliament, Karzai was clearly out of favour with Harper by the time NATO leaders gathered in Lisbon in November 2010. Speaking at the conclusion of the summit, Harper said the Afghan government didn't deserve a "dime" of direct foreign aid money until it ran a corruption-free show.[16] More pointedly, Harper appeared during that same period to lose faith in the whole enterprise and bluntly told a US television interviewer he had deep reservations and would not recommit Canadian troops to combat beyond the 2011 deadline. "We are not going to ever defeat the insurgency," Harper told CNN's Fareed Zakaria.[17]

Nearly a year after the US interview, Harper was more specific. In one of his increasingly infrequent exchanges with Canadian media, he told Canwest News that after 2011 the country's involvement in Afghanistan would be entirely diplomatic and oriented around development and that Canada would "not be undertaking any activities that require any kind of military presence, other than the odd guard guarding an embassy." But the Obama administration had other ideas and quietly lobbied for involvement in a Kabul-based NATO training mission meant to stand up a 352,000-strong Afghan security force of both troops and police. Harper eventually relented and committed to it. The result: Canadian troops—up to 900 of them—stayed until 2014.[18]

It was a defiant, but perhaps more thoughtful, Stephen Harper who stood before troops in the blazing 44°C Afghan sun at Kandahar Airfield on May 30, 2011, and argued that despite "successes and failures," the war had achieved its objective. "Afghanistan," he declared, "is no longer a threat to the world."

American troops had flooded into Kandahar beginning in 2009. And by the time of the Harper government's withdrawal from combat, the Canadian sector had shrunk to a tiny spit of sand in the western Panjwaii district. In a nod to the spilling of blood that remained ahead, Harper acknowledged Afghanistan was "still a violent place, a dangerous place for its citizens. … But this country does not represent a geo-strategic risk to the world. It is no longer a source of global terrorism. This is a tremendous accomplishment, one that obviously serves Canadian interests."[19]

It was far from a declaration of victory, and the security gains, as interceding years would show, were tenuous.

The Backlog

Much has been written and likely will be written about the Harper government's record on military procurement. What is little appreciated is how the backlog of unfinished projects and unfulfilled promises can be partially attributed to the amount of time, political energy and bureaucratic horsepower that was diverted to the war in Kandahar. There were, however, other factors at play—some of them ideological, some of them budgetary—that contributed to the gridlock.

The Conservative platform in the 2006 election, entitled "Stand up for Canada," promised $5.3 billion in increased spending on defence over five years, beyond what the Martin government had already committed; a "complete transformation of military operations and defence administration;" and a "reduced rank structure, review civilian and military HQ functions, and increase frontline personnel."[20]

Even before he was elected, Stephen Harper thought the military and National Defence was full of administrative deadwood. At the time, the media glommed on to promises to increase the size of the regular force to 75,000 and the reserves to 35,000, as well as the pledge to build armed icebreakers and treat the Arctic as another potential conflict zone.

The military did a detailed analysis of the Conservative defence plan soon after the election, and it was the subject of discussion at command council meetings among the senior leadership in the spring of 2006. Some portions of the analysis were later released under access to information legislation and showed that the Arctic proposals alone would require nearly $843 million per year in additional operating revenue.[21] Growing the force was also an expensive proposition. Soldiers cost money. And within two years of taking office, recruiting plans were quietly revised to reflect a force of 70,000 regular and 30,000 reserves—figures that were never achieved, despite the hawkish Conservative reputation on defence. The number of full-time members has hovered in the range of 68,000, while part-timers added up to between 26,000 and 27,000, depending on the year. In the spring of 2016, the auditor general determined that the reserve force, under the Conservatives, had become a hollow army with only a fraction of the troops properly trained, equipped and fit for international and domestic operation. Michael Ferguson discovered there were 21,000 part-time members on the books and only 13,944 of them were considered ready for active service.

The war in Afghanistan prevented Harper from tackling what was perceived to be the bloated defence bureaucracy. It wasn't until the combat mission ended and a new chief of defence staff installed that a fundamental administrative overhaul was undertaken, and it was done under the political guise of cutting the deficit, even though it was clearly a long-standing policy aim.

"The Forces must be restructured to ensure administrative burdens are reduced and resources freed up for the front line," Harper said at the October 29, 2012, swearing in of General Tom Lawson. "The Canada First Defence Strategy must continue to advance, and as I've said before, with the constant search for more teeth and less tail."[22]

A year prior to that speech, the Harper government had been handed a blueprint for cuts by the former army commander, Lieutenant-General Andrew Leslie. The transformation report supposedly received good reviews in the PMO but a cool reception by National Defence, which eventually appeared to cherry-pick from the strategy in producing its own Defence Renewal Plan that proposed cuts and an internal reallocation of as much as $1.2 billion annually. To satisfy the desire to cull the bureaucracy, the plan called for 4,800 jobs to be either cut or reassigned as "frontline" positions.[23]

What the mania about overhead failed to take into consideration was the fact that some staff positions were absolutely vital in the planning and execution of technically complex, major capital projects. A milestone research paper, co-written in January 2015 by the Conference of Defence Associations Institute and the Macdonald-Laurier Institute, examined—perhaps for the first time—why the military's politically charged procurement system was so dysfunctional. The researchers assigned much of the blame to staffing cuts by both Liberal and Conservative governments in the acquisitions branch at National Defence. The numbers were stark. In the early 1990s, there were 9,000 staff dedicated to buying military equipment. Over the course of successive Liberal budgets, that number had been slashed by more than half to about 4,200 in 2004. The number inched up slightly to 4,355 after the Conservatives took power, but the volume of complex projects they wanted to ram through the system doubled. The increase also appeared to be artificial because many positions—especially uniformed ones—remained vacant. Experienced military planners were serving overseas and the ossified system of hiring civilian federal employees guaranteed that quotas were rarely met. Following the mission, and as the "more teeth, less tail" mantra took hold, a further 400 staff positions were cut while projects piled up. "Set against this significantly increased workload, there is simply not enough capacity in the acquisition workforce to manage it," the report said.[24]

Throughout the Harper years, individual projects were dissected and critiqued by various groups and researchers, many of them looking at the subjects through their own political prisms and agendas. They talked about long-delayed maritime helicopters, close combat vehicles and Arctic patrol ships.

However, none were more written about—or caused as much political angst—as the plan to buy sixty-five F-35 stealth fighters under a complex international program that bundled the purchase of the jets with industrial benefits and diplomatic expectations. The "intention" to purchase, announced in the summer of 2010, stalled in a debate over the cost, which the Conservatives pegged at $16 billion for the planes and lifetime support.[25] Prior to the 2011 election, the Parliamentary Budget Office, to the delight of the opposition, challenged the figures, but the issue did not become politically toxic until Auditor General Michael Ferguson weighed in during spring 2012 with an analysis that accused defence and public works of understating the lifetime cost, which he estimated around $45 billion.[26] Perhaps more pertinently, he also accused them of not doing the requisite staff work to assure taxpayers the F-35 was the best choice. The issue was so damaging that the Conservatives pushed off a final cabinet decision on the replacement of the existing CF-18s, originally slated for 2014–15, until after the 2015 election. They gave themselves further room by ordering a life extension to the 1980s vintage Hornets that would keep them flying until 2025.[27]

Some of the political wounds of the F-35 debate were self-inflicted. As with Afghanistan, the Harper Conservatives chose to use the jet as a political wedge issue to paint their opponents as "not supporting the men and women in uniform." Part of the problem was that the stealth fighter, one of the most complex and costly war machines ever conceived by the Pentagon, was still in development and subject to all kinds of bugs and setbacks. Delays and huge cost overruns were a magnet for critics and competitors in Washington and it became the same in Ottawa. Yet, the Canadian government's political messaging remained strident to the point where Julian Fantino, the associate minister of defence in 2011, declared during a visit to the Lockheed Martin plant in Fort Worth, Texas, that the Conservatives would never back down and were "part of the crusade." [28] After Michael Ferguson's report, the messaging became more nuanced and cautious. But political damage had been done to the Conservative brand of being sensible, prudent managers of the public purse.

Although not named specifically in its marquee defence policy of 2008, the F-35 figured prominently behind the scenes in the Harper's government ambitious agenda to rearm the military after what Conservatives frequently described as a "decade of darkness" under the Chrétien-Martin Liberals. The Canada First Defence Strategy (CFDS) proposed $490 billion in spending over two decades. It was mostly in line with what the Conservatives promised in the 2006 election campaign, but the numbers and more importantly the capabilities had been run through the bureaucratic machinery. Critics at the time argued the strategy was short on strategic vision and long on politically saleable equipment purchases that could be tied to Canadian industry. The strategy at its core promised "stable and predictable" funding increases for the baseline budget of 2 per cent per year after 2011.[29] Subsequent analyses, released under access to information legislation, show the ink was barely dry on the strategy before the Conservatives realized their shopping list of equipment for the military was unaffordable.[30] And while the promised cost "escalator" remained, later cuts elsewhere under the government's Strategy Review and Deficit Reduction Action Plan (DRAP) saw the increases more than offset, to the point that by 2014 the defence appropriation was between $2.1 billion and $2.5 billion per year less than had been originally forecast.[31]

If the F-35 demonstrated the perils of political rhetoric, the new defence strategy illustrated the maxim of not over-promising and under-performing. The strategy proposed not only new fighter jets but a complete recapitalization of Navy and other hardware. In order to accomplish that, the Conservatives set about organizing the National Shipbuilding Procurement Strategy, a program that established contractual relationships with two preferred shipyards to build all of the federal fleet—military and civilian.[32] The framework was heralded as a success, but the absence of steel being cut and the shrinking defence budgets of 2012–14 had analysts questioning whether the program would live up to its billing. The first class of ships, due for construction in 2015, were the Arctic Offshore Patrol Ships (AOPS), which is what the Conservative promise of three armed icebreakers had morphed into during the interceding decade. Under the original concept, the Conservatives had envisioned heavy warships capable of operating in multi-year ice and able to fight when necessary. What they got were light patrol ships, with more of a constabulary design that allows them to cut through first-year ice and operate in the North for only part of the year.

The Arctic, despite not possessing a direct military threat, was to receive a deep-water refuelling station and an Army winter warfare centre. Both proved harder than expected to realize. The port at Nanisivik is still years away from operation thanks to environmental concerns, while the training centre in Resolute Bay, a joint venture with Natural Resources Canada, opened only in 2013.[33]

Harper's government did deliver heavy-lift C-17 transport planes, medium-lift C-130J Hercules, CH-47F Chinook battlefield helicopters and a variety of armoured vehicles for the Army during the Afghan War, including replacement Leopard tanks and mine-clearing trucks. Conservatives were able to claim by the time they faced voters in the fall of the 2015 that they were on track to solve the two-decade-old dilemma of replacing the air force's twenty-six CH-124 Sea King helicopters with twenty-eight CH-148 Cyclones, which despite a decade of development and contract extensions would only have basic capabilities for the first few years of operation. But they had failed to deliver fixed-wing search-and-rescue planes; new maritime surveillance aircraft; some form of long-term drone capability; and, perhaps most importantly, replacements for the Navy's 1960s-vintage supply ships.

As the clock ticked toward the 2015 election, Harper's government became increasingly touchy about criticism of its spending record, be it on veterans, military procurement or the defence budget in general. Faced with pressure from the US and Britain to meet NATO's two per cent of gross domestic product benchmark for spending, Stephen Harper concluded the September 2014 leader's summit by declaring he was willing to wage war on the Islamic State and stand up to Russian aggression in Ukraine, but would do so on a budget.

"I don't in any area of government set a budget and say we'll spend a certain amount and go out and try to spend it no matter how we can spend it," Harper said in Newport, Wales. "That's not how we do business and I'm certainly not going spend on a massive military expansion for the sake of doing so. As I say, our allies can be assured and are assured that Canada will spend what is necessary."[34]

The problem was that by early 2015, the Parliamentary Budget Office was telling Canadians the Harper government had put in place a military structure that was unaffordable with the kind of leaner budgets they had delivered. The annual defence appropriation of $21.5 billion—or 1.1 per cent of GDP—would needed to be increased by $3 billion per year, just to keep the same number of troops and equipment. It was the kind of politically unscripted research that ran contrary to the Conservative narrative. In the budget that followed a few weeks after the PBO report, Harper promised more money for the military beginning in 2017.[35]

The Burden

If the difference between rhetoric and reality on defence spending is described as a gap, then it's safe to characterize the difference on veterans' issues as a canyon.

Approximately 40,000 Canadian troops served in Afghanistan between 2001 and 2014. The war came with an incremental cost of approximately $13 billion.[36] [37] Combat, accidents and suicides related directly to the military campaign claimed 158 lives over the twelve and a half years of involvement. The last reported figures show there were 1,859 wounded up to 2011.[38]

During the 2008 election campaign, the Parliamentary Budget Office caused a stir by postulating the war could eventually cost taxpayers between $13.9 billion and $18.1 billion in incremental costs, which are figures over and above the expense of maintaining a standing military force. The Conservatives, unsurprisingly, disagreed with the eye-popping figure and claimed it was much lower. Kevin Page, the budget officer at the time, defended his numbers by saying a lack of cooperation by government departments made it tough to come up with a precise estimate. His report, however, was broader in scope than just the numbers eventually reported by National Defence. What Page and his team attempted to do in 2008 was capture the human cost by measuring future liability to the veterans' affairs system in terms of treatment and benefits for wounded. Those figures could take years or even decades to emerge, particularly when it came to post-traumatic stress cases. The best they could do at the time was rely on mounting data south of the border as Washington struggled to tabulate what Iraq and Afghanistan was costing its treasury. The figures, even when filtered for the Canadian experience, were jaw-dropping.

"While a direct comparison with the results of this US-based study is very difficult, these numbers, applied to the Canadian deployment, would indicate costs of a rough order of magnitude of $10 billion for death, disability, health-care and PTSD related costs alone," the PBO report predicted.[39]

If questions about the conduct of the war preoccupied Harper during minority government years, the government's financial commitment to the treatment of veterans—both of Afghanistan and previous deployments—would, at times, consume the political agenda during majority government days.

The source of grievances, from a policy perspective, can be traced back to the fundamental overhaul of legislation governing veterans' benefits in 2005—the artfully dubbed New Veterans Charter. It was conceived under Paul Martin's government in the waning days of Liberal stewardship, but it was enacted in April 2006 and championed for years by the Conservatives. That was, until 2014, when the complaints—public outrage over a string of suicides among soldiers and a class-action lawsuit by Afghan veterans—prompted Stephen Harper to characterize the charter in the House of Commons as a "Liberal policy." The attempt to disown the charter, which had enjoyed all-party support, spoke loudly.[40] Conservatives were both frustrated and politically wounded by the criticism from veterans.

One of the fundamental revisions ushered in by the charter affected the wounded, and it poisoned public perception almost from the outset. The switch from lifetime pensions to lump-sum payments as compensation for non-economic loss was a trend among other Western nations, including Britain and Australia.[41] And it was seen by the bureaucracy as sound fiscal policy and a vehicle in dismantling the gigantic veterans administrations built up by each nation in the twentieth century. Wars were no longer fought on an industrial-sized scale, and the smaller, leaner professional militaries of today were being reflected in the veterans' support system. Very much like insurance companies and workers' compensation systems, soldiers wounded on the battlefield would be compensated for lost limbs and damaged minds with individual sliding-scale payments depending on the degree of injury.

The notion that soldiers were being "nickel and dimed" roared on to the public stage when the Harper government decided not to renew the term of outspoken veterans ombudsman Pat Stogran, a former Army colonel and the first Canadian ground commander in the Afghan War. Appointed in 2007 with much fanfare to fulfill a Conservative election promise, Stogran's take-no-prisoners style in the backrooms—with both the federal bureaucracy and later Conservative politicians—saw him increasingly isolated by the time his tenure drew to close in 2010. He claimed that not only were modern soldiers being "cheated" by a less generous system, but so were their families, who were called upon more often to bear the burden of care.

"It is beyond my comprehension how the system could knowingly deny so many of our veterans the services and benefits that the people and the government of Canada recognized a long, long time ago as being their obligation to provide," Stogran said on August 17, 2010.[42]

Recognizing the political liability ahead of the spring 2011 election, the Conservatives enacted a series of improvements under Bill C-55, including a more generous permanent impairment allowance for the most critically wounded and easier access to a separate fund known as the Exceptional Incapacity Allowance. It also gave veterans the option to take their disability award as a single lump sum or as an annual payment. For the critics, it was tinkering at best, and at worst, pure political window-dressing.[43]

While the Conservatives struggled to tame the bureaucratic beast at Veterans Affairs, they faced a separate equally vexing problem at National Defence. Warned by two reports in the late 1990s that the military health care system was in need of improvement, the federal government embarked on a decade-long series of initiatives, beginning in 2000.[44] The overhaul coincided with the onset of the Afghan war. Among the proposed actions adopted in 2002 was the desire to have 450 mental health staff to treat the anticipated wave of post-traumatic stress casualties. At the same time, the war brought into sharp focus the military's universality of service policy, which requires all members of the Armed Forces to be physically and mentally fit to deploy. A soldier wounded and sidelined to the Joint Personnel Support Unit has three years to fully recover and return to duty under the policy.[45]

The military issued about 1,000 medical releases during each year of major combat, compared to a total of approximately 5,000 soldiers who muster out annually.[46] By the time the Harper government called it quits in Kandahar in July 2011, many of the soldiers wounded at the beginning and at the height of the fighting were on the line. Medical release notices—known as 3Bs in Defence Department lingo—started to trickle out in 2012 and 2013, many to young soldiers who'd specifically joined to fight the Taliban. They had only few years in uniform and no shot at a direct, indexed military pension. It was another unforeseen circumstance. The resulting stories in the media made the Harper government look heartless and were followed with demands for exceptions to be made to universality of service, but the Conservatives faced pushback from within the military, which believed any kind of exemption meant that they'd be required to accept recruits with disabilities.[47] Unlike other federal institutions, the military has the authority to deny disabled applicants.[48]

If the Harper government was taken by surprise on the issue of universality of service, it could claim no such ignorance when it came to the state of the military's medical system. Throughout the war years, the Conservatives faced a mounting stack of reports, analyses and audits from a variety of federal watchdogs that found deficiencies in the system, despite a fresh investment of cash. The auditor general found in 2007 that the military was unable to demonstrate it provided quality care, and expressed concern about accreditation and qualification of medical staff. More pointedly, in testimony before a House of Commons committee, former auditor Sheila Fraser noted, "Unfortunately, the department has not been able to staff its mental health services with all the professionals required."[49] It was a theme that returned over and over during the next seven years, culminating in perhaps the most politically damaging episode. A series of soldier suicides gripped the military in late 2013 and early 2014. More than most, this installment created an impression of indifference in the minds of the public as both Stephen Harper and former defence minister Rob Nicholson's offices were flooded with angry letters and emails from horrified constituents. That the government had been repeatedly warned about the issue was undisputed.

Aside from Fraser, the military ombudsman twice weighed in on the need for more mental health staff. The Conservatives, in the fall of 2012, responded by putting $11.4 million into the system, specifically to hire staff. Eighteen months later, at the height of the string of suicides, the number of mental health staff remained the largely the same at roughly 380. New hires were tied up in bureaucracy and an internal Defence Department turf war over staffing levels during the deficit-slashing times. Only the embarrassment of the suicide crisis prompted bureaucrats to remove the obstacles.[50]

To its credit, the Harper government did shower the military with millions of dollars in programs meant to not only get people the treatment they needed, but also reduce the stigma associated with mental illness. But it proved tougher than expected to get individuals, steeped and hardened in a macho culture of stoicism and perseverance, to put up their hands. Sometimes it was stubbornness. Other times it was dread of how such an admission would reflect on one's career that forced soldiers to keep silent.

Where the Harper government faced its biggest political and policy challenge with ex-soldiers, however, was at Veterans Affairs, where by 2012 the full extent of the new charter was being felt. The disparity between what was received by ex-soldiers from previous wars and peacekeeping duty what was received by the new generation that fought in Afghanistan gave rise to a series of online assistance groups, notably Canadian Veterans Advocacy, which went by the motto "One Veteran, One Standard." Louder and less likely to be mollified when compared with traditional organizations, such as the Royal Canadian Legion, the groups became a fixture on Parliament Hill, lobbying anyone who would listen.

Eventually, some of these patchwork groups assembled behind a class-action lawsuit launched by six Afghan veterans, who claimed the new charter discriminated against them. The case flew somewhat below the political radar until the summer of 2013, when federal lawyers filed their statement of defence, which among other things said, "at no time in Canada's history has any alleged 'social contract' or 'social covenant'" involving the state's duty to care for war wounded ever been enshrined in legislation or the constitution.[51] Aside from claiming the government had no special obligation to veterans, the lawyers went on to say current and future governments could not be held to the political promises of care from past administrations, notably the pledges of former prime minister Sir Robert Borden in the First World War.

Although legally correct in their defence, the argument was a PR disaster for Harper's government, one made worse by the appointment of former Toronto top cop Julian Fantino to the veterans portfolio. His brusque personality and testy televised public exchanges with ex-soldiers over the closure of nine regional veterans' offices further cemented the unsympathetic perception in the public's mind and overshadowed many of the policy changes the Conservatives wanted to enact. While Fantino twisted in the public spotlight for eighteen months, the new veterans' ombudsman Guy Parent quietly laid out a series of suggested policy changes in several well-researched reports. He compared benefits between the new and the old systems, noting that the most severely wounded would be plunged into poverty after retirement because of the way the system was structured, and that less than half of those eligible to collect disability allowances were getting them because of tight restrictions.[52]

It was left to a new, media-savvy minister, Erin O'Toole, to introduce a series of initiatives—targeted at the most critically injured and their families—on the eve of the 2015 election in order to rebuild bridges. In some respects, it may have been too late politically.[53] One group of veterans pledged to campaign against the Conservatives in the 2015 election—a strategy O'Toole claimed was funded by public service unions angry at job cuts and their perceived harsh treatment at the hands of the Conservatives.[54] Unions dismissed his "straw man" political argument as an attempt to distract the party's base from the complaints of ex-soldiers, who used to be counted among the core Conservative constituency. That the support of the military community, a natural ally, was in question before the 2015 vote spoke volumes about how badly both the policy and political issues were handled.

If there was a moment when that sense of disappointment crystallized in the military community, it happened around the innocuously christened National Day of Honour on May 9, 2014, which had the feeling of being written on the back of a napkin. Unlike the Conservatives' splashy $28-million War of 1812 celebrations, the end of thirteen frustrating and heartbreaking years in Afghanistan was announced and delivered within a six-week space, and it showed. The Royal Canadian Legion was asked to throw open its doors at branches across the country with only a few weeks' warning.[55] Families of the war dead were invited to Parliament Hill for the main commemoration but were initially told to pay their own way—a decision quickly reversed.[56] A closed-door reception for them was sponsored by a private charity. And most tellingly, the Conservatives, who politically live and die by advertising, put few resources into promoting the day outside of Ottawa. In terms of getting the word out, the government only put money into print and radio ads in eastern Ontario. Jason MacDonald, Harper's director of communications, said there would be no national advertising campaign.[57] That turned the event into an Ottawa-centric production on Parliament Hill, attended mostly by the inhabitants of National Defence headquarters. There were certainly small, heartwarming moments in Legion halls elsewhere in the country, intimate tributes for local heroes. But it came nowhere close to the national day of recognition envisioned by the military when commemoration plans were first drawn up in 2011.[58]

The Man and the Military Myth

Stephen Harper's war in Afghanistan had a profound effect on the Canadian military. The army emerged with a cadre of both battle-tested soldiers—both officers and non-commissioned officers—the first in almost two generations. It was reasonably well equipped with new armoured vehicles and artillery and had acquired skills in a range of warfare. The Air Force—at least the helicopter crews—gained valuable experience both in transport and in combat. Even Navy clearance divers, who acted as bomb-disposal technicians, were given a taste of life under fire. When it came to public perception, the military believed the blood spilled in Afghanistan had removed the stain of the Somalia torture and murder scandal more than a decade and a half earlier.

There were political lessons too, and they became apparent when Harper joined the US-led coalition in the military campaign to confront the Islamic State, which in late 2013 and early 2014 had swept across vast swaths of Iraq and Syria, creating a tangible dominion that al-Qaeda had only dreamed about. The prime minister made sure the contributions were modest and politically manageable. Deploying up to sixty-nine Special Forces trainers to Iraq and allowing CF-18s to participate in a bombing campaign against IS positions, equipment and formations was the perfect kind of low-cost, high-publicity war that appealed to them.

Specifically ruling out, in the Parliamentary motion on Iraq, the deployment of regular Army troops to participate in a ground campaign was a sign that Harper had learned from the excruciating political experience of Kandahar. And unlike in Afghanistan, the media in Iraq was kept at a distance, barred by Kuwaitis from the airfields where the planes launched and prohibited from covering the elite Special Forces as they trained Kurdish Peshmerga fighters in Irbil.[59] The Special Forces had, on rare occasion, allowed glimpses into its capacity-building missions in Africa and the Caribbean, but there would be none of that in Iraq.[60] Having media hanging around, as they did in Kandahar, only increased the potential for an unforeseeable and uncontrollable political crisis.

The mythology built up around Harper and the Conservatives as the most ardent defenders of the military institution and its people is open to question, considerable debate and even skepticism. The "we support the troops" mantra made it tough for the opposition and the media to hold the Harper Conservatives to account, even in comparison with past governments that had treated the military with either benign neglect or even outright contempt. The absence of a defence white paper in the latter years of majority government, or even an overarching strategy to articulate where military power fits into Canadian foreign policy, allowed Harper considerable policy manoeuvring room both in where to employ the Forces and in purchasing equipment. But the absence of a clearly defined policy cut both ways. The public's interest in a nasty, far-away guerilla war in Afghanistan was harder to explain, as was the need to buy stealth fighters. Outside of the policy framework, the poisoned politics practised over Kandahar and other files made it impossible to reach a national consensus on defence and security, matters that should—inarguably—be regarded in the interest of all citizens.

If Harper's objective was to fundamentally reshape the Canadian military in terms of bureaucratic organization, funding and equipment, then the job is only half-done. If the objective was to restore the military as a respected national institution post-Somalia, then he succeeded, but some would argue it was the army's conduct in the killing fields of Kandahar and not the machinations of Ottawa that accomplished that. If the objective was political and to secure a long-term voting bloc among those in uniform and veterans, in much the same way the Conservatives have courted the immigrant vote, then it has been sabotaged by his government's inherent contradictions on both the defence budget and the treatment of veterans.

Justin Trudeau's Liberal government faces many of the same problems Stephen Harper inherited from Paul Martin when it comes to defence and foreign policy. There is an unfinished war, under uncertain international leadership; and a military that despite billions of dollars in investment is still in need of new equipment and financing. The major difference, unlike in 2006, is that there's a growing population of veterans with complex, long-term health needs, and who will require the institutional and political attention of not only the next government, but subsequent administrations well into the future.

British philosopher Bertrand Russell reportedly once said, "War does not determine who is right—only who is left." It is safe to say that those who are left coming out of Stephen Harper's wars—against the Taliban, the Islamic State and even government bureaucracy—have yet to fully appreciate or reflect upon the experience.

MONEY

8

Review of Economic Performance and Policy during the Harper Years

David Dodge and Richard Dion

How did the Canadian economy perform during the Harper government years, what factors drove this performance and what role did Harper government policies play in achieving broad economic objectives? In this chapter, we first compare the performance of the economy during the years of the Harper government (2006–15) with that of the preceding twenty-two years[1] and then identify which factors drove this performance, so that we can assess the importance of federal interventions. Then we examine these policies and their effects in the light of objectives that any central government should pursue: stabilization, long-term growth, income distribution and sound public finances.

Broadly speaking, our assessment reveals that Canada's overall economic performance during the Harper years was largely driven by external forces, while domestic policy initiatives played a relatively minor role except during 2008–10. We would argue that the Harper government's economic policies met the objective of strengthening Canada's fiscal position without jeopardizing the goal of income redistribution. After 2010, however, in the face of a persistently slow recovery of demand, the Harper government unduly sacrificed economic growth, in particular public investment, in order to improve a debt position that was already solid.

Canadian Economic Performance during the Harper Years

During the period of the Harper government (2006–15), real GDP growth was markedly slower than during the preceding twenty-two years (table 8.1), a result of the sharp recession that occurred between the fourth quarter of 2008 and the second quarter of 2009, and of the period of sluggish recovery that followed. A slide in the demand for Canadian exports is a central part of this GDP story.

Table 8.1
Contributions to Average Annual Growth in Real GDP in Canada

	1984–2005	2006–2015	2006–2007	2008–2009	2010–2015
GDP Growth	**2.97**	**1.65**	**2.34**	**-0.98**	**2.29**
Contributions from:					
Household consumption	1.64	1.43	2.30	0.78	1.36
Housing	0.16	0.10	0.19	-0.40	0.24
Government	0.46	0.46	0.70	0.92	0.23
Business fixed investment	0.54	0.17	0.69	-1.06	0.40
Sub-total: final domestic demand	**2.87**	**2.19**	**3.87**	**0.30**	**2.27**
Exports	1.91	0.27	0.37	-2.89	1.30
Imports	1.93	0.77	1.77	-1.97	1.35
Sub-total: net exports	**-0.03**	**-0.50**	**-1.40**	**-0.92**	**-0.06**
Inventories	0.11	-0.05	-0.08	-0.35	0.07
Average excess demand (+) or supply (-)*	0.08	-0.57	1.16	-1.28	-0.90

*Based on Bank of Canada estimates of the output gap: multivariate filter measure over 1984–1990 and average of the multivariate filter and integrated framework measures over 1991–2015.
Sources: Statistics Canada, Cansim matrix 380–0100, and Bank of Canada.

On average, the Canadian economy experienced significant slack during the Harper years in contrast to the rough balance between aggregate demand and potential output from 1984 to 2005.[2] Although the Canadian economy during the Harper government years worsened on most fronts, it did quite well when compared with foreign advanced economies. Many of these economies faced severe internal problems such as broken financial systems and collapsed housing markets, while the Canadian economy essentially had to cope only with weak external demand. As a result, not only was the 2008–09 recession less severe in Canada than in most other advanced economies, but the recovery in Canada was also stronger, especially prior to 2013.

Moreover, between 2006 and 2016 employment grew faster in Canada than in the US and other advanced economies. Canada had a lower unemployment rate in 2006–15 than in 1984–2005, reflecting a fall in the underlying structural unemployment rate. The policies and structural developments that were at the root of this fall unfolded well before the Harper government years.

Finally, in contrast with 1984–2005, the amount of money Canadians had left over for themselves after inflation, personal income taxes and transfers grew relative to that of Americans.[3] In fact, not only was the growth rate of real disposable income per capita double that of the United States in 2006–15, it was also much faster than during the Mulroney-Chrétien-Martin years as a whole.

Drivers of Canadian Economic Performance during the Harper Years

Canadian macroeconomic performance during the Harper government years was driven largely by global economic developments, while federal economic policy had a relatively minor effect on Canadian performance, except during 2008–10.

To understand some of the external forces and built-in domestic political, social and economic structures that shaped Canada's economic performance during the Harper years, we'll take a look at seven key drivers—of which only one, discretionary fiscal policy, was within the control of Canadian governments.

Fig. 8.1
Growth in Foreign Activity and Canadian Exports

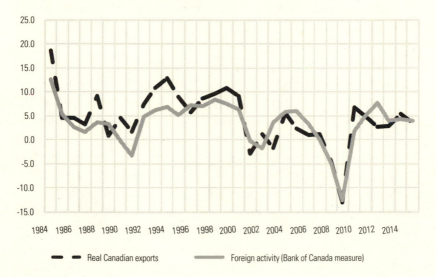

Source: Statistics Canada, Table 380-0064—Gross domestic product, expenditure-based, annual (dollars unless otherwise noted)

Global Economic Growth

The first force acting on Canadian real GDP growth was external activity growth, which drives demand for Canadian exports.[4] Foreign activity growth collapsed during the Harper government years, compared to the previous two decades, due to the severe recession in the United States in 2008–9 (figure 8.1). The direct impact on Canadian exports was a key source of the weaker Canadian real GDP growth during 2006–15.[5]

Industry-specific trends or shocks were also involved: an uptrend in real exports of crude oil and bitumen, a continued downtrend in real exports of forestry products, a significant restructuring of the North American automotive industry in 2008 and 2009, and continued weakness in real exports of electronic products following the sharp drops that resulted from the burst of the dotcom bubble in the early 2000s.[6]

Commodity Prices

Canada's real income as a country got a boost from rising global commodity prices because more goods and services could be purchased out of the revenues from Canadian sale of commodities, notably oil. The implied gain in profits and labour earnings in Canada supported stronger growth in domestic spending and production. Resource industries had a greater incentive to invest than other sectors and, indeed, substantially contributed to growth in business fixed investment during 2006–13. The sharp drop in commodity prices in 2015 set in motion a reverse process of falling real income and spending in Canada, and a collapse of investment in the oil and gas sector.

Cost Competitiveness

A substantial loss of Canadian cost competitiveness depressed Canadian real net exports and hence real GDP in the Harper government years relative to 1984–2005. It also contributed to a fall in Canada's market share of US manufacturing imports.

Measured in terms of unit labour costs (in US$) in Canada versus the US, relative to the 1984–2005 average, a loss of Canadian cost competitiveness in the business sector emerged in 2004 (3.7 per cent). This loss (represented by the black line in figure 8.2) grew to a peak of 49 per cent in 2011 before retreating to 16 per cent in 2015. A substantial appreciation of the Canadian dollar accounted for 70 per cent of the total loss of competitiveness during 2006–15. This appreciation was largely driven by a sharp increase in commodity prices, notably oil prices. A slower rate of labour productivity growth in the business sector relative to the US, which on its own would have accounted for 60 per cent of the competitiveness loss, was half offset by slower wage growth in Canada.

Fig. 8.2
Sources of Loss of Canadian Cost Competitiveness

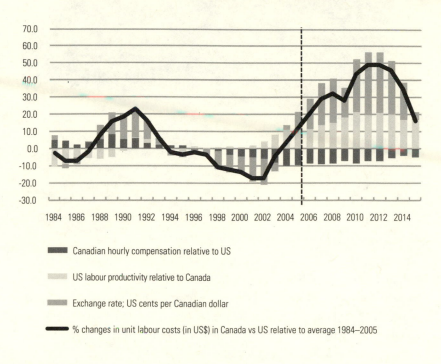

Sources of Losses of Canadian Cost Competitiveness in the Business Sector
Relative to 1984–2005 Average (Percentage Point Contributions)

■■ Canadian hourly compensation relative to US

░░ US labour productivity relative to Canada

▒▒ Exchange rate; US cents per Canadian dollar

— % changes in unit labour costs (in US$) in Canada vs US relative to average 1984–2005

Sources: Statistics Canada, Cansim matrices 383-0008 and 176-0064, and US Bureau of Labor Statistics

Interest Rates and Canadian Monetary Policy

Lower interest rates during the Harper years, shaped by monetary policy from the Bank of Canada, contributed to growth by lowering the cost of paying down debts for households, businesses and governments and boosting domestic asset prices and net worth. The target overnight rate reached a peak of 4.5 per cent in July 2007 and started a steep slide before reaching 1 per cent or less in 2009–15.

Lower interest costs relative to government revenues gave more room to the Harper government (and to provincial governments) for spending on direct programs and transfers, and at the same time they let the government reduce taxes without increasing the federal (or provincial) deficit (figure 8.3).

Fig. 8.3
Shares of Total Federal Government Spending

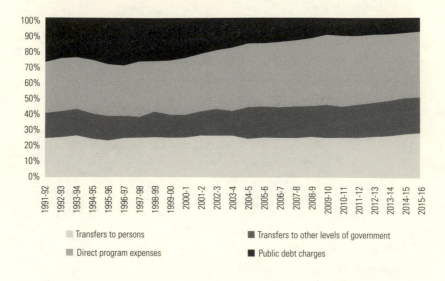

Transfers to persons

Direct program expenses

Transfers to other levels of government

Public debt charges

Sources: Department of Finance Canada, Fiscal Reference Table 2015 and Budget 2016

Canadian Financial Sector

The stability of the Canadian banking system meant that private spending was not restricted by credit constraints, as was the case in other countries. Nor did the federal government have to spend tens of billions of dollars to bail out failing financial institutions, as was the case elsewhere.

The financial stability Canada enjoyed in that period was built on measures put in place before the Harper government came to power. Since the late 1980s, the supervisory regime in the financial sector had evolved and improved to include clearer goals, improved incentives, more accountability as well as increased flexibility for relevant financial authorities to intervene earlier with troubled institutions.. At the outset of the global financial crisis, Canadian banks held fewer toxic assets[7] and had strong capital ratios, higher levels of liquid assets as a share of total assets, and a high ratio of depository funding compared with their international competitors.[8]

Housing Market

The relative buoyancy of the Canadian housing market also helped to buttress the Canadian economy during the Harper years. This buoyancy was reflected in low rates of mortgage delinquencies and defaults and in a significant rise in the value of household real estate to disposable income (figure 8.4).[9] This strong performance stemmed from several factors: the housing price cycle was relatively subdued, and real house prices in particular rose much less in Canada than in the US over 1997–2005, without collapsing in subsequent years as in the US; the quality of verification and documentation demanded by lenders was high; and mortgage lending standards were relatively high until the mid-2000s. Mortgage insurance standards were inappropriately loosened in 2006 but too late for a significant sub-prime market to develop. The Harper government reversed course and tightened these standards between 2008 and 2012 as the global financial crisis unfolded.

Fig. 8.4

Household Real Estate as Per Cent of Disposable Income in Canada

Source: Statistics Canada, Cansim Matrix 378-0123—National Balance Sheet Accounts, financial indicators, households and non-profit institutions serving households, annual (per cent)

The buoyancy also meant that the contribution of housing expenditures to real GDP growth wasn't nearly as negative in Canada compared with the US from 2006 to 2009, and was more positive from 2010 to 2014. It also meant that Canadian households felt far less need after the crisis to put money away and reduce their family debt levels than those in the US. Along with firmer growth of real disposable income in Canada, this led to a stronger contribution of household consumption to real GDP growth in Canada than in the US during the Harper government years.

Fig. 8.5
Fiscal Policy Stance

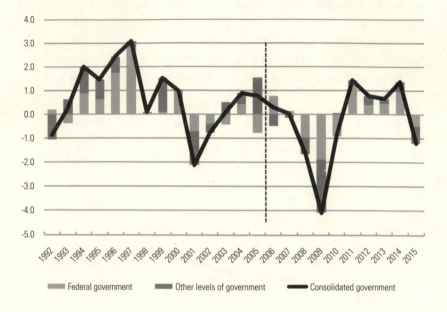

Fiscal Policy Stance: Changes in Net Lending as % of GDP
(+) = drag, (-) = stimulus

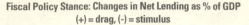

Source: Statistics Canada, Cansim matrices 385-0032 and 380-0064

Government Fiscal Policies

A final force at play was the fiscal policies of governments in Canada. Beyond the effects of automatic stabilizers such as employment insurance and income taxes, the discretionary fiscal policies of federal and provincial governments helped to substantially mitigate the recession in 2008–2010 but actually slowed the recovery afterwards. Fiscal policy by all levels of government was slightly restrictive in 2006, neutral in 2007 and expansionary in 2008–10, with the federal government accounting for nearly 60 per cent of the total stimulus during those three years (figure 8.5). Fiscal policy turned moderately restrictive in 2011–14, with the federal government accounting for about three quarters of the resulting fiscal drag, before becoming mildly expansionary in 2015 due to the effects of automatic stabilizers. Thus, the Harper government's Economic Action Plan helped to support growth in 2009–10, but on balance slowed the pace of the economic recovery in subsequent years, as we shall see in the next section.

Economic Policies of the Harper Government

In this section we concentrate on the Harper government's record on fundamental economic objectives: stabilization, long-term growth, income redistribution and maintenance of a sustainable ratio of public debt to GDP. In organizing our analysis on the basis of these fundamental objectives, we follow the classic framework for analyzing economic policy set out by Richard Musgrave.[10]

Stabilization Policy

Stabilization policy can be divided into three key elements:

- monetary policy—the setting of interest rates by the central bank, which in Canada is organized around a clear inflation target
- fiscal policy—the balance of expenditures and revenues
- financial and "macro-prudential" policies

Policy should try to steer the economy on a middle course between excess demand and excess supply to avoid excessive inflation or anemic economic activity.

Monetary Policy

Monetary policy, based on the inflation-targeting policy executed by the Bank of Canada, played a stabilizing role in 2006–15. In 2006, a longstanding inflation-targeting agreement between the government and the Bank of Canada, which states that the central bank will aim for an inflation target of two per cent, was renewed on essentially the same terms as those agreed previously. That agreement was renewed again in 2011. A lot of research work supported such renewals, and the Harper government made the right decision in going ahead with them.

However, because monetary policy is conducted independently by the Bank of Canada, we will confine our analysis of stabilization to fiscal and macro-prudential policies that are actually conducted by the government.

Fiscal Policy

A government deploys its fiscal policy to "lean against the wind" in order to contribute to keeping aggregate demand as close as possible to potential output, while ensuring that public debt remains sustainable. Simply put, the goal is to contribute to growth within a reasonable speed limit; otherwise inflation or anemic activity can result.

Stabilization requires that a government incurs growing deficits in relation to GDP during periods of increasing slack in the economy, incurs increasing surpluses in relation to GDP as excess demand grows, and stops providing stimulus as higher private demand boosts growth enough to bring aggregate demand closer in balance with potential output.[11]

Because of the structure of ongoing tax, transfer and expenditure policies, the fiscal balance automatically changes to provide some fiscal stimulus when the economy slows and some fiscal drag when the economy grows faster. Such automatic stabilization may be inadequate during a severe downturn, and governments may lower tax rates or increase growth in program spending to boost aggregate demand.[12] Conversely, during a boom, governments may raise tax rates or cut growth in program spending to cool the economy.

However, achieving the proper timing and size of discretionary fiscal policy initiatives on stabilization is a challenge, given that readings of the output gap—that is, the amount of slack in the economy—as well as economic forecasts are subject to large errors. In addition, the size of, and lags in, the effects of fiscal policy measures are variable,[13] and flexibility is limited when adjusting fiscal policy to changing circumstances.

Probably the best that can be reasonably expected is (1) that a government provides a stimulus to growth during a downturn by expanding the deficit in relation to GDP with discretionary measures to supplement automatic stabilizers; (2) that a government refrains from introducing measures to quickly reduce this deficit in relation to GDP before excess supply is substantially eliminated, thereby giving the recovery a chance; and (3) that during periods when inflationary pressures mount (generally after several years of strong growth), a government should at the very least not exacerbate excess demand through expenditure increases or tax cuts that further fuel aggregate demand growth.

On the basis of these minimal expectations, the Harper government's fiscal policy turned out to be appropriately restrictive, but unintentionally so, in 2006–7; it was appropriately expansionary, but fortuitously so, in 2008; it was appropriately and intentionally very expansionary in 2009–10; and finally, it was intentionally restrictive, but inappropriately so, over 2011–15 as a whole (figure 8.5).

The Canadian economy was in significant excess demand from the second half of 2005 through to the third quarter of 2008, although excess demand was considerably smaller in the first three quarters of 2008 than in 2007, according to one measure of the output gap.[14] While the Bank of Canada was raising its policy interest rate to stem inflationary pressures from rapidly increasing excess demand in 2006 and 2007, the federal government added to inflationary pressures by cutting taxes and maintaining a strong pace of program spending during these two years.[15] The strategy of the government was to use the strong tailwind provided to revenues by an economy in boom to grant tax relief and allow robust expenditure growth without compromising further decline in the net debt/GDP ratio. In the end, the federal government increased its net lending (surplus) by 0.8 per cent of GDP in 2006 and 0.1 per cent in 2007,[16] but only because of the stronger than anticipated economy. Discretionary measures taken by the government reduced the size of the surpluses that should have been generated if the government had given priority to stabilization.

The federal government relaxed its fiscal stance by 1 per cent of GDP in 2008, mostly through reductions in the GST rate from 6 to 5 per cent and through cuts in personal and corporate income taxes that were announced in the 2007 economic statement. Again, these measures were not introduced with stabilization in mind. Indeed, in view of the solid growth forecast for 2008 and 2009 in the economic statement, these measures were inappropriate for stabilization because they would have exacerbated excess demand if the forecast had been realized. As it turned out, these tax cuts fortuitously helped stabilize the Canadian economy in 2008 as the US economy started a downturn early in the year, thereby exerting a drag on the Canadian economy as the recession finally set in late in the year in Canada, contrary to expectations. Thus, the federal fiscal stance in 2008 turned out to be appropriate for stabilization only because of planning errors (i.e., the forecasts for growth in the short term proved far too optimistic).

Growth forecasts were adjusted downward again between the 2007 economic statement and 2008 budget, but the projected slowdown was limited largely to 2008 as a rebound in growth to near the 2007 rate was forecast for 2009. Even after further downward adjustments to growth forecasts for 2008, 2009 and 2010, the November 2008 economic statement still predicted real GDP growth in 2009 and did not introduce any significant new measure to support aggregate demand. This was a major error in light of the severity of the downturn that had clearly begun in the US in the first quarter of 2008, although the coming crisis was starting to be evident to Canada only in the fourth quarter of 2008. Indeed, the policies set out in the November economic statement were generally seen as so inappropriate that they triggered a threat by the opposition parties to defeat the minority Harper government, a threat that was thwarted only by the prorogation of Parliament.

It was only at the end of January 2009 with the Economic Action Plan that substantive new measures to stimulate the economy were introduced to fulfil Canada's commitment at the Washington G20 summit in November 2008. With the Economic Action Plan (in addition to limited additional initiatives in the 2010 budget) and the effects of the automatic stabilizers, the federal government appro-priately generated additional fiscal stimulus of 1.9 per cent of GDP in 2009 and 0.9 per cent of GDP in 2010, at a time when the economy was in large excess supply.

As GST rates had already been reduced by two points and cuts in income taxes for 2009 had been introduced, the main discretionary stimulus action had to come from the spending side. One key action was to spend more on infrastructure projects. An ongoing infrastructure program was ramped up, its core consisting of "shovel-ready" projects that had to be completed within two years or a little more to be eligible for federal support. Because the focus of the infrastructure program was "stimulus" pure and simple, the quality of many of these "shovel-ready" projects was modest for what was most needed to support long-term growth. The core program also effectively ended in 2011, too soon in light of the fact that excess supply in the economy resumed increasing in 2012 to reach to significant levels in 2012–15 as economic growth fell to sub-par rates on average.[377] Other important actions taken in 2009 by the federal government to provide a stimulus to the economy included the bailout of GM Canada and Chrysler Canada in 2009 (in collaboration with the Ontario government) and the introduction of the one-year Home Renovation Tax Credit.

The federal government and private forecasters repeatedly overestimated short-term growth rates in Canada, presumably because they did not take into account the persistent negative effects of the financial crisis on growth in advanced economies and the detrimental effect of the loss of Canadian competitiveness. In any event, the federal government steadily trimmed its net borrowing (deficit) in relation to GDP over 2011–14 by the equivalent of 0.8 per cent of GDP per year, thereby slowing the recovery and exacerbating excess supply. In a more typical recovery setting, when actual growth greatly exceeds potential growth, this would have had a relatively benign effect. But in the muted recovery setting that followed the recent global financial crisis, even a moderate fiscal drag was unwelcome. In spite of the government's stated goal of putting emphasis on jobs and the economy, the Economic Action Plan over 2011–15 was in fact an economic inaction plan that subordinated the stabilization goal of growth to the goal of returning to balanced budgets through cuts in direct program spending, an inappropriate focus given the sluggishness of the economic recovery.

Contributing effectively to stabilization with discretionary fiscal policy is admittedly a difficult task. In spite of its incomprehensibly misguided November 2008 statement, the Harper government did a good stabilization job over the 2008–10 period of global financial crisis, although only fortuitously so in 2008. But because it was obsessively focused on reducing the federal deficit over fiscal years 2011–12 through 2015–16, the Harper government unnecessarily contributed to a slower, rather more muted recovery in Canada through to 2015 than a more appropriate fiscal policy would have produced.

Macro-Prudential Policy

Macro-prudential policy consists of rules for financial institutions, markets and instruments (e.g. mortgages). Its aim is to reduce the risk and the macroeconomic costs of financial instability.

One key macro-prudential measure pursued by the Harper government was mortgage lending standards (e.g. maximum amortization period and maximum loan-to-value ratio). The government allowed mortgage insurers to significantly loosen these standards in 2006. This freedom not only exacerbated already strong housing investment through 2006–8 but greatly increased the risks to financial stability. The government reversed course two years later, thereby reducing the risks of financial instability and correcting the error made earlier.

From July 2007 to January 2009 the Harper government played an important role in effectively managing the asset-backed commercial paper (ABCP) crisis[18] so that it did not spread to other parts of the financial markets. In 2009, it also managed well the Canada Mortgage and Housing Corporation (CMHC) securitization of bank-held mortgages. This action helped to prevent an extreme squeeze on the capacity of Canadian banks to lend, which banks in the United States and Europe experienced during the height of the financial crisis. Because of these actions and because, even more importantly, Canadian banks had been well managed and regulated for many years, the federal government did not have to use up fiscal room to bail out the banking system. Budgetary deficits that were incurred in 2009–10 directly increased domestic demand and prevented a more serious collapse in Canadian output and income.

After 2009, the federal government moved to tighten regulation of financial institutions. This undoubtedly reduced the risk of future banking crises. However, it also reduced banks' capacity to lend, although the price and non-price lending conditions offered by banks still improved in 2010–14 and stabilized in 2015.[19]

Following the crisis, the federal government moved to establish a national securities regulator with a goal of improving the functioning and stability of financial markets, and in particular fixed-income markets, which globally had performed disastrously prior to and during the crisis. While its initial attempt was rebuffed by the Supreme Court, a co-operative federal-provincial capital markets regulatory authority is now (2016) in the process of being created. This new authority should not only reduce the risk of future instability but also improve market efficiency and hence contribute to growth.

On macro-prudential policy, therefore, the federal government during the Harper years continued to strengthen previous governments' policies to promote a stable financial sector, although unfortunately with a more rules-based approach to prudential supervision as opposed to our previous principles-based approach. The initiative of creating a capital markets regulatory authority jointly with several provinces was an innovative step toward promoting a more stable and efficient financial sector.

Structural Policy: Promoting Long-Term Growth

Having discussed the macroeconomic overview of the Harper government years, as well as policy choices on the goal of stabilization, we can now turn to the second important economic role of the federal government, which is to implement a structural policy framework that fosters maximum long-term growth, thereby supporting a durable improvement in the living standards of Canadians. The goal is to promote increases in the size of the pie to be shared by Canadians.

Some aspects of this structural policy framework affect incentives and resource allocation across a wide spectrum of markets and industrial sectors—tax policy, trade policy and competition policy, for example. Others are aimed at particular markets, such as labour market policy and financial market policy. Still others are aimed at particular industrial sectors—policies related to transport and communications, oil and gas, and agriculture, for example. The Harper government was active in all these policy fields,[20] but in this section we confine our review to policies on tax, labour market, trade, competition, oil and gas, and infrastructure.

Taxation

The structure of taxation in Canada is set largely by the federal government. Tax policy is perhaps the most important policy lever that the federal government has to influence long-term growth. The Harper government was very active both in modifying the structure of taxation and in reducing the level of federal taxation. Here we confine our review to a few key issues.

While greatly reducing taxes overall, the Harper government decreased its relative reliance on broad-based consumption taxes and increased its relative reliance on income taxes.[21] This broad structural shift, which reversed the thrust of the Mulroney government tax reform, was somewhat detrimental to long-term growth because it limited the scope for reductions in personal and corporate income taxes that would have been more favourable to long-term growth than reductions in consumption taxes. Notably, some of the high effective marginal rates of personal income tax (and rates of clawback of personal transfer payments) could have been reduced more had the GST rate not been reduced from 7 per cent to 5 per cent.[22] Lower effective marginal rates of income tax would have enhanced incentives for individuals to work and save. Importantly, however, the federal government provided the incentives needed for Ontario to join the harmonized sales tax, thereby enhancing economic efficiency.

The Harper government introduced a large number of micro tax measures that should somewhat strengthen tax compliance and in so doing generate fiscal savings for the government.[23] Moreover it announced in the 2013 budget the rationalization of several business tax preferences over the subsequent several years.

Overall, these measures should buttress the integrity of the tax system, although the reduction in the small business tax rate announced in the 2015 budget certainly does not.

On the other hand, the Harper government introduced a large number of "boutique" tax preferences targeted to special groups (e.g., transit and sports equipment credits). These introduced unwarranted complexity and inefficiency into the system. A reduction of general rates of comparable magnitude would have been economically (although not necessarily politically) preferable.

The Harper government introduced on a restricted basis two measures that began to fundamentally change the structure of the personal income tax system: income splitting and the tax-free savings account (TFSA). On income splitting, the government first permitted pension income splitting, effective as of the 2007 tax year. Then in October 2014 it announced limited income splitting for couples with children under the age of eighteen, effective as of the 2014 tax year. These income-splitting measures have resulted in a partial shift from an individual-based system to a family-based one for certain groups but not others, while leaving in place the progressive rate structure designed for individual-based taxation. Whether the individual-based system is preferable to a well-structured family-based one is a matter of debate,[24] but it is clear that by introducing limited income splitting the Harper government has left Canada with a hybrid system in urgent need of reform.

A second measure of equal fundamental significance was the introduction of the TFSA in January 2009, ostensibly to increase the incentive for working individuals to save for retirement. While this provision is a clear gift to higher-income older workers and seniors who have accumulated substantial savings in non-registered accounts, there is little evidence that it has or will actually increase household saving. What is clear is that many individuals now face a difficult choice as to which form of registered vehicle is likely the most tax advantageous, TFSA or RPP/RRSP. Moreover, to the extent that moderate-income workers today use the TFSA rather than the RPP/RRSP as a registered savings vehicle (and thus will have non-taxable income in retirement), the integration of the tax and OAS/GIS system has been broken.[25] With the introduction of the TFSA—and the increase in the annual contribution limit to $10,000 contained in the 2015 budget—the Harper government created a muddled retirement savings and income support system with perverse incentives, a system that cries out for reform by governments in the future.

In summary, the Harper government tinkered with the structure of the tax system, introducing major measures based largely on political philosophy and many boutique provisions based on narrow group interests. It did reduce the

GST rate, thereby giving some boost to household consumption, particularly for lower-income groups (see the later section on income redistribution). It also reduced corporate and personal income tax rates somewhat, thereby improving economic efficiency and long-term growth. What is unfortunate from the point of view of economic efficiency is that the revenue lost through the reduction of the GST from 7 to 5 per cent limited the ability of the government to further reduce marginal effective rates of income tax.

Labour Market

The Harper government introduced measures that aim to affect labour market behaviour and could enhance potential growth as a result. One was new EI rules in 2013 that clarify what a reasonable job search for suitable employment means and that aim to reduce repeat use of EI through more stringent job-search criteria. Another was to prohibit federally regulated employers from setting mandatory retirement ages, starting in 2011. A third one was to raise to sixty-seven the age of eligibility for the OAS. These last two measures have the potential to raise labour force participation of older workers. A fourth one was the introduction in 2007 and enhancement in 2009 of the Working Income Tax Benefit (WITB), which aims to help overcome work disincentives created by the high effective marginal income tax rates faced at low earning levels. The WITB also has significantly affected progressive income redistribution (see the next section). Finally, it should be noted that the Harper government's support to post-secondary education and research moves in the direction of improving productivity growth and hence the longer-term economic outlook for Canada.

Competition

The record of the Harper government in competition policy is mixed. In the area of telecommunications, it worked hard to increase competition in the market for cellular services by reserving spectrum for players other than the big three. It also lifted foreign investment restrictions for telecommunications companies that hold less than 10 per cent of the telecommunications market. These measures may improve competition and increase efficiency, although there is only limited evidence that this has occurred. On the other hand, the government took no action to reduce the restrictions (e.g., cabotage) on competition in the airline industry.

The government continued previous governments' supply-management policies to protect our inefficient dairy and poultry industries and to deny them access to foreign markets. This unwillingness to tackle dairy and poultry competition undermined the government's ability to secure trade deals, which would enhance the efficiency of Canadian business and stands in sharp contrast to its successful efforts to end the monopoly of the Canadian Wheat Board. Moreover, in the proposed Trans-Pacific Partnership trade deal, "compensation" promised to dairy producers would totally eliminate any efficiency for the sector or benefits to consumers. Finally, the government showed surprising willingness to restrict foreign investment in Canada, such as in oil sands and potash. While the rhetoric of the Harper government was decidedly pro-consumer and pro-competition, overall its domestic policy actions appear to have accomplished little in terms of increased competition in Canada.

Trade

Like the Mulroney government, in principle and in rhetoric, the Harper government was decidedly in favour of trade liberalization. Trade liberalization is favourable to long-term growth because it enhances competition in the domestic market and facilitates access of Canadian exporters to foreign markets. Both effects tend to stimulate labour productivity growth. The Harper government's record in trade negotiations was somewhat trade and growth enhancing. This government secured an important agreement with the European Union, although some hurdles still remain as we move along the road to implementation. It also affected (a little late) a major free trade agreement with South Korea. While this is an important achievement, it should be recalled that this agreement allowed Canada only to catch up with the United States, which had completed its negotiation with Korea several years earlier.

Not having secured a bilateral trade agreement with Japan, the Harper government entered late into negotiations between the United States, Japan and other Pacific nations for the Trans-Pacific Partnership agreement. As we write this chapter, it is too early to assess the impact that the agreement would have if ratified and what effect the adjustment expenditures for the automotive and supply-managed (dairy, poultry) industries would have on Canada. What is clear is that for both the Harper government and the Canadian economy, the option of not being part of the TPP was far worse than accepting the terms of an agreement negotiated largely among the United States, Japan and other countries.

It is particularly unfortunate that the Harper government shunned suggestions from the Chinese to engage in negotiations for some form of Canada-China free trade agreement. In this regard, Canada has fallen behind Australia and New Zealand in securing access to the world's second-largest market.

Overall, the Harper government was long on rhetoric in favour of liberalized trade agreements, but short on both the expenditure of political capital and the application of negotiating muscle to achieve greater concrete results during its mandate.

Industrial Policy

All governments adopt policies (either explicitly or implicitly) that tend to favour expansion of industries or sectors of the economy that are perceived to be most important for further growth. For much of the quarter-century prior to 2005, federal governments pursued policies with a mild bias toward manufacturing and processing sectors (especially high-tech industries).[26] The Harper government dramatically changed this policy bias.

Following the stated objective of making Canada a global energy superpower, policies of the Harper government have been directed toward the development of the oil sands. A number of technical income tax preferences favourable to the mining, oil and gas sectors have been maintained and extended. Pipeline construction has been encouraged, and until near the end of its tenure, the government was reluctant to tighten safety regulation on oil shipment by rail. The Harper government failed in its clumsy efforts to promote Keystone XL in Washington, DC, and in doing so drew down on the limited goodwill of the Obama administration to deal with other economic issues important to Canada.

Most importantly, the Harper government did not impose environmental regulations that would increase the cost of extracting and processing bitumen from the oil sands. Consistent with his pre-election promises, Harper rejected out of hand any form of carbon tax. In general, the government adopted the stance that Canada would not meet previously endorsed greenhouse gas reduction targets and would not agree to even moderately restrictive targets over the next decade. While many in the oil industry viewed these environmental policies as favourable to oil sands development, clearly they were viewed by customers abroad as inappropriate and thus have reduced foreign (in particular, American) willingness to purchase Canada's "dirty oil." As an approach to marketing Canadian oil abroad and securing agreement for pipelines within Canada, these environmental policies were totally unhelpful during the Harper years and will continue to make it more difficult to market Canadian bitumen for many years to come.

It is clear that federal (and Alberta) policies were designed to accelerate the pace of oil sands development from 2006 to the first half of 2014, precisely the period during which rising prices of crude oil were already providing the incentive for accelerated investment in the oil sands.[27] The combination of federal "energy superpower" regulatory and tax policies exacerbated wage and cost pressures in Alberta that were already severe and further contributed to the strength of the Canadian dollar. During the period of high oil prices and favourable terms of trade, these federal policies may have contributed marginally to overall growth in Canadian output and incomes (labour market and other capacity constraints in Alberta would have limited the gains), but definitely had the effect of fostering a more unbalanced industrial structure. Across the economy as a whole they had a negative impact on cost competitiveness.[28]

Infrastructure

Infrastructure investment results in efficiency gains in the private sector and hence buttresses long-term growth in Canada. Net acquisition of new fixed capital by the federal government in relation to Canadian GDP, although rising in 2008–10, remained modest during the Harper years relative to the period preceding the fiscal consolidation years of the Chrétien government. By contrast, provinces and municipalities increased their new capital spending in relation to the Canadian GDP during the Harper years, compared to earlier periods. By 2013, they would have accounted for 46 per cent and 40 per cent respectively of total infrastructure investment in Canada against only 14 per cent by the federal government, even after taking into account federal transfers to other levels of government for infrastructure.[29] This information suggests that the federal government under-spent on infrastructure during the Harper years, directly or indirectly, and after 2011 could have provided greater support for provincial and municipal spending on infrastructure, especially since the federal government was the lowest cost borrower of all governments.

Income Redistribution

Governments are expected not only to help increase the size of the pie to be shared by their citizens but also to ensure that the pie is distributed appropriately among them. This involves income redistribution through taxes and transfers toward lower-income groups. Governments affect household income distribution directly and indirectly through a wide range of transfers and taxes, but mainly through their transfers to persons and their personal income taxes. Governments can also affect real income distribution through changes in the levels and structure of sales and excise taxes and the credits related to these taxes.

The Harper government implemented several measures with potentially favourable distributive impact on lower-income groups, of which four are probably the most important. First, the federal government maintained the GST credit level when it reduced the GST rate from 7 per cent to 6 per cent in July 2006 and to 5 per cent in January 2008. It also introduced the Universal Child Care Benefit in 2006, a taxable universal benefit of uniform amount provided to parents of children up to the age of six. In 2007 it launched a new Child Tax Credit of uniform amount for each child under eighteen.[30] Finally, the Working Income Tax Benefit introduced in 2007 and enhanced in 2009 provided a wage subsidy to persons at low earnings levels who face high effective marginal tax rates if at work.

Estimating the impact of government taxes and transfers on income redistribution is a complex exercise that is beyond our range of expertise. Heisz and Murphy[31] have recently worked out such estimates for Canada for the period from 1976–2011, the last year for which they had the micro-data necessary for their calculations. From our perspective, their key finding is that income redistribution toward lower-income groups through federal and provincial taxes and transfers tended to increase modestly during the Harper years of 2006–11, relative to the first half of the 2000s. No doubt federal taxes and transfers played an important role in this increased redistribution, although Heisz and Murphy do not factor in their calculations the effect of the reductions in the GST rate implemented by the Harper government. Their results indicate that the increase in income redistribution was due entirely to transfers, the effect of which on redistribution rose to markedly higher levels over 2009–11.

Heisz and Murphy estimate that income inequality before taxes and transfers tended to rise slightly over 2006–11 but that income inequality after taxes and transfers remained the same. Thus, redistribution through taxes and transfers fully counteracted the rise in income inequality due to market forces.

What we take from these results is that the Harper government contributed to an increase in income redistribution in favour of lower-income groups during the 2006–11 period, in part by beefing up child benefits and further increasing the overall progressivity of the tax system, even as average tax rates were falling. This redistribution counteracted a small increase in market income inequality (before taxes and transfers) in Canada over this period.

Low-Tax Balanced-Budget Objective

In pursuing its fundamental objectives of stabilization, long-term growth and income redistribution, any central government must ensure that its debt remains on a sustainable path. The Harper government made the pursuit of an annual balanced budget a primary element of its economic agenda. It went further than targeting a lower debt/GDP ratio. A balanced budget with lower taxes was the key strategy for the medium term. And this the Harper government did achieve.

However, this accomplishment was made possible in large part by the reduction in the tax revenues needed to finance the dramatically lower public debt charges that came out of Chrétien-Martin budget surpluses from 1997 to 2005, and the sharp fall in global interest rates—neither of which was the result of Harper government actions.

Tax revenues during the 2006–14 Harper years represented about 12 per cent of GDP compared to about 13.5 per cent during the Chrétien-Martin years (1993–2005), while at the same time federal program spending actually increased marginally from 12.8 to 12.9 per cent. Over the period from 2006–14, the Harper government ran a deficit of 0.8 per cent of GDP on average, but this was small enough that the net debt/GDP ratio of 31 per cent at the end of 2014 was lower than the 36 per cent it had inherited from the Martin government at the end of 2005. Thus, even if it did not deliver on the growth objective, the Harper government did deliver on its low-tax balanced-budget promise while actually increasing program spending as a share of GDP.

The fact that the Canadian federal government has remained in much better fiscal shape than any other G7 central government is an achievement of the Harper government.[32] We note that, as it went to the polls in October 2015, the Harper government left behind underfunded directly delivered federal programs (e.g., defence, Aboriginal health) and a revenue system that relied overly on strong resource prices to buttress personal and corporate income tax revenues. With slowing growth due to an aging population and lower resource prices, this legacy will make it very difficult for any future federal government to deliver a public debt performance similar to that delivered by the Harper government in 2011–15.

Summary and Conclusion

Relative to the 1984–2005 period, Canadian economic performance during the Harper government years worsened on most aggregate measures of growth and jobs, despite the fact that it was much better than American performance in 2007–11. On the other hand, relative to the earlier period, the growth rate of real disposable income per capita in Canada during the Harper years was much faster. Income growth per capita was also double the rate in the United States over 2006–15.

Canadian macroeconomic performance during the Harper government years was driven largely by global economic developments; federal economic policy initiatives played a relatively minor role in shaping Canadian performance, except during 2008–10. A severe US recession and sluggish US recovery along with a sizeable loss of Canadian cost competitiveness depressed Canadian growth. The drag was offset only partly by the positive effects of stronger prices for commodities and lower global and domestic interest rates. The resilience of the Canadian banking system and the relative buoyancy of the Canadian housing market, which owed little to Harper government policies, helped to preserve financial stability and buttress economic growth, in contrast to what happened in many other advanced economies.

Contributing effectively to stabilization with discretionary fiscal policy is a difficult task. The federal government ran an overly expansionary discretionary policy in 2006 and 2007, a fortuitously but appropriately expansionary policy in 2008, and an appropriately very expansionary policy in 2009–10. Because it was too focused on reducing deficit over 2011–15, its policy contributed to an unnecessarily slow, rather muted recovery in Canada.

There are many channels through which a government can foster long-term growth, including taxation, measures affecting labour market behaviour and product competition, trade policy, industrial policy and investment in infrastructure and research. The Harper government took policy action in all these areas with mixed results. Reductions in the effective rates of personal and corporate taxation were favourable to long-term growth. However, a decreased reliance on broad-based consumption taxes, whose rate was cut twice by the Harper government, was somewhat detrimental to long-term growth both because it limited the scope for reductions in personal and corporate income taxes that could have taken place otherwise, and because it limited growth-enhancing expenditures.

Changes in the structure of employment insurance and a future rise in the retirement age for the Old Age Security program, if these were to be maintained by subsequent governments, would improve the functioning of the labour market over the longer term. Changes in the regulation of financial markets and institutions will enhance financial stability and market efficiency. On the other hand, the record of pro-consumer competition policy was decidedly mixed. Actions on trade policy, though slow in implementation, should contribute to future growth. Action in foreign investment review was confused and created uncertainty, and that uncertainty will likely constrain future investment and hence lead to slower growth.

With the exception of 2009–10, the Harper government under-spent on infrastructure, thereby constraining future growth. Policy on development of the oil sands and related environment policies fostered unbalanced growth over the last decade.

The Harper government contributed to a modest increase in income redistribution toward lower-income groups in the 2006–11 period, in part through beefing up child benefits and maintaining the GST credit while cutting GST rates. In so doing it helped prevent an increase in inequality in disposable income (after taxes and transfers), as occurred in market incomes.

Finally, the Harper government did deliver on its low-tax balanced-budget promise while actually increasing program spending. This accomplishment was facilitated by the greatly reduced public debt charges that arose from budget surpluses in 1998–2005 and a sharp fall in interest rates—neither of which was the result of Harper government actions.

In any period, a central government faces trade-offs when deciding which economic objectives they should prioritize. The Harper government made four major choices that brought some benefits but inevitably entailed costs in the form of sacrificed opportunities:

- Lower taxes in relation to GDP worked toward supporting long-term growth but also lowered levels of public services that could otherwise have been provided directly or indirectly (e.g., via transfers to provinces).
- A lower GST rate (while keeping the level of GST credit) helped redistribute income toward lower-income groups but deprived the government of revenues that could have better financed public services directly and indirectly and provided more support to long-term growth through lower marginal income tax rates and increased spending on growth-enhancing physical and human infrastructure.
- Trying to achieve a balanced budget strengthened the already strong federal fiscal position, but it did so at the cost of appreciably weaker economic growth at a time of significant slack in the economy in 2011–15.
- Harper government policies, by favouring the development of the oil sands and neglecting environmental regulations, likely contributed indirectly to Canada's loss of overall cost competitiveness.

The Harper government promised a low-tax, balanced-budget plan that could grow jobs and increase output and income. The government delivered better per capita real disposable income growth than its predecessors, but worse employment and output growth. And this record was determined largely by factors other than federal policy. The Harper government's economic policies during 2006–15 met the objective of a strengthened fiscal position without sacrificing the goal of income redistribution, but had decidedly less success in meeting the goal of jobs and growth. In the end, a verdict on the degree of success of the Harper government's economic policies hinges on the relative values that one attributes to the various economic objectives. In our own judgment, after 2010 the Harper government unduly sacrificed growth in order to improve a debt position that was already solid.

9

Canadian Trade and Investment Policy under the Harper Government

Laura Dawson

Throughout Stephen Harper's time as prime minister, trade issues figured prominently in his governing agenda. After nine years, under-the-radar trade issues had progressed furthest, while the Harper government's policy had swung widely between pragmatism and populism on matters that attracted more public attention.

Prime Minister Harper's trade policy followed the trajectory set in motion by his predecessors, beginning with the 1989 Canada–United States Free Trade Agreement (CUFTA). In many respects, he refined and improved on the liberalizing, outward-oriented trade agenda that he inherited by focusing on the trading partners with whom Canada had a clear economic interest. He helped to diversify Canadian trade with new partners and develop markets for non-traditional exports, and he reduced barriers to foreign investment while still retaining oversight in sensitive sectors.

Stephen Harper was lucky. His preferred trade policy was expansionary and focused on competitiveness. It sought to reduce barriers abroad and protectionism at home. This dovetailed perfectly with the opportunities provided by the rise of emerging markets and globalizing supply chains during the early years of his leadership.

Stephen Harper was also unlucky. He governed through one of the worst economic downturns in recent memory—a period of shrinking trade and plummeting investment—when there were no good trade policies, just less-bad ones.

The Harper trade policy is not without missteps and missed opportunities. Some of the areas that could have been better managed are supply management, foreign investment review and trade relations with China. Measured in absolute terms, Canada took many positive steps to increase trade during the Harper era, but global market access is measured in relative terms. As a relatively small, trade-dependent nation attempting to diversify away from trade that is reliant on a few products and a few buyers, Canada needs not only to get to the goal, but to get there ahead of its competitors.

Setting the Stage: Canada's Trade Policy Legacy

The operational principles of trade agreements have changed very little since they were set in the 1948 General Agreement on Tariffs and Trade (GATT). They include non-discriminatory treatment of trading partners, transparency (rules should be consistent and accessible) and progressive liberalization (barriers should be reduced over time through continuing negotiations with trading partners).

The players have grown from a core group of 23 relatively wealthy GATT contracting parties to a group of 159 members of the World Trade Organization (WTO)—of which the majority are emerging markets. The exports are also changing. Canada is transforming from a resource-centric trader to a more diversified trading economy. While Canada's exports are still led by commodities such as oil, gas, minerals and timber, there is now much more focus on adding value to raw materials, diversifying manufacturing, integrating into global value chains and expanding cross-border service exports in such sectors as construction and banking. Moreover, as more Canadian firms seek new markets, investment agreements that provide protection to Canadian firms operating in high-risk markets are just as important as tariff-reducing trade agreements.

Canadian trade officials helped to launch the GATT, and over the seven decades since then, Canada has continued to produce world-class negotiators. Trade officials have tended to stay within trade and economic departments throughout their careers, fostering de facto apprenticeships where even junior officials can make meaningful contributions to the shape of a final deal. Maintaining this type of expertise has kept trade policy on track through political ebbs and flows, and has helped Canada foster a reputation for punching above its weight in international trade negotiations even as its relative influence in other foreign policy arenas has slipped.[1]

For some of the more politically sensitive aspects of trade and investment policy, ideological alignment between Harper, an economist, and senior DFATD (Department of Foreign Affairs, Trade and Development) and Finance Department officials prevented the type of clashes with the Prime Minister's Office that other departments experienced. For trade officials, the most frequent area of conflict with the executive was the management of issues that were elevated to the prime minister's attention because of political optics. One instance where optics clashed with bureaucratic prudence was the decision to formally and publically announce the completion of the Canada-EU Comprehensive Economic and Trade Agreement well before the final negotiations were completed.[2]

Senior trade officials had been used to a fair amount of trade negotiating autonomy within an agreed-upon set of objectives. Having even the smallest decisions vetted by the Prime Minister's Office rankled. Thus, the Harper years were noteworthy for the number of senior trade officials who retired early or accepted international assignments far from Ottawa.

The exodus of senior officials weakened Canada's overall capacity, but junior and mid-level officials rose to the occasion. The large number of trade and investment agreements that Canada has negotiated over the past twenty-five years gave even junior officials the experience they needed to deliver high-quality policy support to the government even without a full roster of veteran negotiators.

Stephen Harper's Trade Policy Inheritance

When Stephen Harper became prime minister in 2006, he inherited a trade policy that was fairly clearly mapped out. Beyond continuing the pace of tariff and non-tariff barrier reduction that began with the GATT, one of the objectives of trade negotiations is to depoliticize international commercial transactions and minimize political intervention. For example, most exporters will admit that they can operate their businesses around various tariff and technical barriers as long as the barriers are consistent and predictable. More serious damage is done to competitiveness when barriers appear and disappear from one day to the next on the basis of political whims.

Because of the lengthening reach of international trade agreements, politicians now have to actively violate their own countries' trade rules in order to raise protectionist barriers that may buy votes from a few constituents but will disadvantage the economy as a whole. With the framework of Canadian trade policy already well in place, the policy decisions Harper faced were less a matter of what to do, but how fast to do it and where to start. There were offensive interests—what new markets to pursue and sectors to promote—and defensive interests—what sectors and geographic regions to protect from international competition.

Harper's own policy instincts favoured liberalization, open markets and negotiated solutions to trade disputes. These were in line with the economic realities of a small-market economy with a rich resource endowment but a relatively small consumer base. Export orientation is necessary for prosperity—relying on domestic sales is not sufficient to sustain domestic standards of living and rules are needed to mitigate against maltreatment by more powerful economies.

The Canada-US Free Trade Agreement was the first real liberalized trade agreement between any two advanced economies in the world. It followed the model of the GATT but with significantly deepened and modernized commitments. The agreement was expanded to include Mexico in the 1994 North American Free Trade Agreement and many of the new commitments worked out by the three countries, such as on services and intellectual property, were later built into the WTO Agreements.[3]

The NAFTA and the WTO set the stage for Canada's current trade policy infrastructure. Virtually all of Canada's trade and investment agreements are based on a NAFTA-WTO template. Once the major agreements of the 1990s were negotiated, the focus of global trade policy turned to implementing the commitments. No major expansions to the NAFTA-WTO model were made until businesses and government institutions had a chance to catch up with new rules and regulations.

Even for experienced trading economies such as Canada, the work of implementing the WTO and NAFTA was a heavy lift. Domestic rules had to be changed, institutions updated and traders educated about the new procedures. For emerging economies, the process was much more difficult. Dozens of new countries entered the international trading system in the 1980s and 1990s and the biggest challenge was building the capacity to implement new commitments. The late 1990s and early 2000s also saw trade liberalization conceptually linked with democratic development and social and political transitions in Latin America, Asia, Africa and states of the former Soviet Union.

Canadian leaders during the late 1990s made a conceptual link between trade and development, even when there was not a strong economic case to pursue an agreement with a new partner. The prevailing wisdom was that good trading partners made good (and stable) neighbours because poverty is a major contributor to political turmoil. The best example of a trade initiative started primarily for development reasons was the Free Trade Area of the Americas (FTAA), launched in 1999. Although never completed, the negotiations provided a master class in tradecraft for officials from newly democratizing and developing economies in Latin America and the Caribbean. The lessons learned from the FTAA about how to negotiate with neighbours formed the basis of the bilateral agreements that Canada completed with Chile, Colombia, Honduras, Peru, Panama and Costa Rica.

The Chrétien and Martin eras were characterized by consolidation of big trade commitments and an expansion of getting-to-know-you agreements with new trading partners, which, although they did not yield much in the way of immediate benefits, would set the stage for future trade engagements.

Trade in the Harper Era

During the 2006 election campaign, Harper's trade policy platform focused on expanding Canada's roster of free trade agreements, reducing subsidies for business and privatizing Crown corporations that competed with comparable private sector businesses.[4] The Harper record for new trade agreements is impressive. Under his watch, Canada concluded ten sets of free trade negotiations (see table 9.1) and numerous Foreign Investment Protection and Promotion Agreements (FIPAs).[5]

Table 9.1
Canada's Completed Free Trade Negotiations

Trading Partner	Year Concluded
TPP	2015
EU (CETA)	2015
Ukraine	2015
South Korea	2015
Honduras	2014
Panama	2013
Jordan	2012
Colombia	2011
Peru	2009
European Free Trade Area (Iceland, Norway, Switzerland and Liechtenstein)	2009

Source: Global Affairs Canada
Note: Table designates concluded agreement. At the time of writing, neither the CETA nor TPP were in force.

The success of the early years of Harper's trade policy was due in large part to a period of global trade expansion. The government's 2009 Global Commerce Strategy was a self-congratulatory ode to having the right policies at the right time. Two-way trade with the world was growing by about 5 or 6 per cent a year, and dependence on the US declined from 73 per cent of total trade in 2004 to 68 per cent in 2008. Inward Foreign Direct Investment (FDI) was strong, although still largely dependent on the US, but signs of investment diversification could be seen through the rising share of Canadian outward-oriented investment.[6] Although the government expressed concern about new competitors rising in emerging markets, they prepared to counter these with new policies to capitalize on emerging market growth opportunities.

However, Canada's days of trade prosperity were numbered. The 2009 financial crisis put the brakes on the expansionary policies of the early Harper years. The United States and the European Union bought more than 80 per cent of Canada's exports and the crisis caused their demand to plummet. The crisis also pushed up the price of oil, so Canada's overall export numbers were buffered somewhat by resource exports, masking the reality that Canada's manufacturing sector was in trouble and emerging market growth was slowing down.

In response, the government's 2011 Economic Action Plan was focused not on big ambitions, but on incremental strategies for riding out the storm. These included economic stimulus and access to credit at home, and measures to reduce border frictions and regulatory costs with the United States.

By 2012, the Harper government was confident enough in the recovery to relaunch an expansionary outward agenda. Although it had the new title of Global Markets Action Plan, there were very few differences from the 2009 Global Commerce Plan. Among its major focus points:

- targeting select markets in Asia Pacific, Latin America, the Middle East, Africa and Europe/Eurasia
- assisting Canadian businesses abroad through the Trade Commissioner Services and other tools
- encouraging innovation, especially in science and technology, through tax breaks and seed capital
- building market access and protection for Canadian investors through new trade and investment agreements

Although it is beyond the scope of this analysis to say whether Harper's trade policy was optimal for the conditions of the global economy, it appears to have been appropriate for the times—expanding in the right directions when times were good, and providing pragmatic alternatives when times were not.

The Unfinished Agenda

Stephen Harper successfully met his 2006 election campaign objective of providing Canada with more trade agreements. The more challenging questions are how well these agreements helped to build Canadian competitiveness and what might have been left off the agenda. Some of the weak spots and challenges that have emerged in Canada's external economic policy during the Harper era are persistent trade distortions due to supply management, continuing irritants with the United States and a need to find a balance between investment promotion and defending sovereignty over sensitive sectors such as cultural industries, where foreign investment was not welcome. As well, the aging NAFTA agreement has raised questions over how to expand to new markets while maintaining the advantages we already have. Some of these challenges were within the government's power to influence; some were not.

Supply Management

For years, most trade officials have privately agreed that supply management policies in dairy and poultry are a drag on an otherwise aggressive and outward-oriented trade policy. Many observers believed that Harper would dial back management policies sometime during his tenure. Supply management provided concentrated benefits to well-organized producer groups but generated little consumer backlash because the benefits had been embedded for so long. Eliminating them would not be easy. Aside from the economic cost of compensating dairy farmers for the loss of more than $20 billion in dairy quota, there would also be political costs, since the majority of quota holders are from a small number of ridings concentrated in Quebec and Ontario.

Until Canada began negotiations with the European Union, there were few trading partners demanding that Canada change its supply management policies. In order to exempt supply management from WTO challenges while still maintaining import barriers, Canada had to agree not to export dairy products. (Otherwise the government supports holding supply management in place would have been considered an unfair subsidy that makes Canadian exports less expensive than those of competitors.) This allowed Canada to continue to impose tariffs of some 250 per cent on certain imported dairy products, especially cheeses.

Even though being denied access to Canada's 34 million consumers irritated dairy exporters in the European Union, the United States and New Zealand, it wasn't until the Canada-EU Comprehensive Economic and Trade Agreement (CETA) and Trans-Pacific Partnership (TPP) negotiations that trading partners overtly targeted Canada's trade-distorting dairy regime.

Through the course of the CETA negotiations (2009–14), Canada conceded a certain amount of tariff-free market access to the EU. This appeared to be a clear sign from the Harper government that supply management's days were numbered. However, the access granted to the EU came from new market growth and did not cut into the market share that Canadian producers were already guaranteed.

Demands for supply management reform were front and centre in the TPP negotiations.[7] The US and New Zealand both framed the inclusion of dairy market access by Canada as a quid pro quo for Canada's being able to sign on to a final agreement.

During the TPP negotiations, the Harper government indicated that hard decisions might have to be made on supply management[8] but made it clear that the final deal would have to offer clear benefits to Canada across sectors before dairy concessions would be offered. However, in CETA, Canada opened up about 4.5 per cent of its cheese market to duty-free access,[9] so some degree of market opening in the TPP was anticipated.

In the end, Canada agreed to offer up 3.25 per cent of its total dairy market to TPP partners while providing compensation to Canadian dairy farmers of $4.3 billion. (This generous adjustment assistance package has raised eyebrows in Canada,[10] opening the question of whether Prime Minister Trudeau will honour the commitment of his predecessor.)

Softwood Lumber

Softwood lumber is a persistent irritant in the Canada-US trade relationship—an irritant that has gone on so long that it has spawned a complicated set of institutional mechanisms to help manage, but never solve, the problem.

The US has long argued that Canada's stumpage fees to cut lumber on Crown land do not reflect market rates and are therefore an unfair subsidy provided by the government. Canada, for its part, maintains that the fees are fair and that Canada's endowment of abundant, accessible and high-quality timber allows Canadian lumber to be brought to market at a lower cost. However, US complaints about public subsidies stem from the fact that 70 per cent of Canadian timber comes from public land, compared to some 15 per cent from public land in the United States.[11]

While there are other aspects to the dispute, such as different systems used in different provinces and disputes over how lumber is graded,[12] since 1986 Canada and the United States have agreed to disagree on softwood lumber—exempting the sector from free trade agreements and using instead a series of voluntary export restraints (VERs).[13] The basic terms of the VER are that the US agrees to let a set quota of Canadian lumber into the US market duty free, and any amounts above the quota are assessed progressively higher tariffs.

There is very little that any Canadian prime minister could do to solve the softwood lumber dispute, given that Canada simply has more abundant lumber resources and that resource management is constitutionally allocated to the provinces, but federal leadership could help to minimize provincial differences, providing Canada with a united front in dealing with the United States.

The most recent softwood lumber agreement expired in October 2015. Market conditions have contributed to higher prices through new US housing starts and demand from China, as well as reduced Canadian supply due to pine beetle infestation, provincial conservation policies and lower yields from new-growth forests. The US has shown little interest in negotiating a new deal, perhaps because high prices and low Canadian export volumes have reduced US fears about Canadian exports flooding the market.[14] Nevertheless, in the absence of a predictable rules-based agreement on softwood, Canada is more vulnerable to US trade challenges, which are costly to adjudicate and disruptive to supply chains.

More Trouble with the Neighbours: COOL and Buy American

From 2013 onward, op-eds focused on the frosty relations between Harper and Obama, and it is now hard to remember that when he was elected in 2006, Stephen Harper promised a new level of cordiality in relations with the United States. During the mid-2000s, such an open-handed approach was appropriate: the NAFTA was still making positive contributions to the integration of North America; and Canada-US trade at the beginning of 2006 was valued at about US$500 billion—more than the value of EU-US trade and double that of Canada-US trade in 1994 when the NAFTA was launched.[15]

Most of the irritant-driven trade agenda that emerged during the later years of the Harper government can be attributed to the global financial crisis, which caused outward-looking economic policies to swing toward domestic protectionism, but some aspect of the cool relations can be blamed on a disconnect between the leaders.

First, there has traditionally been a stronger connection between Canadian Conservatives and US Republicans. While Canadians are more inclined to agree with Democratic social policies and attitudes, the economic policies of the Democrats tend to favour domestic protectionism and the trade-restricting interests of organized labour.

Secondly, the match between a folksy and confident George W. Bush and an eager-to-prove-himself new prime minister was better than the one between a more demanding Harper and a cautious Obama, who was not willing to spend domestic political capital to keep the peace with the northern neighbours.

This polarization played out in the issue of the US Country of Origin Labeling (COOL) law for food products, which had a major negative effect on the Canadian beef and pork sector. The market reality was that an integrated supply chain had emerged wherein animals would move across the border several times during their lives. COOL obligations required labels that said, for example, "Born in Canada. Raised in the United States. Slaughtered in the United States."[16] Not only did this create onerous labelling requirements, it also increased costs because Canadian animals had to be processed separately from US animals to prevent intermingling of Canadian and US meat.

As a result, demand for Canadian, Mexican and other foreign meat products dropped sharply in the US. While US grocery retailers and food processors protested, the COOL provisions were kept in place by political pressure from the US beef and pork producers. The introduction of COOL emerged at about the same time as the scandal involving melamine in Chinese milk. Politicians were highly sensitized to public demands to know the origins of food products.

In 2009, Canada and Mexico launched a successful challenge in the WTO, claiming that COOL rules constituted an unnecessary barrier to trade. The US lost the challenge and the appeal, and in December 2015, a bill to repeal COOL passed through both houses of Congress. While Canada appears to have won the battle, Canadian producers have also lost billions of dollars' worth of market access.

Just as concerns about the safety of Chinese products contributed to public support for COOL, concerns about the US being flooded with Chinese goods and services added fuel to the uptake for "Buy American"[17] measures in the 2009 American Recovery and Reinvestment Act (ARRA). The act and other US economic stimulus programs introduced after the financial crisis contained carve-outs to ensure that supplies and suppliers for US government contracts originated in the United States. This made for good politics but poor economics as established supply chains were disrupted in order to ensure that no foreign pipes or bolts found their way into US public works projects.

Since the North American Free Trade Agreement provided little guaranteed market access to government procurement contracts, Canadian suppliers are vulnerable to the relatively unpredictable application of Buy American language in government contracts. (When Buy American provisions are not specifically included, government entities are free to buy from the most qualified bidder, no matter where they are located.) Among the most troubling examples of Buy American was the removal of Canadian-made pipes from the Camp Pendleton marine base in 2009 and the threatened use, in early 2015, of Buy American rules to ensure that only US steel was used in the construction of a ferry terminal owned by the state of Alaska but located in Prince Rupert, British Columbia.[18]

Elsewhere in the world, liberalized trade in government procurement is notoriously hard to achieve. However, the lack of bilateral will and effective consultative mechanisms for procurement have allowed for very little movement between Canada and the United States over the past twenty years, and the issue will continue to haunt future Canadian leaders.

Foreign Investment Review

Over the past two decades, Canada's system of foreign investment review has been pared down from a relatively rigorous screening system designed to deter foreign, primarily American, influence to a more open system that reserves the government's right to intervene on certain large investments deemed to be detrimental to Canada's interests.

The changes to a more open environment for foreign direct investment began in the 1980s when the calculation was made that if Canada was going to be a global player it needed a greater volume of capital flowing into the economy. Foreign direct investment (FDI) brings not only new capital but also new technologies and know-how. Canada was struggling with high unemployment and low growth, and the Pierre Trudeau–era foreign investment review policies were too slow and cumbersome. The Mulroney government streamlined the process with the 1985 Investment Canada Act (ICA). The ICA allowed that only high-value acquisitions and start-ups would be automatically reviewed by the industry minister. The size of the investment that triggers a review has gradually been increased since 1985 and stands today at $600 million for most types of investment.

Foreign investment review considers whether an investment provides a net benefit to Canada such as increased production, employment or technology transfer. Opponents of the ICA suggest that any form of screening creates a chilling effect on investment. Today, unless an investment is particularly large or in a sensitive sector, federal authorities require only that they are notified about the intended investment.

The ICA has been used twice—both while Harper was prime minister—to block the potential takeover of a Canadian company by a foreign entity. In 2008, the ICA was used to stop Alliant Techsystems' bid for MacDonald, Dettwiler and Associates, a Vancouver technology company best known as the manufacturer of the Canadarm. In 2010, Saskatchewan's Potash Corporation was about to be acquired by Australian mining giant BHP Billiton, but the company withdrew its bid after it learned that the minister of industry[19] would disallow the application if it went forward.

Although hundreds of foreign investments have been approved since 2005, the rejection of the Alliant and BHP Billiton applications is a reminder that political discretion is still a factor in Canada's investment policy regime. As well, Canada maintains a set of exceptions—sectors in which foreign investment is prohibited or severely curtailed—that are kept in place even though the public policy rationale for the exception may no longer be relevant. These include telecommunications and the financial sector.

In addition to concerns about policy sovereignty, the Harper government was faced with a new set of challenges on foreign investment. While previous prime ministers had to grapple with debates over US ownership and the prospects of Canada becoming a branch plant economy, Stephen Harper had to deal with the rhetoric and reality of Chinese investment in the resource sector.

Unlike investment from the US, much Chinese investment is linked to state-owned enterprises (SOEs). As China became a major player in global acquisitions, Canada and other countries have been forced to evaluate whether SOE investment should be treated differently.

These concerns led to the addition of special SOE guidelines to Canada's investment rules in 2012. In addition to net-benefit criteria, the government also takes into account the applicant company's governance structure, and whether or not the government plays a role in the commercial activity, financing or decision-making of the company.[20] Although evaluation criteria remains highly subjective, the government must be convinced that the applicant company's activities are sufficiently separate from government interference before an investment will be approved.

For the most part, Canada's concerns about SOEs are in response to Chinese investment in the extractive sector. China's Sinopec owns nearly 10 per cent of Canadian oil sands giant Syncrude. Recent Chinese acquisitions include PetroChina's purchase of the MacKay River Project from Athabasca Oil Sands Corp., Sinopec's acquisition of Calgary-based Daylight Energy Ltd, and CNOOC's acquisition of the oil sands technology company OPTI in 2011 and Nexen, an oil and gas company, in 2013.

Since these acquisitions have all been approved by the industry minister as meeting the net-benefits test, including the additional considerations for state-owned enterprises, there is reason for optimism that Chinese investment in Canada will continue to be beneficial for both sides. However, it may be too soon to judge since, to date, there are very few cases of Chinese investment arbitration at forums such as International Centre for Settlement of Investment Disputes (ICSID) to evaluate.[21]

Harper presided over a period of ambivalence toward economic engagement with China. A 2015 poll by the Asia-Pacific Foundation indicated that only 42 per cent of Canadians supported investment from China, but Canadians also vastly overestimate the extent of Chinese investment. They assume that it is somewhere around 25 per cent when in fact it is closer to 3 per cent.[22]

Investor-State Dispute Settlement

As the first prime minister operating in an era of truly globalized trade, Stephen Harper faced his share of challenges. Even as Canada sought to attract new investment to develop new areas of comparative advantage at home, and to open new markets for Canadian products and innovators abroad, Canada faced a growing number of investment lawsuits of its own.

Since the 1994 NAFTA, Canada's has permitted investor-state dispute settlement (ISDS), meaning that a company that feels it has been wronged can initiate legal proceedings against a government on its own. It does not have to wait for its home government to take up the cause on its behalf.

Just as there are rules to regulate the behaviour of investors, ISDS provides a layer of protection against excessive or arbitrary behaviour by states. The Harper government has defended its policies on ISDS on the basis of providing legal protections to Canadian investors seeking to invest in markets without reliable rule of law. In such cases, ISDS is a hedge against unwarranted expropriation and allows companies to have their cases heard by impartial tribunals. But, in exchange for protections for Canadians abroad, it also means that foreign companies can challenge Canada's domestic policies as well.

Early on, there were fears that investor-state dispute settlement would result in big American multinationals overturning Canadian public policy in critical areas such as health and education. The reality has been much more mundane. Since the NAFTA came into force, Canada has had a few cases filed against it every year, and Canadian companies have done the same in Mexico and the US. Most cases are withdrawn as unwinnable but some move ahead to arbitration. Canada wins some and loses some. In the 2010 Chemtura case, Canada successfully defended its right to ban a hazardous pesticide, but that same year, Ottawa paid compensation to AbitibiBowater for water and hydroelectric assets expropriated by the government of Newfoundland. (Ottawa offered the settlement voluntarily rather than let the case drag on for years.) But, after more than twenty years of ISDS, Canada's ability to regulate in the public interest remains relatively unchanged and its health and educational supports remain intact.

ISDS is now a feature of most Foreign Investment Protection Agreements (FIPAs) and trade agreements signed by Canada. While ISDS is intended to provide more legal certainty to Canadian firms wishing to invest abroad, it remains controversial at home and in new negotiating forums such as the TPP and CETA.

FIPAs

By the end of 2015, Canada had signed Foreign Investment Protection and Promotion Agreements with more than thirty countries, from Barbados to Senegal, eighteen of which were signed or brought into force during the Harper era.[23] FIPAs provide some basic assurances that if a Canadian establishes or acquires a company in another country, then the Canadian has a right to legal recourse if the company is expropriated without compensation (or if the country changes its rules and makes it impossible for the Canadian company to continue doing business). In exchange, we offer these same rights to foreign investors in Canada.

A FIPA does not provide a firm with permission to invest in Canada, nor does it exempt an investor from local laws; it just provides legal options for companies who believe they have been treated unfairly. Canada has been particularly keen to negotiate these agreements with developing countries because they give Canadian investors the option to use international arbitration panels in countries where the local courts are weak or corrupt. One of the most contentious FIPAs to be negotiated during the Harper era, and perhaps any other, was the FIPA with China brought into force in October 2014.

Even though Canada had negotiated thirty prior FIPAs, the deal with China was different. At thirty-eight times the Canadian population, China's sheer size is formidable. Opponents were concerned that Canada would be outmatched in any agreement with a country the size of China, but the alternative way of looking at it is that Canada will always be outmatched in any transaction with China that isn't governed by a clear, rules-based framework.

Since China has only participated in the global trading system since 1999, when it entered the WTO, there isn't a long history of compliance to evaluate. However, China's compliance with WTO transparency and reporting requirements has been very good. Where there are rules, China has given strong indications that it will follow them. It is in the absence of rules that smaller countries such as Canada will always struggle.

Updating the NAFTA

The 1994 NAFTA governs Canada's largest trading relationship with the United States and Mexico. In 1993, trilateral trade within the North American region was US$288 billion. In 2014, total trilateral merchandise trade exceeded US$1.12 trillion.[24] Covering more than 75 per cent of Canada's exports, the NAFTA provides effective coverage of most of Canada's traditional trade in manufactured goods and agricultural products. However, because it has not been updated in any significant way in more than twenty years, the NAFTA has little to offer to new trade issues such as services trade in the digital economy, reduction of regulatory barriers, energy trade and movement of people.

Unlike the EU, which has supranational governance through the European Parliament and European Council, the NAFTA contains no updating mechanism except through working group meetings on relatively routine technical matters such as tariff classification. Because the NAFTA has become a media scapegoat for the ills of globalized production, politicians in the US dare not reopen the NAFTA for fear that it would never close again. Canada and Mexico have reluctantly accepted the argument that the NAFTA would have to be updated through indirect mechanisms, such as through the Trans-Pacific Partnership.

Since the TPP negotiations included trade subjects not covered in the NAFTA (such as state-owned enterprises) and because Canada, the United States and

Mexico are all negotiating parties in the TPP, any rules in the TPP that go beyond the NAFTA rules will effectively replace them.[25]

The problem with the indirect approach, however, is that the interests of twelve TPP countries from around the world do not line up with the core concerns of the North American political economy. The US side deal with Japan on TPP rules of origin—which was concluded without consultation with Canada and Mexico even though the sector is fully integrated on a trilateral basis—illustrates this sort of challenge.

Border Initiatives

The bilateral Beyond the Border and Regulatory Cooperation Council (BTB/RCC) initiatives launched by Stephen Harper and Barack Obama in 2011 are perhaps the most important Canada-US economic initiatives that no one has ever heard of. BTB serves as a mechanism to have entry and exit decisions made before goods and people even arrive at the border, and to implement common standards of access at the North American perimeter. The major focus areas of BTB include expanding pre-clearance arrangements for trusted traders and travellers, sharing border entry-exit information and increasing pre-clearance capacity in airports and other ports of entry.

The RCC is a mechanism to streamline inspection and certification for traded goods. Based on principles of mutual recognition, RCC seek to achieve the goal of "inspected once, cleared twice" for products crossing the border. The RCC began with a core group of concerns such as automotive emissions, rail safety, medical devices and meat inspection and created tools for problem solving and cooperation among businesses and regulators on both sides of the border. The next steps, currently underway, are formalized collaborative mechanisms between US and Canadian regulators.

The problem with the BTB/RCC initiatives is that because they operate below the political radar, it has always been a challenge to muster sufficient resources to continue their important work. Now as legacy projects of Harper and Obama, it is not clear whether they will continue under new leaders in both countries.

Diversification: Atlantic and Pacific

A core theme of Harper's trade policy was to build effective trade diversification of new markets to move beyond trade for development purposes and to seek economically substantive markets. The CETA and the TPP, which provide diversification in the East and the West, are the capstones of this effort. As the time of writing, the status of the Canada-EU Free Trade Agreement remains uncertain. CETA ratification has been expected for some time, but it appears that in addition to the routine matters of legal review and translation, there is considerable pressure from some EU member states to reopen the investment chapter. Some EU parties are pressing Canada to adopt measures more in line with the EU's proposed ISDS measures in the United States–European Union Trans-Atlantic Trade and Investment Partnership (TTIP) currently being negotiated, even though the final form of the TTIP investment chapter is far from settled.

The continuing delays to the EU agreement are a loss to Canadian businesses that participated in the design of the deal, which would offer clear market access gains in such areas as agriculture, fish and seafood and forest products.

Although the agreement with the European Union is important for some Canadian industries and for its role in upgrading trade rules of interest to advanced industrialized economies, the EU market has relatively static levels of growth and demand. Most new growth will come through trade with emerging economies. This is why the Trans-Pacific Partnership, for which the negotiations concluded in October 2015, is such an important stepping stone for Canada's future trade opportunities.

True, Canada already had trade agreements with most of the economies in the TPP, but Japan is the largest new trading economy and the most promising in the short term.[26] In the longer term, emerging economies such as Vietnam are important sources of new growth and demand.

The Harper government invested considerable political and material resources in the completion of both the CETA and the TPP. If they are successful in the decades ahead, Harper's efforts will be considered prescient and sound. If not, he will be accused of pursuing paper agreements that did not effectively deal with the changing nature of the global economy and Canada's changing fortunes as a commodities exporter.

The China Quandary

One of the missed opportunities of the Harper trade policy was the failure to engage consistently with China on its offer of a strategic economic partnership with Canada. Canada took some steps in closer economic engagement with China, such as the negotiation of a FIPA and the establishment of a renminbi hub, making Canada the first country in the Americas to offer full convertibility in local currency. But with the Harper government perhaps spooked by the large amount of Chinese investment in the energy sector, its policy of ambitious engagement with emerging markets seemed to skid when it came to China. Despite warm initial overtures, Canada did not act on China's proposed high-level economic dialogue, which would have put Canada on the path to a bilateral free trade agreement such as was recently completed by Australia—a competitor to Canada in many respects.

Quantitative analysis suggests that Canada stands to gain $7.8 billion in new exports annually by 2030, as a result of an FTA with China.[27] Canada's pork, oilseeds and green technology industries stand to make particular gains. Focused engagement with China is one area in which the new Trudeau government could succeed where the Harper government fell short.

Conclusions

The Harper government was challenged by a period of turbulent economic events, chief among them the rise of emerging markets, the global disaggregation of supply chains and the transformation of manufacturing from labour-intensive assembly lines to technology-intensive advanced manufacturing techniques.

These challenges were exacerbated by the financial crisis of 2009, which sent shockwaves through the trading system as buyers stopped buying and investors stopped investing. Some of the reverberations from the financial crisis included shrinking demand from Canada's largest trading partner, the United States, and protectionist policies such as Buy American restrictions on government contracts and Country of Origin Labeling in the meat sector.

One of the things that became clear during the Harper era is that free trade agreements are important to a functional, externally oriented trade policy, but they are just one piece of a larger puzzle. Whereas in the 1980s and 1990s, when Canada was negotiating its first trade agreements with the United States and Mexico, tariffs on imports were a significant drain on competitiveness, today the greatest challenge is non-tariff barriers. These include regulatory and certification issues, product safety and labelling issues, and uneven interpretation of rules by different national and sub-national authorities. The developing countries that are the keys to growth for Canada also need the greatest attention to trade facilitation and implementation measures, so that the formal market access negotiated by Canada can be effectively utilized by Canadian exporters.

The new Trudeau government inherits a set of trade policies and agreements that are consistent with an outward-oriented, diversifying economy. Beyond implementation of the CETA and the TPP, the next step for Trudeau could be the serious consideration of a bilateral agreement with China. The continuing challenge for Prime Minister Trudeau is that although Canada has been diversifying its trading partners, its trade profile is largely dependent on oil and gas (about 25 per cent of total goods exports). Taking office during a period of serious volatility in the oil and gas sector, the new prime minister faces the question of how to diversify Canada's trade of other goods and services and better integrate value-added trade with Canada's knowledge economy.

PEOPLE

10

The Harper Influence on Immigration

Ratna Omidvar

The immigration reforms introduced during the Stephen Harper era have radically, but quietly, changed who gets into Canada and how. The immigration system has undergone a small revolution. The name, the Immigration and Refugee Protection Act, is merely the skin of the old system. Inside is a very different beast.

Over the course of a decade in office, Stephen Harper undertook a sweeping overhaul of policies, rules, regulations, systems and process, all without tabling a new Immigration Act. In so doing, he is credited with bringing efficiencies, dismantling backlogs and restoring public confidence in the system. Not surprisingly, these changes have come at a price and with outcomes, whether intended or unintended, that may well shore up Canada's ability to succeed in the short term, but could compromise it in the long term as a successful nation for—and of—immigrants.

The Harper years were not without vision. The transformation of the immigration system under his watch matches the view that immigration is an instrument to grow the economy. The stated goal of the government's efforts to transform the system was "to build a fast and flexible immigration system whose primary focus is on meeting Canada's economic and labour market needs."[1] The changes aimed to make the system "proactive, targeted, fast and efficient."[2]

The primary instrument of change in the Harper era involved a dramatic shift toward market-driven policy-making, with a new focus on immigrants who can hit the ground running and a new role for employers in their selection. It changed who gets into Canada and how they get in. It did away with some sacred cows in processing applicant files to gain efficiencies. Backlogs were eliminated, remarkably at a time when the federal government was reducing its departmental spending.

The Harper era also linked immigration to security with a major overhaul of citizenship policies, making citizenship "harder to get and easier to lose."[3] It favoured refugees from overseas at the cost of refugees who made their claims inland, lending credibility to the criticism that the Harper era had a fixed image of a good refugee (one who was selected from a camp overseas) and a bad refugee (one who found the resources to come to Canada and make a claim on our soil). It favoured a law-and-order approach to fraud in the family reunification stream, catching a few but penalizing many, particularly immigrant women who come to Canada as spouses of permanent residents and Canadian citizens.

Most notably, much of this was accomplished by the successful use of anecdote over evidence. It was done with a precise focus on specific changes followed by more specific changes, at high speed and without meaningful consultations with the public. Major regulatory changes were repeatedly buried in omnibus bills, with little or no public consultation. Keith Banting, one of Canada's most knowledge-able scholars on immigration, has characterized this as immigration policy by stealth or "government by surprise."[4]

A review of the decade finds pockets of great innovation. There were positive, forward-thinking policies, but elsewhere there were poor and even cruel ones. In the Harper era, there are examples of good, bad and ugly decisions.

Some of those decisions leapt to an unusual place, front and centre in the fed-eral election. Unprecedented in modern campaign history, the 2015 election was decided in part by immigration issues. In his victory speech, Prime Minister-designate Justin Trudeau nodded to them: "Our enviable, inclusive society didn't happen by accident and won't continue without effort." In reference to controver-sial citizenship policies of his predecessor, he repeated the campaign hallmark that "a Canadian is a Canadian is a Canadian."[5]

After the Conservative defeat to the Liberal Party, Canadians turned to a ques-tion of legacy on immigration. Will Harper's Canada survive beyond Harper?

Stories around the Globe

To view the shape and mechanics of Canada's immigration system today, it helps to first step outside, to cast around in the wider world for the forces shaping public policy and public opinion on migration. Out there, in other rich nations, what's happening with human movement? The answer, of course, is a thousand things, colliding and influencing each other, as happens in our interconnected world. But a few stories stand out.

In the summer of 2015, a sad milestone passed the world's media pages. The number of refugees from the four-year-long crisis in Syria reached four million. Even when the total had sat closer to three million, it was labelled the world's largest refugee crisis since the Second World War. Still more people are expected to flee to safety, with no clear end to the power wielded by the Islamic State or Syrian dictator Bashar al-Assad. From a population of about twenty million people at the start of the crisis, the four million now outside Syria are clustered mostly in neighbouring countries, while a quarter million Syrians have applied for asylum in Europe.[6] Relative to the whole crisis, that's not very many—but on a beach on Lampedusa or a highway in Calais, it's called a "flood."

At the same time that Syrians are crossing the Mediterranean into Europe, others from various parts of Africa and the Middle East are too, fleeing instability and poverty. In October, the International Organization for Migration (IOM) reported that already in 2015, some 557,899 people had made the journey and over 2,987 had died trying.[7]

Let's move farther inland, to the German city of Dresden, a stronghold of the anti-Islamist, anti-immigration Pegida movement. In English, that's Patriotic Europeans against the Islamisation of the West, and in January 2015, Pegida protesters rallied across the country, calling for fewer immigrants—which in Germany, a long-time destination for Turks, is code for fewer Muslims.[8] Dresden is just one expression of a continental antagonism. The last few years have witnessed a growing voter base for right-wing parties in liberal democracies in Europe. Right-wing parties are particularly large in France and Denmark but have found new support in Austria, Finland, Greece, the Netherlands and Switzerland.[9] The weight of the anti-immigrant movement is difficult to measure against its counterpart movements, most notably in Germany under the leadership of Chancellor Angela Merkel. Indeed, if the United Nation's Nansen Refugee Award goes for the second time in its history to a whole people (the first recipients were Canadians), it could be awarded to the people of Germany.

Down under, migrant boats are never long out of Australia's headlines. Since the government of Tony Abbott implemented Operation Sovereign Borders in 2013 to "stop the boats," arrival rates plummeted.[10] But the operation has led to strained relations with Australia's neighbours, since the boats that Canberra turns away need somewhere else to go. Domestic and international disapproval has been loud. Australia faces allegations of inhumane treatment of desperate migrants, along with criticism centred on the cost of the whole-of-government operation, which stood at over $3 billion in 2014.[11] Nonetheless, new prime minister Malcolm Turnbull, already tested by Australia-bound boats, has backed his predecessor's stance.[12]

Canada has been spared this tension, whether as an accident of our remote geography or by virtue of our history as a nation still in the making. In the past decade, while the Conservative Party held power, Canada's immigration system faced nothing like the strain experienced by other destination countries. There was no serious challenge to the status quo. No "flood" or crisis that launched a public outpouring of anger at domestic immigration management.

But global events do influence public policy and public opinion elsewhere, for better and for worse. Here, on the election trail, Harper made a promise to increase the number of Syrian refugees to Canada as Canadians watched in horror the human crisis unfolding in Europe, symbolized in a single photo of a lifeless toddler on a beach in Turkey—a boy named Alan Kurdi, with grief-stricken relatives in British Columbia. Meanwhile, security fears prompted a ban on travel by Canadians to certain countries, catching in this net not only would-be threats to national and global security, but also Canadians who hail from these parts of the world.

But for the most part, it is remarkable and laudable that the outlook of Harper's Conservative Party remained liberal and pro-immigrant in a growing global anti-immigrant environment.

More Immigrants, Diverse Immigrants: Harper's Liberal Immigration Policy

In 2010, Chancellor Merkel said that multiculturalism in Germany had "utterly failed."[13] In Canada the following year, Harper gave a very different answer during a televised leaders' debate. Asked about the party position on reasonable accommodation of immigrants, Harper replied, "We favour multiculturalism."[14]

"People who make the hard decision to [come here], they first and foremost want to belong to this country, that's why they come. ... They also at the same time will change our country, and we show through multiculturalism our willingness to accommodate," Harper said. "That's why we're so successful integrating people as a country."

The conclusion is that a Canadian political party, even an economically and socially Conservative one, cannot both survive politically and be anti-immigrant. To be anti-immigrant in highly diverse Canada is tantamount to abdicating on the immigrant-rich ridings in and around metropolitan Vancouver, Toronto, Montreal and, increasingly, beyond. No surprise, then, that Harper's Conservative Party pivoted from the direction of the Reform Party. The political strategy that brought him his majority in the 2011 election focused to a great extent on converting immigrant votes into Conservative votes. With the creation of an additional thirty new ridings by the Fair Representation Act of 2011, many of which are in the dense immigrant suburbs of British Columbia and Ontario, the political clout of the immigrant voter is even more intensified.

It is therefore also no surprise that immigration levels rose under Harper (figure 10.1). For many years, immigration hovered at around 250,000 people each year. But in 2015–16, the projected rise was between 260,000 and 285,000.

Fig. 10.1
Permanent Residents to Canada

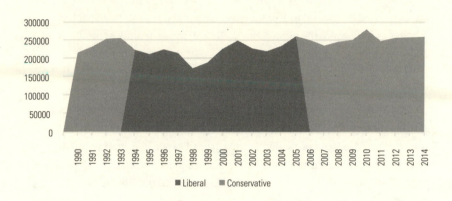

Source: Immigration, Refugees and Citizenship Canada, "Facts and figures 2014—immigration overview, permanent residents"

The mix of immigrant type is more or less consistent, with the biggest change happening to refugee numbers. The Conservatives continued a policy of previous Liberal governments to concentrate immigration in the economic over the family stream, but presided over a new decline in the proportion of refugee arrivals. The level fell from 13 per cent of the total in 2006 to 9 per cent in 2014.

Both the overall immigration level and the Immigration Department's messaging around it speak to a pro-immigration agenda. In an Immigration Department report on plans for 2015–16, we're told that immigrants "enhance Canada's social fabric, contribute to labour market growth and strengthen the economy."[15] This is typical Harper government messaging on immigrants. The positive tone goes up a notch when diaspora and diplomacy intersect.

On a state visit by the president of the Philippines in May 2015, Harper told the press, "Filipino-Canadians adapt to this country very quickly because they exhibit the very best of our shared values. Generous and hardworking, they raise strong families ... and they uphold and promote our shared ideals of freedom, democracy and justice. We are a stronger and better country as a result of their presence."[16] It seems remarkable, in contrast to rhetoric in Europe, that Canada's prime minister could say with a smile, "Tagalog is today the most rapidly growing language in our country." Remarkable until we remember that Filipinos are a quickly growing demographic. The Philippines sends the third-largest number of immigrants to Canada, above Pakistan and beneath only India and China.[17]

The same praise emerged for Indian immigrants during the visit of the rock star Indian prime minister Narendra Modi in April 2015. Harper told a dinner crowd in Vancouver, "Canadians of Indian origin have helped to build a vibrant economy and a dynamic society here in British Columbia. ... [T]he success of the Indo-Canadian community stems from the fundamental traits our two countries share: A belief in hard work, the pursuit of excellence, commitments to family and faith, and to community and country."[18]

Harper's Conservatives not only raised Canada's immigration levels, but as these examples hint, they continued sourcing from a diversity of countries. Since racial discrimination inside the immigration system was eliminated with the introduction of the points system in 1967, immigrants increasingly came from all over the world instead of predominantly from Europe and the English-speaking Commonwealth countries. China, India, the Philippines, Pakistan and Iran are the top five home countries of immigrants to Canada. This diversity is a point of pride too. Multiculturalism Minister Jason Kenney tweeted to his 45,000 followers in March 2015, "overall immigration levels, & immigration of Muslims to Canada, has increased under this Conservative govt."

A markedly different tone emerged in the final months of the 2015 campaign. The debate about niqabs in citizenship ceremonies, the new "barbaric cultural practices" tip line and the focus on non-Muslim refugees from Syria and Iraq stank of distinct if indirect Islamophobia. But even this strategy was suspected to target immigrant votes. *Globe and Mail* columnist Doug Saunders argued that the Conservatives made "a calculated bid to make gains among Hindu, Sikh, Buddhist and Christian diasporas by playing on their atavistic fears of their Muslim neighbours."[19] It was, as Saunders noted, a dangerous game. Canadians soundly rejected identity politics by voting in a Liberal majority.

Despite their election play, however, the Conservatives overall walked in step with public support for diversity. Public opinion consistently falls between 50 and 60 per cent in favour of the immigration level, according to the immigration department's annual tracking survey.[20] Public opinion and political agendas have a reinforcing relationship, and the Harper government deserves credit for its leadership on maintaining Canadians' positive outlook on immigration.

One caveat to the rosy picture came from polling firm EKOS, which released a less promising survey in March 2015. In it, 46 per cent of respondents, polled on the question of whether Canada receives too few, too many or just the right number of immigrants, said too many—which is nearly double how many gave that answer in 2005.[21] A further cynical note is that it's possible Canadians hold relatively good views of immigration because, as the *Ottawa Citizen* put it, most "don't seem to have the foggiest notion of how many immigrants and refugees this country admits every year."[22] In the 2013–14 federal tracking survey, for instance, one third of those polled thought fewer than 100,000 immigrants come to Canada each year.

The Minister for Curry in a Hurry

Deserving an honourable mention for his role in the Harper government's immigration agenda is Jason Kenney, who held the immigration portfolio in the past and maintained his role as minister for multiculturalism throughout the Harper years. That a member of Harper's inner circle—and a man once touted as a contender for future Conservative Party leadership—held the multiculturalism file speaks to its great importance, and its great sensitivity.

Kenney proved a deft manager of the file through a decade of rising anti-immigrant sentiment in other parts of the world and tightening security laws here in Canada. He earned the fond moniker "Minister for Curry in a Hurry" because of an almost superhuman ability to appear when it mattered (hint: it always mattered) at community events, festivals, parades, dinners and national days of some two hundred nations all across the country. Facebook photos showed him outfitted in the colourful dress of who knows what tradition. He once added to his Twitter account the Arabic character "ن" or "N" meaning Nazarene, to show solidarity with Christian Iraqis targeted by the Islamic State.[23] The gesture demonstrated Kenney's ability to walk a fine line, showing support for one group without alienating others.

The Minister for Curry in a Hurry became a powerful tool for immigrants to see themselves recognized by the Conservative Party. Here was a high-profile minister in the prime minister's inner circle who came to their events, who celebrated their contributions and who wooed their support and donations. His dedication to them was rewarded. Of the top thirty ridings with the highest proportion of visible minority voters in the 2011 election, sixteen elected a Conservative.[24]

The new importance of the multiculturalism file was a Harper-Kenney innovation. The multiculturalism post was traditionally a soft one, always secondary to the immigration portfolio. It now matters in a new way. It was attached to Kenney, no matter whether he was minister of human resources and development or defence. Under his leadership, the post morphed into a quasi-diplomatic one, with Kenney playing the government's ambassador to a domestic, multi-nation diaspora. The portfolio has been folded into the Heritage Ministry under the Liberals, so we won't know how a Kenney successor would compare. To come close to his performance, a minister would need foreign policy fluency and be the ultimate retail politician, happy to don a turban, dance a tarantella and chow down on just about anything.

The maturing of the multiculturalism portfolio was not accidental. It was political. It followed the increasing diversity of Canada in general, and the diversity of key ridings in particular. In his recent book mining Canadian immigration data, Andrew Griffith highlighted the growing importance of immigrant communities to federal parties, as well as the new and different ways political parties target immigrant voters. In addition to the regular pocketbook issues, Griffith named some of the community-specific interests the Conservative Party tapped into. For example, there was the five-year community historical recognition program established in 2008, which intended to educate Canadians on the "experiences of ethno-cultural communities affected by wartime discriminatory measures and immigration restrictions."[25] The legacy includes a *Komagata Maru* monument in Vancouver's Harbour Green Park and a travelling exhibit on Italian-Canadians in the Second World War.

Policy-making around community interests is something all parties do, and it's not necessarily a bad thing. Rather, responsiveness to community concerns is an expectation of political representatives, and it can be a healthy sign of engagement with constituents. But as Griffith pointed out, the Harper Conservatives deviated in an important way from previous governments in their approach to immigrant vote shopping. "The [Harper] government is making more one-sided choices in … international disputes than previous governments in its response to diaspora concerns," Griffith argued.[26] One might think of Canada's response to the crisis in Ukraine, to the conflict in Sri Lanka involving the Tamil Tigers and to various conflicts and disputes involving Israel and its Middle Eastern neighbours. In each case, the bias on display for one side is typically overt and passionate, however unhelpful that may be in reducing the tempo of the conflict.

Immigrants in Parliament

Having an immigrant's man like Kenney in office is not the same thing as having an immigrant in office. Under-representation of visible minorities and immigrants is a problem that plagues all political parties in Canada. In a study that took a snapshot of Parliament in 2014, we learned visible minorities made up 10.2 per cent of Tories, 14.4 per cent of the NDP and 13.4 per cent of Liberals.[27] In total, visible minorities made up only 12.3 per cent of the House and Senate. Other research reveals that the number of visible minority candidates running for the major parties in the past four elections remained mostly flat, despite the increase in our population's diversity since 2004.[28]

Yet Harper took a promising step by creating thirty ridings to account for the population rise in Canada's cities and surrounding suburbs. The new ridings were an opportunity for visible minority candidates because of the high diversity in these areas. Not surprisingly, the parties put forward visible minority candidates in some of these new ridings. The candidates selected in ridings like the Greater Toronto Area's Brampton East (Raj Grewal, Naval Bajaj, Harbaljit Kahlon) and Don Valley North (Geng Tan, Joe Daniels, Akil Sadikali) underscore the intersection of representation and winnability. Where visible minority candidates were elected, some of these new ridings collapsed the timeline for a visible minority candidate to be elected, enabling them to skip at least one major barrier, incumbency. Through the combined impact of new ridings and the Liberal Party's diversity policies, the 42nd Parliament is the most diverse yet, with visible minorities in 14 per cent of the 338 seats.[29] This is near parity with the visibility minority makeup of the Canadian population, and is unrivalled in other countries of migration. So far, Liberal Party diversity is not confined to the back benches, but is visible in Trudeau's first cabinet appointments.

From the Best and the Brightest to the Most Ready: Market-driven Selection

Underemployment of immigrants is a problem that, by one estimate in 2011, costs the Canadian economy $30.7 billion.[30] For virtually all visible minority groups, unemployment is higher than it is for non-visible minorities. Millions of dollars get poured into the settlement services sector each year by government in order to find solutions. Calls for proposals for federal money have centred on finding ways to improve immigrant employment. But perhaps the most significant intervention to date is a government one, in the form of the express entry system in effect in January 2015, which Immigration Minister Chris Alexander called the "biggest watershed in Canadian immigration" since the points system.[31]

Express entry is Canada's new tool for managing who gets permanent residence. Gone are the days of first come, first served. Express entry provides a market-driven, competitive and evergreen pool of candidates. It involves a new distribution of points, with greater emphasis on traits that show employability. The system functions more like a bell curve than a simple pass-fail because a candidate's worth depends on the others in the pool. But the primary departure from the old system is the new centrality of the employer in selection. The highest points go to applicants already connected to an employer, meaning that anyone with a job offer gets launched to the front of the line. There, the candidate gets an invitation to apply for permanent residence.

The effects of this watershed on Canada's largest immigration stream will not be evident for some time, when patterns will begin to emerge. But there are three noteworthy observations.

One is that immigrants who are younger, who speak good English or French and who have job offers are the immigrants who will hit the ground running, contribute to our economy and meet our labour market shortages in an efficient and effective manner. These are the immigrants who employers are looking for.

However, the new emphasis on employability, including on the applicant's language skills and pre-existing network, could bias selection in favour of those from places with a similar linguistic or cultural makeup. Early evidence from Australia—the model along with New Zealand for Canada's express entry regime—indicates the new requirements do favour immigrants from English-speaking countries. Researchers in Melbourne and Waterloo, Ontario, looked into why immigrants under the Australian express entry cohort performed better than previous immigrant groups. They discovered not a skills gap, but a language one.[32] The early data shows Canada may be heading in the same direction. The immigration department's numbers on the first six months of express entry selection show that while India maintained its top spot, more citizens from the United Kingdom and Ireland had an invitation to apply than from China.[33]

A third observation about the new system is that a job offer alone can't ensure the best candidates get in, but it is nonetheless the new deciding factor. In the recalibrated points system, candidates can earn a maximum of 1,200 points: 600 for a job offer, and 600 for work experience, education, language and other skills. An analysis by the *Toronto Star* pointed out that someone who scores 649 points can be the weaker choice than someone with 599 points, if the latter earned that total with personal qualities instead of a secured job in Canada.[34] Bottom line: a job offer is the ticket to an invitation to apply.

It is still early days of express entry. It is certain the program will change the immigration landscape, but the scope and variety of consequences are not yet known. At the heart of the drive to marketize Canada's immigration system we find the changing ideal immigrant: Young; reasonably wealthy, educated and skilled; English- or French-speaking; networked; and job-ready or entrepreneurial. Not someone who will be in the middle class, but someone who already is. Someone who perhaps chooses to try out Canada and then maybe leaves for greener pastures.

As always, there are unintended outcomes. The focus on the immediately employable comes at a cost to international students, who many would argue are a better and safer long-term bet, given their Canadian education and credentials. But under the new system, they are not able to compete with someone who has years of experience and a guaranteed job offer.

Other changes are smart and savvy, like the redesigned investor programs, which open immigration to those with start-up businesses or venture capital. Demetrios Papademetriou of the US-based Migration Policy Institute singled out

Canada for its innovative 2015 Immigrant Investor Venture Capital Pilot Program, ahead of the United States, European countries and others who are testing their own programs to attract immigrant capital.[35] Canada's venture capital program aims to attract high-net-worth immigrants to invest in Canada-based start-ups, and demands more of the immigrant than earlier versions, since scrapped for their reputation as cash-for-citizenship deals. The Canadian program is so far one of a kind, and Papademetriou thinks it could be the future of global investor immigration.

Families, Spouses, Children, Parents and Grandparents

Moving beyond the economic stream, the scale of the instrumentalist approach gets clearer. Consider the new rules for sponsoring parents and grandparents, the largest group in the family stream, topping spouses and dependents combined. A longstanding objective of the family stream is "to see that families are reunited in Canada."[36] For many immigrants over the years, the ability to bring an elderly parent or grandparent to Canada meant the end of a tough and extended period of family separation. But backlogs were long, sometimes taking more than a decade to process.

The creation in 2011 of the "super visa" was a masterstroke of inventive public policy. First, it enabled parents and grandparents to come to Canada, not as permanent residents, but as longer-term tourists, for up to two years. Second, it allowed their files to be processed much more quickly because they did not have to go through long and cumbersome security and medical checks. This was warmly greeted by most immigrant communities, who welcomed their parents and grandparents (and the Conservative Party as their friend).

However, it also favoured middle-class families—families whose parents and grandparents could prove that they had no intention of staying permanently in Canada (and therefore of adding costs to an overburdened health care system). They had to prove attachment to their source country, usually through demonstrating ownership of homes or businesses, and they had to buy private health care insurance. It can be argued that low-income immigrants may well need family reunification more urgently than their middle-class counterparts, with parents and grandparents in low-income families acting as informal supports for children. Researchers Naomi Alboim and Karen Cohl concluded that the government's objective appeared to be "excluding those who are perceived as a potential drain on the economy," in spite of their role as economic contributors.[37]

Supporting this conclusion was the new age cut-off for dependent children. Effective in 2014, the Harper government lowered the age of dependents from 22 to under 19. Here is another demonstration of the ideal immigrant. Data show that the economic outcomes of sponsored immigrant children negatively correspond to their age on arrival in Canada. The older the children, the less likely they are to adapt to the Canadian labour market or, in other words, to reinvent themselves. This is, by the way, the government's own and public analysis. A 2013 bulletin on the age change explained, "reducing the age of dependent children would support Canada's immigration priorities by placing more emphasis on younger immigrants, who integrate more rapidly into the labour market and who would spend a greater number of years contributing to the economy."[38]

The Harper government also took on a festering sore in the immigration portfolio, that of spousal sponsorship and instances of fraud, also known as "marriages of convenience." In October 2012, the government announced a new conditional permanent resident stream for sponsored spouses. It required couples to stay in the relationship for a period of two years before permanency is granted. Meant to enforce the rules against fraud, it may well create a different set of problems. There are exceptions for cases of abuse or neglect, but in practice, this could result in victims of spousal abuse needing to stay in relationships for fear of leaving their partners, and so having to leave the country.

Faster, but Fairer?

Speed will be one of the legacies of the Harper era in immigration. Some of the efficiencies deserve high credit, while others are rightly criticized. One of the fixes to the system was working through a large backlog in applications across all streams—economic, family and humanitarian. Backlogs were a growing frustration for immigrants awaiting permanent residence or citizenship, and for those still on the outside such as sponsored family members.

There has been progress. In December 2014, the immigration department reported it had processed more citizenship applications in the previous twelve months than in the two years prior.[39] It set a goal of a twelve-month average processing time for citizenship in 2016, and an even faster processing time for the economic stream's new way of passage. The "express" in express entry will be earned if the department meets its goal of processing candidate applications in six months or less.

Another expression of "faster" is how rapidly changes to the system were introduced. At times, the Conservatives acted with remarkable speed to respond to Canadian concerns, such as the overhaul of the system governing temporary foreign workers. When serious problems surfaced in the spring of 2014, the program was halted and then gutted, a feat of responsive governance. However, it is interesting to note what prompted the overhaul: it was not the treatment of temporary foreign workers, well documented by civil society and the media, but the treatment of Canadians and the misuse of a business model by employers. The issue boiled over when Canadians publicly accused some employers of giving priority status and even their jobs to temporary residents. Changes to the program sought to discourage employers from hiring temporary workers over Canadians.

With speed come sacrifices. And one sacrifice that many critics have accused the government of making is that of fairness. Nowhere does the accusation hold more weight than the refugee file. Canada has two refugee systems, inland and overseas, and the harshest changes occurred in Canada's inland system, primarily through the Balanced Refugee Reform Act (2010) and the Protecting Canada's Immigration System Act (2012). Many of the changes affected not status refugees but claimants: people who may or may not be refugees, but who are nevertheless entitled to certain rights in Canada as their cases are being decided. A few of the harsher policies that affected this group were the removal of federal health care coverage for certain types of claimants, condensed timelines to prepare a claim in Canada and the creation of a so-called safe country list, where nationals of "safe" countries such as Mexico or France face different treatment under Canadian law.

Some "cruel and unusual" changes, in the words of Federal Court Justice Anne Mactavish, have already been struck down.[40] Other changes are now facing or are likely to face constitutional challenges, and still others have been or will be repealed by the Trudeau government.

Accompanying the inland refugee system overhaul was a campaign to steer the refugee narrative in the government's favour. This narrative held that real refugees wait in camps abroad for Canada's protection—they don't show up in Canada and ask for protection, and they don't have money or connections to get them anywhere—and that bogus refugees take advantage of Canada's generosity.

With repetition, the narrative seemed to hold more truth, and the government's language spread to the media too: *bogus, fraudulent, queue jumpers, associated with organized crime.* The narrative oversimplified problems, at times issued outright false information and often couched the government's position in double-speak. Peter Showler, a refugee lawyer and former head of the Immigration and Refugee Board, wrote, "every draconian government measure has been introduced with the word 'generous,'" attempting to make palatable "measures that are distinctly not generous."[41]

Here is a taste of this narrative: Quoted in a 2012 press release to introduce the Protecting Canada's Immigration System Act, aimed partly at countering smuggling, Kenney, then–immigration minister, said, "Canadians take great pride in the generosity and compassion of our immigration and refugee programs. But they have no tolerance for those who abuse our generosity and seek to take unfair advantage of our country."[42] The law allowed the minister to designate a group of people arriving together as an "irregular arrival," creating different treatment for claimants based on how they arrived.

Another: "Canadians can be proud of the fact that Canada has one of the most generous refugee systems in the world," Alexander said in a 2014 press release to name additions to the safe country list.[43]

And in 2014, Alexander gave a speech on the day his government tabled Bill C-24, which would revoke citizenship of dual nationals convicted of certain crimes. He began, "our Government has implemented significant changes to Canada's generous immigration system."[44]

Was there evidence that these harsh policies would work? Not much.

Andrew Griffith called it "policy by anecdote." Stories instead of numbers were used to justify unpopular decisions. Stories aren't always a bad tool. They can humanize the impersonal and distill complex information. But they are best deployed to support evidence, not replace it. With the abolition of the long-form census, Harper's government relied less on science and more on anecdotal evidence. The rise and fall of the temporary foreign worker program is an excellent example. Another is the government's attention to birth tourism and citizenship fraud, despite only weak evidence that either was a real problem.

The same lack of evidence plagued the Conservative Party's attempt to spotlight the niqab during the election campaign, through their decision to appeal a Federal Court ruling that overturned a 2011 ban on wearing the niqab at citizenship ceremonies. The message to Canadians was that Muslim women in niqabs at ceremonies, and in other areas of public life, are a ubiquitous problem. But according to the Federal Court ruling on the case of Zunera Ishaq, who challenged the ban, the policy affected about one hundred women each year.[45] What's more, only two women have decided not to go through with the ceremony because they are required to show their face privately for verification purposes beforehand.[46] It's a tiny number. And yet, in a French-language leaders debate, the niqab got equal airtime with the crisis in Syria, and more time than the Trans-Pacific Partnership, Russia, China and missing and murdered Aboriginal women.[47]

Whither Integration?

As much as the Harper era is signified by changes to who gets into Canada and how, another important and less apparent legacy of its approach is the centralization of federal control over immigration settlement.

Immigration is shared jurisdictionally, with the federal government responsible for selection, citizenship and aspects of integration, and the provincial governments responsible for labour market training and education. It is a messy relationship, with duplication baked into the system. At times, there is music instead of noise. Over the past years, the provinces have become increasingly vocal about their interest in selecting immigrants, and over time, the vehicle for them to do so, the Provincial Nominee Program (PNP), had grown to account for 27 per cent of all economic stream immigrants in 2013.[48] Manitoba in particular has relied on the program, with over 70 per cent of the province's immigrants in 2011 arriving under the PNP.[49] The provinces select nominees who fit their workforce needs, and the federal government approves nearly all applications.

Another innovation in the federal-provincial relationship comes from Alberta. It's a fund that provides micro-loans to skilled immigrants to help pay for Canadian accreditation, upgrading or training in order to find employment in their field. The operations of the Immigrant Access Fund, launched in 2005, are jointly funded by the Province of Alberta and Citizenship and Immigration Canada, but the actual loan funds come entirely from the private sector. It's had a successful run so far, with a repayment rate of 98 per cent.

The Canadian Immigrant Integration Program is another good practice launched under the Conservatives in 2007. A partnership between the federal government, a national network of community colleges and others, the program gives free orientations to immigrants in certain cities abroad before they leave, to help them prepare for life in Canada. Thus they are better prepared to be successful on arrival.

And there's the Foreign Credentials Referral Office (FCRO), established by the Conservatives in 2007, with a goal of redirecting skilled immigrants in Canada to (typically provincial-level) services for credential assessment and recognition. Credential recognition and licensure remains a sticky problem. Too many immigrants are working below their skill level or in fields outside of their training. But the FCRO is a step in the right direction.

The joint relationship between levels of governments on immigration is not always so smooth, and while the Conservatives have introduced innovative programs and reduced inefficiencies, they have also centralized other services and decision-making. In the last few years, all provinces with immigration agreements (with the exception of Quebec) saw these agreements lapse with no promise of renewal. Instead of pooled federal and provincial funds being managed by the provinces, the federal government has chosen to direct its funding to projects and programs directly. While this may no doubt provide more direct accountability, and possibly leave room for greater innovation, it also creates again a lack of coordination, resulting in service gaps on the one hand and duplication on the other.

Citizenship: The Golden Thimble

By and large, most of the changes noted above were quietly approved and implemented with the public being largely disinterested. Not so when it came to the Citizenship

Act (Bill C-24) passed in 2014. And no wonder, because the changes proposed and passed touched every aspect of citizenship. The new bill increased the length of time required to be resident in Canada from three years of physical presence in the country over the last four years to four years of presence in the last six. It required previously exempt age groups to pass language and knowledge tests, increased the application fees significantly and changed the citizenship exam to reflect a more traditional view of Canada. All this in the context of a two- to three-year backlog of citizenship applications. And so, Bill C-24 made citizenship harder to get.

But it also expanded criminal prohibitions to bar applicants for crimes committed abroad. It gave the government the power to revoke the Canadian citizenship of dual citizens convicted of certain crimes. And it eliminated the right of individuals to fight the revocation of citizenship in a hearing in front of a judge, in favour of a written submission with the final decision being made by government officials—thus making citizenship easier to lose.

Bill C-24 effectively created two classes of citizens in Canada: those who are Canadian, whether or not they were born here and possess only Canadian citizenship, and those with eligibility to seek citizenship elsewhere. Amnesty International has said that the law discriminates against dual citizens by suggesting that they are somehow "less Canadian." In response, a number of court challenges have been launched by civil rights groups and constitutional lawyers.

Canada's exceptionalism in immigration, admired the world over, is to a large extent demonstrated by a high uptake on citizenship. Historically, the average figure is around 80 per cent. However, the most recent studies show an alarming dip. Andrew Griffith points out that the percentage of immigrants taking citizenship dropped to 44 per cent among people who arrived in 2007, and to 26 per cent for those who arrived in 2008. Some of this may well be related to the difficulty of citizenship tests, reflected in pass rates down to 86 per cent from 95. The immigration department has disputed these figures, but not that citizenship uptake has overall declined.

Immigration Is Like a Big Beast:
When You Tickle Its Nose, Its Tail Is Bound to Twitch

So what has been Harper's true legacy on Canada's immigration system? It still remains one of the most open and generous in the world. It continues to attract talented immigrants, who line up for entry under the new rules. Canadian immigrants have an expanded voice on the national political stage and it is generally accepted by many Canadians that strong and prosperous immigrants are necessary for a strong and prosperous Canada. Harper has played a significant leadership role in continuing and expanding this narrative.

But there has been an important and not entirely subtle shift. Canada is now more of a headhunter, more eager to look for the right immigrant, the right refugee, the right spouse, the right citizen who fits neatly into a more one-dimensional world. It is the quick wins that interest us the most. We seem to have lost our patience for the long view, and perhaps for nation-building. We miss a great deal when we too narrowly define the right immigrant. A more expansive definition of "right" should be restored so that we continue to bring people from all over the world, young and old, refugees, family members and independents, wealthy and not. Immigration is a plan for the future. As with most investments, it's better to diversify.

One point of continuity will be the instrumentalism of Harper's approach. This will not change. Reform and efficiency are long overdue.

For his critics, the upside of Harper's piecemeal approach to immigration reform is that changes may be more easily undone. There is no new Immigration Act to raze. Instead, his successor faces individual bits and pieces of legislation to remove or refine.

The immigration system inherited by Harper was inflexible and unresponsive to the needs of a modern economy. The one he left is overly tied to short-term demands. The success of the new prime minister in this policy area depends on finding a better balance between preparing for the long term and being adaptable to fast-paced money, goods, ideas and people.

The management of this file affects all of us. Immigration is Canada's nourishment and is responsible for all of us being here except Indigenous peoples. It's what turned this into a great country, and what draws the eyes of an increasingly cosmopolitan world hungry for a model multicultural society. Canada is the standard in diversity. We have to be—our "peace, order and good government" DNA depends on it, and so does our survival as Canadians age and have fewer children. Canada's future, whatever it may hold, will continue to be shaped by who gets in, and how well they do once they arrive.

11

Law and Order in the Harper Years

Tasha Kheiriddin

Good order is the foundation of all things.
—*Edmund Burke*, Reflections on the Revolution in France *(1790)*

The preservation of law and order has long been a central tenet of conservative philosophy. Conservatives believe that one of the primary duties of the state is to protect order, in part by implementing strong laws to deter and punish crime. At the same time, conservatives value liberty. This tension between order and liberty has produced various factions within the conservative movement, from traditionalists to libertarians, who argue over just how much governments should seek to criminalize and/or control citizens' behaviour.

At the same time, for many conservative parties, an emphasis on law and order represents a means of obtaining electoral support. "Tough-on-crime" agendas respond to concerns about the decline of public security, whether real or perceived. Even in a time of falling crime rates for felonies such as murder, the continual emergence of new types of threats, such as cybercrime and terrorist attacks, can create the impression that crime is growing and reaffirm the need for government response. For conservative parties, fighting crime thus represents a political opportunity as well as a philosophical imperative.

The Harper government's tough-on-crime agenda provides a salient example of a political party's twinning of these objectives. In its nine years in office, the Conservative government sought to transform the Canadian justice system through the passage of victims' rights legislation, mandatory minimum laws and anti-terrorist measures. It also overhauled the workings of the Department of Justice, the Public Prosecution Service and Corrections Canada, changed the judicial appointments process and engaged in an unprecedented number of conflicts with the Supreme Court, both in the courtroom and in the media.

These changes have significantly impacted not only individuals involved in the criminal justice system, but the larger relationship between the executive, legislative and judicial branches of government. In assessing the Conservatives' record, one must ask: Is the justice system fairer today than when the Tories took office? Are Canadian streets safer? And were the benefits worth the price?

2006–11: The Rise of "Tough on Crime"

On December 26, 2005, at the height of the holiday shopping season, two Toronto youth gangs crossed paths on Yonge Street three blocks north of the city's iconic Eaton Centre. Five shots rang out. One hit bystander Jane Creba, a fifteen-year-old high school student. Creba died of her injuries, shocking a city that had already seen a record fifty-two gun homicides that year. But her death would also have national implications, because it happened in the middle of a federal election campaign.

According to pollster Darrell Bricker, "When poor Jane Creba was murdered, that's when the numbers shifted." At a presentation given in Ottawa after the 2006 election, Bricker displayed a graph that showed support for the Liberals and Conservatives diverging on the date of the Creba shooting. Bricker attributed the rise in Conservative support to the differing reactions of Prime Minister Paul Martin and Conservative leader Stephen Harper. While Martin spoke of a "culture of exclusion," which may have prompted the crime, Harper said he wanted to punish the criminals. This resonated strongly with voters in Toronto suburbs, who feared the violence that seemed to have engulfed the city over the previous year.[1]

Ten days after the shooting, on January 5, 2006, Conservative leader Stephen Harper announced that if elected he would "completely overhaul" Canada's justice system, by increasing prison sentences as well as devoting more resources to police and border security. On January 13, 2006, the Conservatives released their campaign platform, which devoted more space to justice, law and order than to the economy.[2]

Under the rubric "Stand up for Security," the Conservatives promised that "serious crime means serious time," that they would "get tough with young offenders" and that they would establish a national ombudsman's office for victims. "A Conservative government will protect our communities from crime by insisting on tougher sentences for serious and repeat crime and by tightening parole. We will ensure truth in sentencing and put an end to the Liberal revolving door justice system."[3]

In the same section, the Conservatives promised to repeal "the wasteful long-gun registry," set up by the Liberal administration of Jean Chrétien. In its place, the Conservatives pledged to impose mandatory minimum sentences for gun crimes and reinvest the savings from scrapping the registry into "hiring front-line law enforcement officers and assisting victims of crime."[4]

In 2006 and again in 2008, the Conservatives won a minority government. In both those mandates, they introduced bills designed to implement the justice agenda set out in the 2006 campaign. Due to a lack of support from opposition parties, however, they were unable to pass some measures into law, including their promise to repeal the long-gun registry.

A significant amount of legislation did receive Royal Assent, however, on subjects as diverse as the age of consent and street racing. Chief among them was an omnibus bill called the Tackling Violent Crime Act, Bill C-2. It raised the age of consent for sexual activity from fourteen to sixteen, imposed mandatory minimum sentences for firearms violations, increased penalties for drunk driving and reversed the onus for declaring a person a dangerous offender.

Two laws addressed cybercrime: Bill S-4, the Digital Privacy Act, which criminalized identity theft; and Bill C-28, Fighting Internet and Wireless Spam, designed to protect consumers and businesses against Internet spammers.

The Tackling Auto Theft and Property Crime Act created a separate offence for auto theft, a new offence for tampering with VINs and offences for trafficking in stolen property.

An Act to Amend the Criminal Code (street racing) created five new offences related to street racing.

And an Act to Amend the Criminal Code (conditional sentence of imprisonment) ended the practice of conditional sentences for offences related to serious personal injury, terrorism and gangs.

The Conservatives also acted to defend the rights of crime victims. As promised, they created the office of the Federal Ombudsman for Victims of Crime. Appointed by the government, the ombudsman's role is to "promote access to federal programs and services for victims and addresses complaints from the public about issues relating to victims of crime ... ensure criminal justice personnel and policy-makers are aware of victims' needs, and identify systemic issues that negatively impact victims."[5]

The Tories also passed several pieces of legislation related to victims' rights. They included the Standing Up for Victims of White Collar Crime Act, which imposed mandatory minimum penalties for white-collar crime as well as provisions for restitution to victims, and an Act Protecting Victims from Sexual Offenders, which allowed police services to use a national sex offender database proactively to prevent crimes of a sexual nature.

In a related move, they introduced the Eliminating Entitlements for Prisoners Act, which stripped convicted criminals of the right to receive Old Age Security while in jail.

The latter bill illustrates the symbolic importance to victims of much of the Conservatives' legislation. The bill affected just 400 federal inmates and 600 provincial inmates, who would be impacted only if the provinces signed on, for a total of between $2 million and $10 million a year. But when Senator Judith Seidman spoke in favour of Bill C-31 in the Senate, she cited several victims' advocates, including Sharon Rosenfeldt, president of Victims of Violence, and the mother of one of Clifford Olson's victims, who said: "It's great to see that this government is putting victims and taxpayers first ahead of criminals. The suspension of OAS benefit payments to inmates does just that."[6] Another parent of an Olson victim, Ray King, remarked that "It's the best news I've heard in a long time. I'm quite pleased the government has actually done something."

2011–15: Majority Rule

In 2011, the Conservatives were re-elected with a majority government. This provided the opportunity to implement the full scope of their tough-on-crime agenda, which the Tories proceeded to do within one hundred days of taking office.

The vehicle they chose was Bill C-10, the Safe Streets and Communities Act. It was an omnibus bill, which bundles together a large number of reforms for a single parliamentary vote. This not only expedited the legislation's passage, but reduced debate, and forced the opposition to pronounce themselves on the whole set of reforms, rather than on individual measures.

C-10 wrought many fundamental changes to Canadian criminal law, including

- establishing mandatory minimum sentences for crimes such as drug offences, sex crimes, crimes against children and some violent offences;
- ending the policy of "least-restrictive measures" for inmates;
- eliminating house arrest as a punishment option for many offences where the penalty was two years less a day incarceration; and
- increasing penalties under the Young Offenders Act, and requiring the Crown to consider adult sentences for young offenders convicted of violent crimes.[7]

Of course, not all bills were introduced as omnibus legislation. Some were also passed in a less typical way, as private members' bills. PMBs typically receive less attention and scrutiny than legislation introduced by the government as a whole. They are also less likely to succeed, as they usually represent the pet causes of individual members, which sometimes run counter to party policy, and which have lower priority on a legislative calendar already full of government business.

One such bill was Bill C-309, introduced by Conservative MP Blake Richards, which banned the wearing of masks during a riot or unlawful assembly without a "lawful excuse," such as religious or medical reasons. Doing so now carries a maximum ten-year prison sentence; the bill originally proposed a five-year sentence but the House of Commons justice committee doubled it.[8]

Another was Bill C-26; although it was a government bill, it had started its life as a private member's bill introduced by NDP MP Olivia Chow in 2010.[9] Chow was responding to the case of Toronto Chinatown grocer David Chen, who had been charged with assault and forcible confinement after making a citizen's arrest of a shoplifter the previous year. Chen had apprehended the man after he returned to his store, not while the crime was being committed, a requirement of the previous citizen's arrest law. The so-called "Lucky Moose" bill, named after Chen's grocery store, was then taken up by the Conservatives after the 2011 election. It amended the Criminal Code to allow people to make a citizen's arrest within a "reasonable" period of time after witnessing a crime,[10] a position criticized by civil liberties groups as potentially leading to abuse of power, particularly by private security guards.

The Conservatives also succeeded in abolishing the long-gun registry, as well as making several changes to protect "law-abiding gun owners." These included Bill C-42, which removed several penalties for gun licensing and transportation and provided a six-month grace period for lapsed licences, but required passage of a firearms course to obtain a gun licence. C-42 also enacted mandatory gun prohibitions for violent offenders and perpetrators of domestic assaults.[11]

The pardons process too saw major changes under the Tories, after public outcry in 2010 over the granting of a pardon to former hockey coach and convicted child sex offender Graham James. Changes included instructing the parole board to no longer grant a pardon that could "bring the administration of justice into disrepute;" instituting a three-strikes rule, whereby a person with three convictions for indictable offences with two-year sentences could never be pardoned; and prohibiting a pardon for child sex offenders. As well, the period of time during which a former offender had to remain "crime-free" increased as did the application fee, which rose from $50 to $631. Not surprisingly, the number of requests for pardons has declined—while the changes have created a processing backlog that in 2014 stood at 10,000 applications.[12]

One of the most significant pieces of legislation passed by the Tories was

Bill C-48, the Protecting Canadians by Ending Sentence Discounts for Multiple Murders Act. *Globe and Mail* justice reporter Sean Fine described it as "the biggest psychological break with Canada's recent past" because "It makes life mean life, or very close to it, in a country that has no death penalty and no penalty of life without parole."[13] Previously, in the case of multiple homicides, a killer would ask for parole after twenty-five years. Under the new law, he or she would have to wait until twenty-five years had passed for each murder—which could effectively keep him or her behind bars for life. The bill also eliminated the so-called "faint hope clause," whereby a killer could request parole after fifteen years, instead of twenty-five.

In 2014, the Conservatives passed Bill C-13, the Protecting Canadians from Online Crime Act. It was most notable for establishing the new offence of "non-consensual distribution of intimate images." The law was inspired by the case of Rehtaeh Parsons, a Nova Scotia teenager who committed suicide following the online sharing of photographs of her being sexually assaulted.

The Conservatives also made additional amendments consistent with their emphasis on victims' rights. In 2014 they enacted Bill C-32, the Victims Bill of Rights Act. It amended the Criminal Code to increase the ability of victims to participate in the criminal trial and sentencing processes, eliminated the concept of "spousal immunity" for those asked to testify against a spouse in criminal proceedings under the Canada Evidence Act and amended the Corrections and Conditional Release Act to increase victims' access to information about the offenders who harmed them.[14]

That same year they enacted the Not Criminally Responsible Reform Act, which created a "high risk" designation process for individuals found not criminally responsible for their crimes due to mental illness. The law came in response to public outcry over cases including that of Vince Li, a man with schizophrenia who beheaded and cannibalized a fellow passenger on a Greyhound bus in Alberta, and Allan Schoenborn, a BC man found not criminally responsible for killing his three children.

Those designated as high-risk not criminally responsible (NCR) individuals now faced, among other things, possible extensions by the review board of the period between reviews, the denial of unescorted passes into the community and the condition that escorted passes could only be granted for medical reasons and were subject to sufficient safeguards to protect public safety. The legislation also ensured that victims be specifically considered in such decisions, notified when the accused is discharged and where they intend to reside, and granted non-communication orders with the accused if desired.[15] While many victims' organizations supported it, mental health advocates were concerned that it criminalized and stigmatized the mentally ill. Testifying before the justice committee, J. Paul Federoff of the Canadian Psychiatric Association cautioned, "For the sake of all victims, including potentially your own relatives, I hope you will reconsider the merits of this bill carefully."[16]

Critics and Champions

From its introduction, the Tories' tough-on-crime agenda, and Bill C-10 in particular, came under heavy criticism from many groups involved in the criminal justice system, including lawyers, prisoners' rights advocates and constitutionalists. "The legislation is more based on punishment than prevention, and that's dramatically new," Errol Mendes, a professor of constitutional and international law at the University of Ottawa, told the *National Post.* "It's one of the most punishment-focused [agendas] in Canadian history."[17]

Prisoners' advocates also took a dim view of the reforms. According to Kim Pate, executive director of the Canadian Association of Elizabeth Fry Societies, Canadians have the wrong idea about who's behind bars. "When most people think of who poses a greater risk to them when they're walking down the street or out at night, they tend not to think of poor, indigenous women who have experienced long histories of violence, including, but not exclusively, residential schools. ... They don't tend to think of people with mental health issues, women with mental health issues, or the homeless. They don't think of the people who are increasingly the ones most likely to be in prison."[18]

Corrections Canada workers also opposed the Conservatives' agenda. The Union of Canadian Correctional Officers (UCCO) campaigned against the Tories in the 2015 federal election to protest changes to the corrections system such as double-bunking and overcrowding. They considered these developments dangerous not only for their members, but for society at large. According to UCCO president Kevin Grabowsky, "Not to say that we actually put out a product, but what kind of a product are we going to be putting out, when inmates aren't getting access to a lot of stuff that they once got? That affects Canadians."[19]

Correctional Investigator Howard Sapers, also highly critical of the increase in both double-bunking and solitary confinement, was equally blunt. "It seems to me that if we are going to spend $117,788 each year, on average, to keep a male offender in custody and $211,618 per year for a federally sentenced woman inmate, then we ought to make sure our society is better for it. The sheer magnitude of that kind of investment should get us something more than just incapacitation."[20]

But not everyone saw the changes in a negative light. Dwight Newman, professor of law at the University of Saskatchewan and a visiting fellow at Princeton, says, "People forget how it used to be. They forget how much concern there was about judicial activism, and how much outrage there was about life sentences, or decisions around particular sentences that were nowhere near what the public thought were warranted."[21] Tom Flanagan, a former adviser to Harper and a professor at the University of Calgary, echoed these comments. "When the Conservatives came to power back in 2006, there were problems with parole and very low sentencing numbers. There were really noteworthy examples of people out on parole, who had been convicted and released multiple times. The thrust of tightening up the system made sense."[22]

That tightening also included a heavy emphasis on the right of the victims of crime. Peter MacKay served as minister of justice from 2013 to 2015. When asked what he was proudest of in his government's agenda, he cited the Victim's Bill of Rights. "Too often victims feel helpless and isolated by the justice system. This Bill not only diminishes that sentiment, it also empowers victims. For the first time in Canadian history, victims have a right to information, participation, protection, and restitution."[23]

As previously cited, victims' rights associations were very supportive of the Harper government's changes, as were members of the legal community who worked with victims. Gary Clewley, a former Crown attorney who frequently represents police officers, saw merit in changes such as those brought by Bill C-48. "The Criminal Code is like a pyramid. … It's important that the most serious offences are treated in the most serious fashion. That sets a standard for everything else."[24]

Crime vs. Sociology

Despite the Conservatives' emphasis on victims' rights, however, not all victims felt equally heard. Chief among these were the families of missing and murdered Aboriginal women, an estimated 1,181 of whom had been killed or had disappeared between 1980 and 2012. The manner in which the Conservatives chose to deal with these deaths, as crimes rather than as a "sociological phenomenon," would prove to be one of the undercurrents of the 2015 election campaign. Unfortunately for the Tories, this buttressed the opposition narrative that "tough on crime" was code for "hard of heart"—or worse yet, racist.

Once again, the issue came to national attention due to the callous killing of a young girl. On August 16, 2014, the body of fifteen-year-old Tina Fontaine was pulled from the Red River in Winnipeg. Fontaine, a member of the Sagkeeng First Nation, had only been in the city for a month before she vanished. Her body was found in bag, dumped near the Alexander Docks. As in the Creba case, the murder horrified the nation and prompted calls for government action. In this case, however, these calls were not for tougher gun laws, but for a public inquiry into the murders and disappearances of Aboriginal women over the previous three decades.

But the government either did not understand this difference or chose to ignore it to further push its "tough-on-crime" agenda. While Harper called Fontaine's death "terrible," his reaction to the renewed call for an inquiry was blunt. At a press conference following the teen's death, Harper said, "We should not view this as a sociological phenomenon. We should view it as crime." He reiterated the commitment his government had made to legislation to protect "all Canadians." "I'm not going to comment on the police investigation. … But as the RCMP has said itself in its own study, the vast majority of these cases are addressed and are solved through police investigations, and we'll leave it in their hands."

The comments fell like a bomb into First Nations communities. The executive director of the Native Women's Association of Canada, Claudette Dumont-Smith, called Harper's remarks "insensitive" and "irresponsible," arguing that he didn't seem to be focused on ways to prevent such tragedies. "Why are there so many aboriginal women that are murdered compared to other women. … Doesn't he think that racism and sexism and colonialism play a part in all that?"[25]

Harper's comments were consistent, however, with those he had made in response to the arrest of two men in 2013 accused of plotting to bomb a VIA passenger train. "[T]his is not a time to commit sociology, if I can use an expression," Harper said. "These things are serious threats, global terrorist attacks, people who have agendas of violence that are deep and abiding threats to all the values our society stands for."[26] Earlier that year, Harper had criticized Liberal leader Justin Trudeau for musing about "the root causes of crime" following the Boston Marathon terrorist bombings,[27] saying that this was not the time to "rationalize or make excuses," but to "condemn it categorically, and to the extent you can deal with the perpetrators you deal with them as harshly as possible. And that's what this government would do if ever faced with such actions."

The "criminalization" of issues from murdered Indigenous women to terror attacks provided the Conservatives opportunities to remind Canadians, particularly their own voter base, of their tough-on-crime agenda. It fed the Conservative narrative that they were the only party who could keep Canadians safe from a variety of threats, under the general umbrella of tough-on-crime policies.

Unfortunately for the Tories, in the 2015 election, the opposition "hard-of-heart" narrative appeared to triumph over the government's "tough-on-crime" narrative. It also appears that the Conservatives may have finally realized this after Harper stepped down. A day after her election as Conservative interim leader, Rona Ambrose announced that the Tories would support the new Liberal government's holding of a public inquiry into murdered and missing Aboriginal women. She noted, "at some point that inquiry became so wholly symbolic of this issue that I do understand why the government has decided to go forward with this."[28]

Bad Blood: Conflict between the Legislature, the Executive and the Judiciary

As with their antipathy to "sociology," many policies and changes wrought by the Conservatives ran counter to prevailing views on crime, punishment and rehabilitation. Implementing these changes required the cooperation of the bureaucracy, which caused significant tension between political staff and public servants. This relationship became more adversarial after the Conservatives obtained their majority in 2011.

In the words of a retired DOJ official, who wished to remain anonymous, "They [the minister's office] didn't listen to us; you felt like your advice was irrelevant." According to a source quoted in *Canadian Lawyer* magazine in 2014, "We were in an uncomfortable period because we were debating things that in many instances we hadn't considered for a long time and there is no question there was a skepticism about the courts and an unwillingness to take as an automatic 'well that shuts the argument down, you tell me there's a risk the court may rule against it.'"[29]

In response, a senior Conservative said that "The Department of Justice is far too prone to tell me why I can't so something instead of how I can do it."[30] According to government lawyers, however, the problem was not only the nature of the ministry's requests, but the tight timeframes in which they were requested. This fueled the sense that the tough-on-crime agenda was a political exercise, not a policy one. "It's been a huge failure," said a source inside the justice system, who also would not go on the record. "It hasn't been well done: the courts are consistently striking down provisions, because they were rushed. There's a bad relationship between the Department of Justice and the PMO: they are pulling the strings, not justice. Justice officials do provide good advice by and large, but where it is inconsistent with agenda, it is ignored."

Things got so bad that the government was even sued by one of its own former prosecutors. On September 20, 2015, Edgar Schmidt took the justice minister, the deputy justice minister and the department to court over the government's system of "Charter-proofing" bills.[31] By law, the justice minister must inform Parliament if a proposed law is not consistent with the Charter of Rights and Freedoms. Schmidt assumed this meant that a law is either consistent, or it is not, but his superiors thought otherwise. "Oh, that's not what we do," he says he was told. "We ask ourselves whether there's an argument." Even if the argument has less than a 5 per cent chance of success in the courts, it might still be considered "consistent"—a position that Schmidt says was tantamount to asking him to break the law.[32]

Despite pushback from the bureaucracy, the Conservatives backed down on very few aspects of their tough-on-crime agenda. One exception was Bill C-30, the Lawful Access Legislation, which would have increased government surveillance powers on the Internet. It died on the order paper after Public Safety Minister Vic Toews' infamous pronouncement that critics "can either stand with us or with the child pornographers," which resulted in online personal attacks against Toews and a sense that the Conservatives had crossed the line by endorsing the idea of warrantless surveillance.[33]

Philosophically, the tough-on-crime agenda was consistent with the party's view that the public would be better protected, and victims' interests better served, by a justice system that emphasized truth in sentencing and restitution, rather than judicial discretion and rehabilitation. But there were also other, more political reasons. Regardless of whether it attained its policy objectives, getting tough on crime also meant getting votes—and raising funds.

In all three successful Conservative election campaigns between 2006 and 2011, justice issues figured prominently in Conservative campaign literature. The year 2015 was no exception: Toronto MP Roxanne James went so far as to send a fund-raising email to constituents entitled "Murderers in your neighborhood?", claiming that only a re-elected Conservative government could keep Canadians safe.[34] Even when Tory initiatives were defeated by the courts, this provided an opportunity for the Conservatives to send supporters similar missives decrying the decisions, emphasizing the importance of re-electing a Conservative government and solic-iting contributions to the party's war chest.

Indeed, over their nine years in office, the Conservatives picked an unprece-dented number of fights with the judiciary. The apex of animosity came in March 2014, when the Supreme Court rejected Harper's appointment of lawyer Marc Nadon to fill the vacancy left by the retirement of Quebec Justice Morris Fish. The high court deemed Nadon ineligible to sit on the bench because he was not a member of the Quebec Bar, as per the Supreme Court of Canada Act. According to author John Ibbitson, this was the "boiling point" for the prime minister. "As far as Harper was concerned, the court under [Chief Justice Beverley] McLachlin had resolved to dismantle as much of his government's agenda as it could get away with," he wrote in his recent biography, *Stephen Harper*. "Staff talked the prime minister down from launching a full, public assault on the impartiality of the court, but he still went pretty far."[35]

That he went "pretty far" was an understatement. Following the court's rejection of the Nadon appointment, the PMO made public a phone call by McLachlin to Harper concerning potential problems with appointing a justice who was not a member of the Quebec Bar. The government made it appear as though the chief justice was attempting to interfere in the appointment, when in reality she had made the call in response to a list of several individuals, well before Nadon was selected. McLachlin was cleared of any wrongdoing or inappropriate behaviour by the International Commission of Jurists, an organization based in Geneva, which condemned the government's slight of the chief justice and urged Harper to apologize.[36] Needless to say, he did not.

Apart from the kerfuffle over the Nadon appointments, the Supreme Court struck down a plethora of laws and regulations and stymied the Harper government's attempts at legal reform.

These included:

- mandatory minimum sentences of one year for drug crimes under Bill C-10, declared unconstitutional on April 15, 2016;
- legislation that mandated that persons denied bail due to previous convictions not receive credit for time served, revoked on April 15, 2016;
- mandatory minimums for handgun possession under Bill C-10, tossed out on April 14, 2015;
- the Criminal Court prohibition on doctor-assisted suicide, overturned on February 6, 2015 (Parliament passed a bill in June 2016 permitting in certain circumstances physician-assisted death);
- the government's Senate reference that proposed unilaterally reforming or abolishing the Red Chamber, rejected on April 25, 2014; such amendments, the court ruled, required provincial consent;
- the Truth in Sentencing Act, which eliminated double credit for time served before sentencing, repudiated on April 11, 2014; the Supreme Court ruled that judges can allocate one and a half days' credit, which they had already started to do;
- Criminal Court prohibitions against brothels, streetwalking and living off the avails of prostitution, struck down on December 20, 2013; the government was given a year to enact a new law; and
- the denial of a renewed exemption to Vancouver's InSite safe-injection site, which forced its closure, overturned on September 30, 2011.

In the long term, Harper's combative approach to the high court may have unintentionally helped the court strengthen its position and secure it from future attempts at interference by the legislature. According to Eugene Meehan, Q.C., a lawyer at Supreme Advocacy LLP in Ottawa, and former executive legal officer to the Supreme Court of Canada, "With the challenge to Justice Nadon's appointment, the SCC seized the opportunity to cement its own power by holding that as a court it had constitutional status. Accordingly, the federal government could not make any substantive changes to the Supreme Court of Canada without unanimous consent of Parliament and the provincial legislatures."[37]

The War on Judicial Activism

The Conservatives didn't just have trouble with the Supreme Court, however. Concomitant with their tough-on-crime agenda was a deeply held antipathy toward activist judges. Philosophically, the Conservatives believed that law should be made by an elected Parliament, not an unelected judiciary. Judges were seen to be usurping the power of Parliament by overturning legislation, most of the time through a liberal interpretation of the Charter of Rights and Freedoms. This was seen as compromising the government's ability to enact a more right-of-centre agenda.

One of the means of sustaining Charter challenges was the Court Challenges Program of Canada, a federal program that granted money to groups wishing to contest government legislation. An examination of the granting history showed that most of the money went to organizations on the political left.[38] After taking office in 2006, the Conservatives abolished the program, reinstating funding only for minority language challenges after complaints from the commissioner of official languages. Similarly, the Conservatives scrapped the Law Reform Commission of Canada, a body whose task was to propose possible legislative changes, which was seen as duplicating the work of government in a generally un-conservative way.

Consistent with this desire to rein in an activist judiciary, many of the tough-on-crime bills were designed to constrain the powers of judges. These included laws on mandatory minimums, which took sentencing power away from judges and limited any ability to be "soft on crime." Another was the requirement to impose a "victim surcharge" of 15 per cent of any fine levied, or a flat amount of $100 or $200 for each offence, regardless of any mitigating factors. According to law professor Lisa Kerr, "Previously, judges could waive the (smaller) victim surcharge if it was clear that the offender was unable to pay or payment would clearly harm others (such as family members whom the offender was supporting). ... But the victim surcharge does not go directly to a victim and victim surcharges apply even when there is no identifiable victim (such as in impaired driving cases or in marijuana cultivation cases)."[39]

Not surprisingly, judges rebelled. A *Globe and Mail* investigation in 2015 found that judges in several provinces refused to force victims to pay the surcharges. "In Edmonton and Vancouver, some judges allowed 50 or even 99 years to pay. In Montreal, a judge found a way to make the surcharge $1.50. An Ottawa judge ruled the law unconstitutional without even giving the government a chance to defend it."[40]

The solution for the government was not to pass tougher laws, but to change the people in charge of enforcing them. And that change lay within the judicial appointment process. As far back as 2007, Harper had told the House of Commons, "We want to make sure that we are bringing forward laws to make sure we crack down on crime and make our streets and communities safer. We want to make sure that our selection of judges is in correspondence with those objectives."[41]

At the head of the legal system sat the Supreme Court of Canada. Though the prime minister retained the power to appoint Supreme Court judges, as directed by the Constitution, the Conservatives opened up the appointments process. They instituted parliamentary hearings and the prime minister nominated several candidates who appeared more favourable to the government's agenda. These included not only the ill-fated Nadon, who had written a dissenting opinion supporting Ottawa's position in a terrorist case, but Alberta judge Russell Brown, who blogged that he hoped Harper had a "hidden agenda" and described Justin Trudeau as "unspeakably awful."[42]

Overall, Harper made eight appointments to the Court. The only members still present from when he took office in 2006 were Chief Justice Beverley McLachlin and Ontario judge Rosalie Abella. Yet the Court in 2015 can hardly be described as small-c conservative; most observers consider it as activist as it has ever been. According to Flanagan, Harper "didn't do the job well of changing the complexion of the judiciary. The only one with a reputation as a conservative was Russ Brown." When asked why Harper did not appoint more overtly conservative judges, Flanagan responded that "He thought he would get political credit for middle of the road choices. Personally, I think it would have been better to appoint people whose philosophy he liked."[43]

That said, the Conservatives have had an impact on the judiciary away from the spotlight of the Supremes. They achieved this in part by changing the appointments process for federal courts. Under previous administrations, judges were appointed on the recommendation of committees formed of eminent minds nominated by provincial bar associations and the legal community. The Conservatives saw this as entrenching an elitist and liberal bias. Their "Judicial Appointment Committees" included both lawyers and non-lawyers, representing different interests and points of view, including that of law enforcement.

These committees could furthermore only offer one of two verdicts: recommended, or not recommended. Previously, applications could be labelled "highly recommended," "recommended" or neither. While this change might seem small, Newman says it was significant. "The 'highly qualified' designation was seen as a means of encouraging particular appointments. Under the new system committees provided a review but the decision rested ultimately in the government's hands."[44]

While it is impossible to say who would have been appointed over the past nine years had a different party been in power, it is fair to guess that some appointments would not have been made under the previous Liberal government. These include a number of judges opposed to extending gay rights through the Charter, such as

Grant Huscroft, newly appointed to the Ontario Court of Appeal in 2015. And then there is Vic Toews, elevated to the Manitoba bench a mere eight months following his retirement from politics. As pointed out by writer Christie Blatchford, the convention is that one waits two years after a person leaves government[45]—unless, apparently, that person is Harper's former justice minister.

Process and Practice

While civil servants criticized many of the government's reforms, not all reforms were poorly received. One that was welcomed was a change to the way crimes are prosecuted by the federal Public Prosecution Service. The irony is that this may not have been what the government intended.

In 2006, one of the major planks of the Conservative platform, in addition to crime and the economy, was accountability. The Liberal Party was reeling under the effects of the sponsorship scandal, which had seen $100 million in public money given to Liberal-friendly advertising firms for little or no work, with a portion allegedly kicked back to the party in the form of donations. Many analysts consider ethics, or the lack thereof, to have been the major factor in the Liberals' fall from power and the Conservatives' consequent ascendancy.

Shortly after taking office, the Conservatives introduced the Federal Accountability Act. While the Act was designed to increase transparency and prevent political corruption, it also had the effect of separating the Public Prosecution Service of Canada (PPSC), formerly the Federal Prosecution Service (FPS), from the Department of Justice. The 500 prosecutors of the PPSC are tasked with prosecuting crimes that constitute offences under federal statutes, including those involving "drugs, organized crime, terrorism, tax law, money laundering and proceeds of crime, crimes against humanity and war crimes, Criminal Code offences in the territories, and federal regulatory offences."[46] The Conservatives subsequently added fraud offences under the Financial Administration Act and offences under the Canada Elections Act to that list. Unlike the FPS, however, which was part of the Department of Justice, the PPSC is an independent organization, reporting to Parliament through the Attorney General of Canada.

According to sources within the PPSC, this was the result of a misperception by the Conservatives that offences involving public officials needed to be handled at arm's length from government. In fact, such offences were prosecuted by provincial attorneys general, not the federal attorney general, which meant there was no need to make the PPSC an arm's length body. One source stated that the change was a result of a "failure to consult with people who really know how the justice system works," something that would unfortunately appear as a running theme throughout the Conservatives' relationship with the administration of justice.

Despite the unsound basis for the change, according to a source within the PPSC, "the result was great." While the federal attorney general could still intervene in a public prosecution, under the act such interference would be made public in the *Gazette*, which had not been the case before. Perhaps not surprisingly, and despite the politically sensitive nature of some prosecutions, such as the robocalls affair, such interference had not happened previously. "Anybody who says 'the prosecutor stayed this case because he was a friend of the Prime Minister'—well no, there would be a record of [such an action]. We get accused of this, such as in the [alleged drunk driving] case of Rahim Jaffer. But that matter wasn't our prosecution: it was done by the government of Ontario, and it had huge Charter problems, it was simply not prosecutable." The prosecution service wound up with greater independence, something the Conservatives may not have intended.

The Fight against Terrorism

As with much of the Conservatives' criminal justice agenda, the fight against terrorist crime accelerated after the Conservatives won their majority in May 2011. According to a public service source close to the Department of Justice, political staff told justice officials, "we're gonna do this [introduce new legislation] and do it in three weeks." The department was less than enthused. The government's Combating Terrorism Act, Bill C-9, was in fact introduced in 2012 and passed in 2013. It allowed police to preventatively arrest persons suspected of engaging in terrorist activities, granted courts the power to hold investigative hearings in secret and imposed a penalty of ten to fourteen years in prison for persons found guilty of leaving or attempting to leave Canada to commit terrorist acts.

Things did speed up after the assault on Ottawa by Islamic radical Michael Zehaf-Bibeau, however. On October 22, 2014, Zehaf-Bibeau gunned down Corporal Nathan Cirillo, who was guarding the National War Memorial, before storming Parliament, where he was killed after injuring a guard. The attack came just days after another terror-related attack in Quebec City, in which Martin Rouleau, a recent convert to Islam who had been on a terror watch list, had rammed his car into two members of the Canadian military, killing one of them and injuring the other.

The two incidents brought the fear of terrorism to Canadians' doorstep. In response the government upped the legislative ante and tightened the timeframe. As one of the sources within the PPSC put it, "After Zehaf-Bibeau, everything changed. Justice officials were told to fix things and come up with proposals in five weeks. The result was that important issues got dropped because they were too difficult."

One example was the "intelligence to evidence problem." As CSIS is involved in virtually every terrorist case, tension exists between protecting secret information and engaging the police so that terrorists are prosecuted. People give CSIS information on the basis that it will be secret, but the criminal justice system is antithetical to secrets because it needs evidence so as not to wrongfully convict people. The result is that either CSIS has information and doesn't share it, or it is forced to share information it shouldn't be forced to share. Navigating this interface is so tricky that it simply wasn't included in Bill C-51. "The department was told to come up with options. One came up but never made it into the bill, because there were only five weeks to put it together. C-51 was not well done because someone set a hard deadline for political reasons."

Another example of the government's focus on terrorism-as-crime was the case of Omar Khadr. Khadr, a Canadian citizen, was convicted of throwing a grenade which killed US sergeant first class Christopher Speer in Afghanistan in 2002. Khadr was fifteen years old at the time, and was seriously wounded in the attack. Nevertheless, he was prosecuted as an adult under US military law for war crimes, to which he confessed, and sent to prison at Guantanamo, Cuba. In 2012 Khadr was returned to Canada to serve the remainder of his sentence, but today he has been free on bail since May 2015 and is appealing his conviction in a US court.

Throughout Khadr's imprisonment, the Harper government consistently opposed his return to Canada and release on bail, characterizing him as an unrepentant killer and a threat to Canadian society. In July 2015, Speer's widow and another soldier partially blinded by the grenade thrown by Khadr won a US$134 million lawsuit against Khadr;[47] Khadr himself is suing the Canadian government for $20 million in damages related to his case.

Khadr's supporters accuse the Harper government of persecuting him to bolster its fight against terrorism. Since his release on bail, Khadr has made several media appearances that appear to contradict the image of a terrorist who hates the West. Nevertheless, a day after his release, Harper maintained the government's position, expressing support for the victims of Khadr's attack. "Mr. Khadr, as we all know, plead guilty to very grave crimes, including murder. At this time our thoughts and prayers are with the family of Sgt. Christopher Speer."[48]

The Conservatives also took a hard line on terrorism in Bill C-24, which amended the criminal code to allow government to revoke the Canadian citizenship of dual citizens convicted of terrorism offences. The issue surfaced during the 2015 election campaign, when several persons affected by the law launched constitutional challenges against it. The Liberals have promised to scrap the law once in office.

Assessment
Is the Canadian justice system fairer today than when the Conservatives took office?

The answer to the question depends on one's view of "fairness," which is, of course, subjective. With regard to criminal law, one person may say that mandatory minimum sentences are fair because that is the penalty prescribed by law for the worst offences, regardless of the circumstances in which they were committed. Another person may counter that removing discretion from judges in sentencing is unfair because it treats all criminals the same, regardless of life experiences, and fails to account for any remorse on the part of the criminal.

According to Newman, "Part of what is at stake is the denunciation of offences. That means offering sentences that respond to crimes, whether or not those prove to achieve deterrence function. When people call for 'evidence based' decision-making, they forget that sometimes there are values at stake that aren't easily part of any so-called evidence."[49]

Those values include the sense that punishment should fit the crime, and that lighter sentences such as house arrest constitute an insult to the community and the victims of crime. A government press release announcing the reintroduction of a bill proposing the end of house arrest for violent crimes quoted Heidi Illingworth, executive director of the Canadian Resource Centre for Victims of Crime: "Victims feel distress when they see offenders, not only those responsible for their own victimization, but also those who commit other serious crimes, sentenced to 'house arrest.'"[50]

Of all the measures the Conservatives have implemented, the most significant change may be the emphasis on increasing victims' rights while reducing those of criminals. This involves not only increased measures for restitution, passage of the Victims' Bill of Rights and creation of the ombudsman's office, but punitive measures against wrongdoers. Some of these are almost symbolic, such as removing prisoners' OAS benefits. Some are more tangible, such as efforts to end the "Club Fed" atmosphere the government claimed existed in certain jails by removing prisoners' privileges. For example, the government shut down six prison farms across Canada and eliminated a pilot project for safe prisoner tattooing.

In former justice minister Peter MacKay's view, fairness was about "protecting the innocent, holding offenders accountable for their crimes, and supporting victims. … We restored confidence in our justice system by eliminating sentences which fail to capture the gravity of the crime. As a result, our justice system offers more protection to victims, families of victims, witnesses, and the general public."[51]

Whether one defines the changes as fairer or does not, there is no question that today there is more attention paid to the rights of victims, and less paid to the rights of criminals, than when the Conservatives took office.

Criminologists argue, however, that while double-bunking inmates and providing fewer recreation or rehabilitation programs may make life meaner on the inside, they won't necessarily make things better on the outside once the inmates in question return to society. In 2011, Correctional Investigator Howard Sapers delivered a scathing indictment of the increasing practice of double-bunking. "Putting two inmates in a single cell means an inevitable loss of privacy and dignity, and increases the potential for tension and violence. It is a practice that is contrary to staff and inmate safety. Crowding is linked to higher incidences of violence, prison volatility and unrest, as well as the spread of infectious diseases."[52] These concerns are echoed by corrections officers, and even the convicted themselves. This raises a concern about the second objective of the tough-on-crime agenda: increasing public safety.

Was Canada Safer in 2015 than in 2006?

One of the main goals of the tough-on-crime agenda, as well as of the anti-terrorism agenda, was to increase public safety. The most rudimentary basis for assessment are Statistics Canada's crime statistics, which have been compiled since 1961.

According to StatsCan's most recent figures, crime rates have been falling in Canada for the past twenty years (figure 11.1). Police-reported crime peaked at just over 10,000 crimes per 100,000 population in 1992 and has declined steadily ever since, to just over 5,000 crimes per 100,000 population in 2013. The period of 2002–3 saw a small uptick of several hundred crimes per 10,000 population before the rate declined again.[53]

Fig. 11.1
Police-reported Crime Rate, Canada, 1962–2013

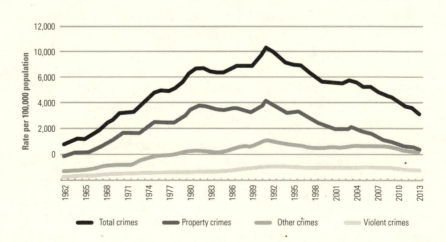

The rate of homicide and attempted murder has declined as well, though not as steadily as the overall crime rate (figure 11.2). Between 1992 and 2013, the homicide rate fell from 2.7 to 1.5 per 100,000 population. However, from 2003 to 2005 it briefly rose from 1.7 to just over 2.0. The attempted murder rate also increased during this time, from 2.1 to 2.6.[54] Both rates began falling again in 2006.

Figure 11.2

Homicides and Attempted Murders, Canada, 1962–2013

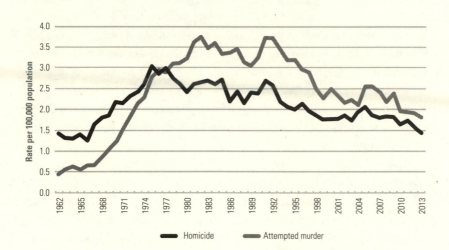

While these percentages are small, in real terms, they represented an increase of 12 per cent in the homicide rate from 2003 to 2004,[55] and 4 per cent from 2004 to 2005.[56] That translated into 73 more murders in 2004 and 34 the following year. And unlike robbery or simple assault, homicide is a crime that makes front-page news. The attention paid to violent crime such as murder and attempted murder can explain the sense, by the election of 2005–6, that crime was once again surging in Canada.

Gun use also exacerbated this fear. Toronto called 2005 "the year of the gun," due to the year-over-year increase in the number of murders and attempted murders involving firearms. But the phenomenon was not unique to Toronto: in Canada in 2005, 222 people were killed by firearms, 49 more than the previous year.[57]

So even though crime rates declined overall during this period, and long-term trends showed crime decreasing, the average citizen could not be faulted for fearing that crime was once again on the rise in Canada. No one knew if the increases in the murder and attempted murder rates were a blip, or whether they were going to keep growing. In 2006, the Conservatives were responding to a real issue and sense in the population that something had to be done about this problem.

"[They] try to pacify Canadians with statistics," Harper said to a party gathering in January 2008. "Your personal experiences and impressions are wrong, they say; crime is really not a problem. These apologists remind me of the scene from the *Wizard of Oz* when the wizard says, 'Pay no attention to that man behind the curtain.'"[58]

Crime statistics also do not necessarily tell the whole story. In a research paper published in 2011, criminologist Scott Newark argued that StatsCan's methods of reporting and analyzing crime data are flawed because they do not report who is committing what kinds of crimes, fail to report the rate of recidivism to assess the impact of rehabilitation and deterrence initiatives, and most importantly, use a model that minimizes the volume of crime committed, by counting incidents as opposed to violations.[59] A gun killing by a gang member, for example, could involve multiple violations, including illegal possession of a firearm, first degree murder and conspiracy to commit murder. But it would only be counted as one "incident" in the database.

Thus, as Newark pointed out, even though an incident may involve multiple crimes and multiple victims, Statistics Canada reports only a single offence. This might be logical in circumstances where the multiple counts are interrelated, such a charge of impaired driving plus a refusal to undergo a blood alcohol test. But, he says, "it is inappropriate and misleading to use it when separate and distinct crimes have been committed for which the individual can be prosecuted and convicted. The result from the current methodology would appear to underreport crime."[60]

So when we ask whether the Conservatives' tough-on-crime reforms reduced the number of crimes committed, the answer is that based on the available evidence, it is impossible to say. While the official overall crime rate declined after the Tories took office, it did not do so more quickly than in the previous decade. Within that rate, however, certain types of offences, such as sexual offences against children, grew in number, while others dropped.

Furthermore, while the Tories made several changes between 2006 and 2011, the majority of their tough-on-crime legislation was only passed after they obtained their majority in 2011. Several of those measures have been overturned by the courts, reducing the scope of their impact. Others are likely to be reversed by the new Liberal government through legislative means. The impact of changes to sentencing laws and mandatory minimums will be impossible to measure if they are undone before they have the chance to have long-term effects.

The Conservatives' policies must also be placed into context. Crime rates are tied to a variety of socio-economic and demographic factors, including age.

Criminologists have consistently found that younger populations commit more crime; recent statistics published by the Federal Bureau of Investigation in the United States show the age of "peak age-crime involvement" to be younger than 25, and the median age for most crimes to be lower than 30.[61] This matters in the Canadian context due to the size of its baby boomer cohort—persons born between 1946 and 1965—relative to the general population.

In 1992, the year that crime began declining in Canada, the youngest of its eight million baby boomers turned twenty-seven. In fact, by that year, the vast majority of them were in their late thirties or early forties—not only a time when they would be less likely to commit crime, but an age at which criminals tend to turn to less-violent illegal activity, such as white collar crime and fraud.[62] Over the past two decades, Canada has witnessed an increase in these types of crime, as well as cybercrime, relative to violent crime.

The only way to measure the specific impact of the Conservatives' policies on the crime rate would be a regression analysis, factoring out variables of age and socio-economic conditions, to determine whether the decline was steeper or not once these variables were removed. It would also take into account the issues raised by Newark, namely multiple offences being reported as one incident, as well as concentrations of crime by age, community and type. Only then could a true picture of the impact of tough-on-crime policies on public safety, such as crime reduction, be accurately determined.

Did Taxpayers Get Value for Money?
While fairness and the impact on safety can be disputed, one thing cannot: under the Conservatives' watch, the incarceration rate greatly increased. And with that, so did its cost to taxpayers.

In 2011, Correctional Service Canada estimated that the Conservatives' existing and proposed legislative changes would translate into a need for 2,700 new prison spaces at a cost of $2 billion. Then–parliamentary budget officer Kevin Page pegged that number at 4,200 prisoners, with a total price tag of $5 billion. This would have the effect of increasing annual prison costs to $9.3 billion by 2015–2016.[63]

An example of how the changes trickled down to the provinces is that of house arrest. According to estimates from the Parliamentary Budget Office, in a typical year, the change would affect 4,500 people trying to avoid jail, half of whom would opt for trial. Six hundred and fifty of those would likely be acquitted; as for those sent to jail, the cost of their incarceration would be $41,000 a year, versus $2,600 a year to keep them at home. The total bill for the provinces would be $135 million, and $8 million for the federal government,[64] because most of the offences for which house arrest was previously imposed were for two years less a day, which would land the offender in a provincial institution.

When it comes to value for money, therefore, it is not clear whether the Conservatives delivered. Canadian streets are statistically safer than in 2006, at least according to Statistics Canada, but they might have been so regardless of the tough-on-crime agenda, and perhaps at a lower cost than $10 billion a year. Additionally, spending the tough-on-crime money on alternative initiatives linked to crime reduction, such as rehabilitative programs or community crime prevention, might have had, and might have continued to have, a greater effect than increased incarceration.

This is the experience of many American jurisdictions, which experimented with tough-on-crime policies only to reverse them when it became evident that they were not deterring crime or increasing public safety. "You will spend billions and billions and billions on locking people up," Texas judge John Creuzot of the Dallas County Court told CBC News. "And there will come a point in time where the public says, 'Enough!' And you'll wind up letting them out."[65]

Not everyone accepts the comparison with the US experience, however. As Flanagan points out, "This comparison needs to be made with great care. The prison population in the US is many times larger per capita than in Canada. Even after various changes, Canada's rate of incarceration is nowhere near the American one. The debate concludes that it has gone too far in the US, but their levels are several times higher than ours. There is a tendency to compare with the US and conclude exactly what Americans have, but there really is no comparison."[66]

Conclusion

If the Conservatives' objective was to increase safety by reducing the crime rate, until a detailed study is done, it is impossible to determine whether this objective was achieved. If their objective was to increase fairness, as defined by augmenting victims' rights and making punishment "fit the crime," they did accomplish this but at a significant cost to taxpayers. Those who define "fairness" differently, however, preferring a more rehabilitative and less punitive approach to justice, will conclude that the government's agenda failed to increase fairness in the system, while unacceptably increasing its costs.

Based on the results of the last election, it is clear that most voters did not share the government's vision, which includes its policies on crime. Key differences on justice issues, such as the holding of a public inquiry on murdered and missing Aboriginal women, as well as the government's appeal of the niqab decision (since dropped by the Liberal government of Justin Trudeau) and proposed criminalization of "barbaric cultural practices," gave many the impression that the

Conservatives were using crime as a wedge issue, instead of focusing on the best interests of Canadians. This ultimately backfired, and the opposition "hard-of-heart" narrative won out over the Tories' "tough-on-crime" storyline. Unfortunately for the Conservatives, the result is a Liberal government bent on undoing much, if not most, of their agenda.

While it might be tempting for the Liberals to swing the pendulum far away from "tough on crime" for political reasons, they might wish to resist this urge and consult all groups who have a stake in the criminal justice system, including victims, before making substantive changes. While critics of the tough-on-crime agenda decried it as mean-spirited, punitive and even "un-Canadian," this should not be the basis on which it is judged.

Instead, the Liberals and future governments should take the evidence-based approach that they promised in all spheres of government. One possibility is a value-for-money audit, to determine if the Conservatives' changes did or did not increase public safety, and if so, whether they were worth the price paid. Though the Liberals should re-inject a measure of the "sociology" so narrow-mindedly decried by the Conservatives, and work to prevent the causes of crime, they should also take pains to maintain deterrence, which is not just the likelihood of getting caught, but fear of being punished for one's actions. While rehabilitation should always be attempted, it is not a cure-all, nor is it, unfortunately, always possible.

Finally, with regard to victims, the new government should strive to ensure that positive advances made under the previous administration are maintained, whatever changes are made. Contrary to the belief of the previous government, it is possible to respect the rights of victims, the accused and the convicted. To say that the latter groups have no rights is short-sighted and below the dignity of a country that values freedom and the rule of law. One can only hope that the new government strikes a balance that preserves the advances made by the previous one, while addressing its shortcomings.

12

Stephen Harper and Indigenous Peoples

Cynthia Wesley-Esquimaux

We also have no history of colonialism. So we have all of the things that many people admire about the great powers but none of the things that threaten or bother them.

—*Stephen Harper, Pittsburgh, September 2009*

As a new government takes over the Crown's fiduciary responsibility for the well-being of First Nations in Canada, it is important to understand what happened to Indigenous affairs under Stephen Harper. But first, a brief review of key government responsibilities is in order.

Formally, Canada is a constitutional monarchy with Elizabeth II, Queen of Canada, as the head of state. In practice, Canada is governed by Parliament and by provisions of the Constitution. Section 35 of the Canadian Constitution, patriated in 1982, recognizes and affirms Aboriginal rights, which include generic and specific Aboriginal rights.

As Osgoode Hall law professor Brian Slattery has explained, generic rights are held by all Aboriginal peoples across Canada and include

- rights to the land (Aboriginal title);
- rights to subsistence resources and activities;
- the right to self-determination and self-government;

- the right to practise one's own culture and customs including language and religion, sometimes referred to as the right of "cultural integrity;" and
- the right to enter into treaties.

Specific rights, on the other hand, are rights held by a specific Aboriginal group or band. These rights may be recognized in treaties or be defined as the result of court decisions.[1]

The Cabinet, a committee of the Queen's Privy Council, exercises the queen's executive authority over Canada through the monarch's representative, the governor general. The Queen and the viceroy are apolitical and their actions tend to be seen as mostly ceremonial. They are largely invisible in Canadian politics and in matters related to governing this country. They appear, however, with the force of law whenever Canada's colonial past, present and future are discussed. As Leonard Rotman noted, "The Canadian Crown's fiduciary duty to First Nations is entrenched in Canadian Aboriginal rights jurisprudence."[2] This is something that is keenly understood by Indigenous peoples, as a "nation-to-nation relationship ... and falling within the domain of international law."[3]

The relationship between First Nations in Canada and the Crown is directed by domestic law, overseen and administered in the Canadian government by the Department of Aboriginal Affairs and Northern Development (now called Indigenous Affairs and Northern Development). By its own admission, Harper's government was aware that "the courts understand treaties between the Crown and Aboriginal people to be solemn agreements that set out promises, obligations and benefits for both parties."[4]

So, how successful was Harper in "overseeing the Crown's fiduciary responsibility" and understanding the treaties as "the solemn agreements" designed to benefit Indigenous peoples in Canada? Was he respectful of the Canadian Constitution (Section 35(1) in particular) and its directives in regard to rights Indigenous peoples continue to express and exercise in Canada? How did Harper use the powers of the Crown, whose responsibility it is to look after the well-being of Indigenous peoples, and from whom it took the land on which Canada now stands?

Before Harper

When Stephen Harper spoke of Canada's colonial past to the Canada-UK Chamber of Commerce that first summer in power, arguing that "the actions of the British Empire were largely benign and occasionally brilliant,"[5] he highlighted and articulated a particular tone-deafness and lack of sensitivity to Indigenous Canada that would characterize his government over the decade in which his party held sway.

In reality, the colonial history of Canada is long, tragic and terrifying. It is beyond the scope of this chapter to trace the contributions of each prime minister to the colonial record of this country, but it's worth noting the legacy of Canada's first prime minister, Sir John A. Macdonald, which remains relevant today as the impact of assimilationist policies still reverberate inside First Nations communities. James Daschuk, professor of kinesiology and health studies at the University of Regina and author of the 2014 book *Clearing the Plains: Disease, Politics of Starvation and the Loss of Aboriginal Life,* found the directives Macdonald sent to federal officials telling them to deny food to the Indigenous people. Throughout his book, Dashuk identified public statements in which Macdonald boasted about keeping the Indigenous population "on the verge of actual starvation"[6] to save government funds.

Macdonald also told the House of Commons in 1883 that residential schools would be one of the main weapons used to eliminate "savages" before they became incorrigible: "When the school is on the reserve the child lives with its parents, who are savages, he is surrounded by savages, and though he may learn to read and write his habits and training and mode of thought are Indian."[7] This passage from the Truth and Reconciliation Commission's report in 2015 also described how residential school student were viewed: "He is simply a savage that can read and write." This policy persisted into the twentieth century and was supported by church leaders of all the Christian denominations running residential schools.[8]

Prime Minister Pierre Trudeau and Minister of Indian Affairs Jean Chrétien responded to the dark history that preceded them by introducing the notorious white paper of 1969, asking to end the special legal relationship between Aboriginal peoples and Canada and to dismantle the Indian Act. They had decided Indians should not be "citizens plus" as the anthropologist Harry Hawthorn's famous 1967 report had suggested,[9] but rather that a "just society" would integrate and accommodate Indigenous peoples as equals without the need for special rights. Their misguided attempt to create a process of integration had the more lasting effect of politicizing Indigenous communities and awakening what had become a sleeping giant of discontent and simmering rage against failed government policy. "In spite of all government attempts to convince Indians to accept the white paper, including additional monies to support their growing political organizations, their efforts failed. They failed, because Indians understood that the path outlined by the Department of Indian Affairs would lead directly to cultural genocide," Harold Cardinal said in his 1969 response, *The Unjust Society.* "We will not walk this path."

Twenty years later, Chrétien would be responsible as prime minister for responding to the Royal Commission on Aboriginal Peoples' final report and its 440 recommendations. Indian Affairs Minister Jane Stewart would issue on behalf of the government a Statement of Reconciliation, part of a new initiative called Gathering Strength—Canada's Aboriginal Action Plan. This plan featured the announcement of the Aboriginal Healing Foundation, with its grant of $350 million to be spent over ten years to support community-based, Aboriginal-directed healing initiatives addressing the legacy of physical and sexual abuse suffered by Indigenous children in Canada's Indian residential school system. Research and funding contributions supported by the foundation were also to focus on the intergenerational impacts of historic and contemporary trauma, and unresolved grief. The Legacy of Hope Foundation spun off from the larger foundation with the mandate of helping Indigenous people overcome the legacy of the residential school system, and the responsibility of educating the public about that painful history.

Chrétien's name is also incontrovertibly tied to the First Nations Governance Act of 2002, overseen by then–minister of Indian and northern affairs Robert Nault. The act would amend the Indian Act to give band councils more power, but it also required them to create rules for picking leaders, as well as for administrative and financial transparency. It was met with serious opposition from First Nations leadership who once again felt that they were not being treated as equal partners in the discussion, and that the changes would degrade their inherent and treaty rights. "It is no small irony that Jean Chrétien's history of involvement with aboriginal policy ended as it began, with an attempt to force through an unpopular change to the *Indian Act*," wrote political scientist Michael Murphy.[10]

Prime Minister Paul Martin was instrumental in completing a comprehensive and long-reaching accord with Indigenous leadership in Canada through a promise to close the existing fiscal gaps with a $5 billion infusion of capital into First Nation coffers. This agreement came to be known as the Kelowna Accord. The accord, announced in November 2005, was the result of an eighteen-month consultative process that involved the federal government, provincial and territorial governments, and five national Aboriginal organizations.[11] That same month, the details of the Indian Residential Schools Settlement were announced, following a long battle in the courts. The settlement included a $2 billion compensation package for victims and triggered the establishment of the Truth and Reconciliation Commission of Canada. Just four days after the First Ministers' Meeting in Kelowna, Parliament would be dissolved.

Enter Harper

Upon winning his first minority government in 2006, Stephen Harper immediately moved away from the Kelowna Accord, an agreement he had opposed while in opposition and against which he had campaigned. Where the Accord would have dispersed $500 million in 2006–7 to improve on- and off-reserve housing,[12] the Conservative budget that same year included just $150 million for housing, education, clean water and other initiatives.

The attitude of the Conservative government toward Kelowna underscored what was to remain a general approach to Indigenous affairs, and to government writ large, which was to move away from large spending projects and look for more practical projects that could be easily evaluated and administered with the least amount of additional bureaucracy. "To understand Harper, you have to understand that he's outcome-oriented," Conservative strategist and former Aboriginal Affairs negotiator Tim Powers said in 2011.[13]

Harper's first high-profile gesture towards Indigenous peoples was well received and included input from then–Grand Chief of the Assembly of First Nations Phil Fontaine. In June 2008, Harper offered a statement of apology to former students of Indian residential schools on behalf of the government of Canada in a solemn ceremony inside the House of Commons. "We now recognize that it was wrong to separate children from rich and vibrant cultures and traditions, that it created a void in many lives and communities, and we apologize for having done this," Harper said. "We now recognize that, in separating children from their families, we undermined the ability of many to adequately parent their own children and sowed the seeds for generations to follow, and we apologize for having done this."[14]

Reaction from within Indigenous Canada to the apology was positive. "The memories of residential schools sometimes cuts like merciless knives at our souls. This day will help us to put that pain behind us," said Phil Fontaine.[15] Mary Simon of Inuit Tapiriit Kanatami was similarly hopeful. "Let us not be lulled into an impression that when the sun rises tomorrow morning the pain and scars will miraculously be gone. They won't," Simon said in Inuktitut. "But a new day has dawned, a new day heralded by a commitment to reconciliation, and building a new relationship with Inuit, Métis, and First Nations."[16] Beverly Jacobs of the Native Women's Association of Canada perhaps best summed up the sentiment at the time, which was that the apology needed to be followed up with action. "When such action is taken by the Canadian government to not only apologize, but to create a process in which it actually acknowledges the harms it's done, then we can accept the Apology," she said. "A process needs to ensure that the financial resources are in place to deal with all of the impacts we are dealing with today."[17]

There was hope for action on a number of fronts, but many of the government's policy initiatives would ultimately alienate First Nations leaders and communities in the process. For example, in 2010 the Harper government would endorse the United Nations Declaration on the Rights of Indigenous Peoples as an "aspirational" document, but would balk at adopting this contemporary treaty throughout its time in power. It argued that parts of the document essentially gave Indigenous peoples a veto over government decisions that involved land, legislation and resource projects, something Ottawa deemed could run counter to other constitutional and parliamentary considerations.

A year later, the government extended the Canadian Human Rights Act to Indigenous people living on reserves after a three-year adjustment period,[18] while simultaneously arguing in the courts that the act did not apply to Ottawa's own provision of services. In other words, cases could be brought against band councils for not providing access for disabled people, but not against the government of Canada.

Also in 2011, the government unveiled its Canada–First Nations Joint Action Plan with the collaboration of the Assembly of First Nations and then–National Chief Shawn Atleo. Chief among its proposals was the creation of a national panel on First Nations education. The move came on the heels of a damning auditor general's report, which said the federal government had made little progress in closing the gap in educational achievement between First Nations people living on reserves and the rest of the Canadian population. It also found that funding formulas were still putting Aboriginal students at a marked disadvantage by failing to take into consideration the number of eligible students in a community and then not ensuring funds dispersed actually went to education.

The national panel's findings echoed the urgency of the AG's report. It found there was no legislative framework governing First Nations education, no support system for the schools, no "context for evaluating success or for regularly making improvements through ongoing assessment of student achievement."[19] Among its recommendations was immediate and increased funding to bring Aboriginal schools up to the same level as provincial educational institutions, something that was never realized, although promises with multiple strings attached were certainly made. It also called for a new "First Nations Education Act" that would entrench Indigenous control over education and protect "the First Nation child's right to their culture, language and identity."[20]

The Harper government responded to the education debacle in the 2012 budget with a commitment of $275 million over three years for school infrastructure and for literacy programming. Still, the Assembly of First Nations pointed out the promises fell far short of what was needed, mainly due to the fact that First Nations education funding had been capped at a 2 per cent increase every year since 1996, "whereas transfer payments to provinces have been increasing by 4.8% annually through to 2011."[21] There was no consideration given to multiple reports and conversations happening across the country, raised by educators and policy advisers of different stripes, which confirmed the inequity of educational dollars and supports for First Nations schools, especially in remote areas of Canada.

Within a year, the government had a new proposal, this time with Atleo very notably by Harper's side at the announcement. It promised $1.9 billion for Aboriginal education over seven years, with a new annual increase or escalator of 4.5 per cent annually. But the money came with some major conditions—a new education act would need to pass with broad First Nations approval, and there would be new educational standards applied to schools. Criticism of the proposal began to percolate almost immediately, with chiefs across the country arguing, sometimes rather dramatically, that they hadn't been properly consulted. When Bill C-33, or the First Nations Control of First Nations Education Act, was proposed in April 2014, it was widely panned and soundly rejected. "Instead of building the capacity of First Nations institutions, Bill C-33 would require an army of federal bureaucrats in the department of Aboriginal Affairs—which hasn't governed First Nations education since residential schools," noted Chief Franklin Paibomsai of the Whitefish River First Nation. "It would actually dramatically increase federal control of First Nations education, by taking power away from First Nations governments and centralizing that power in federal hands."[22]

The Assembly of First Nations executive ultimately dismissed the proposed education bill as "assimilationist." For Indigenous people in Canada, any bill designed without meaningful collaboration with the people whom this bill would affect was just another confirmation that the paternalistic attitudes of the federal government were not relics of the past. In the end, the promised substantial cash injection into the education system never happened.

In the meantime, another highly contested Harper bill had managed to pass in 2013, Bill S-2, the Family Homes on Reserves and Matrimonial Rights or Interests Act. Because provincial laws do not cover real property on reserves, the bill was intended to close that legal loophole and provide protection for women when marriages dissolved or when they were escaping situations of domestic abuse. Previously, properties were left in the hands of men, who were still considered the "heads of household."[23] This issue wasn't a new one. It had been debated for over ten years amongst Indigenous peoples themselves, some of whom had gone ahead and created their own policies, even with the cooperation of the Canadian government, at various points in time.

Former BC regional chief to the Assembly of First Nations (AFN) Wendy Grant-John had been appointed by the government in 2007 to study the issue and talk to a wide range of groups and First Nations. She emphasized the need for consultations on the issue, and that there was a "strong preference for recognition of First Nations' jurisdiction to fill the legislative gap identified, a minimal role for federal legislation and a virtual universal opposition to the introduction of provincial laws (by incorporating them in a federal law) to deal with this issue."[24]

The Harper government's legislation ultimately gave First Nations a year to come up with their own rules around real property or have the federal government impose its own. There were some supporters of the legislation, including the Congress of Aboriginal Peoples. But critics, including the Native Women's Association of Canada, said Ottawa hadn't spent enough time consulting with First Nations communities on the complex issue and wasn't taking into consideration how the legislation fit into the wider context of First Nations governance. They also noted that the government had not given proper consideration to how women would access the justice system to deal with property rights, nor how larger issues of domestic violence were being addressed.[25]

The Chrétien government had angered more than a few Indigenous politicians with what the latter felt was interference in band business through the tabling of the Governance Act in 2002, but their ire was substantially raised with the imposition of the First Nations Financial Transparency Act in 2013 under Harper. Here was an act that flew directly in the face of the governance control and management power that chiefs and their councils felt they had. Requesting the posting of band expenses and audits online for their membership was one thing, and a choice some First Nations across Canada had already made on their own. The demand to post pay schedules and financial statements online from a government that cloaked itself in a thick veil of silence and secrecy was asking too much, and offended even the most compliant chiefs and community members. By the time of the 2015 federal election, 34 per cent of First Nations communities hadn't complied with the act and ran the risk of seeing their funding cut off.[26]

In addition to contentious legislation, the Harper government also eliminated a series of programs and initiatives, or allowed them to lapse. These included:

- the Aboriginal Healing Foundation;
- the National Aboriginal Health Organization, a research and advocacy organization established in 2000 to promote the health and well-being of Indigenous peoples; core funding came from Health Canada;
- the First Nations Statistical Institute, formed in 2006, which helped fill gaps in data on Indigenous communities; the negative impact of the loss was compounded by the axing of the mandatory long-form census in 2010, and the lack of any corresponding move to include more questions on Indigenous people in the remaining mandatory short form; and
- Sisters in Spirit, a Native Women's Association of Canada initiative to research and document murdered and missing Indigenous women; the government said in 2010 that it would focus funds on taking action to address the issue.

The government also cut core and project funding to Indigenous organizations and tribal councils as part of government-wide spending cuts. A 2015 analysis by the Aboriginal Peoples Television Network showed there had been $60 million in cuts over three years, with Inuit groups losing 71 per cent of organizational funding and First Nations groups cut by 65.5 per cent.[27]

Omnibus Trouble

The action that proved to be *the* galvanizing force for Indigenous peoples to unify against Harper was the omnibus federal budget implementation Bill C-45, tabled on October 18, 2012. The bill included unilateral measures that touched on the Indian Act and on environmental laws protecting millions of bodies of water across the country.

The Indian Act changes made it easier for a band to lease designated reserve lands by requiring a majority vote only at a community meeting or in a referendum. This renewed accusations that the government was not properly consulting First Nations when it drafted the changes. "The Parliament of Canada is changing the Constitution and our constitutionally protected lands without our consent," Onion Lake First Nation chief Wallace Fox wrote that year, "There were no meetings. There were no discussions. There was nothing to respect the honour of the Crown."[28]

This omnibus bill also replaced the Navigable Waters Act, first introduced in 1882, with the Navigation Protection Act. The new measures meant that navigation on only 162 waterways, including the three oceans, would be automatically protected from obstruction under federal law. If a government or company wanted to build a bridge or dam on one of the other 2.5 million bodies of water previously covered by Ottawa, they would have to deal with provincial or municipal laws. The change was billed as cutting down on unnecessary red tape, but it was also viewed as giving an unfettered hand to pipeline companies.[29]

If there was any opposition to the omnibus bill among the wider Canadian population, it proved disjointed and ineffective. The Indigenous world, however, stated clearly and unequivocally that Bill C-45 was unacceptable and declared it would fight to ensure the entire country understood why. What started as a series of "teach-ins" organized by four female activists in Saskatchewan snowballed into organized protests and rallies across the entire country.[30]

Unfortunately, the wave of protest that jump-started a global dialogue and ultimately became known as #idlenomore wasn't enough to stop the bill.

"Justice at Last?"

Throughout the decade of intense conversation and imposed change there were occasional glimpses of "Benevolent Harper"—the first prime minister to appoint an Innu person, Peter Penashue, to cabinet. Inuit woman Leona Aglukkaq also became a minister. In 2014, a new school was finally built at the Attawapiskat First Nation after a wait of fifteen years. In 2000, the reserve's elementary school had been closed due to toxic contamination after a fuel pipe under the building ruptured and spilled diesel fuel. The contamination from that spill is believed to date back to 1979.[31]

In spite of what Conservatives themselves would term "good works" during their decade in office, the problem remained that Indigenous people wanted full and proper consultation, not what I have termed the "violence of benevolence," which is violent because it is unwanted, because it is imposed and because it has never delivered what has been promised in its various renditions.[32] The kind of benevolence this government delivered was frequently sticky with injustice and expectations that rarely matched need.

Treaty negotiations fell into this category, and in 2007 the Harper government announced its "Justice at Last" process to address the hundreds of "specific" treaty claims that were backed up in the system. Specific claims deal with legal disputes and grievances First Nations have with the Crown over issues related to their treaty lands. The initiative created a new independent tribunal to help assess whether a particular group had a legitimate case. It was where the parties would turn when First Nations and the government reached an impasse in their negotiations. "Instead of letting disputes over land and compensation drag on forever fueling anger and frustration and uncertainty, they will be solved once and for all by impartial judges," Harper said when he announced the change.

A departmental review of the process, released in 2013, noted that a backlog in claims awaiting assessment had been cleared, and that the total number of claims being negotiated had gone up.[33] Still, the government's data showed the number of settled claims had not yet increased. An analysis by the National Claims Research Directors, supported by dozens of chiefs, tribal councils and Aboriginal organizations, said the government was rejecting a majority of claims, and later presenting that as evidence the backlog was gone. The report also said the number of negotiations had gone up because the department was dealing with only portions of claims.[34]

By 2014, the chair of the tribunal, Judge Harry Slade, was warning the tribunal was on the verge of failure. Where the legislation called for six full-time members, Slade remained the only one, plus two part-time members. "My term expires in December 2015," Slade wrote in his annual report. "Without the appointment of one or more full-time members in the interim there will be no ability to implement a succession plan or service the case load. The Tribunal will fail."[35] As noted throughout this critique, Slade was also critical of the fact that the tribunal's support services were merged along with ten other federal administrative tribunals in a budget cutting exercise, without any prior consultation with First Nations as the legislation required.

This government also stumbled on comprehensive land claims, major land negotiations with First Nations not previously covered by treaties or legal agreements. Most of those ongoing claims are in British Columbia, and they sometimes cover territory highly coveted for resource development. After a high-profile meeting with the AFN in Ottawa in early 2012, the prime minister promised a series of high-level meetings to deal with the snail's pace on treaty negotiations. That fall, then–Aboriginal and northern affairs minister John Duncan announced the government would focus its resources on negotiations that showed the most promise for resolution, a decision that would feel uncomfortably close to judgment calls on merit and on meeting government-determined criteria.

Pressure for action continued to mount, particularly after 2014 with the Supreme Court's historic decision in the Tsilhqot'in case. The court declared Aboriginal title to approximately 1,900 square kilometres in the BC interior, recognizing that the six bands there didn't just have claim over specific, intensively used sites, but over the wider area they had historically occupied. "The notion of occupation must also reflect the way of life of the Aboriginal people, including those who were nomadic or semi-nomadic," the justices noted. The case excited Indigenous nations across Canada because it spoke directly to underlying Aboriginal title. It confirmed the force of long-standing arguments for Indigenous ownership of their traditional territories, and it also raised the bar for governments who wanted to pursue development projects on those lands.

But by 2015, the minister's special representative on renewing the comprehensive land claims policy, Douglas Eyford, reported the system was still moving painfully slow, mired in unnecessary government bureaucracy. He noted that three agreements in principle at BC treaty tables had been held up at cabinet for approval. "The fact these problems persist three decades later demonstrates the absence of a strong commitment by the entire federal government to treaty-making," he wrote. "Without more purposeful leadership, Canada's approach is bound to produce the same disappointing outcomes."[36] When the election was called, the Harper government had succeeded in negotiating six modern treaties. However, Eyford noted that seventy-five claims were still very slowly making their way through the system.

Harper as a Mobilizing Factor

The perception of failed policy and practice came up over and over again throughout the nine years of Harper's tenure, whether it was about consultation, governance or all-important Indigenous education policy and practice. His government's failure to accept the conclusions of the Truth and Reconciliation Commission in May 2015, and its stubborn resistance to holding an inquiry into missing and murdered Indigenous women, would stand in stark contrast to the official Indian residential schools apology of 2008.

Harper's record ultimately helped spur the "Rock the Vote" movement, conceived by Idle No More supporters. Indigenous people across Canada were preparing for the 2015 election, but they faced substantial barriers to voting: poverty, lack of identification and lack of transportation to voting stations. Tania Cameron, an NDP candidate in Northwestern Ontario in 2008 and 2011, turned her attention to helping First Nations overcome those barriers.

The government's 2014 Fair Elections Act required voters to have two pieces of identification and eliminated vouching. Vouching is a process frequently used in First Nation communities to allow a voter to have someone swear to where he or she lives, because the lack of street addresses and electricity in far too many places translates to a lack of household bills with addresses, and in remote northern communities, where a status card frequently suffices for health access, there is a lack of provincial health cards.

Cameron began the monumental task of having chiefs write a letter of confirmation of residence to virtually every individual on every First Nation to ensure they had a piece of official mail to confirm their address and to state that they lived on the reserve where they were registered to vote. In addition, she set up a Facebook page called "First Nations Rock the Vote," where people could find information on what qualified as identification. She also provided Elections Canada information online.[37] Prior to the 2015 election, the Assembly of First Nations identified fifty-one ridings across Canada as potential swing ridings where, according to AFN national chief Perry Bellegarde, the outcome could be determined by the turnout of Aboriginal voters.[38] And Bellegarde, after first declaring himself a non-voter due to political restrictions, reversed his decision and made a commitment to getting out the vote and casting a ballot himself.[39]

Conclusion

Indigenous communities ultimately viewed Harper as initiating acts that hurt their interests and limited their vision for the future. They saw benign neglect in significant sectors of the government that directly impacted Indigenous affairs. They saw outcome-oriented Harper deliberately denying any future of self-determination and self-governance even though the Canadian Constitution guaranteed them both as rights of Indigenous peoples living in this country. And most importantly, as I mentioned before, Indigenous people wanted full and proper consultation on matters of critical importance.

The act of consulting and accommodating means stepping directly into the circle of Indigenous leadership with an attitude of respect and equanimity, and engaging in a dialogue that is mutually expressive, mutually inclusive and mutually determining. And while it might be concluded that Harper made some small effort at being magnanimous throughout his term, the larger story remains, at best, an expression of tightly controlled concessions.

If there is to be meaningful progress when it comes to Indigenous affairs and the inclusion of Indigenous interests in socio-economic development and prosperity, it has to come, at a minimum, with recognition and implementation of the following four critical areas:

- recognition and implementation of the government-to-government treaty relationship through the immediate settlement of specific and comprehensive lands claims
- recognition of territorial jurisdiction and title to Indigenous lands and resources
- an equitable sharing of mutually developed natural resources and wealth
- full and proper consultation and accommodation of Indigenous interests, especially in regard to the development or disturbance of natural resources on traditional Indigenous territories

The Liberal government under Justin Trudeau inherits a fragile relationship between Indigenous people and the Crown. New Indigenous and northern affairs minister Carolyn Bennett's mandate letter stated that "It is time for a renewed, nation-to-nation relationship with Indigenous Peoples, based on recognition of rights, respect, cooperation, and partnership." Trudeau also directed that an inquiry be held into missing and murdered Indigenous women, and Bennett told the United Nations that her government would provide unqualified support for the UN Declaration on the Rights of Indigenous Peoples (UNDRIP).

In the meantime, Indigenous youth across Canada and their allies in the Idle No More movement are watching the federal government and are determined to ensure government takes the right path forward by asserting Indigenous influence at every opportunity. In the Anishinabe prophecy of the Seven Fires, Western society comes to a crossroads—with one road leading to global destruction, and the other to be travelled alongside Indigenous peoples. "This path will lead to the lighting of the 8th fire, a period of eternal peace, harmony and a 'New Earth' where the destruction of the past will be healed."[40]

COMMENTARIES

13

The Harper Government and Agriculture

Barry K. Wilson

I t was arguably the signature agricultural policy moment for prime minster Stephen Harper during his almost decade in power.

On November 28, 2011, with majority government finally secured and the parliamentary votes assured, the Harper Conservatives were determined to end the sixty-eight-year-old monopoly on exporting Prairie wheat held by the Canadian Wheat Board (CWB) since 1943. It was the only agricultural file on which urbanite Harper ever seemed to have a personal, rather than political or strategic, interest.

It was a dramatic parliamentary evening and many of the several score Western Canadian Conservative MPs in the House of Commons that night remembered it later as one of their proudest political accomplishments, perhaps in part because of how much it mattered to The Boss.

Of course, through their years in government, the Conservatives introduced and put into effect many other pieces of agricultural legislation, regulation and policy that changed the rules of the agriculture and agrifood industry—an economic sector that contributes more than $104 billion to the annual gross domestic product and employs more than two million Canadians.

More importantly, the government prodded, led and sometimes forced farmers to change the way they think about government. The Harper administration tried, largely successfully, to alter the view of government's role in the agrifood industry from being there mainly to step in and bail out farmers in troubled times to instead creating rules and conditions that would theoretically allow efficient, well-run operations to prosper.

That paradigm shift is the Conservatives' main agricultural policy legacy.

Dismantling the Canadian Wheat Board

For sheer political drama and importance to the Conservative rural agenda, no issue resonated like the Canadian Wheat Board vote, and Stephen Harper was in the thick of it.

As an MP and then as president of the National Citizens Coalition in the 1990s, he had made the Wheat Board monopoly a personal cause. It was a piece of ideological baggage he brought into government.

Harper considered the marketing monopoly an affront to the freedom of agricultural businesspeople who wanted the ability to sell their grain to the highest bidder, not a government-imposed monopoly that took the grain, sold it and paid farmers a price that averaged the highs and lows.

For several decades, it had been the most divisive issue in the Prairie farm economy.

The majority of affected farmers consistently indicated through farm group resolutions and CWB board of directors elections that they preferred to work within the wheat board system because of its equity principle that gave all farmers— whether near the United States market or 300 miles north of the border—equal access to world markets and pooled prices. They saw the board as a powerful marketer able to compete against big private grain companies in world markets and to stand up to the railways on farmers' behalf.

A vocal minority opposed it as a violation of their property rights as entrepreneurs to sell their produce to whomever they wanted, whenever they could and at the best price they could get, with the money in hand at time of sale rather than arriving through the staggered payment system used by the CWB. That system saw final disbursements from the pool flowing more than a year after a sale. In some celebrated cases, a handful of farmers defied the law to make a point and paid a legal price. They saw the board as a vestige of another era and another ideology out of step with modern-day business principles.

Ironically, most of those CWB-supporting Prairie farmers also consistently voted Conservative on issues other than the wheat marketing system.

In the early months of the Conservative government's third term and without conducting a vote promised to affected farmers, Harper and his agriculture minister, Gerry Ritz, seized the moment to act.

November 28, 2011, was the final Commons vote on Bill C-18—the Marketing Freedom for Grain Farmers Act.[1]

It was an historic night on Parliament Hill. Speaker Andrew Scheer, a thirty-two-year-old rural-urban Saskatchewan MP who had personally campaigned against the Wheat Board's monopoly in his four successful election campaigns but was now sworn to uphold parliamentary decorum that raucous evening, presided over the events.

The applause from Conservative MPs began just after 7 p.m., when Harper rose in the House of Commons to cast the first vote in favour of the final reading of Bill C-18. The applause lasted for more than fifteen minutes as 152 other Conservative MPs rose to vote in favour of ending the marketing monopoly of the Winnipeg-based CWB.

The final tally was 153–120.

The wheat board monopoly ended August 1, 2012, and by 2015, its assets and control had been sold to an American–Saudi Arabian corporate consortium.

The Contradiction: Supply Management

Harper and his MPs, meanwhile, had no trouble throughout their years in power supporting and defending another agricultural monopoly—supply management. On November 22, 2005, on the eve of World Trade Organization negotiations in Hong Kong, all Conservative MPs were part of a unanimous House of Commons vote that demanded no changes to supply management.

It is a forty-year-old system that forces dairy, chicken and egg producers to buy quota that limits production to domestic demand, and requires that they sell to the marketing agency and take a cost-of-production-based fixed price for their produce.

The quid pro quo is that they are largely protected from foreign competition in the domestic market through border tariffs that in some cases exceed 200 per cent.

The system promises affected farmers a predictable income. It also has made supply management farmers among the most indebted in the industry, albeit asset (quota) rich. In dairy, while the price of quota varies between provinces, quota that allows production from one cow per year typically costs more than $25,000.

While the system is national, it is concentrated in vote-rich Quebec and Ontario and sports an influential and well-financed lobby that works the halls of Parliament Hill relentlessly.

Conservative MPs who instinctively were against protectionism often justified the government support for one monopoly (supply management) but not another (the CWB) by arguing that farmers involved in the supply managed business support the system and besides, it is voluntary. Of course, it also helps that supply management ensures that its farmers receive their money from consumers and not from government payments.

Prairie grain farmers working under the CWB consistently elected a majority of directors who supported the single desk. Still, Ritz resisted calls for a vote by farmers on the issue and dismissed a plebiscite held by the Wheat Board in 2011 as non-binding. As to supply management being "voluntary," skeptics scoffed that farmers who tried to work outside the quota system soon found themselves in court. Critics saw politics and voter pandering in constituencies the Conservatives needed to win as the real motive for dismantling the Wheat Board but preserving supply management.

Whatever the reality, the Conservative government was an unwavering supporter of supply management in the breach, aggressively pursuing trade agreements that would help agricultural exporters while fiercely defending the protected sectors of the industry. All the while, it was quietly telling industry leaders that some weakening of the system was inevitable in an increasingly trade-dominated economy and efforts should be made to preserve the foundational principles of supply management (production controls, cost-of-production-influenced pricing and predicable import levels). At the same time, the government was pursuing reform of some of the more rigid import restrictions and the high quota costs that hampered efforts to attract new entrants and undermined those who defended the system against its free trade detractors.

And when trade negotiations with the European Union (2014) and members of the Trans-Pacific Partnership (2015) resulted in agreement to allow a controlled and modest increase in imports of supply managed products from abroad, the Conservatives promised financial compensation for any damage, including a 2015 election campaign pledge of $4.3 billion over fifteen years to compensate for lost domestic market share and potential quota price decreases.

To the end, supply management farm leaders praised the Harper Conservatives for supporting, defending and nudging the system to reform, even if some of their members grumbled. For adamant Wheat Board supporters, on the other hand, Tory became the ultimate four-letter word.

Legislative Moves

The bitter and emotional CWB legislation and debate aside, the Harper years were not a period of sustained legislative activism. Instead, the government pursued its agenda in agriculture by pushing for a general shift in attitude. Much of that shift came from more subtle legislative initiatives and changes to federal rules.

Notably, there was a strengthening of plant breeders' rights protection against unauthorized planting of patented seeds without paying royalties, potentially benefitting mainly large multinational agribusiness seed companies, which fund most seed research. As well, there were changes to the Canada Grain Act that that reduced some of the regulatory requirements for the Winnipeg-based Canadian Grain Commission and turned other traditional inspection services over to the private sector.[2] The Grain Commission, created more than a century ago to protect farmers and customers from grain industry bad habits, retained its core role of setting and overseeing standards and performance in the industry including grading and inspecting grain headed to terminals or ports.

Both legislative initiatives were embedded in controversial omnibus bills, so beloved by the Conservatives, and both were denounced by critics as a weakening of farmer protection and a gift to big industry. Supporters, including most national farm organizations, representing the majority of farmers, defended the moves as a way to attract private sector investment into the plant breeding business and to increase the efficiency and lower the cost of grain industry oversight regulations.

Despite some loud opposition from the National Farmers Union, Canadian Wheat Board supporters and rival MPs, both bills were approved with little lingering uproar.

Late in its final term, the Conservative government also produced and passed legislation designed to deal with a perennial Prairie grain sector issue that has bedeviled farmers and governments for close to a century—the performance of Canada's national railways in moving the multi-billion-dollar crop that is produced each autumn by Prairie grain, oilseed and lentil farmers.

The 2014 Fair Rail for Canadian Farmers Act required the Canadian National and Canadian Pacific railways to move a minimum of 500,000 tonnes of product each week or face the prospect of fines that by law could reach $100,000 for each day the goal was not reached.[3] In the end, the legislative bark was far worse than its bite and railway fines were a fraction of what farmers and grain companies expected. The legislation also promised more shipper protection in contracts with the railways.

Political pressure for legislative action came during the winter of 2013–14, when farmers who had produced a huge 2013 crop found their bins full, their grain elevators packed and millions of tonnes stranded and unsold. Meanwhile, ships waited at port charging demurrage fees that farmers ultimately paid in lower prices as worldwide customers complained about Canada's reliability as a supplier.

Railways blamed the winter weather, the size of the crop and anything else that would deflect blame from their performance.

For rural Prairie Conservative MPs, many of whom were grain farmers, the bottom line was that their constituents reported an estimated $7 billion worth of unsold grain in their elevators and on-farm storage sites, creating cash-flow problems while they prepared for their 2014 spring planting. The government acted, although many farm lobbyists thought the response was too tepid.

The government also announced a review in 2014 of the Canada Transportation Act led by former Conservative trade minister David Emerson to look at whether more fundamental regulatory or legislative change was necessary to hold the railways to account. The conclusions of the review and any government action fell into the new Liberal government's lap, and in early 2016, the Liberals' reaction to recommendations for stronger regulations left wiggle room for future action.

Gerry Ritz: The Face of Change

These legislative changes were all part of the puzzle, but the bigger sea change that the Harper years brought to the agricultural industry was a change in attitude, a change in what farmers could expect from government and a transformation in what or how much the government was prepared to offer.

Agriculture minister Ritz was the government face of that change. In many ways, the transformation began the day in late February 2008 when he made clear to the country's largest farm lobby that he would get his way whether it supported him or not. Ritz, a former Saskatchewan grain farmer appointed the previous summer as Canada's thirty-second agriculture minister and eventually becoming the sixth-longest serving, was making his first appearance before Canada's oldest, largest and traditionally most influential farm organization—the Canadian Federation of Agriculture (CFA).

Through provincial and commodity group members, the CFA claimed to represent 200,000 Canadian farmers and farm families. It once called itself "the House of Agriculture." Its leaders, policy decisions and political demands guided generations of federal agriculture ministers.

But on this cold Ottawa morning, a grim-faced Ritz stood before CFA leaders and delegates with a no-holds-barred message. The issue, of course, was the Canadian Wheat Board and Ritz's determination to begin its dismantlement by removing malting barley from its marketing monopoly.

The CFA was divided on the issue, even though the CWB was a member. It insisted Ritz had no right to act without farmer approval through a vote.

The minister began by listing the groups and provinces he was consulting on the issue—all opposed to the monopoly and all his allies—and then insinuated that the absence of a firm CFA position combined with its call for a vote to let farmers decide showed a lack of leadership and was in defiance of the tide of history.

"This is no time to sit on the fence," Ritz lectured the silent farm audience. "Barley marketing freedom is coming and it's time to lead, follow or get out of the way."[4] Then he stormed off the stage without taking questions.

CFA delegates were stunned at this unprecedented affront. Yet after some grumbling, its leaders took a measure of the man and realized that if they were to have influence and access, they had to either mount a fierce counterattack with thousands of farmers demonstrating on the street against Ritz policies—as they had organized against previous ministers—and risk failure, or learn how to accommodate this strong-willed minister with an agenda and little tolerance for opposition.

Less than two years later, CFA president Laurent Pellerin concisely articulated the conclusion of the painful internal debate. "We don't have to play the same role as opposition parties," he said. "They have a job to do criticizing the government. It is our job to work with the government."[5]

So having earned his alpha-politician spurs early on, Ritz developed a good relationship with most farm leaders, who understood the new rules of the game, over his next eight years in office (except, of course, with leadership of groups that opposed his agenda, including the National Farmers Union and Friends of the Canadian Wheat Board, whom he ignored or ridiculed).

He met with supportive or acquiescent farm leaders often, consulted frequently, listened to and often acted on complaints, went to bat for them when they were under siege from foreign government policy or domestic critics and invited them along on his dozens of trade and trade negotiation trips. Ritz was a relentless trade promoter, logging hundreds of thousands of miles in trade missions and in negotiating market-opening deals for Canadian food products.

Ritz's early show of stubborn strength was one factor that accounted for the long period of relative peace in farmer-government relations.

The other was a red-hot farm economy.

Capitalizing in Boom Years to Change Mindsets

After years of price catastrophe (grain and hogs) and disease-related industry disasters (beef and hogs) through the 1990s and most of the first decade of the twenty-first century, the Conservative government presided over a period of unprecedented price and income highs in many key sectors.

When the Harper Conservatives first took office in 2006, farm cash receipts nationally totalled $37 billion, but realized net farm income (receipts minus operating costs and depreciation, essentially farm-retained earnings) barely hit the $1 billion level.

Over the next nine years, those numbers steadily climbed until by 2011, cash receipts (gross income from the farm) had reached $49.6 billion, and by 2014 had exploded to $57.8 billion—a record by a country mile. Realized net income followed the same path, hitting $5.5 billion in 2011 and $7.7 billion in 2014—an astounding eight-fold increase in eight years. It also was a period of sharp increases in asset values on the farm as the value of land and machinery increased. Average farm size grew as farmers expanded or amalgamated operations, and farm numbers continued their seventy-five-year decline that started during the Great Depression of the 1930s and continues apace.

Ironically, despite the recent boom years in much of agriculture during the latter Conservative government, farm debt continued to grow, escalating a trend that began in 1993. Through the 1980s and early 1990s, national farm debt remained stable in the $22 billion range. By 2006, the accumulated farm debt had more than doubled to $52.4 billion. By the time the Conservative years ended, the farm debt load exceeded $90 billion as farmers borrowed to expand, to consolidate and to replace equipment while taking advantage of record low interest rates.

When those rates begin to increase, there will be significant sector exposure to higher debt servicing costs.

Still, political discontent on the farm diminishes when financial times are good.

It was an opportune time for the government to implement a quiet revolution of changing farm sector expectations of what governments can and should do for farmers.

The Conservative government insisted that farmers be willing to manage more of their own risks as businesses are supposed to do, rather than turning to the government for bail-outs when markets sour, prices decline or business decisions turn out to be faulty.

Insurance, hedging, forward pricing and market watching were to be the go-to tools for farmers.

The agriculture industry mindset about how much it could lean on government when times got tough shifted. The Conservatives set out to impose a business model rather than a tradition of "farming the mail box," as Ritz liked to call it.

For many decades, most farmers have by instinct been a conservative constituency whatever the ideological stripe of the government, but that support came with irony. They also were quick to expect government to bail them out when times were tough. At a large boisterous rally of 1,000 farmers in Saskatoon in 1993 during a grain price trough, one producer went to the microphone to tell Progressive Conservative agriculture minister Charlie Mayer: "All we're asking for is a lousy billion bucks." Years later when Liberal minister Lyle Vanclief went before the Canadian Federation of Agriculture annual meeting to announce a half-billion-dollar injection of funds because of low prices, some delegates called for his resignation because it wasn't the demanded $1 billion.

The Harper government was determined to change that mentality.

The philosophy was relatively simple: governments have an obligation to help the farm sector when catastrophe strikes, whether in the form of disease, extreme weather or pernicious political protectionism by foreign governments. The bovine spongiform encephalopathy (mad cow disease) outbreak that closed markets around the world and crippled the Canadian beef industry for years, and the battle against Country of Origin Labeling (COOL) laws in the United States that stripped Canadian beef and hog producers of billions of dollars, are two examples.

But Ritz also insisted that business principles, rather than the expectation of government payments, govern farm decisions as a key to financial sustainability.

It was government's responsibility to create market conditions that allowed efficient farmers and the food industry to survive and thrive, not to prop them up.

Reducing the Government's Footprint

In a political system in which agriculture is a rare shared federal-provincial jurisdiction, Ritz forged an unusually collaborative relationship with provincial agriculture ministers that replaced the often-combative relationships of the past.

The result was a 2012 federal-provincial deal on a new five-year federal agricultural policy framework that changed the rules to significantly reduce potential program payouts. Farm leaders grumbled about a lower level of protection and a lack of consultation, but there was little aggressive farm lobby pushback.

The focus of research funding shifted to shorter-term projects with a quick product-development focus and industry direction rather than longer-term basic research. The ranks of public researchers became thinner.

Net program payments per farm were $20,344 in 2006 when the Conservatives took power and $10,347 in 2013. That was due in large part to better market returns, but also to a deliberate policy plan.

And as Agriculture Canada budgets fell compared to the farm payment–bolstered spending estimates inherited by the Conservatives in 2006, so did the profile of the department diminish during the Harper years. The government moved both the Canadian Food Inspection Agency and the Pest Management Regulatory Agency from Agriculture Canada to Health Canada.

The government's agenda, largely accomplished, was to reduce the department's footprint in the industry. In the final Agriculture Canada spending estimates and planning document tabled in Parliament before the government was defeated in 2015, Ritz promised more of the same.

"Working with our portfolio partners, along with governments and industry, we'll continue to drive transformative change so Canada's innovative farmers and food processors can maximize opportunities in the global marketplace while generating jobs and growth for Canadians," he wrote. While Ritz meant it as a prediction, it has become what he no doubt hopes will be a legacy statement.

The October 2015, federal election offered one early snapshot of farmer judgment on the Harper government's agricultural policy record. While Canadian voters turned massively against the Conservatives, the bulk of rural seats from

Ontario west, including the vast majority of Canadian farmers, stayed loyally Tory. Adding a handful of rural seats from Quebec, rural or rural-influenced ridings sent 70 per cent of the ninety-nine-member Conservative caucus to Ottawa.

Unfinished Business

The Liberal government that replaced the Conservatives November 4, 2015, inherited some serious unfinished agricultural business started by the previous government.

With two key trade deals for agriculture—the Canada–European Union deal and the Trans-Pacific Partnership deal—awaiting approval or rejection, the new government faces a dilemma that has challenged Canadian governments for half a century. It will need to balance the interests of supply managed dairy, poultry and egg sectors against those producers that stand to gain through increased export sales and prices—namely grain, pulse crops, oilseed and livestock.

The new government, largely shut out of the rural Prairies, inherits the Prairie grain transportation file and will have to decide what to do about the recommendations of the Canadian Transportation Act review. Farmers, grain companies and international buyers will be watching.

Perhaps the biggest agricultural challenge will be to decide whether to reverse some of the cuts made to federal-provincial "Growing Forward" farm support programs that were triggered in 2013 and will end in 2018. Federal-provincial agriculture ministers' negotiations on the new policy framework have started and will intensify as the 2017 deadline for a deal approaches.

In an economy as volatile and cyclical as agriculture, which is susceptible to weather, world prices, global economic developments, currency values, disease and political events, the income boom of recent years almost certainly will weaken and the impact of reduced program support levels agreed to in 2012 will become obvious as farm incomes drop. An inevitable interest rate increase will make the cost of servicing more than $90 billion in debt an uncompetitive one.

The question is, will future governments be prepared to commit more farm support money and spend political capital to try to convince the provinces to do the same?

14

Harper on Health Care: A Curious Mix of Continuity, Unilateralism and Opportunity Lost

Michael B. Decter

Prime Minister Stephen Harper's record on health care was the result of foundations laid by his predecessors, the vagaries of electoral politics and a smattering of definitive public policy moves in the file. Harper inherited the health summit legacy of prime ministers Jean Chrétien and Paul Martin, but the portfolio was shaped by his pursuit of a majority government and balanced budgets, and his eleventh-hour interest in innovation. He avoided making health care a major political issue by treating the provinces generously on transfers and by not engaging them on other health issues.

When Harper was first elected in early 2006, the policy context of health care was largely set by the health accords of Chrétien (2003) and Martin (2004)—both the results of an active health policy agenda that followed the austerity of the 1990s—and two landmark policy reports on the future of health care in Canada.

The first of these reports, by the Commission on the Future of Health Care in Canada, headed by former Saskatchewan NDP premier Roy Romanow, was released in 2002 after less than two years of public hearings and research activities. Commissioner Romanow argued persuasively that the Canadian health care system was sustainable only with renewed federal funding, substantial structural reforms and a broadening of coverage.

The other report—or more precisely "reports," as it was composed of five reports in total—came from the Senate Committee on Social Affairs, ably chaired by Senator Michael Kirby. Both the Kirby and Romanow reports urged governments to maintain public insurance for health services, but they parted company on delivery of health services. Romanow recommended that health services remain largely publicly delivered, while the Kirby Committee advocated for a mix of public and private providers under the umbrella of public insurance. The Senate Committee researched areas such as mental health and the role of academic medical centres in detail. Their recommendations in these areas were deeper and more specific than those found in the Romanow report.

These two reports underpinned the debates and negotiations that eventually led to the 2003 and 2004 intergovernmental health accords and foreshadowed the substantial increases in federal transfers in health funding that followed.

The 2003 Health Accord was described by then–Manitoba premier Gary Doer as "take it or leave it federalism." With Chrétien coming to an end of a lengthy tenure in office, he made it clear that he had money for the provinces for health care but little appetite for any negotiation. Take it or leave it was the mood. In the end, Alberta premier Ralph Klein did indeed "leave it," departing the 2003 First Ministers' Meeting early for the casino across the river in Gatineau, Quebec. He did, however, remark on his way out the door that Ottawa should "just send us the Alberta share." In that instance, therefore, it was perhaps more a case of "leave it and take it."

The second accord, negotiated by Paul Martin in 2004, was of particular importance to the decade that would follow, both in form and in substance. Negotiating as he was from a minority position in the federal Parliament, and with an eye to the next federal election, Martin addressed the long and deeply held view of the provinces that the federal government had abandoned its financial partnership in Medicare. To address this central concern, he agreed to a new ten-year commitment to increase the Canada Health Transfer each year by 6 per cent. The provinces made few concessions on establishing reliable accountability mechanisms to track how the increases would be spent.

These are the circumstances in which Stephen Harper took the leadership of Canada's health care system as prime minister in 2006. Each in its own way, the reports and accords would help shape the new prime minister's response to what is always an unpredictable policy file. The reports above all highlighted the need for reform. The 2004 health accord, which the party's election platform that year said would fix health care "for a generation," provided the funding basis. And Chrétien's "take it or leave it" approach in 2003 provided a precedent for Harper's approach later in his three mandates.

The First Health Care Challenge for Harper: Wait Times

The health care issue with political traction in the federal elections of 2004 and 2006 was wait times for diagnostic imaging, as well as for cancer, cataract and joint-replacement surgeries. Organized medicine in the form of the Canadian Medical Association (CMA) stepped up with a series of "Taming the Queue" conferences to highlight the issue. The real power of the wait times issue flowed from the ability of individual Canadians (and the media) to measure how long they had been waiting, and their conclusion was too long.

Wait times reduction based on new funding was a central element of the 2004 Health Accord and was the only element with seemingly measureable outcomes. This goal was also one of Stephen Harper's five main campaign commitments in the 2005–6 election. He promised to reduce wait times for key procedures, along with other commitments such as reducing the GST and introducing the Federal Accountability Act.

As "Canada's New Government" took office, the five priorities took on an especially important place in Harper's agenda. But given the need for additional intergovernmental collaboration to make progress on wait times, that promise was largely left behind as the minority government geared up for an election campaign that always seemed just around the corner. Nonetheless, some progress was made. Although not uniform across Canada, each province did measure wait times, and many of them showed a reduction in the key areas that had been identified.[1]

Transition—Implementing Health Accords

Tony Clement served as the Harper government's first minister of health. Not a newcomer to politics, he had served as environment and then health minister in the Ontario government under premiers Mike Harris and Ernie Eves. These posts gave Clement insights into intergovernmental processes and informed his approach to provincial counterparts once he took the federal chair at the intergovernmental table.

One of Clement's early tasks was implementing the 2004 Health Accord and, through it, providing federal funding to initiate wait times reduction projects in the provinces.

The 2004 accord provided predictable funding to the provinces and territories through the Canada Health Transfer, which included an annual escalator of 6 per cent, for a ten-year period. This was the financial stability long sought by provincial and territorial first ministers.

Beyond the specific provisions to fund wait times reductions across the county, however, the accord did not settle the details of how there would be a generational fix to the entire system, as the Liberals had promised. Instead, the accord laid out a series of issues—home care, pharmaceutical care and long-term care—as an agenda for further negotiation by first ministers.

Although the Harper government left the funding formula in place—even extending its duration by three additional years—it did not engage in this agenda, which yet required further negotiation. Harper had no interest in detailed meetings on health policy with the first ministers. In truth, he did not really want to meet other first ministers as a group on any issue. Thus, the agenda to reform the health care system was left largely unaddressed. Money provided by the Canada Health Transfer went to provincial coffers with precious few conditions attached or accountability expected. Rather than "buying" reform, the flow of funds resulted in better pay for doctors and nurses. The federal health minister's non-interventionist approach spoke to the Harper government's deeply held belief that health care was a provincial responsibility in which Ottawa shouldn't meddle.

Wait times declined for the five areas highlighted in the accord in every jurisdiction in Canada. The dedicated funding, and the political prominence of wait times in the mind of voters, led to measurable improvement. A number of provinces also identified a number of additional target areas for wait times reduction that had not been specifically identified in the accord.

Tainted Blood—Unfinished Justice

One of the early achievements of the Harper Government in the health care file was a full and final settlement with the victims of tainted blood in December 2006. The scandal of tainted blood ranks as one of the most tragic failures of what once was a trusted element of Canadian health care. The Canadian Red Cross and the Biologics and Genetic Therapies Directorate at Health Canada failed catastrophically in their responsibility to protect the safety of those dependent on blood and blood products. A partial settlement had been reached with victims under the Chrétien government in 1998. However, a significant group of victims remained outside that settlement. Upon taking office, Harper moved quickly to conclude a full settlement and, in doing so, provide redress for all of the victims of this tragic regulatory failure. "While no amount of money can fully compensate these victims for their pain and suffering, Canada's new government has never wavered in its commitment to compensate all victims of tainted blood, no matter the date of infection," Clement said in a June 2007 news release.

The new Canadian Blood Services organization replaced the Canadian Red Cross as manager of the blood system in 1998, following a recommendation of the Royal Commission of Inquiry on the Blood System in Canada (the Krever Commission).

Investing in eHealth

Although the Harper government had concerns about the Canada Health Infoway (CHI) when it took office, the Conservatives were gradually persuaded to renew Ottawa's commitment to the organization. Canada Health Infoway began in 2001 as the instrument and vehicle for federal investment in electronic health record development and health information infrastructure. Canada Health Infoway support to provincial and territorial health systems was premised on productivity improvements in the sector, long criticized for being overly reliant on paper records and antiquated information technologies. One knowledgeable observer declared Canadian health care in 2015 to still have the largest installed base of fax machines remaining on earth. Despite the enormity of the challenge, Canada Health Infoway has made significant progress in the fifteen years since its creation.

In light of the progress the organization was making, the Harper government invested an additional $500 million dollars in its 2010 budget in Canada Health Infoway, thus renewing its mandate. The pan-Canadian structure of the organization and the fact that the federal government is its sole funder contributed to the successful renewal. The governance of Canada Health Infoway is based on a corporate structure wherein the thirteen deputy ministers of health from the federal, ten provincial and three territorial governments serve as the corporation's members. But because no consultation with the provinces was required at the political level, CHI fit more easily with the Harper government's preference for unilateral action in health policy.

Emergent Unilateralism

With the Canada Health Transfer in place, the Harper government turned its attention to unilateral federal initiatives in health care.

The Canadian Partnership Against Cancer ranks as one of the Harper government's early and lasting achievements. Cancer advocacy groups had pursued the idea of an independent not-for-profit organization committed to combating cancer and sharing best practices across Canada, and the idea found favour with the new government. First established and funded in 2007, it was renewed for a further five years in 2012.

The Mental Health Commission emerged from the 2003 work of the Kirby Senate Committee. In 2007, the Harper Government approved funding for the commission, and Harper asked former senator Kirby to become the first chairman of the not-for-profit commission.

The Global Child and Maternal Health Initiative was Harper's marquee health and development initiative. He unveiled the original $2.8 billion investment in 2010 at the G8 summit, held in Muskoka, Ontario. In 2014, he announced a further

$3.5 billion in funding between 2015 and 2020. "This is a moral imperative to saving the lives of vulnerable women and children in some of the poorest countries around the world when it is in our power to do so," Harper said of the initiative.[2]

The initiatives favoured by the Harper government in health were distinguished by three factors: they allowed the federal government to act unilaterally, they addressed a national health issue and they were beyond the commitments of the Martin health accord.

Cutting Refugee Health Coverage and Veterans' Health Benefits

The Harper government's most controversial decisions in health were not in the intergovernmental sphere but rather in an area of exclusive federal jurisdiction. The cuts to health coverage for refugees and the cuts to veterans' health benefits provoked loud and sustained opposition.

This approach to health coverage for these two vulnerable groups fell within the general philosophy of mean-spirited arbitrary unilateralism for which the Harper government came to be known—as bewildering in its motive as it was in its implementation. It challenged the public's notions of generosity and of the nation's commitment to veterans. The stubbornness with which the Harper government defended its unpopular policies underscored the near Thatcher-like stance of not turning in response to criticism, no matter how valid.

In a small but telling example of how people are drawn into political life, Jane Philpott, a family doctor with international experience wrote editorials opposing the refugee health cuts. Later she ran as a Liberal candidate, became Canada's health minister and reversed the same cuts she had protested.

The Abandonment of Intergovernmental Dialogue on Health Care

Leona Aglukkaq, a former health minister in the Nunavut government, was sworn in as federal health minister in 2008. Throughout her nearly five-year term as minister of health in the Harper government, she was most frequently the voice of that government's view that the primary responsibility for health care rested with the provinces. The federal government's gradual retreat from intergovernmental dialogue on health matters since 2006 caused great concern, but there was an expectation that the need to renegotiate the 2004 Health Accord would force Ottawa back to the table and restart engagement.

Instead, a unilateral decision by the federal government to change the Canada Health Transfer (CHT) was announced by Finance Minister Jim Flaherty on December 19, 2011. To put it mildly, it was not received as a welcome Christmas gift by most provincial finance ministers.

The "take it or leave it" offer was first to extend the annual increase of 6 per cent for an additional three years, after which the annual increase would be the greater of 3 per cent per annum or the annual growth in gross domestic product. On these points, there would be no negotiation.

Many provinces and health provider organizations had been gearing up for a lengthy and spirited negotiation, but the realities of a slowing economy and the fact that provincial health spending had been growing closer to 3 per cent per annum dampened enthusiasm for a protracted debate. The negotiation preparation lost steam and the Harper government achieved their goal of having the provinces focus on managing down the cost of health care services.

The Search for Innovation at No or Little Cost

Rona Ambrose was appointed federal health minister in mid-2013 and served for over two years. One of her most notable achievements was the formation of an Advisory Panel on Health Care Innovation. The mandate of the Advisory Panel was to identify the five "most promising areas of innovation in Canada and internationally."[3] A further part of its mandate was to recommend how the federal government could support innovation in these five areas, and they were directed to recommend no financial investments of any scale. David Naylor, former president of the University of Toronto and dean of its medical school, was appointed as chair of the Advisory Panel on July 24, 2014.

Ignoring the "no additional funding" stipulation in its mandate, the Advisory Panel recommended that up to $1 billion dollars per year be allocated from both existing spending and new dollars to the implementation of their recommendations. Chief among those recommendations was a bringing together of three existing agencies—Canada Health Infoway, the Canadian Foundation for Health Care Improvement and the Patient Safety Institute—into a new organization focused on innovation. The recommendation of the Advisory Panel was to fund the spread of innovation across Canadian health care in a much more deliberate and accelerated pace. Their recommended antidote for arrested development was accelerated innovation.

The Advisory Panel report was delivered to Minister Ambrose in July 2015, a few short weeks before the start of the federal election campaign. She made no statements upon receiving the Panel's report beyond simply acknowledging its receipt, and took no position on the report's analysis or recommendations.

Conclusion

The Harper government rejected the "sleeves rolled up" working agenda on health care contemplated by Prime Minister Paul Martin at the time of the 2004 Health

Accord, but preserved and in some case enhanced key elements of the accord. It is somewhat ironic that the Harper government, having inherited both a reform agenda and a funding formula, felt politically bound not to alter the financial aspect but ignored the working agenda for change, based on a clear belief that the provinces had stewardship of the good ship health care delivery. Time and again, Harper's health ministers stressed the provincial responsibility for health care delivery.

As it remained wholly untouched by the Harper government that initiated it, the Naylor panel report may well have provided the Trudeau government with an agenda and plan to foster innovation in Canadian health care. Having described Canadian Medicare as being in "arrested development," the panel offered decision-makers the stark choice of trending down toward worse outcomes or scaling up toward innovation.

The Harper government may have been on the cusp of a new and more constructive direction in health policy at the time of its defeat. Certainly the Advisory Panel on Health Care Innovation laid out a powerful and plausible direction for modernizing Canadian health care. But in politics as in life, the maxim "too soon old, too late wise" has in itself great wisdom. Battered by the challenge of managing two successive minority governments, Harper finally won his majority in 2011. But with that majority government, health policy became more unilateral and at times was driven more by narrow-minded cost containment than by modernization.

With a few important exceptions—the tainted blood settlement, the Canadian Partnership Against Cancer and the Mental Health Commission—the Harper government's health policies could fairly be described as the river of federal money: the increase in the Canada Health Transfer flowed on at a steady rate of six per cent per year even as provincial spending slowed, but the health policy agenda continued to experience arrested development, as noted in the Naylor report.

Sadly, Harper was unwilling to seize the opportunity to lead the much-needed reform of Canadian health care, believing that provincial governments needed to be fully accountable for reforming health service delivery. He did leave a more realistic financial framework for transfers to the provinces and an enlightened Advisory Panel Report for the Trudeau government to tackle.

15

Unsustainable Development:
Energy and Environment in the Harper Decade

George Hoberg

Stephen Harper's policies on energy and environment were guided by a free market, decentralist ideology designed to promote economic growth through natural resource development. He was reluctant to use governmental power to intervene in the market, and he resisted using the federal government to play a leadership role in intergovernmental relations. While Harper sought to create a policy and a political environment that would foster such resource-driven economic growth, political and market forces, both domestic and international, conspired against his ambitions. In the end, his record was only partially successful. His success in forestalling significant climate action reduced the costs of business, but it also backfired. His inaction on environmental issues, especially on climate, intensified domestic opposition and tarnished Canada's environmental record internationally. As a result, he was unable to accomplish his goal of transforming Canada into an energy superpower.

Four interrelated groups of strategies guided the Harper era in the energy-environment field: relaxing environmental laws to facilitate project approval, evading meaningful action on climate change, undermining the federal government's own capacity on environmental issues and vacating intergovernmental relations. Harper's core goal seemed to be to advance the interests of the resource sector as much as possible by minimizing regulatory costs and marginalizing opponents, but he pursued the strategy well past the time that it appeared to be fruitful.

Responsible Resource Development

Shortly after forming government in 2006, Harper famously pronounced in a speech in London that Canada was an "emerging energy superpower."[1] His core strategy to pursue that vision was to expand the oil sands, and an essential step toward that was to expand pipeline capacity into growing markets. During his time as prime minister, four major pipelines were proposed, but none of them were under construction or in operation when he left office. Still, his efforts to promote oil sands expansion transformed Canadian environmental law and politics.

The first, TransCanada's Keystone XL, was proposed to connect the oil sands to the Gulf Coast of the United States. Because it crossed national boundaries, however, it was subject to American jurisdiction. Bill McKibben, the head of the US-based climate action group 350.org, decided in mid-2011 to target the pipeline as "the poster child for the kind of stuff that's going to have to stay in the ground."[2] Reframing the pipeline controversy as a climate issue brought the oil sands and Canada's weak climate record to American attention.

US law requires a presidential "national interest" determination, and that allowed activists to target their campaign directly at President Obama. Environmentalists were a critical part of Obama's electoral coalition. The strategy was successful at mobilizing an anti-pipeline movement that was influential enough to get the regulatory decision postponed until after the 2012 presidential election. The pipeline became a flashpoint between the Democratic president and the Republican Congress, as well as one of the most divisive issues in Canadian-American relations in recent history. The Keystone XL pipeline—the one Harper once referred to as a "no-brainer"—was ultimately rejected by Obama in November 2015.

As the Keystone XL pipeline got bogged down in cross-border controversy, the Canadian oil sector, and its allies in government, began placing more emphasis on the Northern Gateway pipeline proposal, which would run from Edmonton to the North Pacific coast at Kitimat, BC. The proposal ran squarely into a well-organized coalition of environmentalists and First Nations who were intent on keeping oil tankers away from the coast and thwarting oil sands expansion. The proposal was submitted by Enbridge in 2010, and the government established a joint review panel to conduct the regulatory review and environmental assessment. Activists launched a "mob the mic" campaign to mobilize participation of opponents at the hearings. Roughly 4,200 individuals and groups registered to give oral statements, overwhelming the expectations of the joint review panel. In response, in late 2011, the panel extended the timeline for project review by a year.

The Harper government was incensed by this development and responded forcefully the following spring, when it introduced Bill C-38, the Jobs, Growth and Long-term Prosperity Act, and its companion, Bill C-45. These mammoth omnibus budget bills rewrote much of Canadian environmental law in order to implement the government's Responsible Resource Development Plan. The stated purpose of the plan was to "create jobs, growth, and long-term prosperity" by "streamlin[ing] the review process for major resource projects."[3] Bill C-38 amended the Canadian Environmental Assessment Act and the National Energy Board Act to streamline regulatory approvals, provide strict timelines for review and limit participation in the process to those who are "directly affected" or have, in the regulators' judgment, "relevant information and expertise."

These bills also moved the final decision on pipeline approval from the National Energy Board (NEB) to cabinet, weakened the Fisheries Act to remove much of the protection afforded to fish habitat, and insulated pipelines from the provisions of the Navigable Waters Protection Act.[4] These sweeping budget bills, unprecedented for the scope of their impact on authorizing legislation, provoked a massive outpouring of criticism and protest from the environmental community. They also outraged First Nations, some of whom responded by mobilizing behind the Idle No More movement.[5]

In December 2014, the Harper government granted approval to the Northern Gateway pipeline with 209 conditions. By that time, however, the accumulated opposition to the pipeline (including that of BC premier Christy Clark) led many to conclude that the pipeline would never be built despite the conditional authorization. Initially the oil industry had more hope for the Kinder Morgan Trans Mountain Expansion project, but it ran into the same political dynamic that the Northern Gateway pipeline did. Despite the mandated timetables, that project review ran over as well, in part the result of self-inflicted wounds by the Harper government. Harper's surprise appointment of an NEB member who had acted previously as a witness for Kinder Morgan required the NEB to take a pause to deal with the conflict of interest issues.[6] The NEB recommended its approval with conditions eight months after Harper left office (the pending final decision is with the Trudeau government).

The Energy East pipeline, from Edmonton to New Brunswick, was formally proposed in October 2014. Regulatory review is currently underway and a decision is expected in mid-2018. The Responsible Resource Development Plan was intended to facilitate the approval and construction of critical infrastructure like oil sands pipelines, but it ultimately failed to do so. The Harper government did strengthen tanker safety rules in 2013 and 2014, but that had little apparent affect on the adamant opposition to new oil sands pipelines among Indigenous people, environmentalists and many residents of affected communities.

Evading Climate Action

Harper's record is one of evading meaningful policy actions to tackle climate change. He came into office in 2006 criticizing the previous Liberal government for agreeing to targets without a plan to attain them, and promised to develop a "made in Canada" policy. In May 2006, Environment Minister Rona Ambrose announced that it would be "impossible for Canada to reach its Kyoto targets,"[7] setting the stage for Canada's formal withdrawal from the Kyoto Protocol five years later.

The Harper government replaced the nation's Kyoto Protocol commitment to reduce emissions by 6 per cent below 1990 levels by 2012 with a new goal of a 20 per cent reduction below 2006 levels by 2020 (equivalent to 2 per cent below 1990 levels).[8] In April 2007, the Harper government proposed their "turning the corner" plan, which was a regulatory approach requiring large emitters to reduce their carbon pollution per unit of production by a specified percentage each year. That proposed plan was perhaps the most ambitious action on climate change ever proposed by the Harper government, under John Baird. The plan was never implemented, however, and instead Harper turned the corner on any ambition to undertake meaningful climate action.

The 2008 election campaign featured Liberal leader Stéphane Dion's ill-fated "green shift," a proposal for a revenue-neutral carbon tax. Dion's weak communication skills were no match for Harper's relentless criticism. The 2008 world economic crisis further undermined the political viability of Dion's proposal, and Harper made the most of it: "It is like the [1980] national energy program in the sense that the national energy program was designed to screw the West and really damage the energy sector—and this will do those things. This is different in that this will actually screw everybody across the country."[9] Harper went on to win his second minority government.

Harper's success against Dion changed the politics of climate change as he came to believe that opposition to carbon taxes and aggressive climate policy was a winning political strategy. As global climate policy momentum began to increase, Harper adopted the strategy of limiting policy change and castigating proposals for greater ambition.

During the Copenhagen rounds of international climate talks in 2009, Harper abandoned his "made in Canada" rhetoric for deference to the position of the United States. In January 2010, then–environment minister Jim Prentice announced Canada's new national target—a 17 per cent reduction below 2005 levels by 2020. Not only was that target weaker than the previously announced 6 per cent below 1990 (2020 emissions would be 6 per cent higher), but the new position was striking for how it tied itself to US actions: the target was "to be aligned with the final economy-wide emissions target of the United States in enacted legislation." In his Calgary speech announcing the new targets, Prentice stated, "Our determination to harmonize our climate change policy with that of the United States also extends beyond greenhouse gas emission targets: we need to proceed even further in aligning our regulations. ... [W]e will only adopt a cap-and-trade regime if the United States signals that it wants to do the same. Our position on harmonization applies equally to regulation. ... Canada can go down either road—cap-and-trade or regulation—but we will go down neither road alone."

In 2010, the legislative effort in the US to develop a cap and trade program died in the US Senate.[10] As Republican control of Congress increased, and environmental politics (like everything else in America) became more polarized, President Obama's only choice was to pursue his regulatory authority under the existing Clean Air Act. The two most important areas of authority over greenhouse gases were regulation of coal-fired power plants and of automobiles. Recognizing that cap and trade was dead in the US, the Harper government committed to pursuing regulations, focusing on the three most substantial components of Canada's emissions: coal-fired power plants, the oil and gas industry, and automobiles.

Harper actually got out ahead of the US government by adopting regulations for coal-fired electricity. In 2012, Ottawa enacted regulations (to be brought into force in 2015) for new coal-fired power plants. The regulations effectively banned new coal-fired power plants that did not capture and sequester their carbon. The problem, however, is that the regulations would not affect existing power plants unless the operator was planning to extend their life beyond their normal "useful life" of forty-five to fifty years. As a result, given their age, no existing plants would be affected before 2030. Nothing in the regulations required or encouraged existing coal generation to be shut down.[11] When it came to automobiles, the Harper government—following a long tradition of Canadian governments—chose to adopt the new vehicle standards adopted by the Obama government in 2012. Given the integrated nature of the North American vehicle market, it would have been both costly and disruptive for Canada *not* to adopt the new standards. It is this action—following the US lead on auto regulations—that is the single most consequential action by the Harper government in reducing greenhouse gas (GHG) emissions.

In contrast to the coal and vehicle sectors, where Harper did enact at least some regulations, he never enacted regulations on Canada's fastest growing GHG sector, the oil and gas industry. Harper's commitment to develop GHG standards for the oil and gas sector dates back to 2007. It was the third pillar in the government's regulatory approach, and it became salient as the Keystone XL controversy with the United States was increasingly focused on the climate implications of oil sands expansion, and Canada's lax climate policies.

While a regulatory proposal was never published, it was widely circulated that the federal government was considering a proposal to go beyond Alberta's oil sands GHG regulation. The Alberta regulation required emitters to reduce pollution 12 per cent below certain emission targets per barrel, and if they couldn't meet that, pay $15 a tonne for the amount in excess of the target. The federal government proposal was to increase the emission rate target reduction to 30 per cent and increase the penalty for not meeting that to $30 a tonne.[12] But the Harper government never moved forward with that proposal, or any other GHG rule for the oil sands. Initially, Harper justified his reluctance based on that fact that the US had yet to enact similar recommendations. Shortly after that justification had been shown to be false,[13] the price of oil began its spectacular decline. In December 2014, Harper essentially closed the book on the possibility of issuing a regulation, stating: "Under the current circumstances of the oil and gas sector, it would be crazy, it would be crazy economic policy to do unilateral penalties on that sector. We are clearly not going to do it."[14]

Fig. 15.1
Canada Not on Track to Meet Emissions Target

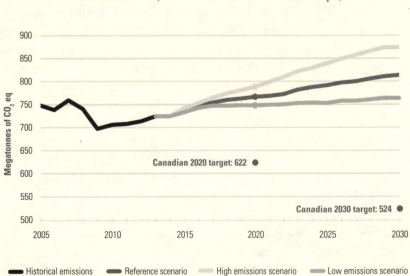

Historical greenhouse gas emissions and projections to 2030 with measures of September 2015, Canada, 2005 to 2030 (Mt CO_2 eq)

Source: Environment and Climate Change Canada, *Canada's Second Biennial Report on Climate Change* 2016, 19, available at www.ec.gc.ca.

When the sector was booming and the price of oil soaring, Harper didn't regulate GHG emissions from the oil sands, nor did he when the price of oil collapsed. Harper never acted to address Canada's fastest growing source of emissions, and the single biggest symbol domestically and internationally of his government's climate evasions. He did enact regulations on future coal plants that would have no impact until 2030. He did adopt US regulations for the auto sector. As a result, Canadian climate policy has lagged behind other countries and become a potent symbol of the Harper government's poor environment record. Figure 15.1 shows Canada's progress towards its 2020 and 2030 international targets. Its 2020 targets already out of reach, Canada will only be able to achieve its 2030 targets with significant new policy measures (the different levels in the projections reflect different assumptions of economic growth and oil prices). In an international comparison of sixty-one countries on climate policy, Canada' ranking is very poor—fifty-sixth of sixty-one countries measured. Of all OECD countries, only Korea, Japan and Australia ranked lower.[15]

Undermining Capacity

One of the most striking features of Harper's record was his eagerness to undermine the capacity not just of his political opponents but of his own government as well. He actively worked to delegitimize environmentalists and used the government's tax machinery to intimidate them. He reduced funding for the environment compared to other programs, and he eliminated a prestigious government forum for non-partisan advice. He also restricted his own government scientists from commenting publicly.

As resistance to Harper's developmental priorities grew, his government initiated an explicit attack on the credibility and legitimacy of environmental critics of oil sands expansion. The flashpoint was the Northern Gateway Pipeline, described above. On the eve of the joint review panel hearing on the pipeline, then–natural resources minister Joe Oliver published an open letter directly attacking the pipeline's opponents. He referred to "environmental and other radical groups" that "threaten to hijack our regulatory system to achieve their radical ideological agenda" with the help of "funding from foreign special interest groups."[16]

The prime minister himself reiterated a similar theme, and Environment Minister Peter Kent accused environmental groups of "laundering" money from foreign special interests to undermine the regulatory review process.[17] Environmentalists were also alarmed when the Harper government's 2012 anti-terrorism strategy listed "eco-extremists" as threats. In 2014, an RCMP Critical Infrastructure Intelligence Assessment listed the "anti-Canadian petroleum movement" in its document on "Criminal Threats to the Canadian Petroleum Industry."[18]

The Harper government also used the tax code to discourage environmentalists and other critics of his administration from politically challenging the government. Many environmental groups are registered charities under tax law, and that status puts limits on what fraction of a group's funding can be used for political advocacy. Part of Bill C-38, the omnibus bill that changed so much of the regulatory framework, provided a specific budgetary authorization for the Canadian Revenue Agency to audit registered charities. Many of the environmental opponents of Harper's agenda were subjected to rigorous scrutiny; conveniently, conservative charities appeared to be insulated from the audits.[19] When announcing the winding down of the special audit program in January 2016, the Trudeau government's minister of national revenue announced the results of audit: "To date, of the 30 completed political activities audits, only five resulted in a determination to revoke registration, all of which were primarily based on factors that were beyond their involvement in political activities."[20]

Fig. 15.2
A Clean and Healthy Environment, Federal Spending

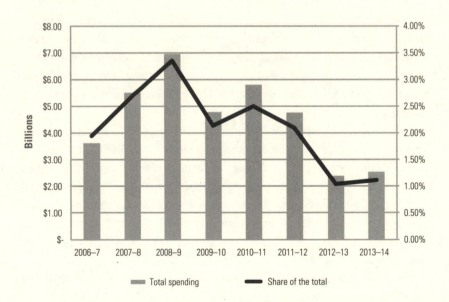

Based on an analysis of the federal public accounts by the Institute for Fiscal Studies at the University of Ottawa. Used with permission.

While attacking political opponents, Harper was also undermining the capacity of his own government to produce effective environmental regulation. Budgets for environmental programs were reduced relative to other government priorities. Figure 15.2 shows trends in the function of a "clean and healthy environment." Funding in the last year of data (2013–14) was 1.1 per cent of overall program spending, down from its peak in 2008–9 of 3.4 per cent, and from the 2.0 per cent in its starting year of 2006–7.

The government also terminated a prestigious non-partisan research organization. The National Roundtable on the Environment and the Economy was created by the Mulroney government in 1988 to provide advice and analysis for how to promote sustainable development in Canada. The Harper government cut funding to the organization in 2012 and went so far as to scrub the organization's content from the web. While the decision was initially justified by budgetary concerns, John Baird, then–minister of foreign affairs, stated in the House that the decision was linked to the roundtable support for carbon pricing. In a remarkably blunt characterization of his government's view of value of independent advice, he stated: "It should agree with Canadians. It should agree with the government. No discussion of a carbon tax that would kill and hurt Canadian families."[21]

The Harper regime became notorious for "muzzling" its own scientists. In the past, it was common practice for federal research scientists to be able to talk directly to the media or to attend conferences and openly discuss science-policy issues. The Harper government changed that by centralizing communications and prohibiting scientists from engaging with the media and others outside the government without first getting approval from agency communication officials. Criticism emerged as the practice became more widespread and its implications for the media and working scientists became more apparent.[22] Harper's clampdown on federal scientists drew the attention of the international science community, becoming the subject of an editorial in the prestigious journal *Nature* and of a special session of the American Association for the Advancement of Science.[23] The strategy also became the target of political mobilization, giving birth to a new NGO called Evidence for Democracy and spawning headlines like "Scientists March on Canadian Parliament."[24] Evidence-based decision-making became an issue in the 2015 election.

Vacating Intergovernmental Relations

The fourth essential feature of Harper's energy and environmental record was his government's refusal to engage directly in intergovernmental discussions. Canada's constitution establishes a complex division of power between the federal government and the provinces. Since the 1980 National Energy Program debacle, Canadian federal governments have been reluctant to play a strong role in energy policy. But federal caution is unlikely to be effective at fostering the country as an "emerging energy superpower," nor is it likely to be productive at resolving complex issues requiring difficult choices with strong regional distributional consequences. Harper's unwillingness to provide national leadership on these critical issues, driven in large part by his decentralist ideology, stymied effective policy and national conflict resolution.

The leadership vacuum resulting from Harper's unwillingness to engage with the provinces was evident in both climate and energy policy. On climate, Harper's goal was to evade meaningful policy, so the lack of engagement was at least consistent with his policy goals in the short term. His unwillingness to engage on energy issues is more puzzling. As early as 2007, initiatives began to emerge, both among the provinces and within civil society, to advance a national energy strategy of some kind. The initiatives began to take on momentum in 2012 when Alberta, anxious to create conditions for pipeline expansion, took on a leadership role. But the province's interests in oil sands expansion were not consistent with the interests of Ontario, Quebec and British Columbia, provinces that were keen to show leadership on fighting climate change. The premiers of BC and Alberta ended up in a bitter conflict in 2012 over the Northern Gateway pipeline, yet Harper simply stood on the sidelines.[25] In July 2015, the provinces did succeed in producing a document called the Canadian Energy Strategy,[26] but it was too vague to resolve any of the enduring conflicts that characterized the Harper era, and seems to have been quickly forgotten.

Conclusion

These four strategies are interrelated, and their effects compounded to backfire against Harper's agenda. The Responsible Resource Development Plan was designed to facilitate project approval, but instead inspired a powerful resistance movement that was able to thwart pipeline expansion, at least during Harper's time in office. His efforts to evade meaningful action on climate change were designed to reduce the costs to business and facilitate oil sands expansion. But the black eye he gave Canada's environmental record made it harder to get the market licence the sector needed. He sought to ridicule, marginalize and intimidate opponents in the environmental community, but at the end of his reign the Canadian environmental movement was more robust and resourceful than when he took office. By vacating intergovernmental relations, deep differences among provinces, and about Canada's identity, simply festered.

At the end of the day, Harper seemed to privilege his own ideology over the interests of not only the oil sands sector that drove the wealth of his home province, but also his own political fortunes. His desire to limit government regulation of the market, and avoid infringing on what he considered provincial responsibilities, prevented him from taking actions that would have benefited the energy sector and, potentially, his electoral fortunes in 2015. His legacy in the energy and environmental field is one of neglect in addressing the core challenges of sustainable development in the twenty-first century.

Conclusion

Jennifer Ditchburn and Graham Fox

It is impossible to capture the "Harper Factor" over a broad range of policy areas with a single adjective. His impact after a decade in power is not one thing. In an important way, that is the point of this book: the measure of a prime ministership does not neatly fit into a single box defined as negative or positive, deep or shallow.

For instance, his attention to victims' rights and some of his reforms to the immigration system can be seen as largely positive. His intensely partisan approach to politics, his curtailing of access to government information and his conduct of foreign affairs, in contrast, were not.

If there is one overarching conclusion we have reached as co-editors, it is that Stephen Harper was not, in the end, a transformational prime minister.

While he was certainly a polarizing political figure—perhaps the most polarizing of his generation—it would be difficult to argue that his government fundamentally changed the course of public policy in Canada. This is not to say that some of his decisions weren't controversial, or didn't break with the past, and as David Zussman's chapter explored, Harper did alter the *way* in which policy was developed inside government. But the analyses in this volume have shown that in many cases there was a significant gap between the scope of change announced by his government (or decried by his opponents) and the amount of change that was actually implemented. Murray Brewster's examination of the government's commitment to re-equipping the military is just one example. Even in cases where the change was more dramatic, it doesn't necessarily follow that the change will be lasting.

Stephen Harper's approach to politics is far more likely to be a defining feature of his legacy than are the policies he introduced as prime minister. Short-term political objectives often dictated the policy outcome and, in a few cases, will prove to have deeper consequences for the country. For example, the revenues lost through the cutting of the GST, one of the Conservative Party's five key promises in the 2005–6 election campaign, prevented the government from introducing other measures that would have contributed to longer-term growth. Canada's relationship with China never quite recovered from Harper's initial public repudiation of Beijing in 2006. The impact of favouring mandatory minimum sentencing over a rehabilitative approach to corrections will be borne out in the years to come as incarcerated Canadians rejoin their communities.

The supremacy of politics over policy also manifested itself in the proliferation of micro or retail policies during his time in office. These tailored measures were aimed at small pockets of accessible voters in target constituencies. The tax credit for children's sports equipment was marketed as a tool to encourage physical activity, but it was largely about impacting the electoral choice of parents in the suburbs of Toronto. Likewise, barring certain refugee applicants from health care services appeared designed to resonate with certain elements of the party's base of support.

Winning three consecutive mandates and remaining in office almost ten years is a feat few Canadian political leaders have achieved, and so Harper is assured a place in history. But that is a political achievement, not a policy achievement. During his time in office, he made a great many decisions—some of them good or even great, others bad or worse—but we are at a loss to note one signature policy achievement that will, in future years, define his prime ministership. The Federal Accountability Act, his government's first item of business after the 2006 victory, might prove to be the most durable. Despite the growing body of evidence that the law is in serious need of fundamental reform, the mythology built around the Act will make it very difficult indeed for future governments to make the necessary changes.

Still, the short-termism that guided so many decisions will have an impact on how Canadians look back on the mark Harper made on the country. Changes implemented in haste to address the needs of the moment may not stand the test of time. At the time of this writing, the Trudeau government was already dismantling many Harper policies—the Liberals reinstated the long-form census, announced an inquiry on missing and murdered Indigenous women, and restored health care services to all refugees. As well, Trudeau met with the premiers and improved access to the media. One wonders, what will be left of the Harper legacy after even one Trudeau term?

To conclude that Harper's time in office was not transformational is not in itself a judgment on the quality of the decisions he made. To state the obvious, not all long-serving prime ministers have been transformational. Whether it was by choice or by force of personality or both, Harper opted for a more incremental, transactional approach to governing. As prime minister, he *managed* the country, in many cases competently. But transformation requires a public leadership beyond even highly competent management.

As Prime Minister Brian Mulroney said in a 2014 speech in Ottawa, "[l]eadership is the process, not only of foreseeing the need for change, but of making the case for change. Leadership does not consist of imposing unpopular ideas on the public but of making unpopular ideas acceptable to the nation." On many issues, Stephen Harper did not try to rally the country together or bring opposing sides to some sort of consensus. Susan Delacourt has explored how Harper was guided by an electoral strategy that focused on micro-targeting voters, rather than inviting Canadians into a big tent.

Consultations on important points of public policy such as Indigenous affairs, the immigration system and the environment were thin (or non-existent, as with the elimination of the long-form census). Environmentalists became traitors, people who criticized defence policy were friends of the Taliban or not supportive of our troops, those who had problems with the justice file were soft on crime, Canadians who advocated for diplomacy just wanted to "go along to get along" and all sorts of policy thinkers were summarily dismissed as "elites." With so many groups of Canadians not invited to Harper's table while he was in power, and with a communications strategy that throttled the flow of information, it will make it difficult for the public to settle on a shared understanding of his contribution even years from now.

Transformational impact on public policy requires that at least some of the major changes a prime minister introduces last beyond her or his time in office. Indeed, each long-serving prime minister who has had that kind of impact in the last half-century had a signature policy achievement that was celebrated ten, twenty and thirty years after its implementation: Diefenbaker's Bill of Rights, Pearson's Medicare, Pierre Trudeau's Charter of Rights and Freedoms, Mulroney's free trade agreements and acid rain treaty. Those signature achievements have ensured each of them has shaped the lives of Canadians well after leaving office.

While unforeseen events may, in future, change current public perceptions of a specific Harper policy, it is difficult at this stage to identify what that lasting contribution to Canadian public policy would be. Longevity in office allowed Stephen Harper to have a significant impact on Canadians while he was prime minister. But his focus on the transactional means that impact will not likely be felt much beyond the current generation.

Contributor Biographical Notes

Co-Editors

Jennifer Ditchburn is the editor-in-chief of *Policy Options*, the online magazine of the Institute for Research on Public Policy (IRPP). An award-winning journalist, she spent more than two decades covering national and parliamentary affairs for the Canadian Press and for CBC Television. She is a three-time winner of a National Newspaper Award, and the recipient of the prestigious Charles Lynch Award for outstanding coverage of national issues. Jennifer is a frequent contributor to television and radio public affairs programs. She holds a Bachelor of Arts from Concordia University and a Master of Journalism from Carleton University. Her research on the history of the Canadian Parliamentary Press Gallery appeared in the 2016 book *Sharp Wits & Busy Pens*.

Graham Fox is President and CEO of the Institute for Research on Public Policy (IRPP)—an independent, non-partisan think tank headquartered in Montreal. He is a former a strategic policy adviser at the law firm of Fraser Milner Casgrain, where he provided public policy analysis and government relations advice to firm clients. Before that, Graham was vice-president of the Public Policy Forum, executive director of the KTA Centre for Collaborative Government and director of communications at the IRPP. In politics, Graham contested the 2007 Ontario general election as a candidate in the constituency of Ottawa-Orléans. He was also chief of staff to the Rt. Hon. Joe Clark, leader of the Progressive Conservative Party of Canada, and press secretary to the Hugh Segal campaign for the leadership of the PC Party. A policy entrepreneur, Graham's research interests include federalism and intergovernmental affairs, parliamentary reform, democratic renewal and citizen engagement. He holds an undergraduate degree in history from Queen's University, where he was a Loran scholar, and a master's degree in political science from the London School of Economics.

Contributors

Murray Brewster is a defence and foreign policy correspondent in CBC's parliamentary bureau. He spent fifteen months in Afghanistan during the five-year Kandahar combat mission, travelling with troops and unilaterally throughout the country while working as a reporter with the Canadian Press. Murray's book, *The Savage War: The Untold Battles of Afghanistan*, was published in 2011 by John Wiley and Sons, and he was the lead writer on the documentary *Kandahar Journals*, which aired on CBC Documentary Channel and was released in the US in the fall of 2015. He has won twelve regional and national Radio and Television News Director Awards, two Atlantic Journalism Awards and the Ross Munro Award for war corresponding (2010); appeared as a finalist twice in the Michener Awards for public service in journalism (1989 and 2014); and was a finalist in the National Newspaper Awards for beat reporting (2010).

Laura Dawson is Director of the Canada Institute at the Wilson Center in Washington, DC. The Canada Institute is North America's only organization dedicated to research and discussion on the full spectrum of Canada-US issues. Laura is a speaker, writer and thought leader on US-Canada and international economic issues. She was named one of Canada's Top 100 Foreign Policy Influencers by Ottawa's *Hill Times* in 2014 and is founder of the Ottawa-based policy research company Dawson Strategic. Previously, Laura served as a senior adviser on economic affairs at the United States Embassy in Ottawa and program director at the Centre for Trade Policy and Law. She has taught at the Canadian School of Public Service and at Carleton University. She is a Fellow at the Canadian Defence & Global Affairs Institute and is Chair of the Council of the Great Lakes Region. Laura holds a PhD in political science.

Michael B. Decter is a Harvard-trained economist with over three decades of experience as a senior manager. He served as Cabinet Secretary in the Government of Manitoba and Deputy Minister of Health in the Government of Ontario. He is a leading Canadian expert on health systems, with a wealth of international experience. As a Senior Research Scholar at the Centre for Bioethics, University of Toronto, Michael authored the book *Healing Medicare: Managing Health System Change—The Canadian Way*, published in 1994. His second health book, *Four Strong Winds—Understanding the Growing Challenges to Health Care,* was published in June 2000. His third book, *Navigating Canada's Health Care*, co-authored by Francesca Grosso, was published in December 2006. Michael was the Founding Chair of the Health Council of Canada and former Chair of Saint Elizabeth Health

Care. He also served as the Chair of the Canadian Institute for Health Information, the Ontario Cancer Quality Council and Wait Times Data Certification Council of Ontario. In 2004, Michael was awarded the Order of Canada. In 2013, he was named Chancellor of Brandon University.

Susan Delacourt is a freelance columnist whose work appears in iPolitics and the *Toronto Star*. Over her career, she has worked at some of the top newsrooms in the country, from those of the *Star* and the *Globe and Mail* to the *Ottawa Citizen* and the *National Post*. She is the author of four books, and her latest—*Shopping for Votes*—was a finalist for the Hilary Weston Writers' Trust Prize for Nonfiction in 2014. A frequent political panellist on CBC Radio and CTV, Susan has taught classes in journalism and political communication at Carleton University. She is the winner of the 2011 Charles Lynch Award, an annual award presented to a Canadian journalist in recognition of outstanding coverage of national issues as selected by their colleagues in the Canadian Parliamentary Press Gallery, and the prestigious 2014 Hyman Solomon Award for Excellence in Public Policy Journalism.

Richard Dion is a senior Business Adviser, Economic Analyst and Forecasting Adviser at Bennett Jones LLP. He provides economic analysis and forecasting for clients with business interests in Canada and abroad. Prior to joining Bennett Jones, Richard worked as an economist for the Bank of Canada (for over thirty years in various departments), the Department of Foreign Affairs and International Trade, and Energy, Mines and Resources Canada.

During a distinguished career in the federal public service, David Dodge held senior positions in the Central Mortgage and Housing Corporation, the Anti-Inflation Board and the Department of Employment and Immigration. After serving in a number of increasingly senior positions at the Department of Finance, including that of G7 Deputy, he served as Deputy Minister of Finance from 1992 to 1997. In 1998, David was appointed Deputy Minister of Health, a position he held until his appointment as Governor of the Bank of Canada in 2001. He is Chancellor Emeritus of Queen's University, and a senior adviser at Bennett Jones LLP.

George Hoberg is a political scientist and professor in the Liu Institute for Global Issues at the University of British Columbia. He specializes in environmental and natural resource policy and governance. Before joining the Liu Institute, George taught public policy and American politics in the Department of Political Science for thirteen years, and forest and energy policy in the Faculty of Forestry from

2001 to 2016. His research interests include environmental policy, energy policy, forest policy and more generally the design of policies and institutions to promote sustainability. George's current research focuses on the clean energy transformation, and he's writing a book on the resistance to oil sands pipelines and the challenges and opportunities of the clean energy transformation.

A familiar face to followers of Canadian politics, Tasha Kheiriddin is the host of *The Tasha Kheiriddin Show*, airing weekday afternoons on AM640 radio in Toronto. She writes two weekly columns in English for iPolitics.ca, which appear in French on her website, www.tashakheiriddin.com, and provides political analysis for RDI's *Le Téléjournal* and Radio-Canada's *Grands Lacs Café*. She is the co-author of the 2005 best-seller *Rescuing Canada's Right: Blueprint for a Conservative Revolution*. A graduate of McGill Law School, Tasha practised litigation before working as the legislative assistant to the Attorney General of Ontario. In 1998 she began producing television with CBC Newsworld and the Cable Public Affairs Channel (CPAC), winning the Justicia Award for Excellence in Journalism from the Canadian Bar Association in 2003. Tasha subsequently served as Ontario director of the Canadian Taxpayers Federation, Vice-President of the Montreal Economic Institute and Director for Quebec of the Fraser Institute, while lecturing on conservative politics at McGill University.

The Hon. Ratna Omidvar is an internationally recognized expert on migration, diversity and inclusion. In April 2016, Prime Minister Trudeau appointed Ratna to the Senate of Canada as an independent Senator representing Ontario. Ratna is the founding Executive Director and currently a Distinguished Visiting Professor at the Global Diversity Exchange (GDX), Ted Rogers School of Management, Ryerson University. GDX is a think-and-do tank on diversity, migration and inclusion that connects local experience and ideas with global networks. Ratna is a director at the Environics Institute, and at Samara. She is the Toronto Region Immigrant Employment Council's Chair Emerita and was formerly the Chair of Lifeline Syria. Ratna is co-author of *Flight and Freedom: Stories of Escape to Canada* (2015), an Open Book Toronto best book of 2015 and one of the *Toronto Star*'s top five good reads from Word on the Street. Ratna was appointed to the Order of Ontario in 2005 and became a Member of the Order of Canada in 2011, with both honours recognizing her advocacy work on behalf of immigrants and devotion to reducing inequality in Canada.

A former Canadian diplomat, Colin Robertson is a senior adviser to Dentons LLP living in Ottawa and working with the Business Council of Canada. He is

Vice President and Fellow at the Canadian Global Affairs Institute. Colin is an Executive Fellow at the University of Calgary's School of Public Policy and a Distinguished Senior Fellow at the Norman Paterson School of International Affairs at Carleton University. He sits on the advisory councils of the Conference of Defence Associations Institute and the North American Research Partnership, and is an Honorary Captain (Royal Canadian Navy) assigned to the Strategic Communications Directorate. Colin writes a column every two weeks on foreign affairs for the *Globe and Mail* and is a regular contributor to other media.

Cynthia Wesley-Esquimaux is the Vice Provost (Aboriginal Initiatives) at Lakehead University, Thunder Bay & Orillia. She also serves as an Adjunct Asst. Professor for the Faculty of Anthropology and Research Affiliate of the Centre for Health Care Ethics. Her research and academic writing is directed toward understanding the continuing transmission of unresolved intergenerational trauma and grief primarily within the Indigenous community of Canada. Cynthia is a Board Member for Canadian Roots Exchange, Healthy Minds Canada and the Teach for Canada Non-Profit. She is a member of the Governing Circle of the National Centre for Truth and Reconciliation at the University of Manitoba and was inducted as an Honourary Witness by the Truth and Reconciliation Commission of Canada. Cynthia is a member of the Chippewa of Georgina Island First Nation in Lake Simcoe, Ontario, and has dedicated her life to building bridges of understanding between people.

Barry K. Wilson, a Life Member of the Canadian Parliamentary Press Gallery, spent thirty-four years on Parliament Hill as national correspondent for the *Western Producer*, Canada's largest agricultural newspaper, covering agricultural politics and policy, trade and world food issues. He is the author of books on politics (*Politics of Defeat*, 1980), agricultural policy (*Beyond the Harvest*, 1981, and *Farming the System*, 1990) and history (*Benedict Arnold: A Traitor in Our Midst*, 2001). Currently he is working on a biography of Sir Mackenzie Bowell, Canada's fifth prime minister. In 2012, Barry became only the second journalist to be inducted as a member of the Canadian Agricultural Hall of Fame. He holds a Bachelor of Arts, a Bachelor of Journalism and a Master of Arts in Canadian Studies from Carleton University.

Paul Wilson holds a PhD in early modern English history from Queen's University, and has been an associate professor in the Clayton Riddell Graduate Program in Political Management at Carleton University since 2011. From 2009 to 2011, he served as director of policy in the Prime Minister's Office, and also as acting chief of staff during the 2011 election campaign. Paul had previously served as director of policy to the Hon. Diane Finley and the Hon. Monte Solberg at Human Resources and Skills Development, and to the Hon. Vic Toews at both the Department of Justice and the Treasury Board. From 1997 to 2001 he was director of research in the Office of the Leader of the Opposition.

David Zussman is an Adjunct Professor at the School of Public Administration at the University of Victoria and Senior Fellow at the Graduate School of Public and International Affairs (GSPIA) at the University of Ottawa. From 2008 to 2016, he held the Jarislowsky Chair in Public Sector Management at the University of Ottawa. David, who has a PhD in psychology from McGill University, has also been a professor in the School of Public Administration at the University of Victoria and served as Dean of the Telfer Faculty of Management and Director of GSPIA at the University of Ottawa. He was previously President of the Public Policy Forum for seven years, and also served as Executive Vice President and COO of EKOS Research Associates Inc. During the mid-1990s, David led the transition exercise for Prime Minister Jean Chrétien, was appointed Assistant Secretary to the Cabinet for Program Review and Machinery of Government in the Privy Council Office, and served a seven-year term as Commissioner of the Public Service Commission.

Notes

Introduction

1 http://speech.gc.ca/en/content/making-real-change-happen.

2 Bruce Anderson and David Coletto, *Popularity & Prime Ministers* (Abacus Data, January 17, 2016), http://abacusdata.ca/wp-content/uploads/2016/01/Abacus-Release-Current-Past-PMs.pdf.

1 Unfinished Business: The Legacy of Stephen Harper's "Open Federalism"

1 For examples, please see John Ibbitson, *Stephen Harper* (Toronto: McClelland and Stewart, 2015); Bob Plamondon, *Full Circle: Death and Resurrection in Canadian Conservative Politics* (Toronto: Key Porter Books, 2006); Hugh Segal, *The Long Road Back: The Conservative Journey, 1993–2006* (Toronto: HarperCollins Publishers Ltd, 2006); and Paul Wells, *Right Side Up: The Fall of Paul Martin and the Rise of Stephen Harper's New Conservatism* (Toronto: McClelland and Stewart, 2006).

2 Ronald L. Watts, *Executive Federalism: A Comparative Analysis* (Kingston, ON: Institute of Intergovernmental Relations, Queen's University, 1989), 3.

3 Stephen Harper, "Achieving Economic Justice in Confederation" (Reform Association of Canada, 1987), quoted in Ibbitson, *Stephen Harper*, 62–63.

4 All references to political party election platforms cited in this chapter come from the collection of political texts made available at www.poltext.org by Lisa Birch, Jean Crête, Louis M. Imbeau, Steve Jacob and François Pétry, with the financial support of the Fonds de recherché du Québec—Société et culture (FRQSC). Reform Party of Canada, *Principles and Policies: The Blue Book* (Calgary: Reform Fund Canada, 1991), https://www.poltext.org/sites/poltext.org/files/plateformes/can1991r_plt_en_12072011_125340.pdf.

5 Stephen Harper et al., "An Open Letter to Ralph Klein," *National Post*, January 24, 2001.

6 The term "Calgary School" refers to a group of academics and graduates of the University of Calgary who, among other shared views, believe in a more limited role for Ottawa and a stronger role for the provinces within the Canadian federation.

7 For insightful analyses of the dynamics of the YES campaign during the 1995 referendum, please see Chantal Hébert and Jean Lapierre, *Confessions post-référendaires : Les acteurs politiques de 1995 et le scenario d'un Oui* (Montreal: Les éditions de l'Homme, 2014), and Martine Tremblay, *La rébellion tranquille : une histoire du Bloq québécois (1990–2011)* (Montreal: Québec Amérique, 2015), 279–318.

8 Jim Brown, "Chrétien opens constitutional Door," The Canadian Press, October 24, 1995, FP Infomart.

9   Gilles Duceppe was, in fact, the Bloc's third leader. Michel Gauthier was elected to replace Lucien Bouchard in 1996, but internal divisions led, in as many years, to a second leadership contest, which was won by Duceppe.

10   For the text of the Saskatoon Consensus and the Victoria Proposal, see appendices 1 and 2 in *The Canadian Social Union without Quebec: Eight Critical Analyses*, ed. Alain-G. Gagnon and Hugh Segal (Montreal: Institute for Research on Public Policy, 2000).

11   Alain-G. Gagnon and Hugh Segal, "Introduction," in *The Canadian Social Union without Quebec: Eight Critical Analyses*, ed. Alain-G. Gagnon and Hugh Segal (Montreal: Institute for Research on Public Policy, 2000), 2–3.

12   Alain Noël, "General Study of the Framework Agreement," in Gagnon and Segal, *Canadian Social Union without Quebec*, 9.

13   Progressive Conservative Party of Canada, *Let the Future Begin*, Party Platform 1997, https://www.poltext.org/sites/poltext.org/files/plateformes/can1997pc_plt_en._14112008_175654.pdf.

14   Council of the Federation, *Founding Agreement*, December 5, 2003, http://www.canadaspremiers.ca/phocadownload/publications/cof_founding-agreement.pdf.

15   See Conservative Party of Canada, *Demanding Better: Conservative Party of Canada, Platform 2004*, https://www.poltext.org/sites/poltext.org/files/plateformes/can2004pc_plt_en._14112008_171920.pdf.

16   Conservative Party of Canada, *Stand Up for Canada: Conservative Party of Canada Federal Election Platform 2006*, 3, https://www.poltext.org/sites/poltext.org/files/plateformes/can2006pc_plt_en._14112008_165519.pdf.

17   Ibid., 42–43.

18   Ibid.

19   Conservative Party of Canada, "Harper Announces Conservative Platform for Québec," news release, December 19, 2005.

20   Ibid.

21   The five priorities were: (1) passing the Federal Accountability Act, (2) cutting the Goods and Services Tax, (3) introducing mandatory minimum sentences for gun-related crimes, (4) creating the universal child benefit and (5) negotiating with the provinces guaranteed wait times for certain medical procedures.

22   Government of Québec and Government of Canada, "Accord entre le Gouvernement du Québec et le Gouvernement du Canada relatif à l'Organisation des Nations unies pour l'éducation, la science et la culture (UNESCO)," May 5, 2006, https://www.mrif.gouv.qc.ca/content/documents/fr/unesco.pdf.

23   Stephen Harper, "Prime Minister Harper Outlines His Government's Priorities and Open Federalism Approach" (speech delivered to Montreal Board of Trade, April 20, 2006), http://nouvelles.gc.ca/web/article-en.do?crtr.sj1D=&mthd=advSrch&crtr.mnthndVl=1&nid=207899.

24   Ibid.

25   Ibid.

26   Ibbitson, *Stephen Harper*, 227.

27   As part of the research conducted in the preparation of this chapter, the author conducted four interviews with senior officials with responsibility for the intergovernmental file: two at the federal level, one from Quebec and one from a Western province. As the interviews were conducted well before the results of the 2015 election were known, all agreed to the interview on the condition that they not be identified.

28   Conservative Party of Canada, *The True North Strong and Free: Stephen Harper's Plan for Canadians [2008 Election Platform]*, 2, https://www.poltext.org/sites/poltext.org/files/plateformes/can2008pc_plt_eng._13112008_193556.pdf.

29 Ibid., 16.

30 Ibid., 26.

31 Conservative Party of Canada, *Here for Canada [2011 Election Platform]*, 30, https://www.poltext.org/sites/poltext.org/files/plateformes/can2011pc_plt_en_12072011_114959.pdf.

32 Conservative Party of Canada, *Protect Our Economy [2015 Election Platform]*, 154, https://www.poltext.org/sites/poltext.org/files/plateformes/conservative-platform-2015.pdf.

33 Graham Fox, "Harper's 'Open Federalism': From the Fiscal Imbalance to 'Effective Collaborative Management' of the Federation," *Policy Options*, March 1, 2007.

34 Department of Finance Canada, *Restoring Fiscal Balance in Canada: Focusing on Priorities* (Ottawa: Department of Finance Canada, 2006), https://www.fin.gc.ca/budget06/pdf/fp2006e.pdf.

35 Martine Tremblay, *La rébellion tranquille : Une histoire du Bloc Québécois (1990-2011)*, (Montreal: Québec-Amérique, 2015), 511–14.

36 Canadian Intergovernmental Conference Secretariat, "Prime Minister and Premiers Agree on Action for the Economy," news release, January 16, 2009, http://www.scics.gc.ca/english/conferences.asp?a=viewdocument&id=78.

37 Roger Gibbins, "Bridge Building and the New Federalism," *Canadian Political Science Review* 2, no. 3 (2008): 84.

38 Emmett Macfarlane, "The Myth of Federal Health Care Cuts," *Policy Options*, November 15, 2014, http://policyoptions.irpp.org/2014/11/15/the-myth-of-federal-health-care-cuts/.

39 Alain-G. Gagnon, "Canada with Stephen Harper at the Helm: A Mixed Record" (lecture, IACFS Annual Conference 2015, Montreal, October 3, 2015), 6.

40 Paul Wells, *Right Side Up: The Fall of Paul Martin and the Rise of Stephen Harper's New Conservatism* (Toronto: McClelland and Stewart, 2006), 316–17.

41 Ibbitson, *Stephen Harper*, 267–74.

42 Ibid., 271.

43 The data presented at the round table were drawn from Herman Bakvis, "Changing Intergovernmental Governance in Canada in the Era of 'Open Federalism'" (lecture, Conference on Variety and Dynamics of Multilevel Governance in Canada and Europe, Technical University Darmstadt, Germany, June 12–13, 2014), 10.

44 Tremblay, *La rébellion tranquille*.

45 See Claire Durand, "L'appui à la souveraineté du Québec : Où en sommes-nous?" (lecture, Colloque de l'IRPP, Montreal, March 21, 2014), http://www.mapageweb.umontreal.ca/durandc/Recherche/Publications/souverainete_quebec/Presentation_IRPP_durandc.pdf.

46 For examples, see Jean-François Lisée, *Sortie de Secours : Comment échapper au déclin du Québec* (Montreal: Boréal, 2000), and Marc Brière, *Le Québec, QUEL QUÉBEC ?* (Montreal: Stanké, 2001).

47 Michael Atkinson and Daniel Béland, "Farewell to Open Federalism," *Policy Options*, September 9, 2015, http://policyoptions.irpp.org/issues/september-2015/election-2015/farewell-to-open-federalism/.

2 Harper and the House of Commons: An Evidence-Based Assessment

1 *Toronto News*, November 28, 1905, quoted in R. MacGregor Dawson, ed., *Constitutional Issues in Canada, 1900-1931* (London: Oxford University Press, 1933), 121, 123. Thanks to James Bowden who posted this passage on his blog, www.parliamentum.org, on June 13, 2013.

2 W.A. Matheson, *The Prime Minister and the Cabinet* (Toronto: Methuen, 1976), 127.

3 R. MacGregor Dawson, "The Cabinet—Position and Personnel," *Canadian Journal of Economics and Political Science* 12, no. 3 (1946): 275.

4 Donald Savoie, *Governing from the Centre* (Toronto: University of Toronto Press, 1999).

5   Jeffrey Simpson, *The Friendly Dictatorship* (Toronto: McClelland and Stewart, 2001), xi, 3.

6   Lawrence Martin, *Harperland: The Politics of Control* (Toronto: Viking, 2010), 274.

7   Martin, *Harperland*, 272, 275.

8   Michael Harris, *Party of One: Stephen Harper and Canada's Radical Makeover* (Toronto: Viking, 2014), 483.

9   Mark Bourrie, *Kill the Messengers: Stephen Harper's Assault on Your Right to Know* (Toronto: HarperCollins, 2015), 338–40.

10 Mel Hurtig, *The Arrogant Autocrat: Stephen Harper's Takeover of Canada* (Vancouver: Mel Hurtig Publishing, 2015), 1, 9.

11 John Raulston Saul, *The Comeback: How Aboriginals Are Reclaiming Power and Influence* (Toronto: Penguin Canada, 2015), 114.

12 Don Martin, "Tories Have a Book on Political Wrangling," *National Post*, May 18, 2007, National Edition, A1.

13 Gloria Galloway, "Tory Whip Defends Manual on Disrupting Committee Meetings," *The Globe and Mail*, May 21, 2007.

14 For example, Brooke Jeffrey, *Dismantling Canada: Stephen Harper's New Conservative Agenda* (Montreal and Kingston: McGill-Queen's University Press, 2015), 126; Hurtig, *Arrogant Autocrat*, 13.

15 Canadian Association of Income Trust Investors, "CAITI offers $10,000 cash reward for a copy of Harper's 200 page manual," *CAITI-Online* (blog), September 3, 2008, http://caiti-online. blogspot.ca/2008/09/caiti-offers-10000-cash-reward-for-copy.html.

16 Doug Smith, in discussion with the author, September 25, 2011.

17 Bill Graveland, "Martin Points to Differences between Columnists, Reporters at Scud Stud Trial," *Calgary Herald*, December 7, 2015, http://calgaryherald.com/news/local-news/ martin-points-to-differences-between-columnists-reporters-at-scud-stud-trial.

18 Jeffrey, *Dismantling Canada*, 136.

19 Chantal Hébert, "Harper Uses Bouchard Playbook to Muzzle MPs," *Toronto Star*, April 19, 2010, 6.

20 Dan Gardner, "Harper Likes His Ministers Weak," *Ottawa Citizen*, July 6, 2012, A11.

21 Lawrence Martin, "A Rare Show of Courage from Tory Bobbleheads," *iPolitics*, March 27, 2013, http://ipolitics.ca/2013/03/27/a-rare-show-of-courage-from-tory-bobbleheads.

22 Bill Curry, "Turner blasts Tory 'establishment'," *The Globe and Mail*, October 19, 2006, A5; Garth Turner, *Sheeple: Caucus Confidential in Stephen Harper's Ottawa* (Toronto: Key Porter, 2009).

23 Brent Rathgeber, "Why I Quit the Conservative Party: Edmonton MP Brent Rathgeber on Why He Chose to Sit as an Independent," *National Post*, June 7, 2013, A10; Brent Rathgeber, *Irresponsible Government: The Decline of Parliamentary Democracy in Canada* (Toronto: Dundurn, 2014).

24 Examples include Leon Benoit's C-291 in 2006; Ken Epp's C-484 in 2007; Rod Bruinooge's C-510 in 2010; Stephen Woodworth's M-312 in 2012.

25 Chantal Hébert, "Stirrings of Dissent Should Worry Harper," *Toronto Star*, March 27, 2013, A8.

26 Canada, House of Commons, *Order and Notice Paper*, 41st Parliament, 1st session no. 154 (September 27, 2012): VII.

27 Canada, *House of Commons Debates*, 41st Parliament, 1st session, vol. 146 no. 229 (March 26, 2013): 15189.

28 John Ibbitson, "Why the Tory Backbench Won't Remain Tight-Lipped," *The Globe and Mail*, April 18, 2013; Aaron Wherry, "The Backbench Spring," *Maclean's*, April 15, 2013, http://www. macleans.ca/politics/ottawa/the-backbench-spring.

29 Bill Curry and Stuart Thompson, "Voting Records Show Tory MPs More Apt to Break Ranks," *The Globe and Mail*, February 4, 2013, A4.

30 On February 16, 2015, Liberal MP Mauril Belanger voted in favour of an NDP amendment (vote 332) to a government motion supporting integrated security in the parliamentary precinct.

31 See R. Paul Wilson, "Minister's Caucus Advisory Committees Under the Harper Government," *Canadian Public Administration* 58 no. 2 (June 2015): 227–48.

32 For example, Angelo Persichilli, "Harper Wants Tory Caucus Involved in Policy-Making," *Hill Times*, August 16, 2010, 1, 10; Jane Taber, "Harper Tories to Vet Potential Political Landmines," *The Globe and Mail*, September 11, 2010, A7; Paul Wells, *The Longer I'm Prime Minister: Stephen Harper and Canada, 2006-* (Toronto: Random House, 2013), 389.

33 *A Drafter's Guide to Cabinet Documents* (Privy Council Office, 2013), 28, http://www.pco-bcp. gc.ca/docs/information/publications/mc/docs/dr-guide-eng.pdf.

34 Personal interview with minister, October 23, 2012.

35 Personal interview with MP, May 22, 2013.

36 C.E.S. Franks, *The Parliament of Canada* (Toronto: University of Toronto Press, 1987), 128–32. For a history of the evolution of rules with respect to closure and time allocation, see also chapter 14, "The Curtailment of Debate," in *House of Commons Procedure and Practice*, 2nd edition, ed. Audrey O'Brien and Marc Bosc (Ottawa: House of Commons, 2009), 647–75.

37 Franks, *Parliament of Canada*, 117.

38 O'Brien and Bosc, eds., *House of Commons Procedure and Practice*, 647.

39 Franks, *Parliament of Canada*, 131–32.

40 François Plante, "The Curtailment of Debate in the House of Commons: An Historical Perspective," *Canadian Parliamentary Review* 36 no. 1 (2013): 31–33.

41 Canada, *House of Commons Debates*, 41st Parliament, 1st session, vol. 147 no. 109 (September 15, 2014): 7317.

42 Plante, "Curtailment of Debate," 32, 34.

43 Ibid., 34.

44 Aaron Wherry, "Why Is the Harper Government Using Time Allocation So Often?," *Maclean's*, June 24, 2014, http://www.macleans.ca/politics/why-is-the-harper-government-using-time-allocation-so-often.

45 Laura Stone, "'It Is Not Appropriate to Manhandle Other Members': House Speaker Admonishes Trudeau after PM Ignites Fracas by Grabbing Tory Whip, Elbowing NDP MP," *The Globe and Mail*, May 19, 2016, A1.

46 C.E.S. Franks and David E. Smith, "The Canadian House of Commons under Stress: Reform and Adaptation," in *New Political Management to New Political Governance: Essays in Honour of Peter C. Aucoin*, ed. Herman Bakvis and Mark D. Jarvis (Montreal and Kingston: McGill-Queen's University Press, 2012), 88.

47 O'Brien and Bosc, eds., *House of Commons Procedure and Practice*, 725.

48 Michel Bédard, *Omnibus Bills: Frequently Asked Questions* (Library of Parliament, October 1, 2012), 4–5.

49 O'Brien and Bosc, eds., *House of Commons Procedure and Practice*, 724.

50 Bédard, *Omnibus Bills*, 3.

51 O'Brien and Bosc, eds., *House of Commons Procedure and Practice*, 724.

52 Josh Paterson et al., "Letter to the Standing Committee on Finance," May 10, 2010, http://miningwatch.ca/sites/default/files/letter_to_finance_committee_re_budget_0.pdf.

53 Aaron Wherry, "A Short History of Budget Implementation Acts," *Maclean's*, May 4, 2012, http://www.macleans.ca/politics/ottawa/a-short-history-of-budget-implementation-acts/.

54 Rachel Aiello, "We 'Don't Have a Clue' What's in Omnibus Bills, Say MPs," *The Hill Times*, March 2, 2015, 15.

55 Canada, *House of Commons Debates*, 35th Parliament, 1st session, vol. 133 no. 45 (March 25, 1994): 2775.

56 C.E.S. Franks, "Omnibus Bills Subvert Our Legislative Process," *The Globe and Mail*, July 14, 2015, A17; Franks, *The Parliament of Canada*, 128–32.

57 See for example Paul Wells, *Right Side Up: The Fall of Paul Martin and the Rise of Stephen Harper's New Conservatism* (Toronto: McClelland and Stewart, 2006), 302–10; Bourrie, *Kill the Messengers*, 65–91.

58 Andrew MacDougall, "Why Conservatives Really Shouldn't Treat the Media Like Donkeys," *Ottawa Citizen*, June 11, 2016, D4.

59 Personal interview, October 1, 2015.

60 *Toronto News* in Dawson, *Constitutional Issues in Canada*, 124.

61 Paul Wells, "The Gray Fog Rolls Out," *Maclean's*, April 21, 2014, http://www.macleans.ca/politics/ottawa/the-gray-fog-rolls-out.

62 Canada, *House of Commons Debates*, 41st Parliament, 2nd Session, vol. 147 no. 114 (September 26, 2014): 7900.

63 Editorial, "Democratic respect? Resistance is futile," *The Globe and Mail*, September 26, 2014, A10.

64 Louis Massicotte, "Omnibus Bills in Theory and Practice," *Canadian Parliamentary Review* 36, no. 1 (2013): 16.

65 Andrew MacDougall, "Putting the PMO in Its Place: How Central Control Spun Out of Control," *Ottawa Citizen*, October 31, 2015, C1.

66 See American Dialect Society, "Truthiness Voted 2005 Word of the Year," http://www.americandialect.org/truthiness_voted_2005_word_of_the_year.

67 Andrew Coyne, "Writing About Harper: Two New Books Expose the Limits of Polemic," *Literary Review of Canada*, April 2015, 4.

68 Lorne Gunter, "Social media does not bring down governments or win elections," *National Post*, April 15, 2011, http://news.nationalpost.com/full-comment/lorne-gunter-social-media-does-not-bring-down-govts-or-win-elections.

69 Steve Chase, "Tories openly criticize party performance: After 12 years of strict message control under Harper, Conservatives now speak more freely about internal disagreements," *The Globe and Mail,* October 23, 2015, A3.

3 Stephen Harper and the Federal Public Service: An Uneasy and Unresolved Relationship

1 See, for example: Peter Aucoin, "New Political Governance in Westminster Systems: Impartial Public Administration and Management Performance at Risk," *Governance* 25, no. 2: 177–99; Donald Savoie, *Power: Where Is It?* (McGill-Queens Press, 2010); Eddie Goldenberg, *The Way It Works: Inside Ottawa* (Toronto: Douglas Gibson Books, 2007); and Paul Wells, *The Longer I'm Prime Minister: Stephen Harper and Canada, 2006-* (Toronto: Random House, 2013).

2 This includes attending annual meetings like the G7, G20, APEC and the Commonwealth as well as leading delegations to the UN or on trade missions.

3 The technological revolution (personal computers and high speed communications) that has swept across the globe and disrupted almost all conventional industries has had a particularly profound impact on the functioning of government.

4 The mergers were with the Progressive Conservative Party of Peter MacKay, the Canadian Alliance led by Stockwell Day, and Preston Manning's Reform Party. See Bob Plamondon, *Full Circle: Death and Resurrection in Canadian Conservative Politics* (Toronto: Key Porter Books, 2006).

5   Campbell Clark, Gloria Galloway, and Brian Laghi, "Harper: Don't fear a majority," *The Globe and Mail*, January 18, 2006, http://www.theglobeandmail.com/news/national/harper-dont-fear-a-majority/article965075/.

6   Susan Delacourt, "The Harper Government vs. the Public Servants," *Toronto Star*, July 12, 2013, http://www.thestar.com/news/insight/2013/07/12/the_harper_government_vs_the_public_servants.html.

7   These were: to clean up the government through the Federal Accountability Act; to cut the GST; to crack down on crime; to deliver a Conservative daycare plan; and to establish patient wait times guarantee. Of the five projects, three were delivered.

8   See Eddie Goldenberg's book on the Chrétien approach to working with the public service: *The Way It Works: Inside Ottawa* (Toronto: Douglas Gibson Books, 2007).

9   Kathryn May, "Harper's Suspicions of PS Hint at Rocky Relations to Come," *Ottawa Citizen*, January 18, 2006.

10 There is a longstanding tradition in Canada of newly elected governments being suspicious of the neutrality of the public service. See David Zussman, *Off and Running: The Prospects and Pitfalls of Government Transitions in Canada* (Toronto: University of Toronto Press, 2013).

11 Ian Brodie, Personal Communication, April 6, 2014.

12 Prime ministers are very powerful in Canada and Harper had full discretionary powers to organize and compensate the public service.

13 This includes all departments, agencies, boards and commissions.

14 See the Appendix following the chapter for additional detail regarding affected federal entities.

15 The EAP was a success because of the commitment, skill and professionalism of the public service in allocating resources across the country with little loss or errors but its accomplishments did not resonate in the PMO or in ministers' offices.

16 For a more detailed discussion, see David A. Good and Evert Lindquist, "Canada's Reactive Budget Response to the Global Financial Crisis: From Resilience and Brinkmanship to Agility and Innovation," in *The Global Financial Crisis and Its Budget Impacts on OECD Nations*, ed. John Wanna, Evert Lindquist, and Jouke de Vries (Cheltenham, UK: Elgar, 2015).

17 Stephen Harper, "Accountability and the Public Service" (speech to public servants, Ottawa, ON, March 23, 2006).

18 The hiring of outside advisers to do the analysis was a blow to the confidence of the public service, which does not have a tradition of using outside experts. For a detailed analysis of the cost containment exercises see David A. Good, *The Politics of Public Money*, 2nd ed. (University of Toronto Press, 2014).

19 These Public Accounts are hosted online by Library and Archives Canada: http://epe.lac-bac.gc.ca/100/201/301/public_accounts_can/index.html.

20 They have also said that they would improve access for serious illness.

21 Ian Lee, "The Alleged Downsizing of the Federal Public Service under the Harper Conservatives," in *How Ottawa Spends, 2013–2014*, ed. Christopher Stoney and G. Bruce Doern (Montreal: McGill-Queen's Press, 2013).

22 In this sense, it was similar to Program Review.

23 Personal interview with the author, September 15, 2015. For a complete review of different budgetary systems in Canada, see Chapter 10 of Good, *The Politics of Public Money*.

24 The role of the Treasury Board has changed over the years as a function of the government's need to limit spending and the political strength of the presidents of the Treasury Board vis-à-vis their colleagues.

25 Ian Lee, "The Alleged Downsizing," 98.

26 For a full analysis of this conflict, see Kevin Page, *Unaccountable: Truth and Lies on Parliament Hill* (Toronto: Viking Press, 2015).

27 Paul Tellier served as Secretary to the Cabinet from 1985 to 1992.

28 May, "Harper's Suspicions of PS."

29 David Zussman, "Political Advisors," paper presented for the Expert Group on Conflict of Interest, Public Governance Committee, OECD, Paris, 2009.

30 Quoted in Jennifer Ditchburn, "Duffy Trial Sheds Light on PMO Power, Hand-holding of MPs," *Maclean's*, August 26, 2015, http://www.macleans.ca/politics/ottawa/duffy-trial-sheds-light-on-pmo-power-hand-holding-of-mps/.

31 Attributed to Mike Duffy when describing his experiences working with the PMO.

32 This was not always the case but the longstanding tradition in Canada is for exempt staff to enable as well as provide political advice to their ministers.

33 Critics inside the government have had a remarkably short shelf-life and faced lonely and bruising attacks on their character and competency. For a discussion of the fate of many of these people see Aaron Wherry, "How they do it," *Maclean's*, August 18, 2010, who provides a list of 12 individuals who were fired or persuaded to leave their government posts. They include Linda Keen, Bernard Shapiro, Kevin Page, Munir Sheikh, Robert Marleau, and Richard Colvin.

34 Susan Delacourt, "Tory Government Takes Aim at Bureaucracy," *Toronto Star*, January 17, 2008, https://www.thestar.com/news/2008/01/17/tory_government_takes_aim_at_bureaucracy.html.

35 Wells, *The Longer I'm Prime Minister*, 32.

36 David Zussman, "Ethics, Corruption, Good Government and the Management Styles of Prime Ministers," speech presented to the Third Annual Conference of the Canadian Association of Programs in Public Policy and Administration (CAPPA), Queen's University, Kingston: May 21, 2014.

37 The Association of Professional Executives of the Public Service of Canada, *Perspectives of Public Service Executives on Their Evolving Work* (February 2014), 1.

38 Although some proposed nominations appear to have been rejected, these cases may well have been judgments on competence or suitability to the task rather than political reliability.

39 Ralph Heintzman, *Renewal of the Federal Public Service: Toward a Charter of Public Service*, Canada 2020, 2015.

40 Wells, *The Longer I'm Prime Minister*, 23.

41 David Zussman, "The Precarious State of the Federal Public Service," in *How Ottawa Spends, 2010–2011*, ed. G. Bruce Doern and Christopher Stoney (Montreal: McGill-Queen's University Press, 2010), 195–218.

42 Stephen Harper (Speech, Conservative Convention, Calgary, November 1, 2013), http://ipolitics.ca/2013/11/01/verbatim-stephen-harpers-speech-to-the-calgary-convention/.

43 Stephanie Levitz, The Canadian Press, "Harper Gives Forceful Denunciation of Liberals in Final Pitch Before Election," *iPolitics*, October 18, 2015, http://ipolitics.ca/2015/10/18/harper-gives-forceful-denunciation-of-liberals-in-final-pitch-before-election/.

4 Government News Management and Canadian Journalism

1 Jennifer Ditchburn, "Harper's Opaque Communications Strategy Stymies Reporters at APEC Summit," The Canadian Press, November 19, 2006, FP Infomart.

2 Catherine Cullen, "Harper Meets Castro, but We Had to Look to Cuba for the Photo," *CBC News*, April 13, 2015, http://www.cbc.ca/news/politics/harper-meets-castro-but-we-had-to-look-to-cuba-for-the-photo-1.3031064.

3 Gerry Nicholls, *Loyal to the Core: Stephen Harper, Me and the NCC* (Toronto: Freedom Press Canada, 2009), 109.

4   Jennifer Ditchburn, "Journalistic Pathfinding: How the Parliamentary Press Gallery Adapted to News Management Under the Conservative Government of Stephen Harper," Master of Journalism, Carleton University, 2014, https://curve.carleton.ca/31240d56-a0eb-41ba-a8f7-ffb8828c43f0.

5   Wilfrid Eggleston, Press Gallery Dinner Pamphlet, 1947, MG30 D 282 Vol. 12, Wilfrid Eggleston Fonds, Library and Archives Canada, Ottawa, Canada.

6   Anthony Westell, "Access to News in a Small Capital: Ottawa," in *Secrecy and Foreign Policy*, ed. Thomas M. Franck and Edward Weiband (New York: Oxford University Press, 1974), 256.

7   Colin Seymour-Ure, "An Inquiry into the Position and Workings of the Parliamentary Press Gallery in Ottawa" Master of Journalism, Carleton University, 1962. See also Canada, Task Force on Government Information, *To Know and Be Known: The Report of the Task Force on Government Information* (Ottawa: Queen's Printer, 1969).

8   Allan Levine, *Scrum Wars: The Prime Ministers and the Media* (Toronto: Dundurn Press, 1993), 213.

9   Seymour-Ure, "An Inquiry," and Peter Desbarats, *Guide to Canadian News Media* (Toronto: Harcourt Brace Jovanovich, 1990).

10 Paul Rutherford, *The Making of the Canadian Media* (Toronto: McGraw-Hill Ryerson Ltd., 1978), 109.

11 Canada, *The Report of the Task Force*.

12 Jonathan W. Rose, *Making "Pictures in Our Heads": Government Advertising in Canada* (Westport, CT: Praeger, 2000).

13 Anthony Westell and Carman Cumming, "Canadian Media and the National Imperative," in *Government and the News Media: Comparative Dimensions*, ed. Dan Nimmo and Michael W. Mansfield (Waco, TX.: Baylor University, 1982).

14 Kirsten Kozolanka, "The Sponsorship Scandal as Communication: The Rise of Politicized and Strategic Communications in the Federal Government," *Canadian Journal of Communication* 31, no. 2 (2006): 350.

15 Robert E. Denton Jr. and Gary C. Woodward, *Political Communication in America*, 3rd ed. (Westport, CT: Praeger Publishers, 1998).

16 Kenneth L. Hacker, Maury Giles, and Aja Guerrero, "The Political Image Management Dynamics of President Bill Clinton," in *Images, Scandal and Communication Style of the Clinton Presidency*, ed. Robert E. Denton Jr. and Rachel L. Holloway (Westport, CT: Praeger Publishers, 2003).

17 Edwin Diamond and Robert Silverman, *White House to Your House: Media and Politics in Virtual America* (Cambridge, MA: MIT Press, 1997), 5.

18 Margaret Scammell, "The Media and Media Management," in *The Blair Effect: The Blair Government 1997-2001*, ed. Anthony Seldon (Cambridge: Cambridge University Press, 2001) and Raymond Kuhn, "The First Blair Government and Political Journalism," in *Political Journalism: New Challenges, New Practices*, ed. Raymond Kuhn and Erik Neveu (London: Routledge, 2002).

19 Helen Ester, "The Media," in *Silencing Dissent: How the Australian Government Is Controlling Public Opinion and Stifling Debate*, ed. Clive Hamilton and Sarah Maddison (Crows Nest, NSW: Allen & Unwin, 2007), 112.

20 Jennifer Ditchburn, "Harper Looks to His Aussie 'Mate' for Model of Conservative Success," *The Canadian Press*, May 18, 2006, FP Infomart.

21 Tim Harper, "PMO Backs Down on Threat to Bar Journalist for Asking Stephen Harper a Question," *Toronto Star*, October 2, 2013, http://www.thestar.com/news/canada/2013/10/02/pmo_backs_down_on_threat_to_bar_journalist_for_asking_stephen_harper_a_question_tim_harper.html.

22 Mike Blanchfield and Jim Bronskill, The Canadian Press, "Documents Expose Harper's Obsession with Control," *Toronto Star*, June 6, 2010, http://www.thestar.com/news/canada/2010/06/06/documents_expose_harpers_obsession_with_control.html.

23 Lawrence Martin, *Harperland: The Politics of Control* (Toronto: Viking Canada, 2010).

24 Paul Thomas, "Communications and Prime Ministerial Power" (Presentation, Conference Honouring Donald Savoie, Bouctouche, NB, June 8–10, 2011).

25 The Canadian Press, "Information Services Staff Has Grown 15% under Harper," *CBC News*, June 23, 2013, http://www.cbc.ca/news/politics/information-services-staff-has-grown-15-under-harper-1.1319930.

26 Jay G. Blumler and Michael Gurevitch, *The Crisis in Public Communication* (New York: Routledge, 1995), 35.

27 Hélène Buzzetti et al., "An Open Letter to Canadian Journalists," Canadian Association of Journalists, June 2010, http://www.caj.ca/an-open-letter-to-canadian-journalists/.

28 Anthony Sabato, *Feeding Frenzy: How Attack Journalism Has Transformed American Politics* (Toronto: The Free Press, 1991).

29 Henk Pander Maat, "How Newspaper Journalists Reframe Product Press Release Information," *Journalism* 14, no. 3 (2012).

30 Scott Althaus, "When News Norms Collide, Follow the Lead: New Evidence for Press Independence," *Political Communication* 20, no. 4 (2003).

31 Suzanne Legault, interview by Michael Enright, *The Sunday Edition*, CBC Radio, February 10, 2013.

32 Murray Brewster, The Canadian Press, "Harper Government Considers Soldiers on Viagra a Cabinet Secret," *CBC News*, September 14, 2014, http://www.cbc.ca/news/politics/harper-government-considers-soldiers-on-viagra-a-cabinet-secret-1.2766012.

33 Canadian Media Guild, "Canadian Media Guild: Job Cuts in the Print Media Industry," and "Canadian Media Guild: Job Cuts in the Broadcast Industry," November 2013.

34 *Canada's Digital Divides* (Communications Management Inc., August 20, 2015), http://media-cmi.com/downloads/CMI_Discussion_Paper_Digital_Divides_082015.pdf.

35 Craig Aaron, "Public Media to the Rescue?," in *Will the Last Reporter Please Turn out the Lights?: The Collapse of Journalism and What Can Be Done to Fix It*, ed. Robert. W McChesney and Victor Pickard (New York: The New Press, 2011).

36 *A New Age for Newspapers, Diversity of Voices, Competition and the Internet: Hearing Before the Subcommittee on Courts and Competition Policy of the Committee on the Judiciary House of Representatives*, 111th Cong. (April 21, 2009), https://judiciary.house.gov/_files/hearings/printers/111th/111-38_48745.pdf.

37 Michael J. Copps, "What About the News? An Interest in the Public," in *Please Turn out the Lights*, ed. McChesney and Pickard.

38 Canada, Parliament, "Proceedings of the Senate Standing Committee on Transport and Communications," Issue 3, Evidence, February 26, 2014, http://www.parl.gc.ca/content/sen/committee/412%5CTRCM/03EV-51227-E.HTM.

39 Dennis Dawson et. al, *Time for change: The CBC/Radio-Canada in the Twenty-First Century* (The Senate Standing Committee on Transport and Communications, July 2015), http://www.parl.gc.ca/Content/SEN/Committee/412/trcm/rep/rep14jul15-e.pdf.

40 Hubert T. Lacroix, "Speaking Notes for Hubert T. Lacroix, President and CEO, CBC/Radio-Canada, at the Public Broadcasters International Conference, Munich, Germany," *CBC News*, September 10, 2015, http://www.cbc.radio-canada.ca/en/media-centre/2015/09/10/.

41 Susan Milligan. "The President and the Press," *Columbia Journalism Review*, March/April 2015, http://www.cjr.org/analysis/the_president_and_the_press.php.

42 Leonard Downie Jr. "The Obama Administration and the Press: Leak investigations and surveillance in post-9/11 America," Committee to Protect Journalists, October 10, 2013, https://cpj.org/reports/2013/10/obama-and-the-press-us-leaks-surveillance-post-911.php.

43 Canada, Treasury Board Secretariat, "Policy on Communications and Federal Identity," May 11, 2016, https://www.tbs-sct.gc.ca/pol/doc-eng.aspx?id=30683.

5   Permanent Marketing and the Conduct of Politics

1 Brad Lavigne, *Building the Orange Wave: The Inside Story behind the Historic Rise of Jack Layton and the NDP* (Madeira Park, B.C.: Douglas & McIntyre, 2013), 133–34, and Susan Delacourt, *Shopping for Votes: How Politicians Choose Us and We Choose Them* (Madeira Park, B.C.: Douglas & McIntyre, 2013), 246–47.

2 Michael Ignatieff, *Fire and Ashes: Success and Failure in Politics* (Toronto: Random House, 2013), 120.

3 Alex Marland, *Brand Command: Canadian Politics and Democracy in the Age of Message Control* (Vancouver: UBC Press, 2016).

4 Ibid., 379.

5 André Turcotte, "Under New Management: Market Intelligence and the Conservative Party's Resurrection," in *Political Marketing in Canada*, ed. Alex Marland, Thierry Giasson, and Jennifer Lees-Marshment (Vancouver: UBC Press, 2012), 84.

6 Delacourt, *Shopping for Votes*, 205

7 Sandra Buckler, interview with Emmanuele Latraverse,Stephanie Rubec, and Isabelle Rodrgrigue, March 27, 2006, http://www.politicswatch.com/gallery2-mar27-2006.htm.

8 John Ibbitson and Oliver Moore, "Partisan Cheques Put Tories in Hot Water," *The Globe and Mail*, October 14, 2009, http://www.theglobeandmail.com/news/politics/partisan-cheques-put-tories-in-hot-water/article4316924/.

9 Marland, *Brand Command*, 307.

10 Richard Nimijean, "Domestic brand politics and the modern publicity state," in *Publicity and the Canadian State: Critical Communications Perspectives*, ed. Kirsten Kozolanka (Toronto: University of Toronto Press, 2014), 172–194.

11 Donald J. Savoie, *Governing from the Centre: The Concentration of Power in Canadian Politics* (Toronto: University of Toronto Press, 1999).

12 Tom Flanagan, "Something Blue: Conservative organization in an era of permanent campaign," *Inroads* 28 (2011): 98.

13 Ibid., 94.

14 Alfred Apps, *Building a Modern Liberal Party: a Background Paper for discussion among Members of the Liberal Party of Canada* (Liberal Party of Canada, 2011), http://www.liberal.ca/files/2011/11/BuildingaModernLiberalParty.pdf.

15 Lavigne, *Building the Orange Wave*, 178.

16 Laura Payton, "Conservative Party Fined for Breaking Election Laws," *CBC News*, November 10, 2011, http://www.cbc.ca/news/politics/conservative-party-fined-for-breaking-election-laws-1.1076877.

17 Don Martin, "Don Martin: Tories Have Book on Political Wrangling," *National Post*, May 17, 2007, A1.

18 Josh Visser, "NDP MP Pat Martin Signs off of Twitter after Epic Anti-Tory Tirade," *National Post*, December 20, 2012, http://news.nationalpost.com/news/canada/canadian-politics/rat-faced-whores-ndp-mp-pat-martin-launches-epic-twitter-tirade-against-tories-vic-toews.

19 See: "Stephen Harper, Conservative MP for Calgary Heritage," OpenParliament.ca, accessed August 30, 2015, https://openparliament.ca/politicians/stephen-harper/.

20 Evan Sotiropoulos, "The Use and Misuse of Members' Statements," *Canadian Parliamentary Review* 32, no. 3 (2009): 14, http://www.revparl.ca/32/3/32n3_09e_Sotiropoulos.pdf.

21 Ibid., 11.

22 Keith Beardsley, "Congratulatory Message to Attack Piece—BLOG—A Look at Canadian Politics," *ATory01: A Tory First: Looking at Politics in Canada through a Conservative Lens* (blog), September 25, 2012, http://www.atory01.com/blog/2012/9/25/congratulatory-message-to-attack-piece.html.

23 Flanagan, "Something Blue," 94.

24 Colin Bennett and Robin Bayley, *Canadian Federal Political Parties and Personal Privacy Protection: A Comparative Analysis* (Office of the Privacy Commissioner of Canada, March 1, 2012), https://www.priv.gc.ca/information/research-recherche/2012/pp_201203_e.pdf.

25 Steven Chase, "CEOs Assail Wireless Rules That Give Edge to Verizon," *The Globe and Mail*, July 29, 2013, http://www.theglobeandmail.com/report-on-business/top-ceos-call-on-harper-to-level-wireless-playing-field/article13475552/.

26 Kenneth Whyte, "Bay Street No Longer Matters in Ottawa," *Maclean's*, November 6, 2013, http://www.macleans.ca/news/canada/bay-street-no-longer-matters-in-ottawa/.

27 Tom Flanagan, "The Emerging Conservative Coalition," *Policy Options* June-July 2011: 104–108.

28 Delacourt, *Shopping for Votes*, 214.

29 John Ibbitson, *Stephen Harper* (Toronto: McClelland & Stewart, 2015), 308.

30 McEwing v. Canada (Attorney-General) 2013, FC 525 (CanLII), accessed August 28, 2015, http://www.canlii.org/en/ca/fct/doc/2013/2013fc525/2013fc525.html.

31 Melissa Williams et. al., "An Open Letter on the Fair Elections Act," *The Globe and Mail*, April 23, 2014, http://www.theglobeandmail.com/globe-debate/an-open-letter-from-academics-on-bill-c-23/article18114166/.

32 Laura Payton, "Election Chief Marc Mayrand Fears Canadians Could Be Denied Vote," *CBC News*, March 6, 2014, http://www.cbc.ca/news/politics/election-chief-marc-mayrand-fears-canadians-could-be-denied-vote-1.2562153.

33 Alex Boutilier, "Pierre Poilievre Attacks Head of Elections Canada," *Toronto Star*, April 8, 2014, http://www.thestar.com/news/canada/2014/04/08/conservative_minister_launches_personal_attack_on_elections_chief.html.

34 Delacourt, *Shopping For Votes*, 326.

35 Ibid., 308.

6 Rising Power: Stephen Harper's Makeover of Canadian International Policy and Its Institutions

While this piece is entirely my responsibility, it was much improved after consultation with scholars and former practitioners including Chris Waddell, David Bercuson, David Perry, Denis Stairs, Ian Brodie, Jack Granatstein, Peter Harder and Roland Paris, as well as the editors. In terms of published works on Stephen Harper I benefitted from John Ibbitson's *Stephen Harper: Making of a Prime Minister*, Random House, 2015, and Lawrence Martin's *Harperland: The Politics of Control*, Penguin, 2011.

1 Laura Payton, "Harper speech fires up convention crowd," *CBC News*, June 10, 2011, http://www.cbc.ca/news/politics/harper-speech-fires-up-convention-crowd-1.976268.

2 John Ibbitson, "The Harper Doctrine: Conservative foreign policy in black and white," *The Globe and Mail*, June 12, 2011, http://www.theglobeandmail.com/news/politics/ottawa-notebook/the-harper-doctrine-conservative-foreign-policy-in-black-and-white/article615115/

3 Stephen Harper, "Address by the Prime Minister at the Canada-UK Chamber of Commerce" (speech, London, July 14, 2006).

4   David Akin, "Harper mounts fierce defence of muscular foreign policy," *Toronto Sun*, May 25, 2015, http://www.torontosun.com/2015/05/25/harper-mounts-fierce-defence-of-muscular-foreign-policy.

5   Colin Robertson, "Canada's dynamic, blunt-talking Foreign Minister practices a unique but effective brand of diplomacy." *Inside Policy*, Macdonald-Laurier Institute, December 2013, http://www.macdonaldlaurier.ca/files/pdf/Inside%20Policy%20December%202013.pdf

6   Philippe Lagassé, "When Does Parliament Get to Vote on Military Deployments?" *CIPSBLOG* (blog), Centre for International Policy Studies, September 8, 2014, http://www.cips-cepi.ca/2014/09/08/when-does-parliament-get-to-vote-on-military-deployments/.

7   Jennifer Ditchburn, The Canadian Press, "Tories oust Hugh Segal from key Senate post," *Toronto Star*, February 21, 2007, http://www.thestar.com/news/2007/02/21/tories_oust_hugh_segal_from_key_senate_post.html.

8   Talia Chung, "Afghanistan: Chronology of Canadian Parliamentary Events," Library of Parliament, November 20, 2007, http://www.lop.parl.gc.ca/content/lop/ResearchPublications/prb0724-e.pdf.

9   Allan Woods, "Conservatives, Liberals extend Afghanistan mission," *Toronto Star*, March 14, 2008, https://www.thestar.com/news/canada/2008/03/14/conservatives_liberals_extend_afghanistan_mission.html.

10 Mark Kennedy, "Parliament votes 149-129 to widen Canada's mission against ISIS to Syria and extend it for a year," *National Post*, March 31, 2015, http://news.nationalpost.com/news/canada/canadian-politics/parliament-votes-149-129-to-widen-canadas-mission-against-isis-to-syria-and-extend-it-for-a-year.

11 Ramsay Cook, *Teeth of Time: Remember Pierre Elliott Trudeau*. (Montreal & Kingston: McGill-Queen's University Press, 2006), 63.

12 When Prime Minster Justin Trudeau visited the Pearson Building after taking power, he was mobbed in a scene reminiscent of a pop star amongst groupies an episode that further confirmed Conservative suspicions about the Foreign Service. See editorial, "Civil Servants don't get to pick their government. That's up to voters," *The Globe and Mail*, December 2, 2015, http://www.theglobeandmail.com/globe-debate/editorials/civil-servants-dont-get-to-pick-their-government-thats-up-to-voters/article27571139/.

13 Global Affairs Canada, "Harper Government Launches New International Trade Plan," news release, November 27, 2013, http://news.gc.ca/web/article-en.do?nid=796219.

14 Campbell Clark, "Why the Conservative approach to diplomacy misses the target," *The Globe and Mail*, April 16, 2014, http://www.theglobeandmail.com/news/politics/globe-politics-insider/why-conservatives-rejection-of-old-fashioned-diplomacy-doesnt-work/article18036403/.

15 Author's discussion with senior PMO official after the 2009 election.

16 Aaron Wherry, "The Argument of Force," *Maclean's*, September 1, 2011, http://www.macleans.ca/politics/ottawa/the-argument-of-force/.

17 "Canada's casualties in Afghanistan," *CBC News*, May 2014, http://www.cbc.ca/news2/interactives/canada-afghanistan-casualties/.

18 Jeffrey Simpson, "The Harper Government Loves the Military—in theory," *The Globe and Mail*, January 28, 2014, http://www.theglobeandmail.com/globe-debate/the-harper-government-loves-the-military-in-theory/article19355276/.

19 David Perry, *The Growing Gap Between Defence Ends and Means: The Disconnect between the Canada First Defence Strategy and the Current Defence Budget* (CDA Institute, June 2014), 1, http://www.cdainstitute.ca/images/PerryBudgetJune2014.pdf.

20 Peter Weltman, *Fiscal Sustainability of Canada's National Defence Program* (Office of the Parliamentary Budget Officer, March 26, 2015), 15-16, http://www.pbo-dpb.gc.ca/files/files/Defence_Analysis_EN.pdf.

21 Dave Perry, *Putting the "Armed" into the Canadian Armed Forces: Improving Defence Procurement in Canada* (CDA Institute, January, 2015), http://cdainstitute.ca/images/vimy-paper-21.pdf.

22 Global Affairs Canada, "Harper Government Launches New International Trade Plan," news release, November 27, 2013, http://news.gc.ca/web/article-en.do?nid=796219.

23 James Bradshaw, "As Ottawa pushes for foreign students, universities worry about spaces for Canadians," *The Globe and Mail*, January 16, 2014, http://www.theglobeandmail.com/news/national/education/as-ottawa-pushes-for-foreign-students-critics-worry-about-how-schools-will-handle-them/article16378000/.

24 Kim Mackrael, "Canada's foreign aid doesn't exist to keep NGOs afloat," *The Globe and Mail*, November 28, 2012, http://www.theglobeandmail.com/news/politics/canadas-foreign-aid-doesnt-exist-to-keep-ngos-afloat-fantino-says/article5751774/.

25 OECD Development Assistance Committee, *DAC Peer Review of Development Cooperation, 2012* (Secretary General of the OECD, 2012), http://www.oecd.org/dac/peer-reviews/peer-review-canada.htm.

26 OECD, "Canada's development aid: focused and effective but should be more generous and efficient," news release, June 19, 2012, http://www.oecd.org/dac/peer-reviews/canadasdevelopmentaidfocusedandeffectivebutshouldbemoregenerousandefficient.htm.

27 OECD Development Assistance Committee, *Peer Review*, 15.

28 Robert Greenhill and Megan McQuillan, "Assessing Canada's Global Engagement Gap," *OpenCanada*, October 6, 2015, https://www.opencanada.org/features/canadas-global-engagement-gap/.

29 The Canadian Press, "Harper wraps up 'nation-building' trip to Arctic," *Red Deer Advocate*, August 28, 2010, http://www.reddeeradvocate.com/news/national/harper_wraps_up_nation-building_trip_to_arctic_101673933.html.

30 Government of Canada, "Statement on Canada's Arctic Foreign Policy: Exercising Sovereignty and Promoting Canada's NORTHERN STRATEGY Abroad," Global Affairs Canada, last modified June 3, 2013, http://www.international.gc.ca/arctic-arctique/arctic_policy-canada-politique_arctique.aspx.

31 Steven Chase, "Harper orders new draft of Arctic seabed claim to include North Pole," *The Globe and Mail*, December 4, 2013, http://www.theglobeandmail.com/news/politics/harper-orders-new-draft-of-arctic-seabed-claim-to-include-north-pole/article15756108/.

32 Steve Rennie, The Canadian Press, "Arctic naval base plans scaled back after costs soared: document," *CBC News*, September 8, 2014, http://www.cbc.ca/news/canada/north/arctic-naval-base-plans-scaled-back-after-costs-soared-document-1.2759743.

33 David Pugliese, "Can the National Shipbulding Procurement Strategy deliver the maritime fleets Canada needs?," *Ottawa Citizen*, December 7, 2015, http://ottawacitizen.com/news/national/defence-watch/can-the-national-shipbuilding-procurement-strategy-deliver-the-maritime-fleets-canada-needs.

34 "WHO | Work with the G8 and G20," World Health Organization: The Partnership for Maternal, Newborn, & Child Health, accessed July 5, 2016, http://www.who.int/pmnch/about/20111129_work_with_G8/en/.

35 See "Canada's Leadership in Maternal, Newborn and Child Health—The Muskoka Initiative (2010-2015)," Global Affairs Canada, last modified December 18, 2014, http://mnch.international.gc.ca/en/topics/leadership-muskoka_initiative.html.

36 "Mulroney honoured for environmental record," *CBC News*, April 20, 2006, http://www.cbc.ca/news/canada/mulroney-honoured-for-environmental-record-1.616580.

37 See Denis Stairs, *Being Rejected in the United Nations: The Causes and Implications of Canada's Failure to Win a Seat in the UN Security Council* (Canada Defence & Foreign Affairs

Institute, March 2011), https://d3n8a8pro7vhmx.cloudfront.net/cdfai/pages/43/attachments/original/1413677044/Being_Rejected_in_the_United_Nations.pdf.

38 See "Statements by President Barack Obama and Prime Minister of Canada Stephen Harper of Canada," (speeches delivered at the White House, Washington, DC, December 7, 2011), https://www.whitehouse.gov/the-press-office/2011/12/07/statements-president-barack-obama-and-prime-minister-canada-stephen-harp.

39 Mark Brown, "How much thicker is the Canada–US border? The cost of crossing the border by truck in the pre- and post-9/11 eras, 1994 to 2009," Statistics Canada, July 24, 2015, http://www.statcan.gc.ca/daily-quotidien/150724/dq150724a-eng.htm.

40 Elaine Smith, "Personal relationships key to successful diplomacy: Mulroney," *U of T News*, October 13, 2011, https://www.utoronto.ca/news/personal-relationships-key-successful-diplomacy-mulroney.

41 Gloria Galloway, "Harper rebukes U.S. envoy over Arctic dispute," *The Globe and Mail*, January 27, 2006, http://www.theglobeandmail.com/news/national/harper-rebukes-us-envoy-over-arctic-dispute/article702554/.

42 Bloomberg News, "Harper 'confident' Keystone pipeline will be built" *Financial Post*, September 21, 2011, http://business.financialpost.com/news/energy/harper-confident-keystone-pipeline-will-be-built; Joanna Slater, "Harper 'won't take no for an answer' from U.S. on Keystone XL," *The Globe and Mail*, September 26, 2013, http://www.theglobeandmail.com/report-on-business/harper-wont-take-no-for-an-answer-from-us-on-keystone-xl/article14547474/.

43 Ben Wolfgang, "Keystone Pipeline: Obama bashes pipeline while in Myanmar," *Washington Times*, November 14, 2014, http://www.washingtontimes.com/news/2014/nov/14/keystone-pipeline-obama-bashes-project-while-in-my/.

44 Mark MacKinnon, "The remaking of Harper's China Gambit," *The Globe and Mail*, February 3, 2012, http://www.theglobeandmail.com/news/world/the-remaking-of-harpers-china-gambit/article543845/.

45 John Ibbitson, "China publicly scolds Harper for taking too long to visit," *The Globe and Mail*, December 3, 2009, http://www.theglobeandmail.com/news/politics/china-publicly-scolds-harper-for-taking-too-long-to-visit/article4312718/.

46 Timothy Appleby, "Harper greets pandas at airport, calling them 'national treasures,'" *The Globe and Mail*, March 25, 2013, http://www.theglobeandmail.com/news/toronto/harper-greets-pandas-at-airport-calling-them-national-treasures/article10279675/.

47 Steve Chase and Kim Mackrael, "Canada, India agree to $350 million uranium supply deal," *The Globe and Mail*, April 15, 2015, http://www.theglobeandmail.com/news/politics/canada-india-agree-to-major-uranium-supply-deal/article23967494/.

48 Jane Taber, "PM brands Canada an 'energy superpower,'" *The Globe and Mail*, July 15, 2006, http://www.theglobeandmail.com/news/national/pm-brands-canada-an-energy-superpower/article18167474/.

49 Ben Doherty, "G20: Canadian prime minister shirtfronts Putin instead," *The Guardian*, November 15, 2014, http://www.theguardian.com/world/2014/nov/15/g20-canadian-prime-minister-shirtfronts-vladimir-putin-instead.

50 Laura Payton, "Canada closes embassy in Teheran, expels Iranian diplomats," *CBC News*, September 7, 2012, http://www.cbc.ca/news/politics/canada-closes-embassy-in-iran-expels-iranian-diplomats-1.1166509.

51 "VIDEO: Stephen Harper's speech to Israeli Knesset," *CBC News*, January 20, 2014, http://www.cbc.ca/news/politics/stephen-harper-s-speech-to-the-israeli-knesset-1.2503902.

52 Department of Foreign Affairs, Trade and Development (Global Affairs Canada), "Evaluation of the Americas Strategy," January 2011, http://www.international.gc.ca/department-ministere/evaluation/2011/tas_lsa11.aspx.

53 Tonda MacCharles, "Is Africa on Stephen Harper's radar?," *Toronto Star*, June 11, 2010, http://www.thestar.com/news/canada/2010/06/11/is_africa_on_stephen_harpers_radar.html.

54 Geoffrey York, "Canada targets South Africa as priority market in Africa," *The Globe and Mail*, June 23, 2014, http://www.theglobeandmail.com/report-on-business/international-business/african-and-mideast-business/canada-stands-by-south-africa/article19301859/.

55 Global Affairs Canada, "Minister Fast Announces Export Development Canada to Expand Its Footprint into Africa," news release, June 23, 2014, http://news.gc.ca/web/article-en.do?nid=860809.

56 Stephen Harper, "The Best Country in the World," (election victory speech to Conservative supporters, June 1, 2011, Calgary), http://policyoptions.irpp.org/issues/the-winner/the-best-country-in-the-world/.

57 John Noble, "Has Canada become a diplomatic scold?," *iPolitics*, November 15, 2013, http://ipolitics.ca/2013/11/15/has-canada-become-a-diplomatic-scold/.

58 The Canadian Press, "Ottawa turns to digital diplomacy to reach Iranians," *CBC News*, May 10, 2013, http://www.cbc.ca/news/politics/ottawa-turns-to-digital-diplomacy-to-reach-iranians-1.1394508.

59 *James Eayrs, "'A Low, Dishonest Decade': Aspects of Canadian External Policies in External Affairs," in The Growth of Canadian External Policies in External Affairs*, ed. H.L. Keenleyside et al. (Durham, N.C.: Duke University Press, 1960), 79.

60 Mike Blanchfield, The Canadian Press, "Trudeau tells Canadian diplomats he relies on their judgment," *Toronto Star*, November 5, 2015, http://www.thestar.com/news/canada/2015/11/05/trudeau-tells-canadian-diplomats-he-relies-on-their-judgment.html.

61 Jim Bronskill, The Canadian Press, "'We're back,' Justin Trudeau says in message to Canada's allies abroad," *National Post*, October 20, 2015, http://news.nationalpost.com/news/canada/were-back-justin-trudeau-says-in-message-to-canadas-allies-abroad.

7   The Strange Voyage: Stephen Harper on Defence

1 See, e.g., "National Defense—Page 1 | GOP," Republican National Committee (web site), accessed July 5, 2016, https://www.gop.com/issue/national-defense/canonical/.

2 Stephen Harper, "Address by the Prime Minister to the Canadian Armed Forces in Afghanistan, March 13, 2006" (speech, Ottawa, ON, March 13, 2006), http://www.forces.gc.ca/en/news/article.page?doc=address-by-the-prime-minister-to-canadian-forces-in-afghanistan/hnocfoh3.

3 Alan Woods, "Canada's Elite Commandos and the Invasion of Afghanistan," *Toronto Star*, April 25, 2010, http://www.thestar.com/news/canada/2010/04/25/canadas_elite_commandos_and_the_invasion_of_afghanistan.html.

4 Murray Brewster, The Canadian Press, "U.S. warned Canada about Taliban surge before Kandahar," *CTV News*, October 16, 2011, http://www.ctvnews.ca/u-s-warned-canada-about-taliban-surge-before-kandahar-1.712028.

5 Murray Brewster, *The Savage War: The Untold Battles of Afghanistan* (Toronto: John Wiley & Sons, 2011), 91–92.

6 Ipsos-Reid, survey of opinions and attitudes towards the Canadian Forces (commissioned by Department of National Defence), March 2008. Released to The Canadian Press under Access to Information and Privacy.

7 Ipsos-Reid, survey of opinions and attitudes towards the Canadian Forces (commissioned by Department of National Defence), March 2009. Released to The Canadian Press under Access to Information and Privacy.

8 Jack Granatstein, "[Opinion] Canada Needs NATO—and It Needs Us," *The Globe and Mail*, September 24, 2007, http://www.theglobeandmail.com/opinion/canada-needs-nato---and-it-needs-us/article725446/.

9   Steve Chase, "Canada complicit in torture of innocent Afghans, diplomat says," *The Globe and Mail*, November 18, 2009, http://www.theglobeandmail.com/news/politics/canada-complicit-in-torture-of-innocent-afghans-diplomat-says/article1347481/.

10 Special Committee on the Canadian Mission in Afghanistan, "Minutes," 40th Parliament, 2nd session, no. 015 (November 18, 2009), http://www.parl.gc.ca/HousePublications/Publication.aspx?DocId=4236267&Language=E.

11 Graeme Smith, "From Canadian custody into cruel hands," *The Globe and Mail*, April 23, 2007, http://www.theglobeandmail.com/news/world/from-canadian-custody-into-cruel-hands/article585956/.

12 Daniel Leblanc, "Liberals' 'passion' is with Taliban, PM says," *The Globe and Mail*, March 22, 2007, http://www.theglobeandmail.com/news/national/liberals-passion-is-with-taliban-pm-says/article961657/.

13 John Manley et. al., *Independent Panel on Canada's Future Role in Afghanistan* (Ottawa: Foreign Affairs and International Trade, 2008), http://publications.gc.ca/collections/collection_2008/dfait-maeci/FR5-20-1-2008E.pdf.

14 Jean-Christophe Boucher, "Evaluating the "Trenton Effect": Canadian Public Opinion and Military Casualties in Afghanistan (2006–2010)," *American Review of Canadian Studies* 40, no. 2 (2010): 237–58.

15 Lloyd Axworthy, "Time for a civilian surge," *The Globe and Mail*, December 16, 2009, http://www.theglobeandmail.com/globe-debate/time-for-a-civilian-surge/article1209832/.

16 The Associated Press, "Harper calls for more action to stamp out corruption in Afghanistan," *CP24*, November 20, 2010, http://www.cp24.com/harper-calls-for-more-action-to-stamp-out-corruption-in-afghanistan-1.577074.

17 "Canada's Harper doubts Afghan insurgency can be defeated," *CNN*, March 2, 2009, http://www.cnn.com/2009/WORLD/asiapcf/03/02/canada.afghanistan/index.html.

18 Aaron Wherry, "A short history of the Harper government changing its mind on the mission in Afghanistan," *MacLean's*, April 25, 2012, http://www.macleans.ca/politics/ottawa/a-short-history-of-the-harper-government-changing-its-mind-on-the-mission-in-afghanistan/.

19 Campbell Clark, "PM's farewell to Kandahar: 'Afghanistan is no longer a threat to the world'," *The Globe and Mail*, May 30, 2011, http://www.theglobeandmail.com/news/politics/pms-farewell-to-kandahar-afghanistan-is-no-longer-a-threat-to-the-world/article581554/.

20 Conservative Party of Canada, *Stand Up for Canada: Conservative Party of Canada Federal Election Platform 2006*, 45, https://www.poltext.org/sites/poltext.org/files/plateformes/can2006pc_plt_en._14112008_165519.pdf.

21 Murray Brewster, The Canadian Press, "Flag in the Arctic could cost Forces $843 million a year: documents," *Toronto Star*, January 22, 2009, http://www.thestar.com/news/canada/2009/01/22/flag_in_the_arctic_could_cost_forces_843_million_a_year_documents.html.

22 Stephen Harper, "Statement by the Prime Minister of Canada at the Chief of Defence Staff Change of Command ceremony," October 29, 2012, http://news.gc.ca/web/article-en.do?nid=704069.

23 See "Defence Renewal Overview," National Defence and the Armed Forces, last modified March 11, 2016, http://www.forces.gc.ca/en/about/defence-renewal.page.

24 Dave Perry, *Putting the "Armed" into the Canadian Armed Forces: Improving Defence Procurement in Canada* (CDA Institute, January, 2015), 8, http://cdainstitute.ca/images/vimy-paper-21.pdf.

25 "Canada to spend $9B on F-35 fighter jets," *CBC News*, July 16, 2010, http://www.cbc.ca/news/canada/canada-to-spend-9b-on-f-35-fighter-jets-1.908494.

26 John Ivison, "Auditor-General's report shows flaw in Tories' reflex to never retreat or apologize," *National Post*, April 3, 2012, http://news.nationalpost.com/full-comment/john-ivison-auditor-generals-report-shows-flaw-in-tories-reflex-to-never-retreat-or-apologize.

27 Murray Brewster, The Canadian Press, "CF-18 upgrades will keep jets flying until 2025, Ottawa says," *CTV News*, September 30, 2014, http://www.ctvnews.ca/politics/cf-18-upgrades-will-keep-jets-flying-until-2025-ottawa-says-1.2031683.

28 Colin Horgan, "'We're part of the crusade', Fantino says on F-35," *iPolitics*, November 10, 2011, http://ipolitics.ca/2011/11/10/were-part-of-the-crusade-fantino-says-on-f-35/.

29 *Canada First Defence Strategy* (National Defence and the Armed Forces, May 12, 2008), http://www.forces.gc.ca/assets/FORCES_Internet/docs/en/about/CFDS-SDCD-eng.pdf.

30 Lee Berthiaume, "Tories knew last year shopping list of military equipment was 'unaffordable', documents show," *National Post*, June 4, 2012, http://news.nationalpost.com/news/canada/tories-knew-last-year-shopping-list-of-military-equipment-was-unaffordable-documents-show.

31 Murray Brewster, The Canadian Press, "National defence cuts could tally $2.5B," *CBC News*, September 30, 2012, http://www.cbc.ca/news/politics/national-defence-cuts-could-tally-2-5b-1.1229454.

32 See Public Works and Government Services Canada, "Government of Canada announces National Shipbuilding Procurement Strategy," news release, June 3, 2010, http://news.gc.ca/web/article-en.do?nid=537299.

33 "Arctic naval facility at Nanisivik completion delayed to 2018," *CBC News*, March 4, 2015, http://www.cbc.ca/news/canada/north/arctic-naval-facility-at-nanisivik-completion-delayed-to-2018-1.2980312.

34 Murray Brewster, The Canadian Press, "Canada sending dozens of military advisors to Iraq to help counter ISIS's 'murderous rampage'," *National Post*, September 5, 2014, http://news.nationalpost.com/news/canada-sending-several-dozen-military-advisors-to-iraq-as-nato-ramps-up-defences.

35 Peter Weltman, *Fiscal Sustainability of Canada's National Defence Program* (Office of the Parliamentary Budget Officer, March 26, 2015), http://www.pbo-dpb.gc.ca/files/files/Defence_Analysis_EN.pdf.

36 Joe Sterling, "Canada ending battle mission in Afghanistan," *CNN*, July 7, 2011, http://www.cnn.com/2011/WORLD/asiapcf/07/05/canada.afghanistan.troops/.

37 Murray Brewster, The Canadian Press, "Canadian training mission in Kabul estimated at $522 million," *CBC News*, March 7, 2013, http://www.cbc.ca/news/canada/canadian-training-mission-in-kabul-estimated-at-522-million-1.1308393.

38 Jean-Rodrigue Paré, *Post-Traumatic Stress Disorder and Mental Health of Military Personnel and Veterans* (Library of Parliament Background Papers, October 14, 2011), http://publications.gc.ca/collections/collection_2011/bdp-lop/bp/2011-97-eng.pdf.

39 Ramnarayanan Mathilakath, Ashutosh Rajekar, and Sahir Khan, *Fiscal Impact of the Canadian Mission in Afghanistan* (Office of the Parliamentary Budget Officer, October 9, 2008), http://www.pbo-dpb.gc.ca/files/files/Publications/Afghanistan_Fiscal_Impact_FINAL_E_WEB.pdf.

40 Murray Brewster, The Canadian Press, "Stephen Harper partially disowns veterans charter amid demands Fantino resign," *CBC News*, December 10, 2014, http://www.cbc.ca/news/politics/stephen-harper-partially-disowns-veterans-charter-amid-demands-fantino-resign-1.2866858.

41 Gloria Galloway, "Benefits for wounded Canadian veterans do not stack up," *The Globe and Mail*, March 9, 2015, http://www.theglobeandmail.com/news/politics/benefits-for-wounded-canadian-veterans-do-not-stack-up/article23381161/.

42 CTV.ca News Staff, "Ombud blasts government's treatment of veterans," *CTV News*, August 17, 2010, http://www.ctvnews.ca/ombud-blasts-government-s-treatment-of-veterans-1.543393.

43 See Department of Veteran Affairs, "'New Chapter in the New Veterans Charter Receives Royal

Assent'—The Honourable Jean-Pierre Blackburn," news release, March 24, 2011, http://www.veterans.gc.ca/eng/news/viewrelease/1101.

44 See Lieutenant-Colonel Joane Simard, "Canadian Forces Health Services Unit Commanding Officers: The Lynchpin of Reform" (Canadian Forces College, May 27, 2005), http://www.cfc.forces.gc.ca/259/290/291/287/simard.pdf.

45 Department of National Defence, "Fit to Serve: Universality of Service and Related Support Programs," Backgrounder, June 29, 2010, http://www.forces.gc.ca/en/news/article.page?doc=fit-to-serve-universality-of-service-and-related-support-programs/hnps1uk2.

46 Jungwee Park, Statistics Canada, "A profile of the Canadian Forces," *Perspectives on Labour and Income [Statistics Canada]* 9, no. 7 (July 2008): 17–30, http://www.statcan.gc.ca/pub/75-001-x/75-001-x2008107-eng.pdf.

47 Murray Brewster, The Canadian Press, "Injured Canadian troops booted from military before qualifying for pension," *Toronto Star*, October 29, 2013, http://www.thestar.com/news/canada/2013/10/29/injured_canadian_troops_booted_from_military_before_qualifying_for_pension.html.

48 See Canada, *Debates of the Senate [Official Report]*, 41st Parliament, 2nd session, vol. 149 no. 64 (May 29, 2014), http://www.parl.gc.ca/Content/Sen/Chamber/412/Debates/pdf/064db_2014-05-29-e.pdf.

49 Sheila Fraser, Auditor General of Canada, "Opening Statement to the Standing Committee on National Defence," Office of the Auditor General of Canada, March 6, 2008, http://www.oag-bvg.gc.ca/internet/English/osh_20080306_e_30183.html.

50 Murray Brewster, The Canadian Press, "Turf war hindered hiring of mental-health staff at National Defence, sources say," *The Globe and Mail*, January 26, 2014, http://www.theglobeandmail.com/news/politics/turf-war-hindered-hiring-of-mental-health-staff-at-national-defence-sources-say/article16506941/.

51 Kristen Everson, "Veterans don't have social contract, Ottawa says in lawsuit response," *CBC News*, March 18, 2014, http://www.cbc.ca/news/politics/veterans-don-t-have-social-contract-ottawa-says-in-lawsuit-response-1.2577053.

52 Murray Brewster, The Canadian Press, "Guy Parent finds badly wounded soldiers not getting disability cheques," *CBC News*, August 19, 2014, http://www.cbc.ca/news/politics/guy-parent-finds-badly-wounded-soldiers-not-getting-disability-cheques-1.2741190.

53 Veterans Affairs Canada, "Government of Canada improves Veterans' access to job opportunities," press release, May 26, 2015, http://news.gc.ca/web/article-en.do?nid=980069.

54 Anna Mehler Paperny, "Veterans' anti-Conservative campaign fuelled by 'union money,' Minister says," *Global News*, September 30, 2015, http://globalnews.ca/news/2250076/veterans-anti-conservative-campaign-fuelled-by-union-money-minister-says/.

55 Leslie MacKinnon, "Afghan mission Day of Honour planning catches legion off guard," *CBC News*, April 28, 2014, http://www.cbc.ca/news/politics/afghan-mission-day-of-honour-planning-catches-legion-off-guard-1.2624268.

56 The Canadian Press and National Post Staff, "'Your attendance would be at your own expense': Tories backtrack after asking dead soldiers families to pay own way to 'National Day of Honour,'" *National Post*, April 3, 2014, http://news.nationalpost.com/news/canada/your-attendance-would-be-at-your-own-expense-government-backtracks-after-asking-families-of-killed-soldiers-to-pay-own-way-to-national-day-of-honour.

57 Murray Brewster, The Canadian Press, "Rick Hansen to MC day of honour for Canada's Afghan mission," *CTV News*, April 28, 2014, http://www.ctvnews.ca/canada/rick-hansen-to-mc-day-of-honour-for-canada-s-afghan-mission-1.1795727.

58 Department of National Defence, PowerPoint presentation (Spring 2011) obtained by The Canadian Press in March 2012.

59 Kelsey Berg, "DND Decides that Silence is the Best Policy," NATO Association of Canada, August 28, 2015, http://natoassociation.ca/dnd-decides-that-silence-is-the-best-policy/.

60 David Pugliese, "Canada's secret soldiers: Special Forces' work takes place under the radar," *Ottawa Citizen*, December 30, 2014, http://ottawacitizen.com/news/national/canadas-secret-soldiers-special-forces-work-takes-place-under-the-radar.

8 Review of Economic Performance and Policy during the Harper Years

A digital version of this chapter, including expanded data on the drivers of Canadian economic performance, will be published in *Policy Options* magazine simultaneously with the release of *The Harper Factor*. We would like to thank, without implicating, several people for their valuable input to this chapter: Michael Horgan, Mark Jewett, John Weekes, Michael Kergin and Anne McLellan, all colleagues at Bennett Jones, and Bruce Little.

1 The comparison period for growth starts in 1984, partly because this was the start of the Mulroney government. But the main reason is to permit a long enough period (twenty-two years) to properly reflect long-run trends in the data. Available national accounts data start in 1981, but it was appropriate to exclude the years of recession in the early 1980s. Note also that our analysis essentially rests on annual data.

2 During 1984–2005, there were years of large excess supply, as in 1991–1993 and 1996–1997, and years of large excess demand, as in 1988–1990 and 1999–2000. We interpret the small average excess demand over the whole period (0.08) as indicating a rough balance overall, especially since estimates of the output gap have a large confidence interval about them.

3 Statistics Canada, *Table 380-0072—Current and capital accounts—Households*, CANSIM (database); Statistics Canada, *Table 380-0066—Price indexes, gross domestic product*, CANSIM (database), household final consumption expenditure deflator; Statistics Canada, *Table 051-0005—Estimates of Population, Canada, provinces and territories, (persons)*, CANSIM (database); and US Bureau of Economic Analysis.

4 The foreign activity measure is compiled by the Bank of Canada. "The foreign activity measure captures the composition of foreign demand for Canadian exports by including components of US private final domestic demand and economic activity in Canada's other trading partners. The Bank of Canada uses it to predict demand for Canada's exports" (Bank of Canada).

5 Statistics Canada, *Table 380-0100—Contributions to per cent change in real gross domestic product, expenditure-based, annual (per cent)*, CANSIM (database), and Bank of Canada.

6 Statistics Canada, *Table 380-0105—Contributions to per cent change in real exports and imports of goods and services, annual (per cent)*, CANSIM (database).

7 A crisis erupted in the non-bank asset-backed commercial paper market (ABCP) in August 2007 but was aptly resolved through the mediation of federal public authorities.

8 Lev Ratnovski and Rocco Huang, "Why are Canadian Banks More Resilient?," *IMF Working Paper*, WP/09/152, July 2009, http://www.imf.org/external/pubs/ft/wp/2009/wp09152.pdf.

9 Some fear, however, that housing is overvalued and that a price correction is due sooner or later.

10 Richard Musgrave, *The Theory of Public Finance* (New York: McGraw-Hill, 1959).

11 Fiscal stimulus here refers to an *increase* in net borrowing (deficit + net acquisition of non-financial assets) as a percentage of GDP. Although it does not measure the impact of the increase in deficit on real GDP growth directly, clearly this impact is correlated with the size of the fiscal stimulus as defined here.

12 The incentive to mitigate a downturn is all the greater if it is believed, as several economists do,

that pronounced slack in the economy leads to persistent slower potential growth as a result of lower investment, degradation of skills, etc.

13 The size of the effects per dollar of fiscal measure (the fiscal multiplier) depends, among other things, on the composition of the fiscal measures by type of expenditures, taxes and other revenues, on the state of the economy and the response of monetary policy, on expectations of the private agents and how they adjust their saving rate, and on the import propensity of the economy. See, for example, Ray Barrell, Dawn Holland, and Ian Hurst, "Fiscal Multipliers and Prospects for Consolidation," *OECD Journal: Economic Studies* 2012, no. 1 (2012): 71–102. In its 2009 Economic Action Plan, the Department of Finance Canada reported multipliers over two years, ranging from 1.5 for infrastructure investment to 0.2 for corporate income tax measures.

14 The two measures of the output gap estimated by the Bank of Canada differ markedly on the size of excess demand during 2008. The "integrated framework" measure indicates much smaller excess demand than the "extended multivariate filter" measure.

15 Among other tax measures, the GST was cut from 7 to 6 per cent in July 2006 and from 6 to 5 per cent in January 2008. Total program spending increased at an average annual rate of 6.9 per cent in 2006–2007 and 2007–2008.

16 Note that these figures include the effects of automatic stabilizers.

17 There were substantial differences between the Bank of Canada estimates of output gap from the integrated framework and those from the multivariate filter, the former indicating much larger output gaps than the latter. Our analysis is based on averages of the two estimates.

18 ABCP stands for asset-backed commercial paper. For an excellent analysis of the management of this crisis, see Paul Halpern, Caroline Cakebread, Christopher C. Nicholls and P. Puri, *Back from the Brink* (Toronto: University of Toronto Press, 2016).

19 See Bank of Canada, *Senior Loan Officer Survey,* various issues.

20 Policies related to financial markets were reviewed in the previous section.

21 Between fiscal years 2005–2006 and 2014–2015, federal tax revenues fell from 13.3 per cent of GDP to 11.6 per cent. At the same time, the share of federal revenues represented by taxes on goods and services (largely GST) fell from 21 to 17 per cent.

22 The reductions of the GST rate in 2006 and 2008 were important measures that will be discussed in the next section on income redistribution.

23 See table A5.4 of Government of Canada, *Strong Leadership [Budget 2015]* (Ottawa: Department of Finance, 2015), http://www.budget.gc.ca/2015/docs/plan/budget2015-eng. pdf, for the list of integrity tax measures introduced since Budget 2010. Unfortunately, the government continued to starve the Canada Revenue Agency's operating expenditures, which reduced its effectiveness in ensuring compliance.

24 While we believe that the individual-based system has clear advantages, some other countries have a well-structured family-based one, a system actually proposed for Canada by the Carter Commission.

25 The old age transfer system—in particular the clawback provisions in OAS and GIS—is predicated on the simple base of income for tax purposes, with no asset test. Because the TFSA will not generate income for tax purposes, some modification of the eligibility rules for the GIS—such as an asset test—may be needed.

26 They also continued to maintain policies highly favourable to mining.

27 This was true except for the brief period in 2008–2009 when global prices fell.

28 See figure 8.5.

29 Government of Ontario, *Building Ontario Up: Ontario Budget 2015* (Toronto: Queen's Printer for Ontario, 2015), 307, http://www.fin.gov.on.ca/en/budget/ontariobudgets/2015/papers_all.pdf.

30 In the Federal Budget 2015 the universal child care benefit was increased, especially for children under age six, and this enhanced program replaces the child tax credit.

31 Andrew Heisz and Brian Murphy, "The Role of Taxes and Transfers in Reducing Income Inequality," in *Income Inequality: The Canadian Story*, ed. David A. Green, W. Craig Riddell and France St-Hilaire (Montreal: Institute for Research on Public Policy, 2016). Their analysis covers 1976–2011 and the effects of key taxes and transfers by the federal *and* provincial governments. Our conclusion on redistribution arising from policies of the Harper government is based on our reading and interpretation of the results and charts provided by Heisz and Murphy.

32 While the federal debt/GDP ratio declined, the fiscal position of the provinces deteriorated during the Harper years so that the general government net debt (book value)/GDP ratio rose.

9 Canadian Trade and Investment Policy under the Harper Government

1 Roland Paris, "Trade Appears Strong Because the Rest Is Weak," *National Post*, December 20, 2013.

2 In October 2013, Canada announced that an "agreement in principle" had been reached with the EU. In September 2014, Canadian and European officials celebrated the completion of a final text. By the end of 2015, not only had Europe's national government's not ratified the deal, but opposition seemed to be growing daily over investor-state dispute settlement and perceived linkage between the CETA and the US-EU free trade agreement being negotiated.

3 The World Trade Organization (WTO) was established in 1995 and oversees the operation and negotiation of the major agreements governing the multilateral trading system, including the GATT, the General Agreement on Trade in Services (GATS) and the Agreement on Trade-Related Aspects of Intellectual Property (TRIPs). Most regional trade agreements, such as the North American Free Trade Agreement, use rules and principles that conform to the WTO model.

4 Conservative Party of Canada, *Stand Up for Canada: Conservative Party of Canada Federal Election Platform 2006*, 3, https://www.poltext.org/sites/poltext.org/files/plateformes/can2006pc_plt_en._14112008_165519.pdf.

5 Between 2006 and 2015, Canada signed, concluded or brought into force FIPAs with more than twenty countries. See Global Affairs Canada, "Foreign Investment Protection and Promotion Agreements," http://www.international.gc.ca/trade-agreements-accords-commerciaux/agr-acc/fipa-apie/index.aspx.

6 DFATD (Global Affairs Canada), "Canada's State of Trade: Trade and Investment Update—2009," http://www.international.gc.ca/economist-economiste/performance/state-point/state_2009_point/2009_4.aspx.

7 These negotiations ran from 2008 to 2015, but Malaysia did not join until 2010. Canada and Mexico joined in 2012, and Japan in 2013.

8 Jennifer Ditchburn, "Harper promises to defend the dairy industry," The Canadian Press, September 29, 2015.

9 Jason Fekete, "Canada's dairy farmers 'angered and disappointed' by EU trade deal that would double cheese imports," *National Post*, October 16, 2013.

10 Dmitry Lysenko and Saul Schwartz, "Does Canada Need Trade Adjustment Assistance?," *IRPP* 57 (December 2015): 1–32.

11 Naomi Christensen, *Branching Out: Preparing for Life Without a Softwood Lumber Agreement* (Canada West Foundation, September 2015), 7, http://cwf.ca/wp-content/uploads/2015/09/CWF_NRP_BranchingOut_Report_SEPT2015.pdf.

12 Grading provides a standard for measuring the number of defects in a lumber product. Disputes arise when lumber is purchased from public lands as lower-grade product and then resold as higher-grade product.

13 Canada agreed to the VER through a 1986 Memorandum of Understanding. In 1996, the first five-year Softwood Lumber Agreement was signed. Following a four-year gap marked by protracted disputes, another agreement was reached in 2006. That agreement had a term of seven years plus a two-year extension agreed to in 2013. It expired in October 2015 but parties agree not to launch a trade action for one year (until October 2016).

14 Christensen, 7.

15 John Herd Thompson and Stephen J. Randall, *Canada and the United States: Ambivalent Allies*, 4th Edition (Athens: University of Georgia Press, 2008), 331.

16 A good summary of the issues is found in Joel L. Greene, *Country-of-Origin Labeling for Foods and the WTO Trade Dispute on Meat Labeling* (Congressional Research Service, December 8, 2015), http://www.fas.org/sgp/crs/misc/RS22955.pdf.

17 Although often used interchangeably, the Buy American Act applies to all US federal goods purchases, while the Buy America Act applies solely to grants issued by the Federal Transit Administration and Federal Highway Administration.

18 The Alaska government cancelled the call for bids in late January 2015.

19 Now the Minister of Innovation, Science and Economic Development.

20 Innovation, Science and Economic Development Act, "All Guidelines—Industry Canada *Investment Canada Act*, http://www.ic.gc.ca/eic/site/ica-lic.nsf/eng/lk00064.html#p2.

21 The International Centre for Settlement of Investment Disputes (ICSID) is a member of the World Bank Group.

22 Asia Pacific Foundation of Canada, *2015 National Opinion Poll: Canadian Views on Asian Investment* (Asia Pacific Foundation of Canada, June 2015), https://www.asiapacific.ca/surveys/national-opinion-polls/2015-national-opinion-poll-canadian-views-asian-investment.

23 Negotiations have been concluded, but agreements not yet signed, for another seven FIPAs.

24 Global Affairs Canada, "NAFTA Fast Facts," http://www.international.gc.ca/trade-agreements-accords-commerciaux/agr-acc/nafta-alena/facts.aspx.

25 Using a software analogy, the TPP offers downloadable patches to update the aging NAFTA.

26 Canada and Japan had previously started negotiations on a bilateral free trade agreement but these were sidelined in favor of the TPP negotiations. Arguably, the results of the TPP would yield deeper commitments, given the larger market opportunities of the regional agreement, but the results would not as focused on the specific bilateral interests of the two economies.

27 Laura Dawson and Dan Ciuriak, "Chasing China: Why an economic agreement with China is necessary for Canada's future prosperity," Dawson Strategic and Ciuriak Consulting, January 2015, http://dawsonstrat.com/files/2016/01/Chasing-China-Web-Ready.pdf.

10 The Harper Influence on Immigration

1 Citizenship and Immigration Canada, "Notice—Transforming the Immigration System," May 25, 2012, http://www.cic.gc.ca/english/department/media/notices/notice-transform.asp.

2 Ibid.

3 Michael Adams, Audrey Macklin and Ratna Omidvar, "Citizenship Act will create two classes of Canadians," *The Globe and Mail*, May 21, 2014.

4 Keith Banting, "Beyond Government by Surprise: Governance in the Immigration Sector" (plenary presentation, 17th National Metropolis Conference, Vancouver, BC, March 26–28, 2015).

5 Justin Trudeau, "Justin Trudeau, for the record: 'We beat fear with hope,'" *Maclean's*, October 20, 2015, http://www.macleans.ca/politics/ottawa/justin-trudeau-for-the-record-we-beat-fear-with-hope/.

6 For the most recent data, see "Syria Regional Refugee Response—Regional Overview," *UNHCR*, last modified July 4, 2016, http://data.unhcr.org/syrianrefugees/regional.php.

7   International Organization for Migration, "IOM Monitors Latest Migrant Arrivals, Deaths in Mediterranean," news release, October 6, 2015, https://www.iom.int/news/iom-monitors-latest-migrant-arrivals-deaths-mediterranean.

8   "Why are thousands of Germans protesting and who are Pegida?" *BBC*, January 13, 2015, http://www.bbc.co.uk/newsbeat/article/30694252/why-are-thousands-of-germans-protesting-and-who-are-pegida.

9   Robert D. Kaplan, "Europe's deep right-wing logic," *Forbes*, June 4, 2014, http://www.forbes.com/sites/stratfor/2014/06/04/europes-deep-right-wing-logic/.

10   "Promise check: We will stop the boats," *Australian Broadcasting Corporation*, July 27, 2014, http://www.abc.net.au/news/2014-07-27/we-will-stop-the-boats-promise-check/5474206.

11   Tim Leslie and Mark Corcoran, "Operation Sovereign Borders: The First Six Months," *Australian Broadcasting Corporation*, March 26, 2014, http://www.abc.net.au/news/interactives/operation-sovereign-borders-the-first-6-months/.

12   Sarah Martin and Peter Alford, "First assault: new boat tests Malcolm Turnbull's resolve," *The Australian*, September 24, 2015, http://www.theaustralian.com.au/national-affairs/immigration/first-assault-new-boat-tests-malcolm-turnbulls-resolve/news-story/b60947ef164664639d451ad17c341138.

13   "Merkel says German multicultural society has failed," *BBC News*, October 17, 2010, http://www.bbc.com/news/world-europe-11559451.

14   Leaders' debate, April 2011, available at: "2011 Canadian Federal Election Debate," YouTube video, originally televised by CTV on April 12, 2011, posted by "Canuck Politics," April 13, 2011, https://www.youtube.com/watch?v=jGYE2d4LJ5M.

15   Citizenship and Immigration Canada, "Report on Plans and Priorities 2015–2016," http://www.cic.gc.ca/english/resources/publications/rpp/2015-2016/index.asp#a2.1.

16   Stephen Harper, "PM delivers remarks during a joint press conference with Benigno Aquino III, President of the Philippines," May 8, 2015. Though the news release has been removed from the Prime Minister of Canada website, a transcript is available at "Gallery: Aquino walks the Hall," *iPolitics*, May 8, 2015, https://ipolitics.ca/2015/05/08/gallery-aquino-walks-the-hall/.

17   Citizenship and Immigration Canada, "Facts and figures 2013—Immigration overview: Permanent residents," http://www.cic.gc.ca/english/resources/statistics/facts2013/permanent/10.asp.

18   Stephen Harper, "PM delivers remarks at a dinner in honour of Narendra Modi, Prime Minister of India, in Vancouver," April 16, 2015, accessed August 9, 2015, http://pm.gc.ca/eng/news/2015/04/16/pm-delivers-remarks-dinner-honour-narendra-modi-prime-minister-india-vancouver (page discontinued).

19   Doug Saunders, "How Tories win immigrant votes using anti-immigrant messages," *The Globe and Mail*, October 9, 2015.

20   Andrew Griffith, *Multiculturalism in Canada: Evidence and Anecdote* (Ottawa: Anar Press, 2015), 47.

21   Frank Graves, "The EKOS poll: Are Canadians getting more racist?," *iPolitics*, March 12, 2015, http://ipolitics.ca/2015/03/12/the-ekos-poll-are-canadians-getting-more-racist/.

22   Don Butler, "Canadians in the dark about immigration numbers: survey," *Ottawa Citizen*, August 27, 2014, http://ottawacitizen.com/news/national/canadians-in-the-dark-about-immigration-numbers-survey.

23   Evan Dyer, "Raif Badawi case: What he has in common with Jason Kenney," *CBC News*, March 3, 2015, http://www.cbc.ca/news/politics/raif-badawi-case-what-he-has-in-common-with-jason-kenney-1.2980113.

24   Griffith, *Multiculturalism in Canada*, Appendix M.

25   Citizenship and Immigration Canada, "The Community Historical Recognition Program," http://www.cic.gc.ca/english/multiculturalism/programs/community.asp.

26 Griffith, *Multiculturalism in Canada*, 116.
27 Kai L. Chan, "Canada's Governing Class: Who Rules the Country?," September 2014, http://www.kailchan.ca/wp-content/uploads/2014/11/Kai-Chan-2014_Canadas-governing-class-who-rules-the-country.pdf.
28 Jerome H. Black, "Racial Diversity in the 2011 Federal Election: Visible Minority Candidates and MPs," *Canadian Parliamentary Review* 36, no. 3 (Autumn 2013): 21–26.
29 Affan Chowdhry, "Record number of visible minority MPs elected to Commons," *The Globe and Mail*, October 20, 2015.
30 Royal Bank of Canada, *Immigrant labour market outcomes in Canada: The benefits of addressing wage and employment gaps* (RBC Economics Research, December 2011), http://www.rbc.com/newsroom/pdf/1219-2011-immigration.pdf.
31 Demetri Sevastopulo and Simon Doyle, "Immigrants Join the Canadian 'Express,'" *Forbes*, June 21, 2015.
32 Andrew Clarke and Mikal Skuterud, "Why Do Immigrant Workers in Australia Perform Better than in Canada? Is It the Immigrants or Their Labour Markets?" *Canadian Journal of Economics* 46, no. 4 (November 2013): 1431–62.
33 Citizenship and Immigration Canada, "Express Entry Mid-Year Report," July 31, 2014, http://www.cic.gc.ca/english/resources/reports/ee-midyear-2015.asp.
34 Nicholas Keung, "Only 1 in 10 candidates invited to immigrate under Ottawa's new Express Entry system," *Toronto Star*, August 6, 2015, http://www.thestar.com/news/immigration/2015/08/06/only-1-in-10-candidates-invited-to-immigrate-under-ottawas-new-express-entry-system.html.
35 Demetrios G. Papademetriou, "The Global Boom in Investor Immigration: Lessons for Canada," webinar presented by The Conference Board of Canada, August 5, 2015.
36 Ninette Kelley and Michael Trebilcock, *The Making of the Mosaic: A History of Canadian Immigration Policy*, 2nd ed. (Toronto: University of Toronto Press, 2010), 438.
37 Naomi Alboim and Karen Cohl, "Shaping the Future: Canada's Rapidly Changing Immigration Policies," The Maytree Foundation, October 2012, 29.
38 "Regulations Amending the Immigration and Refugee Protection Regulations," *Canada Gazette* 147, no. 20 (May 18, 2013), http://www.gazette.gc.ca/rp-pr/p1/2013/2013-05-18/html/reg1-eng.html.
39 Citizenship and Immigration Canada, "Reducing citizenship processing times and backlogs," December 23, 2014, http://www.cic.gc.ca/english/about_us/mandate/citizenship.asp.
40 Canadian Doctors for Refugee Care v. Canada (Attorney general), July 4, 2014, FC 651.
41 Ratna Omidvar and Dana Wagner, *Flight and Freedom: Stories of Escape to Canada*, (Toronto: Between the Lines, 2015), 225.
42 Citizenship and Immigration Canada, "Harper Government Introduces the *Protecting Canada's Immigration System Act*," news release, February 16, 2012, http://www.cic.gc.ca/ftp/pdf/20120216-eng.pdf.
43 Citizenship and Immigration Canada, "Protecting Canada's Asylum System from Abuse," news release, October 14, 2014, http://news.gc.ca/web/article-en.do?nid=892139.
44 Chris Alexander, "Speaking notes for Chris Alexander, Canada's Citizenship and Immigration Minister at a News Conference to Announce the Tabling of Bill C-24: The Strengthening Canadian Citizenship Act," speech, February 6, 2014, http://news.gc.ca/web/article-en.do?nid=842109.
45 Ishaq v. Canada (Citizenship and Immigration), 2015 FC 156 (CanLII), accessed October 21, 2015, http://www.canlii.org/en/ca/fct/doc/2015/2015fc156/2015fc156.html.
46 "Niqab ban prevented 2 women from proceeding with citizenship oath," *CBC News*, September 30, 2015, http://www.cbc.ca/news/politics/niqab-ban-zunera-ishaq-1.3249495.
47 "A French-language transcript of last night's debate," *Maclean's*, September 25, 2015, http://www.macleans.ca/politics/ottawa/a-french-language-transcript-of-last-nights-debate/.

48 Lotf Ali Jan Ali, "Welcome to Canada? A Critical Review and Assessment of Canada's Fast-Changing Immigration Policies," *RCIS Working Paper* No. 2014/6, October 2014, 9, http://www.ryerson.ca/content/dam/rcis/documents/RCIS_WP_Ali.pdf.

49 Stephanie Stobbe and Judith Harris, "Tracking Immigrant Professionals' Experience in Manitoba's Labour Market," *RCIS Working Paper* No. 2013/6, 3, http://www.ryerson.ca/content/dam/rcis/documents/RCIS_WP_Stobbe_Harris_No_2013_6.pdf

11 Law and Order in the Harper Years

1 Elaine Flis, "I am woman; hear me more," *Public Affairs: Your Online Newsletter*, February 2006, http://www.publicaffairs.ca/newsletter-files/feb06.htm.

2 Conservative Party of Canada, *Stand Up for Canada: Conservative Party of Canada Federal Election Platform 2006*, 21–27, http://www.cbc.ca/canadavotes2006/leadersparties/pdf/conservative_platform20060113.pdf. The economy is discussed in pages 15–20.

3 Ibid., 22.

4 Ibid., 23.

5 "Welcome to the Federal Ombudsperson for Victims of Crime," Office of the Federal Ombudsperson for Victims for Crime, accessed July 5, 2016, http://www.victimsfirst.gc.ca/.

6 See Seidman's speech in Canada, *Debates of the Senate [Official Report]*, 40th Parliament, 3rd session, vol. 147 no. 70 (November 25, 2010), http://www.parl.gc.ca/content/sen/chamber/403/debates/pdf/070db_2010-11-25-e.pdf.

7 "What worries critics about omnibus crime bill," *CBC News*, March 6, 2012, http://www.cbc.ca/news/canada/what-worries-critics-about-omnibus-crime-bill-1.1244907.

8 Meagan Fitzplatrick, "Wearing a mask at a riot is now a crime," *CBC News*, June 19, 2013, http://www.cbc.ca/news/politics/wearing-a-mask-at-a-riot-is-now-a-crime-1.1306458.

9 Brendan Kennedy, "MP's bill would expand citizens' arrest rights," *Toronto Star*, October 15, 2010, http://www.thestar.com/news/gta/2010/10/15/mps_bill_would_expand_citizens_arrest_rights.html

10 Timothy Appleby and Jill Mahoney, "New citizen's-arrest law greeted with applause, criticism," *The Globe and Mail*, March 11, 2013, http://www.theglobeandmail.com/news/national/new-citizens-arrest-law-greeted-with-applause-criticism/article9634015/.

11 Bruce Cheadle, The Canadian Press, "Conservatives' gun bill C-42 set to pass before Commons recess," *CBC News*, May 10, 2015, http://www.cbc.ca/news/politics/conservatives-gun-bill-c-42-set-to-pass-before-commons-recess-1.3068589.

12 Bruce Cheadle, The Canadian Press, "Pardon backlog leaves thousands of former offenders in limbo," *CBC News*, November 27, 2014, http://www.cbc.ca/news/politics/pardon-backlog-leaves-thousands-of-former-offenders-in-limbo-1.2851926.

13 Sean Fine, "Five Fundamental Ways Harper Has Changed the Justice System," *The Globe and Mail*, May 6, 2014, http://www.theglobeandmail.com/news/politics/five-fundamental-ways-harper-has-changed-the-justice-system/article18503381/.

14 Lyne Casavant, Christine Morris, and Julia Nicol, *Legislative Summary: Bill C-32: An Act to enact the Canadian Victims Bill of Rights and to amend certain Acts* (Library of Parliament, July 23, 2014), http://www.lop.parl.gc.ca/Content/LOP/LegislativeSummaries/41/2/c32-e.pdf

15 Justice Canada, "Coming into Force of the *Not Criminally Responsible Reform Act*," news release, July 11, 2014, http://news.gc.ca/web/article-en.do?nid=867529.

16 Meagan Fitzpatrick, "10 voices on the 'not criminally responsible' reform bill," *CBC News*, June 6, 2013, http://www.cbc.ca/news/politics/10-voices-on-the-not-criminally-responsible-reform-bill-1.1330502.

17 Kathryn Blaze Carlson, "Crime and punishment: Inside the Tories' plan to overhaul the

justice system," *National Post*, May 31, 2011, http://news.nationalpost.com/news/canada/crime-and-punishment-inside-the-tories-plan-to-overhaul-the-justice-system.

18 Sheena Goodyear, "No One Seems to Care About Prison Reform in Canada," *Vice News*, October 1, 2015, https://news.vice.com/article/no-one-seems-to-care-about-prison-reform-in-canada.

19 Laura Stone, "Prison guards launch campaign against Conservatives in John Baird's riding," *Global News*, September 30, 2014, http://globalnews.ca/news/1590992/prison-guards-launch-campaign-against-conservatives-in-john-bairds-riding/.

20 Howard Sapers, *Annual Report of the Office of the Correctional Investigator 2013-2014* (Office of the Correctional Investigator, June 27, 2014), http://www.oci-bec.gc.ca/cnt/rpt/annrpt/annrpt20132014-eng.aspx#sIII.

21 Dwight Newman, telephone interview with the author, October 8, 2015.

22 Tom Flanagan, interview with the author, October 23, 2015.

23 Peter MacKay, interview with the author, October 20, 2015.

24 Fine, "Five Fundamental Ways."

25 Kathryn Blaze Carlson and Jill Mahoney, "Harper rejects calls for aboriginal women inquiry," *The Globe and Mail*, August 21, 2014, http://www.theglobeandmail.com/news/politics/harper-rejects-calls-for-aboriginal-women-inquiry/article20166785/.

26 Meagan Fitzpatrick, "Harper on terror arrests: Not a time for 'sociology,'" *CBC News*, April 25, 2013, http://www.cbc.ca/news/politics/harper-on-terror-arrests-not-a-time-for-sociology-1.1413502.

27 Leslie MacKinnon, "Harper slams Trudeau for comments on Boston bombings," *CBC News*, April 17, 2013, http://www.cbc.ca/news/politics/harper-slams-trudeau-for-comments-on-boston-bombings-1.1394586.

28 "Conservative Leader Rona Ambrose charts new course to support MMIW inquiry," *CBC Radio*, November 7, 2015, http://www.cbc.ca/radio/thehouse/meet-your-new-government-1.3305229/conservative-leader-rona-ambrose-charts-new-course-to-support-mmiw-inquiry-1.3307494.

29 Elizabeth Thompson, "DoJ hunger games," *Canadian Lawyer*, August 4, 2014, http://www.canadianlawyermag.com/5219/DoJ-hunger-games.html.

30 Ibid.

31 Sean Fine, "Lawyer's lawsuit highlights Ottawa's court clashes over Charter rights," *The Globe and Mail*, September 20, 2015, http://www.theglobeandmail.com/news/national/lawyers-lawsuit-highlights-ottawas-court-clashes-over-charter-rights/article26449862/

32 Ibid.

33 John Ibbitson, "How the Toews-sponsored Internet surveillance bill quietly died," *The Globe and Mail*, May 15, 2012, http://www.theglobeandmail.com/news/politics/how-the-toews-sponsored-internet-surveillance-bill-quietly-died/article4179310/.

34 Paula Loriggio, The Canadian Press, "Harper's 'life without parole' initiative a political move, say critics," *Global News*, March 4, 2015, http://globalnews.ca/news/1863522/new-law-will-ensure-some-life-sentences-are-for-life-harper/.

35 John Ibbitson, *Stephen Harper* (Toronto: McClelland and Stewart, 2015), 385.

36 Tonda MacCharles, "Stephen Harper urged to apologize for spat with Chief Justice Beverley McLachlin," *Toronto Star*, July 25, 2014, http://www.thestar.com/news/canada/2014/07/25/chief_justice_cleared_in_spat_with_stephen_harper_government.html.

37 Eugene Meehan, interview with the author.

38 Tasha Kheiriddin and Adam Daifallah, *Rescuing Canada's Right: Blueprint for a Conservative Revolution* (Toronto: John Wiley & Sons Canada, 2005), 105.

39 Lisa Kerr and Anthony N. Doob, "The Conservative Take on Crime Policy," *The Harper Decade: Canada Has Changed* (blog), August 20, 2015, http://www.theharperdecade.com/blog/2015/8/17/the-conservative-take-on-crime-policy.

40 Sean Fine, "Stephen Harper's courts: How the judiciary has been remade," *The Globe and Mail*, July 24, 2015, http://www.theglobeandmail.com/news/politics/stephen-harpers-courts-how-the-judiciary-has-been-remade/article25661306/.

41 Ibid.

42 Glen McGregor, "The Gargoyle: New Supreme Court appointee blogged on Khadr, called Trudeau 'unspeakably awful,' hoped for Harper majority," *Ottawa Citizen*, July 31, 2015, http://ottawacitizen.com/news/national/the-gargoyle-new-supreme-court-appointee-blogged-on-khadr-called-trudeau-unspeakably-awful-hoped-for-harper-majority.

43 Flanagan interview.

44 Newman interview.

45 Christie Blatchford, "The rot in Canada's system of picking federal judges," *National Post*, April 28, 2014, http://news.nationalpost.com/full-comment/christie-blatchford-the-rot-in-canadas-system-of-picking-federal-judges.

46 Public Prosecutor Service of Canada, "About the Public Prosecutor Service of Canada," last modified May 20, 2015, http://www.ppsc-sppc.gc.ca/eng/bas/index.html#mandate.

47 The Associated Press, "U.S. judge awards $134-million in suit against Omar Khadr," *The Globe and Mail*, July 2, 2015, http://www.theglobeandmail.com/news/national/us-judge-awards-134-million-in-suit-against-omar-khadr/article25242269/.

48 Kim Mackrael and Sean Fine, "Harper unapologetic about Ottawa's efforts to keep Omar Khadr in prison," *The Globe and Mail*, May 8, 2015, http://www.theglobeandmail.com/news/politics/harper-unapologetic-about-governments-efforts-to-keep-khadr-in-prison/article24334556/.

49 Newman interview.

50 Department of Justice Canada, "Government Introduces Bill to End House Arrest for Property and Other Serious Crimes by Serious and Violent Offenders," news release, April 22, 2010, http://news.gc.ca/web/article-en.do?m=/index&nid=526859.

51 Interview with MacKay.

52 Howard Sapers, *Annual Report of the Office of the Correctional Investigator 2011–2012* (Office of the Correctional Investigator, June 26, 2012), http://www.oci-bec.gc.ca/cnt/rpt/annrpt/annrpt20112012-eng.aspx#sIII.

53 Statistics Canada, "Megatrends: Canada's Crime Rate: Two Decades of Decline. Graph: Homicides and Attempted Murders in Canada, 1962–2013," last modified October 12, 2015, http://www.statcan.gc.ca/pub/11-630-x/11-630-x2015001-eng.htm.

54 Ibid.

55 Julie Sauvé, "Crime Statistics in Canada, 2004," [Statistics Canada,] *Juristat* 25, no. 5 (2005): 1-22, http://publications.gc.ca/collections/Collection-R/Statcan/85-002-XIE/0050585-002-XIE.pdf.

56 Mia Dauvergne and Geoffrey Li, "Homocide in Canada, 2005," [Statistics Canada,] *Juristat* 26, no. 6 (2006): 1-25. http://publications.gc.ca/Collection-R/Statcan/85-002-XIE/85-002-XIE2006006.pdf.

57 Ibid.

58 Alexander Panetta, The Canadian Press, "Harper sets economy as key theme in election-style speech," *The Globe and Mail*, January 25, 2008, http://www.theglobeandmail.com/news/national/harper-sets-economy-as-key-theme-in-election-style-speech/article18442679/.

59 Scott Newark, *Why Canadian Crime Statistics Don't Add Up: Not the whole truth* (MacDonald Laurier Institute, February 2011), 4-28, http://macdonaldlaurier.ca/files/pdf/MLI-Crime_Statistics_Review-Web.pdf.

60 Ibid., 9.

61 Jeffrey T. Ulmer and Darrell Steffensmeier, "The Age and Crime Relationship: Social Variations,

Social Explanations," in *The Nurture Versus Biosocial Debate in Criminology*, ed. Kevin M. Beaver, J.C. Barnes, and Brian B. Boutwell (Los Angeles: Sage Publishing, 2014), 377, http://www.sagepub.com/sites/default/files/upm-binaries/60294_Chapter_23.pdf.

62 David K. Foot and Daniel Stoffman, *Boom, Bust & Echo* (Toronto: MacFarlane Walter and Ross, 1996), 139–143.

63 Carson, "Crime and punishment."

64 Sean Fine, "Five Fundamental Ways."

65 Terry Milewski, "Texas conservatives reject Harper's crime plan," *CBC News*, October 17, 2011, http://www.cbc.ca/news/politics/texas-conservatives-reject-harper-s-crime-plan-1.1021017.

66 Flanagan interview.

12 Stephen Harper and Indigenous Peoples

1 Brian Slattery, "A Taxonomy of Aboriginal Rights," in *Let Right Be Done: Aboriginal Title, the Calder Case, and the Future of Indigenous Rights,* ed. Hamar Foster, Heather Raven, and Jeremy Webber (Vancouver: UBC Press, 2007), 111–28.

2 Leonard I. Rotman, "Provincial Fiduciary Obligations to First Nations: The Nexus between Governmental Power and Responsibility," *Osgoode Hall Law Journal* 34, no. 2 (Winter 1994): 735, http://digitalcommons.osgoode.yorku.ca/cgi/viewcontent.cgi?article=1662&context=ohlj.

3 Erin Hanson, "Aboriginal Rights," Indigenous Foundations, University of British Columbia, 2009, http://indigenousfoundations.arts.ubc.ca/home/land-rights/aboriginal-rights.html.

4 Aboriginal Affairs and Northern Development Canada, "Treaties with Aboriginal People," last modified September 15, 2010, http://www.aadnc-aandc.gc.ca/eng/1100100032291/1100100032292.

5 Stephen Harper, "Address by the Prime Minister at the Canada-UK Chamber of Commerce" (speech, London, July 14, 2006).

6 James Daschuk, *Clearing the Plains: Disease, Politics of Starvation, and the Loss of Aboriginal Life* (Regina: University of Regina Press, 2013), 134.

7 Truth and Reconciliation Commission of Canada, *Honouring the Truth, Reconciling for the Future: Summary of the Final Report of the Truth and Reconciliation Commission of Canada* (Winnipeg: Truth and Reconciliation Commission of Canada, 2015), 2, http://www.trc.ca/websites/trcinstitution/File/2015/Honouring_the_Truth_Reconciling_for_the_Future_July_23_2015.pdf.

8 Ibid.

9 Indian and Northern Affairs Canada, *A Survey of the Contemporary Indians of Canada: Economic, Political, Educational Needs and Policies: Part 2 [The Hawthorn Report]* (Ottawa: Queen's Printer and Controller of Stationary, October 1967), https://www.aadnc-aandc.gc.ca/eng/1291832488245/1291832647702.

10 Michael Murphy, "Looking Forward Without Looking Back: Jean Chrétien's Legacy for Aboriginal-State Relations," in *The Chrétien Legacy: Politics and Public Policy in Canada*, ed. Lois Harder and Steven Patten (Montreal: McGill-Queen's University Press, 2006), 161.

11 See *The Canadian Encyclopedia*, s. v. "Kelowna Accord," July 23, 2013, http://www.thecanadianencyclopedia.ca/en/article/kelowna-accord/.

12 Lisa L. Patterson, *Aboriginal Roundtable to Kelowna Accord: Aboriginal Policy Negotiations, 2004-2005* (Library of Parliament, May 4, 2006), http://www.parl.gc.ca/content/LOP/researchpublications/prb0604-e.htm.

13 Kathryn Blaze Carlson, "Stephen Harper's chiefly practical approach to First Nations' issues," *National Post,* December 9, 2011, http://news.nationalpost.com/news/canada/stephen-harpers-chiefly-practical-approach-to-first-nations-issues.

14 Stephen Harper, "Statement of apology to former students of Indian Residential Schools," Indigenous and Northern Affairs Canada, June 11, 2008, https://www.aadnc-aandc.gc.ca/eng/1100100015644/1100100015649.

15 Phil Fontaine, "Indian Residential Schools Statement of Apology—Phil Fontaine, National Chief, Assembly of First Nations [transcript]," Indigenous and Northern Affairs Canada, June 11, 2008, https://www.aadnc-aandc.gc.ca/eng/1100100015697/1100100015700.

16 See Mary Simon's full speech in Appendix A of Jennifer Henderson and Pauline Wakeham, *Reconciling Canada: Critical Perspective on the Culture of Redress* (Toronto: University of Toronto Press, 2013), 338.

17 Beverley Jacobs, "Response to Canada's Apology to Residential School Survivors," *Canadian Woman Studies* 26, nos. 3–4 (2008): 225, http://cws.journals.yorku.ca/index.php/cws/article/view/22138/20792.

18 "First Nations people now covered under rights act," *CBC News*, June 17, 2011, http://www.cbc.ca/news/canada/first-nations-people-now-covered-under-rights-act-1.1103923.

19 Scott Haldane et al., *Nurturing the Learning Spirit of First Nation Students: The Report of the National Panel on First Nation Elementary and Secondary Education for Students on Reserve* (Aboriginal Affairs and Northern Development, 2011), 10, https://www.aadnc-aandc.gc.ca/DAM/DAM-INTER-HQ-EDU/STAGING/texte-text/nat_panel_final_report_1373997803969_eng.pdf.

20 Ibid., vii.

21 Assembly of First Nations, *Federal Budget 2012—Summary and Considerations* (April 5, 2012), 2, http://www.afn.ca/uploads/files/federalbudgetanalysis2012afn.pdf.

22 Chief Shining Turtle, "The First Nations Education Act Is Just a Pretty Face," *Politics Canada* (blog), *Huffington Post*, May 16, 2014, http://www.huffingtonpost.ca/chief-shining-turtle/first-nations-education_b_5337327.html.

23 Standing Senate Committee on Human Rights, *A Hard Bed to Lie in: Matrimonial Real Property on Reserve: Interim Report of the Standing Senate Committee on Human Rights* (Ottawa: Standing Senate Committee on Human Rights, 2003), http://www.parl.gc.ca/Content/SEN/Committee/372/huma/rep/rep08nov03-e.pdf.

24 Wendy Grant-John, *Report of the Ministerial Representative: Matrimonial Real Property Issues on Reserves* (Office of the Ministerial Representative, March 9, 2007), 2, http://www.collectionscanada.gc.ca/webarchives/20071125013543/http://www.ainc-inac.gc.ca/wige/rmr/rmr_e.pdf.

25 Native Women's Association of Canada, "Bill S-2: Family Homes on Reserves and Matrimonial Interests or Rights Act," 2011, accessed December 4, 2015, http://www.nwac.ca/sites/default/files/imce/Final%20NWAC%20Press%20Release%20on%20Bill%20S-2%20November%2025%202011.pdf (page discontinued).

26 Joanna Smith, "Nearly 200 First Nations haven't filed yet under Financial Transparency Act," *Toronto Star*, September 1, 2015, http://www.thestar.com/news/canada/2015/09/01/nearly-200-first-nations-havent-filed-yet-under-financial-transparency-act.html.

27 Jorge Barrera, "Aboriginal organizations hit with $60 million worth of cuts, Inuit faced steepest reduction: AFN Analysis," *APTN..ca*, January 13, 2015, http://aptn.ca/news/2015/01/13/aboriginal-organizations-hit-60-million-worth-cuts-inuit-faced-steepest-reduction-afn-analysis/.

28 "Conservative proposed omnibus Indian Act changes would allow bands to lease out reserve lands without majority community support," *APTN.ca*, November 21, 2012, http://aptn.ca/news/2012/11/21/conservative-proposed-omnibus-indian-act-changes-would-allow-bands-to-lease-out-reserve-lands-without-majority-community-support/.

29 Heather Scoffield, The Canadian Press, "Documents Reveal Pipeline Industry Drove Changes to Navigable Waters Act," *CTV News*, February 20, 2013, http://www.ctvnews.ca/politics/documents-reveal-pipeline-industry-drove-changes-to-navigable-waters-act-1.1164476.

30 See "Timeline: Idle No More's Rise," *CBC News*, October 4, 2013, http://www.cbc.ca/news2/
    interactives/timeline-idle-no-more/index.html.

31 "New Attawapiskat School Opens Today," *CBC News*, August 29, 2014, http://www.cbc.ca/news/
    canada/sudbury/new-attawapiskat-school-opens-today-1.2750480.

32 Cynthia Wesley-Esquimaux, "Legacy: Genocide by Paper," accessed July 5, 2016, https://www.
    academia.edu/3377703/Legacy_genocide_by_paper.

33 Aboriginal Affairs and Northern Development Canada, *Summative Evaluation of the Specific
    Claims Action Plan* (Ottawa: AANDC, April 2013), https://www.aadnc-aandc.gc.ca/eng/1385384
    648312/1385384701998.

34 See National Claims Research Directors, *In Bad Faith: "Justice at Last" and Canada's Failure
    to Resolve Specific Land Claims* (March 2015), http://www.ubcic.bc.ca/files/PDF/InBadFaith_
    JusticeatLast_CanadaFailureResolveSpecificClaims.pdf.

35 Harry Slade, *Annual Report: For Presentation to the Honourable Bernard Valcourt Minister
    of Aboriginal Affairs and Northern Development Canada* (Specific Claims Tribunal Canada,
    September 30, 2014), http://www.sct-trp.ca/pdf/Annual%20Report%202014.pdf.

36 Douglas R. Eyford, *A New Direction: Advancing Aboriginal and Treaty Rights* ([Ottawa:]
    Indigenous and Northern Affairs Canada, 2015), 51, http://www.aadnc-aandc.gc.ca/
    DAM/DAM-INTER-HQ-LDC/STAGING/texte-text/eyford_newDirection-report_
    april2015_1427810490332_eng.pdf.

37 Jody Porter, "First Nations combat 'Un-Fair Elections Act' with Rock the Vote," *CBC News*, July 9,
    2015, http://www.cbc.ca/news/canada/thunder-bay/first-nations-combat-un-fair-elections-act-
    with-rock-the-vote-1.3143801.

38 "First Nations Voters have Chance to Swing Election Results: Cheryl Maloney Urging all Canadians
    to Get Out and Vote in the Upcoming Federal Election," September 7, 2015, http://www.cbc.ca/
    news/canada/nova-scotia/first-nations-voters-have-chance-to-swing-election-results-1.3217916.

39 "Perry Bellegarde Says he will vote in federal election after all," *CBC News*, September 9, 2015,
    http://www.cbc.ca/news/politics/canada-election-2015-bellegarde-voting-first-nations-1.3220841.

40 The Prophecy of the Eighth Fire. See "The 8th Fire," Rites of Passage, accessed December 7, 2015,
    http://the8thfire.org/8thfire/.

13 The Harper Government and Agriculture

1 Barry K. Wilson, "Historic Vote Ends CWB Single Desk," *The Western Producer*, December 1,
   2011, http://www.producer.com/2011/12/historic-vote-ends-cwb-single-desk/.

2 Barry K. Wilson, "Changes to Grain Act to Proceed," *The Western Producer*, December 14, 2012,
   http://www.producer.com/2012/12/changes-to-grain-act-proceed%E2%80%A9/.

3 Canada, Agriculture and Agri-Food Canada, "Harper Government Introduces Legislation to
   Address Rail Capacity Challenges," March 26, 2014, http://news.gc.ca/web/article-en.do?nid=829579.

4 Barry K. Wilson, "Ritz refuses to hear pro-CWB views," *The Western Producer*, March 6, 2008,
   http://www.producer.com/2008/03/ritz-refuses-to-hear-procwb-views/.

5 Barry K. Wilson, "CFA strives to cooperate with feds," *The Western Producer*, February 18, 2010,
   http://www.producer.com/2010/02/cfa-strives-to-cooperate-with-feds/.

14 Harper on Health Care: A Curious Mix of Continuity, Unilateralism, and Opportunity Lost

1 For detailed information on wait times reductions, please consult the Canadian Institute for
   Health Information (CIHI) website at https://www.cihi.ca/en/health-system-performance/
   access-and-wait-times.

2   Mike Blanchfield, The Canadian Press, "PM Harper pledges $3.5 billion to extend maternal, child health initiative to 2020," *Toronto Star*, May 29, 2014, https://www.thestar.com/news/canada/2014/05/29/pm_harper_pledges_35_billion_to_extend_maternal_child_health_initiative_to_2020.html.

3   The Advisory Panel on Healthcare Innovation, *Unleashing Innovation: Excellent Healthcare for Canada: Executive Summary* (July 2015), http://www.healthycanadians.gc.ca/publications/health-system-systeme-sante/summary-innovation-sommaire/alt/summary-innovation-sommaire-eng.pdf.

15 Unsustainable Development: Energy and Environment in the Harper Decade

1   Jane Taber, "PM brands Canada an 'energy superpower,'" *The Globe and Mail*, July 15, 2006, http://www.theglobeandmail.com/news/world/pm-brands-canada-an-energy-superpower/article1105875/.

2   Ryan Lizza, "The President and the Pipeline," *The New Yorker*, September 16, 2013, http://www.newyorker.com/magazine/2013/09/16/the-president-and-the-pipeline.

3   Natural Resources Canada, "Harper Government Announces Plan for Responsible Resource Development," news release, April 17, 2012, http://www.nrcan.gc.ca/media-room/news-release/2012/45/2001.

4   Glen Toner and Jennifer McKee, "Harper's Partisan Wedge Politics: Bad Environmental Policy and Bad Energy Policy," in *How Ottawa Spends, 2014–2015*, ed. G. Bruce Doern and Christopher Stoney (Montreal: McGill-Queen University Press, 2014); Martin Olszynski, "From 'Badly Wrong' to Worse: An Empirical Analysis of Canada's New Approach to Fish Habitat Protection Laws," *Journal of Environmental Law and Practice* 28, no. 1 (2015): 1–52.

5   Terry Wotherspoon and John Hansen, "The 'Idle No More' Movement: Paradoxes of First Nations Inclusion in the Canadian Context," *Social Inclusion* 1 (2013): 21–36.

6   George Hoberg, "Pipelines and the Politics of Structure: A Case Study of the Trans Mountain Pipeline" (paper delivered at the Annual Meeting of the Canadian Political Science Association, Calgary, AB, May 31–June 2, 2016), https://cpsa-acsp.ca/documents/conference/2016/Hoberg.pdf.

7   "'Impossible' for Canada to reach Kyoto targets: Ambrose," *CBC News*, April 7, 2006, http://www.cbc.ca/news/canada/impossible-for-canada-to-reach-kyoto-targets-ambrose-1.583826.

8   Kathryn Harrison, "A Tale of Two Taxes: The Fate of Environmental Tax Reform in Canada," *Review of Policy Research* 29 (2012): 383–407.

9   "PM: Dion's carbon tax would 'screw everybody,'" *CBC News*, June 20, 2008, http://www.cbc.ca/news/canada/pm-dion-s-carbon-tax-would-screw-everybody-1.696762.

10 Ryan Lizza, "As The World Burns," *The New Yorker*, October 11, 2010.

11 Jason Dion, Dave Sawyer, and Phil Gass, *A Climate Gift or a Lump of Coal? The emission impacts of Canadian and U.S. greenhouse gas regulations in the electricity sector* (International Institute for Sustainable Development, September 2014), http://www.iisd.org/sites/default/files/publications/climate-gift-or-lump-of-coal.pdf.

12 See, e.g., Keith Stewart, "Confidential documents detail oil industry lobbying to weaken greenhouse gas rules," *Greenpeace Canada* (blog), November 8, 2013, http://www.greenpeace.org/canada/en/blog/Blogentry/confidential-documents-detail-oil-industry-lo/blog/47293/.

13 Josh Wingrove, "Memo contradicts Harper's stance on emission limits," *The Globe and Mail*, May 22, 2014, http://www.theglobeandmail.com/news/politics/memo-contradicts-harpers-stance-on-emission-limits/article18818653/.

14 Shawn McCarthy, "Harper calls climate regulations on oil and gas sector 'crazy economic policy,'" *The Globe and Mail*, December 9, 2014, http://www.theglobeandmail.com/news/

politics/harper-it-would-be-crazy-to-impose-climate-regulations-on-oil-industry/
article22014508/.

15 Jan Burck, Franziska Marten, Christoph Bals, *Climate Change Performance Index: Results 2016* (Germanwatch and Climate Action Network Europe, 2016), http://germanwatch.org/en/download/13626.pdf.

16 Joe Oliver, "An open letter from the Honourable Joe Oliver, Minister of Natural Resources," Natural Resources Canada, January 9, 2012, http://www.nrcan.gc.ca/media-room/news-release/2012/1/1909. See also George Hoberg, "The Battle Over Oil Sands Access to Tidewater: A Political Risk Analysis of Pipeline Alternatives," *Canadian Public* Policy 39 (2013): 371–91; and Monica Gattinger, "The Harper Government's Approach to Energy: Shooting Itself in the Foot," in *The Harper Era in Canadian Foreign Policy*, ed. Adam Chapnick and Christopher J. Kukucha (Vancouver: UBC Press, 2016).

17 "Harper warns pipeline hearings could be 'hijacked'," *CBC News*, January 6, 2012, http://www.cbc.ca/news/business/harper-warns-pipeline-hearings-could-be-hijacked-1.1150914; "Environmental charities 'laundering' foreign funds, Kent says," *CBC News*, May 1, 2012, http://www.cbc.ca/news/politics/environmental-charities-laundering-foreign-funds-kent-says-1.1165691. See also Toner and McKee, "Harper's Partisan Wedge Politics."

18 Shawn McCarthy, "Ottawa's new anti-terrorism strategy lists eco-extremists as threats," *The Globe and Mail*, February 10, 2012, http://www.theglobeandmail.com/news/politics/ottawas-new-anti-terrorism-strategy-lists-eco-extremists-as-threats/article533522/; Shawn McCarthy, "'Anti-petroleum' movement a growing security threat to Canada, RCMP say," *The Globe and Mail*, February 17, 2015, http://www.theglobeandmail.com/news/politics/anti-petroleum-movement-a-growing-security-threat-to-canada-rcmp-say/article23019252/.

19 Broadbent Institute, *Stephen Harper's CRA: Selective Audits, "Political" Activity, and Right-Leaning Charities* (Broadbent Institute, October 2014), https://d3n8a8pro7vhmx.cloudfront.net/broadbent/pages/16/attachments/original/1430005311/Stephen_Harper's_CRA.pdf?1430005311.

20 Canada Revenue Agency, "Minister Lebouthillier announces winding down of the political activities audit program for charities," news release, January 20, 2016, http://news.gc.ca/web/article-en.do?nid=1028679.

21 The Canadian Press, "Environment panel's end blamed on support for carbon tax," *CBC News*, May 15, 2012, http://www.cbc.ca/news/politics/environment-panel-s-end-blamed-on-support-for-carbon-tax-1.1164935. Reports from NRTEE have been archived: "Reports produced by the National Round Table on the Environment and the Economy (NRTEE)," Newfoundland and Labrador Environmental Industry Association, http://neia.org/national-round-table-on-the-environment-and-the-economy-reports/.

22 Kathryn O'Hara and Paul Dufour, "How Accurate Is the Harper Government Misinformation? Scientific Evidence and Scientists in Federal Policy-making," in *How Ottawa Spends, 2014-2015*.

23 Editorial, "Frozen Out," *Nature* 483, no. 6 (March 1, 2012): 6, http://www.nature.com/nature/journal/v483/n7387/full/483006a.html.

24 Ivan Semeniuk, "Scientists march on Canadian parliament," *Nature Newsblog* (blog), *Nature*, July 10, 2012, http://blogs.nature.com/news/2012/07/scientists-march-on-canadian-parliament.html.

25 Monica Gattinger, "A National Energy Strategy for Canada: Golden Age or Golden Cage of Energy Federalism?," in *Canada: The State of the Federation 2012*, ed. Loleen Berdahl and André Juneau (Montreal: McGill-Queen's University Press, 2015).

26 Council of the Federation, *Canadian Energy Strategy* (July 2015), http://www.canadaspremiers.ca/phocadownload/publications/canadian_energy_strategy_eng_fnl.pdf.